NURSING LAW FOR IRISH STUDENTS

Neil Van Dokkum

GILL & MACMILLAN

Gill & Macmillan
Hume Avenue
Park West
Dublin 12
with associated companies throughout the world
www.gillmacmillan.ie

© 2005 Neil Van Dokkum

ISBN-13 978 07171 3837 1
ISBN-10: 0 7171 3837 2
Index compiled by Julitta Clancy
Print origination in Ireland by O'K Graphic Design, Dublin

The paper used in this book is made from the wood pulp of managed forests. For every tree felled, at least one is planted, thereby renewing natural resources.

All rights reserved. No part of this publication may be copied, reproduced or transmitted in any form or by any means without permission of the publishers or else under the terms of any licence permitting limited copyright issued by the Irish Copyright Licensing Agency.

A catalogue record is available for this book from the British Library.

CONTENTS

Preface v
Acknowledgments vi
Table of Cases vii
Table of Statutes xi

PART ONE: PROFESSIONAL LIABILITY

1 A Statutory Overview 3
2 An Bord Altranais 14
3 The Education of Nurses in Ireland 33
4 The Fitness to Practise Inquiry 37

PART TWO: CIVIL LIABILITY

5 Introduction to Tort Law 57
6 Patient Autonomy and the Tort of Trespass to the Person 64
7 Informed Consent to Medical Treatment 73
8 Capacity of the Patient to give Informed Consent 80
9 The Mentally Incapacitated Adult Patient 87
10 The Consent of Parents to the Medical Treatment of their Child 98
11 Full and Proper Disclosure to the Patient 108
12 Voluntary Consent 125
13 Emergency Treatment 131
14 Negligence – An Introduction 135
15 A Duty of Care 140
16 The Standard of Care 152
17 Damages 172
18 Causation 179
19 The Legal Duty of Confidentiality 192
20 Personal Health Information 204
21 Permitted Disclosure of Confidential Information 209

22	The Consent of the Patient to Disclosure	213
23	Exceptions to the Duty of Confidentiality	220
24	Medical Records and the Common Law	237
25	The Statutory Position Regarding Medical Records: Data Protection and the Freedom of Information	247

PART THREE: CRIMINAL LIABILITY

26	The Distinction between the Civil and Criminal Law	261
27	*Actus Reus and Mens Rea*	270
28	Specific Offences that may arise in the Nursing field	275
29	Drugs	286
30	General Defences in the Criminal Law	304

PART FOUR: ACCOUNTABILITY TO THE EMPLOYER

31	The Contract of Employment	319
32	Termination of the Employment Contract	349
33	Statutory Regulation of Employment	371
34	Discrimination and the Employment Equality Act	383
35	Health and Safety in the Workplace	397
36	Vicarious Liability and the Nurse	415

PART FIVE: DEMONSTRATING YOUR KNOWLEDGE

| 37 | Writing Essays and Answering Exam Questions | 427 |

| Index | | 445 |

PREFACE

The seed for this book was planted whilst preparing my lectures to the nursing students at Waterford Institute of Technology. During my research, it soon became apparent that whilst there were a number of contemporary English and American legal texts written for nurses, the only Irish text was completely out of date, and not in keeping with a four-year degree course.

Whilst it is hoped that this text will go some way toward filling that gap, this work was written with a motive that goes beyond supplying students with an accessible reference when the time comes to research their assignments or swot for their exams.

The message in this book is that nurses are skilled professionals, and it is high time that the related professions, and indeed the country as a whole, recognised this fact. Our nursing students work extremely hard for four years, both in the classroom and in the hospital ward, and emerge with the degree of Bachelor of Science in Nursing. And yet, even with this degree in hand, they are often relegated in their working lives to little more than skivvies to their seemingly more illustrious medical colleagues.

Clearly, in any profession one always starts at the bottom and works upward on the professional ladder. But what constitutes the bottom rung of that ladder should be determined by one's initial qualifications and experience. Our newly qualified nurses enter the professional ranks with an excellent and prestigious degree, and have also completed a substantial number of clinical hours (well in excess of the EU requirement) as part of their studies. They are entitled to the status and privileges enjoyed by other professions with equivalent qualifications and experience, particularly when one considers that many of the everyday duties performed by a nurse are onerous in the extreme.

The United Kingdom is already implementing the process of delegating to nurses some of the tasks previously the preserve of doctors, and it is hoped that Ireland will do the same. Our doctors, particularly junior doctors in State hospitals, often labour under demanding and exhausting workloads. Mistakes are made, and patients ultimately suffer. This makes no sense when in those same hospitals there are a number of nurses who are more than capable of assuming some of those responsibilities.

It is hoped that this book, in some small way, will make people appreciate the enormous reservoir of skill and expertise that is our nursing profession, and I salute the nurses in this country for the fine job that they are performing. May this book be of some use to you.

The law is stated as it was on 31 December 2004.

ACKNOWLEDGMENTS

A lot of people made this book possible.

From a practical point of view, thanks to the good people at Gill & Macmillan for their support and hard work, particularly Marion O'Brien, Aoileann O'Donnell and Thérèse Carrick.

The love and support of those I left behind in South Africa was crucial in those stressful days before emigration, and I owe a special debt to my mother in that regard – thanks Mom. Thanks also to those in Ireland that made the move possible, and here particular mention must be made of Timmy and Kathleen Keating and Keiran Mulvey.

Special mention must go to my neighbour Eddie, a continuous source of wisdom, wit and insight into the fascinating world of the Irish psyche.

Thanks also to the many people who have made me feel very welcome in this beautiful country, and who continue to do so on a daily basis. To my colleagues at WIT, in particular my partners in crime, Walter O'Leary, Grainne Callanan and Albert Keating, many thanks for your infinite patience in answering my million-and-one questions about Irish law and life in general. Special thanks also to Michael Howlett and John Ennis, who have both been unflinching in their support of 'this new fellow from South Africa'.

And finally, and most importantly, the source of my inspiration, my lovely wife Fiona, who unquestioningly accompanied me on the journey to our new home, who supports me in everything I do, and who raised two beautiful sons to boot, I dedicate this work to her.

Neil van Dokkum
December 2004

TABLE OF CASES

Attorney General v Guardian Newspapers Ltd (No. 2) [1988] 3
 W.L.R. 776...228

B (a minor) (wardship: sterilisation), In re [1990] 2 A.C. 1......................94
B (M), In re [1997] 2 F.L.R. 426...92
B v O'R [1991] 1 I.R. 289..128–129
Barnett v Chelsea Kensington Management Committee [1968] 1
 All ER 1068...180–181
Bolam v Frien Barnet Hospital Management Committee [1957] 1
 W.L.R. 582; [1957] 2 All ER 118........................155–157, 161–162, 183
Bolitho (administratix of the estate of Bolitho, deceased) v City and
 Hackney Health Authority [1997] 4 All ER 771.......160–163, 183–184
Boyle v Marathon Petroleum (Ireland) Ltd, unreported, High Court,
 12 January 1999..404–406
Byrne v RHM Foods (Ireland) Ltd, UD 69/1979.....................................353

C (an adult) (refusal of medical treatment), In re [1994] 1
 All ER 819..89–91, 92
Canterbury v Spence 464 F 2d 772 (1972).............110–111, 112, 118, 122
Caparo Industries plc v Dickman [1990] 2 A.C. 605.............................233
Co-Co Engineering v AN Clark (Engineers) [1969] R.P.C. 41...............197
Cody v Hurley, unreported, High Court, 20 January 1999.............175–178
Collins v Mid-Western Health Board [2000] 2 I.R. 154.................163–166
Conole v Redbank Oyster Company [1976] I.R. 191..............................188
Cook v Carroll [1945] I.R. 515...198–200
Crawford v Board of Governors of Charing Cross Hospital,
 The Times, 8 December 1953..137

Daly v Hanson Industries Ltd, UD 719/1986..359
Daniels v Heskin [1954] I.R. 73...113–114, 154
Denny (Henry) & Sons (Ireland) Ltd v Minister for Social
 Welfare [1998] 1 I.R. 34..331–333
Director of Public Prosecutions v. J T [1988] 3 Frewen 141..................217
Donoghue v Stevenson [1932] A.C. 562........................141–142, 143, 152
Dunne (an infant suing by his mother and next friend Catherine Dunne) v
 The National Maternity Hospital and Reginald Jackson [1989] I.R. 91
 ....157–159, 162
Edwards v National Coal Board [1949] 1 All E.R. 743 (CA)................ 403
Egdell case. *see* W v Egdell and others

F (mental patient: sterilisation), In re [1989] 2 All ER 545.......... 92–93, 94
Fairchild v Glenhaven Funeral Services Ltd [2002] 2 All ER 305
.... 184–185
Female Employee, A, v A Hospital [2001] ELR 79...................... 390–391
Franklin v Giddins [1978] Qd. R. 72... 197–198

G. (A.) v Guardian Newspapers (No. 2) [1990] A.C. 109.............. 201–202
Geoghegan v Harris [2000] 3 I.R. 536... 116–119
Gillick v West Norfolk and Wisbech Area Health Authority [1985] 3 All
    ER 402.. 100–102, 105, 106, 107, 257
Griggs v Duke Power Company 401 US 424 (1971)............................... 387

Hennessy v Read & Write Shop Ltd, UD 192/1978...................... 358–359
House of Spring Gardens v Point Blank Ltd [1948] I.R. 611................. 194
Hunter v Mann [1974] Q.B. 767... 222–223

James v Eastleigh Borough Council [1990] I.R.L.R 288........................ 386

K. v An Bord Altranais [1990] I.R. 396... 39, 47
Kavanagh v Cooney Jennings Ltd, UD 175/1983.................................. 360
Kelly v St. Laurence's Hospital [1989] I.L.R.M. 437..................... 167–169
Kennedy v Ireland [1987] I.R. 587.. 195, 200
Kenny v O'Rourke [1972] I.R. 339... 181
Kirby v Burke [1944] I.R. 207.. 152–153
Kirwan v Dart Industries Ltd and Leah, UD 1/80........................... 327–328

Lindsay v Mid-Western Health Board [1993] 2 I.R. 147........................ 138

McCann v Irish Medical Organisation, unreported, High Court,
    2 October 1989... 350–352
McCarthy v Murphy [1998] I.E.H.C. 23.. 189–190
McGee v Attorney General [1974] I.R. 284...195
McGhee v National Coal Board [1972] 3 All ER 1008.......................... 185
McInerney v MacDonald (1992) 93 D.L.R. (4th) 415.................... 241–243
Malette v Shulman (1990) 67 D.L.R. (4th) 321............................. 132–133
Marshall (Thomas) Ltd v Guinle [1979] 1 Ch. 227................................ 197
Marshall v Gotham Company Ltd [1954] 1 All E.R. 937 (HL)...... 403–404
Merrigan v Home Counties Cleaning Ireland Ltd, UD 904/1984........... 360
Mid-Western Health Board v Fitzgerald, unreported, High Court,
    28 November 2003...388–390
Miller v Minister for Pensions [1974] 2 All E.R. 372............................ 268
Miller v Pensions [1947] 2 All ER 372... 136

Murray v Ireland [1985] I.L.R.M. 542...217

N (otherwise K) v K [1986] 6 I.L.R.M. 75.................................... 126–128
Nathan v Bailey Gibson Ltd [1998] 2 I.R. 162.................................... 387
North Western Health Board v HW and C W, unreported, Supreme
 Court, 8 November 2001.. 103–105

O'Ceallaigh v An Bord Altranais (unreported, Supreme Court,
 17 May 2000).. 43, 52
O'Donovan v Cork County Council [1967] I.R. 173..... 153–155, 162, 168
O'Friel v Trustees, St. Michael's Hospital Dun Laoghaire
 [1982] I.L.R.M. 260... 322–325

Palmer v Tees Health Authority, *The Times* Law Reports, 1
 June 1998; [1998] Lloyds Rep. 447 (QBD)................................ 232–234
Parry-Jones v The Law Society [1968] 1 All ER 171............................223
People (A.G.) v Byrne [1974] I.R. 1...268
People (A.G.) v Quinn [1965] I.R. 366..268–269
People (Attorney General) v Whelan [1934] I.R. 518.................... 310–311
People (DPP) v Lawless (1985) 3 Frewen 30.. 288
Ponnampalam v Mid-Western Health Board, UD 300/1979................ 360

R v Department of Health, ex parte Source Informatics Ltd
 [2000] 1 All ER 785...207–208, 209
R v Kemp [1957] 1 Q.B. 399... 308
R v Mid Glamorgan Family Health Services Authority, ex parte
 Martin [1995] 1 All E.R. 356 (CA).. 243–244
Readymix Concrete Ltd v Minister for Pensions [1968]
 2 Q.B. 497..327
Reilly v Ryan [1991] I.L.R.M. 449...418–420, 422
Roe v Ministry of Health and Others; Woolley v Same [1954] 2
 Q.B. 66.. 145–146

S (hospital orders: court's jurisdiction), In re [1995] 3
 All ER 290... 216
Schonloendorff v Society of the New York Hospital 501 NE 92
 (1914)...74
Scott v London and St. Katherine Docks Co. (1865) 3 H. & C.
 569... 137–138
Seager v Copydex [1967] 2 All ER 415..196
Shakoor (administratix of the estate of Shakoor, deceased) v
 Situ (t/a/ Eternal Health Company) [2000] 4 All ER 181... 148–150, 169

Sidaway v Board of Governors of Bethlehem Royal Hospital
[1985] A.C. 871.. 111–113, 122, 244, 245
Sidaway v Governors of Bethlehem Royal Hospital [1985] 1 All
ER 821.. 75, 78
Smyth v Eastern Health Board [1996] ELR 72.............................. 392–394
Sunday Tribune Ltd, In re [1984] I.R. 505..................................... 325, 333
Superquinn Ltd v Bray Urban District Council [1998] 3 I.R.
542...185–187

Tarasoff v Regents of the University of California 131 Cal.
Rptr. 14 (1976) (California Supreme Court)......................230–231, 234
Tierney v An Post, unreported, Supreme Court, 6 October
1999..327
Toal v Duignan [1991] I.L.R.M. 135..245
Traynor v Ryan [2002] 13 ELR 245...367

W v Egdell and others [1990] All ER 835 (CA)......................206, 227–229
Walsh v Family Planning Services Ltd [1992] 1 I.R. 496
.... 75–76, 114–116, 119
Ward of Court, In re [1995] 2 I.L.R.M. 401................................ 84, 95–96
Ward of Court (withholding medical treatment), In re (No. 2)
[1996] 2 I.R. 79...78
Western Health Board v Quigley [1982] I.L.R.M. 390.................... 363–365
Wilsher v Essex Area Health Authority [1987] Q.B. 730........169–170, 183

X v Y [1988] 2 All ER 648..200, 205–207

Z v Finland (1988) 25 E.H.R.R. 371..195–196

TABLE OF STATUTES

CONSTITUTION OF IRELAND
Constitution of Ireland, 1937........3
  Article
  40.3.1..66
  41....................102, 103, 104, 217
  42..............................102–103, 104
  42.5...................................103, 105

STATUTES
Adoptive Leave Act 1995............361
Age of Majority Act 1985..............99
Anti–Discrimination (Pay) Act
  1974......................................391
  s. 7..392
  s. 19..392
Carer's Leave Act 2001...............361
Child Care Act 1990.....................99
Children Act 2001......................306
Civil Liability Act 1961......182–183
Companies Act 1963..................336
Court and Court Officers Act 1995
  s. 45 (1)..................................224
Criminal Damage Act 1991
  s. 6..312
  s. 6 (2)............................312–313
Criminal Justice Act 1960
  s. 2..220
Criminal Lunatics Act 1800
  s. 2..307
Data Protection Act 1988..........239,
  247, 248–251, 253, 256, 257
  s. 2C.......................................249
  s. 4 (1)(a)(i)–(iii)......................250
  s. 4 (8)....................................250
  s. 8..250
  s. 19 (2)..................................249
Data Protection Act 2003..........239,
  247, 250–252, 257
  s. 2B..252

Dentists Act 1985......................252
Employment Agency Act 1971...336
Employment Equality Act 1977
 383
Employment Equality Act 1998
  ....383, 384–396
  s. 2 (a)....................................288
  s. 6.........................286, 384–385
  s. 8........................287, 288, 384
  s. 9..384
  s. 10..384
  s. 11..384
  s. 11 (5).................................. 394
  s. 12..384
  s. 13.............................288, 384
  s. 15..390
  s. 15 (3)..................................390
  s. 22 (1)..................................287
  s. 24 (1)..................................394
  s. 25...............................392, 394
  s. 26..390
  s. 26 (1).................................. 394
  s. 28..394
  s. 33..395
  s. 34..395
Equality Act 2004.....................383,
  384, 395
  s. 14A.....................................390
Freedom of Information Act 1997
  ....254–257, 258
  Part III....................................255
  s. 7..255
  s. 12 (2)..................................255
  s. 17 (1)..................................255
  s. 17 (4)..................................255
  s. 20..255
  s. 21..255
  s. 22..255
  s. 23..255

s. 28...255
s. 28 (3)...255
s. 28 (4)...255
Health Act 1947
  s. 65..292
Health Act 1953
  s. 36..292
  s. 39..292
Health Act 1970......... 11, 320, 349, 357, 360, 363, 367, 368, 369, 370, 372
  s. 14..364
  s. 23..365
  s. 23 (2)...363
  s. 23 (3)...363
  s. 24......................................365, 366
  s. 59..292
Health Acts 1947 to 1985..........292
Industrial Relations Act 1990
  s. 23..335
Industrial Relations Acts 1946–1990 335
Industrial Training Act 1967......321
Infanticide Act 1949................... 284
Maternity Protection Act 1994
  ....355, 361
Medical Practitioners Act 1978
  ....12, 252
Midwives (Ireland) Act 1918......4–5
Midwives Act 1931...............6, 8, 13
Midwives Act 1944...............6–8, 13
  s. 44..9
Minimum Notice and Terms of Employment Acts 1973–1991....341
Minimum Notice and Terms of Employment Acts 1973–1994....372
Misuse of Drugs Act 1977
  ....286, 290, 303
  s. 1...286, 295
  s. 1 (2)....................................286–287
  s. 15..288–289
  s. 15 (2)... 288

s. 16..287
s. 18..287, 297
s. 27..297
s. 29 (1)..287
s. 29 (3)..288
Misuse of Drugs Act 1984
  ....290, 303
National Minimum Wage Act 2000
  .... 338, 361, 372–373, 376–377
  s. 14..376–377
  s. 23..338
  s. 24 (2)...377
Non–Fatal Offences Against the Person Act 1997..................70, 105, 107, 275, 276–285
  s. 2...276–278
  s. 3..278
  s. 4...278–279
  s. 6...279–282
  s. 6 (1)... 281
  s. 6 (2)... 281
  s. 6 (3)... 281
  s. 6 (5)... 281
  s. 7......................................282, 283
  s. 8...282–283
  s. 8 (1)...283
  s. 8 (2)...283
  s. 8 (3)...283
  s. 18..313–314
  s. 18 (1)...313
  s. 19......................................313, 314
  s. 20......................................313, 314
  s. 20 (1)...314
  s. 21..312–313
  s. 23..105–106
Nurses Act 1950........... 8–9, 10, 11, 13, 24
Nurses Act 1961.................9, 10, 13
Nurses Act 1985................. 4, 9–11, 13, 14, 15, 29, 32, 35, 38, 367, 370

Part Four	33, 37–38, 39
Part III	24, 380
Part IV	380
Part V	29
s. 2	11–12
s. 4	11
s. 6	15–18
s. 6 (1)	15–16
s. 6 (2)	16
s. 6 (3)	18
s. 7	18
s. 8	18
s. 9	18–20
s. 10	21
s. 11	21
s. 13	21–22
s. 13 (2)	11, 22
s. 13 (5)	22
s. 15	22
s. 16	22
s. 17	22
s. 25	23
s. 26	12, 23–24
s. 27	12, 24, 29
s. 28	24–25
s. 28 (4)	25
s. 32	33
s. 33	33
s. 34	33
s. 36	33
s. 37	33–34
s. 38	40–44, 47, 49, 50, 51, 53
s. 38 (2)	43
s. 39	23, 44–47, 50
s. 40	47–49, 50
s. 41	49
s. 42	49–50
s. 44	43, 50–52, 53
s. 44 (2)	50
s. 44 (3)	50
s. 45	52
s. 46	52

s. 47	52
Schedule 2	18
Nurses Registration (Ireland) Act 1919	5–6
Nurses Registration Act 1948	8, 13
Organisation of Working Time Act 1997	340, 373–376
s. 3	374
s. 11	374
s. 12	374–375
s. 14	376
s. 15	374
s. 16	375
s. 18	376
s. 19	375
s. 20	376
s. 21	376
Parental Leave Act 1998	361
Payment of Wages Act 1991	338, 372–373
s. 2	373
s. 4	373
Prisons Act 1970	
ss. 2, 4	220
Protection of Employees (Fixed-Term Work) Act 2003	379–381
s. 2	380
s. 5	380
s. 6	380
s. 6 (2)	380
s. 6 (5)	380–381
s. 8 (1)	381
s. 8 (2)	381
s. 9 (1)	381
s. 11	381
s. 17	380
Protection of Employment (Part-Time Work) Act 2001	338, 356, 378–379
s. 7 (2)(a)	378

xiv NURSING LAW FOR IRISH STUDENTS

s. 7 (2)(b) 379
s. 7 (2)(c) 379
s. 9 (2) 379
s. 9 (4) 379
Public Health Act 1947 224
Public Health (Control of Diseases) Act 1984 224
Redundancy Payments Act 1967 359
Redundancy Payments Act 1971 359
Redundancy Payments Act 2003 378
Redundancy Payments Acts 1967–2001 321
Redundancy Payments Acts 1967–2003 377–378
Road Traffic Act 1961 224
Road Traffic Act 1972 222
   s. 168 (2) 222
   s. 168 (2) (b) 222
   s. 168 (3) 222
Safety, Health and Welfare at Work Act 1989 .... 348, 399–410, 414
   Part III 409
   Part V 409
   Part VI 409
   Part VII 409
   Part VIII 409
   s. 2 410–411
   s. 6 399–401
   s. 6 (1) 400
   s. 6 (2) 400
   s. 6–11 .... 399–402, 414
   s. 7 401
   s. 8 401
   s. 9 401–402
   s. 10 402
   s. 11 402
   s. 12 407
   s. 13 409
   s. 16 409

s. 28 .... 399, 410
s. 33 409
s. 34 409
s. 35–37 409
s. 51 (3) 410
Sale of Food and Drugs Act 1875
   s. 10 292
Social Welfare (Consolidation) Act 1981 331–332
Terms of Employment (Information) Act 1984 325
Terms of Employment (Information) Acts 1994 and 2001
   336–338
   s. 3 (1) 336
Unfair Dismissals Act 1977
   .... 363, 364, 366, 367, 370
   s. 1 354–355
   s. 2 356–357
   s. 2 (1)(a) 356
   s. 4 .... 357, 362
   s. 6 357
   s. 6 (1) 361
   s. 6 (2) 361–362
Unfair Dismissals (Amendment) Act 1993 .... 324–325, 356
Unfair Dismissals Acts 1977–1993
   .... 321, 322, 340, 341, 352
Unfair Dismissals Acts 1977–2001
   .... 354, 357, 359
   s. 14 (1) 338

STATUTORY INSTRUMENTS
Data Protection (Access Modification) (Health) Regulations 1989 (S.I. No. 82 of 1989) 239–240, 250
Health (Removal of Officers and Servants) Regulations 1971 (S.I. No. 110 of 1971)
   365–366

Medicinal Products (Prescription and Control of Supply) Regulations 1996 300–301
Mental Hospitals (Officers and Servants) order 1946 (S.I. No. 203 of 1946)....................... 364
   para. 3 (3).............................. 364
   para. 3 (4).............................. 364
Misuse of Drugs Regulations 1979 (S.I. No. 32 of 1979).......... 290
Misuse of Drugs (Amendment) Regulations 1987 (S.I. No. 263 of 1987)....................... 290
Misuse of Drugs Regulations 1988 (S.I. No. 328 of 1988)........ 290
   Part 2....................................... 290
   Part 3....................................... 290
   Part 4....................................... 290
   Articles
   8... 292
   10.. 293
   12.. 294
   13........................ 290, 295, 297
   14........................ 290, 295–296
   14 (3)...................................... 296
   16.. 297
   17 (3)...................................... 293
   20.. 293
   24.. 290
   sched. 1............................ 291, 297
   sched. 2.......... 291, 293, 297, 300
   sched. 3............................ 291, 293
   sched. 4............................ 291, 296
   sched. 5............................ 291, 296
Misuse of Drugs (Amendment) Regulations 1993................ 290
National Drugs Advisory Board (Establishment) Order, 1966 224

National Treasury Management Agency (Delegation of Functions) Order, 2003 421–422
Organisation of Working Time (Exemption of Civil Protection Services) Regulations 1998 (S.I. No. 52 of 1998)......... 375
Organisation of Working Time (Exemption of Transport Activities) Regulations 1998 (S.I. No. 20 of 1998........... 375
Organisation of Working Time (General Exemptions) Regulations 1998 (S.I. No. 21 of 1998)............................. 375
Safety, Health and Welfare at Work (General Application) Regulations 1993 .... 410–414, 414
   Part I...................................... 411
   Part II..................................... 411
   Part IV............................ 412, 413
   Part IX.................................... 414
   Part V..................................... 413
   Part VI.................................... 413
   Part VII................................... 413
   Part VIII......................... 413–414
   Part X..................................... 414
   reg. 7..................................... 411
   reg. 10................................... 412
   reg. 16................................... 412
   reg. 17................................... 412
   reg. 18–20............................. 413
   Schedule 5............................. 412
   Schedule 8............................. 413
   Schedule 9............................. 413
   Schedule 10........................... 413
   Schedule 11........................... 413
   Schedule 12........................... 414

EUROPEAN LEGISLATION
Decisions
  75/365/EEC..............................26
Directives
  75/362/EEC..............................26
  75/363/EEC..............................26
  76/686/EEC..............................26
  77/452/EEC......................25, 26
  77/453/EEC..............................26
  77/454/EEC..............................26
  77/455/EEC..............................26
  78/1026/EEC............................26
  78/1027/EEC............................26
  78/687/EEC..............................26
  80/154/EEC......................25, 26
  80/155/EEC..............................26
  81/1057/EEC............................26
  85/384/EEC..............................26
  85/432/EEC..............................26
  85/433/EEC..............................26
  89/594/EEC..............................26
  93/16/EEC................................26
  2001/19/EEC............................26

Treaty of Nice...............................14
European Convention on Human
  Rights, 1950 Article 8........195

UNITED KINGDOM LEGISLATION
Access to Health Records Act 1990
  ....253, 257
Access to Medical Reports Act
  1988..................218, 253, 257
Midwives Act 1918....................6, 8
National Health Service (Venereal
  Diseases) Regulations, 1974
  (S.I. No. 29 of 1974)..........225

United Nations Conventions
United Nations Convention against
  Illicit Traffic in Narcotic Drugs
  and Psychotropic Substances
 290

PART ONE

PROFESSIONAL LIABILITY

1

A STATUTORY OVERVIEW

> **Learning Outcomes**
> **At the completion of this chapter, the reader should know and understand the following:**
> - What is meant by the term 'legislation'.
> - The evolution of legislation governing Irish nurses and midwives up to the present Nurses Act 1985.
> - The removal of the division between nurses and midwives, leading to the creation of one Nurses' Register.
> - The structure and section headings of the Nurses Act 1985.
> - Some important definitions in the Nurses Act 1985.

Important legal concepts and phrases that are crucial to an understanding of this chapter

'The Legislature' is the group of elected officials who make the laws that govern the population of a country. In Ireland, the legislature is known as the Oireachtas, which was created by the 1937 Constitution of Ireland (Bunreacht na hÉireann) and consists of the President, the House of Representatives (Dáil Éireann) and the Senate (Seanad Éireann).

Dáil Éireann is elected by popular franchise – in other words, they are voted into power by the citizens of the country by either a General Election (when the entire country votes for all the seats in the Dáil), or a Local Election (when one particular seat is empty and needs to be filled). Seanad Éireann consists of sixty members. Eleven of these are appointed by the Taoiseach. Six are appointed by university graduates who have reached the age of eighteen years. The remaining forty-three seats are elected from five panels of candidates who have links to certain interests or services – five are elected from the cultural and education panel, eleven are elected from the agricultural panel, eleven are elected from the labour panel, nine are elected from the commercial panel and seven are elected from the administrative panel. Membership of these panels is restricted and the category of people entitled to elect candidates onto the panels, and thereafter into the Senate, is also restricted.

The Legislature is one of the recognised arms of government, with the other being the Executive (the government, most importantly the Cabinet made up of Ministers) and the Judiciary (the Courts of Law, the most important being the Supreme Court of Ireland).

As Ireland has a Constitution, and that Constitution is supreme, all laws passed by the Oireachtas must not be repugnant (disobey or offend) the Constitution. If such repugnant legislation is passed, it will be declared unconstitutional by the courts.

'Legislation' is the collection of written laws that are passed by the Oireachtas. They are also called 'statutes' or 'Acts'. Legislation may either be superior (sometimes called 'primary') or subordinate (sometimes called 'secondary'). Superior legislation consists of Acts of the Oireachtas, for example the Nurses Act 1985. When that superior legislation grants another organisation or person the power to make laws, these laws are known as subordinate legislation. For example, the Minister of Health and Children can make statutory instruments implementing training programmes for Irish nurses so that they are qualified to practice anywhere in Europe. The Nurses Act would need to authorise the Minister to do this.

Introduction – The evolution of nursing legislation in Ireland

At the beginning of the twentieth century, Ireland was still subject to English rule, with the bulk of Irish legislation being English statutes extended in their application to Ireland. These statutes are easy to identify, as the word "Ireland" was placed in brackets and inserted into the title of the English statute.

After 1922, and the creation of Saorstát Éireann (the Irish Free State), the (Southern) Irish were permitted to legislate on their own behalf. By this time it had become clear that whilst there were similarities between the respective nursing professions in Ireland and England, it was necessary to have specialist legislation pertaining to Ireland. Despite this, the statutes that were passed immediately after 1922 (and some would argue for most of the twentieth century) were by and large copies of similar English legislation. Be that as it may, they were passed by the Irish legislature for the Irish nursing profession.

Midwives (Ireland) Act 1918

This Act was the last English statute governing the practice of midwifery that was extended to Ireland, and it established the Central Midwives Board and the first register for midwives in Ireland, which was called the Roll of Midwives.

In terms of this Act, the powers of the Central Midwives Board were as follows:

- To issue and cancel certificates.
- To make rules and regulations regarding the issue of these certificates.
- To train and examine a midwife for purposes of admission and re-admission to the Roll of Midwives.
- To regulate, supervise and restrict the practice of midwifery.
- To remove a midwife for contravention of the Rules and Regulations as they appeared in the Act, or for misconduct.
- To restore a midwife to the Roll.

Although the Act was in respect of Ireland, it was still subject to English approval, in that the abovementioned rules and regulations were only valid once they had been approved by the Privy Council, which was the highest court with jurisdiction over the governed territories.

This Act is important in the sense that prior to this statute the official thinking had mirrored the thinking of the wider community regarding infant mortality - that the fittest would survive. In practice this meant that a lot of Irish babies (and often their mothers) died.

In 1915, the Irish infant mortality rate was 92 per 1000 born, mainly due to diarrhoea, tuberculosis and other infectious diseases. Most of these deaths were preventable as were the six maternal deaths per thousand live births. (Barrington R., *Health, Medicine and Politics in Ireland 1900-1970*, Dublin: Institute of Public Administration, 1987:75.).

One of the main objectives of this Act was to prevent unqualified women setting up as midwives. At the same time, the question of qualifications was a difficult issue, given that many skills had been passed down by word of mouth through generations, and one can only imagine that the enforcement of this Act must have been extremely difficult, as the midwife was often an influential, even powerful, figure in the community.

This Act created the first nursing register in Ireland, known as the Roll of Midwives, which was published annually by the Central Midwives Board.

Nurses Registration (Ireland) Act 1919

This Act was the last English statute governing the nursing profession that was extended to Ireland, and it established the General Nursing Council for Ireland. The Act specified that there be a register to consist of general nurses and a supplementary register for male nurses, for nurses trained in the nursing and care of persons suffering from mental diseases and for nurses trained in the nursing of sick children. Midwives were placed on a separate roll at that time.

It is interesting to note that even at these early stages of statutory control of nursing, the basic divisions of general health, mental health and paediatric health were established, and these divisions were set to continue for the remainder of the century. Nursing was still seen as being the essential preserve of the female gender with the register of male nurses being regarded as a 'supplementary' register.

The Council was empowered to make rules and regulations in respect of the formation, maintenance and publication of the Register of Nurses, and to educate and discipline nurses. A nurse who was removed from the Register had the right to appeal to the High Court.

Midwives Act 1931

This Act was a supplement to the (English) 1918 Act of the same name, and confirmed the continued existence of the Central Midwives Board. The Act further provided that anybody who attended a birth in a professional capacity had either to be a qualified and certified medical practitioner or midwife, or had to be a person who was attending the birth as part of her formal training as a midwife. Failure to heed this provision was punishable by a fine. There was, however, further provision that persons who were recognised midwives either as a result of training or who were already in the employ of a poor law authority could continue to practise as midwives but only 'under the direction and personal supervision of a duly qualified medical practitioner'. This was a pragmatic recognition that, whilst it was desirable to prevent the practice by unqualified midwives in Ireland, it would leave a huge gap in the childbirth services if all midwives without the requisite qualifications were immediately removed. Such midwives would be allowed to continue to practice, but under the supervision of a doctor.

This Act empowered the Central Midwives Board to frame rules and regulations governing the issue of 'midwives' badges', and made it an offence for anyone other than a midwife to wear such a badge. This had the practical effect of allowing a member of the public, or a patient, to identify the person as a qualified and registered midwife.

Clearly the 1931 Act was created in order to prevent some of the abuses that had continued in Ireland despite the 1918 Act, the most serious being the practice of midwifery by persons without any formal training or qualifications. Whilst some would argue that these unqualified women were invaluable to communities who would otherwise have had no recourse to any help at all, the figures recording the death rate of both infants and mothers was an indication that changes were necessary.

Midwives Act 1944

This Act repealed the Order that created the Central Midwives Board of the previous two Acts, and created a new Central Midwives Board. It is not immediately apparent why the new Board was created, as the Act provides that the previous Board members make up the new Board.

Clearly the emphasis was on regulation, but not at the price of continuity. This Act introduced a number of regulatory measures, including a special seal, regular meetings, a voting procedure, an election of a chairperson, the appointment of seven of the eleven sitting members by the Minister (at least four of these seven appointees had to be midwives) and the election of four medical practitioners to the Board as elected by medical practitioners. In other words, of the eleven members, four had to be midwives (all appointees) and four had to be doctors. Elections were held every five years, commencing in 1949.

The Board was also given the power to make rules. The subject matter of these rules could be 'in relation to any matter or thing referred to in this Act', but the rules could only come into force after approval by the Minister and after the Minister had consulted with the Medical Registration Council, which is an indication of where the real power lay.

The Board maintained the Roll of Midwives, and the Board was given the power to place midwives on, or remove midwives from, the Roll. A midwife could be removed from the Roll if the Board was satisfied that the midwife was guilty of 'infamous misconduct' or 'professional misconduct', or if the midwife had been 'convicted in the State of treason or of a felony or misdemeanour' or had been convicted outside the State of a crime or offence which would be a felony or misdemeanour if committed in Ireland, or if the midwife had been convicted of an offence under the Midwives Act, or if the midwife had disobeyed the rules made by the Board under the Act, or if the Board was satisfied that the midwife was physically or mentally unfit to attend women in childbirth.

The Board could caution, reprimand or suspend a midwife instead of removal from the Roll. A midwife who was dissatisfied with the Board's decision could appeal to the Minister or to the High Court, but not both.

The Board could also reinstate a midwife onto the Roll for any reason they considered sufficient. All midwives on the previous Roll under the previous Act were immediately placed on the new Roll.

Despite the practice of issuing Midwife Badges, which continued under this Act, the Act in addition provided that the Board would issue certificates to all midwives confirming their eligibility to practise as midwives. These midwife certificates were clearly very valuable as the Act provided that the person who had custody of the midwife's certificate on the death of that midwife committed an offence if he or she failed to return that certificate to the Board.

The Board was also empowered to stipulate the nature and extent of the qualifying examinations necessary to practise as a midwife, including refresher courses for practising midwives.

Immediate control of midwives was vested in the local supervising authority of the district in which the midwife practised.

An interesting part of this Act was the part dealing with the question of the procedure to be followed by a midwife when faced with 'an emergency'. The Board was tasked with formulating rules setting out which circumstances would constitute an emergency. When faced with such emergency, the midwife was legally obligated to call in a doctor.

The Act also provided, as did the previous Act, that only midwives or doctors or persons training to be such could attend a birth, but added an extra category, namely a person acting in an emergency without payment. This Act repealed the 1918 and 1931 Acts.

Nurses Registration Act 1948

This Act was passed in order to carry out one specific task – the extension of the term of office of the members of the General Nursing Council who were in office at the time that the Act became effective.

This was essentially a holding pattern pending the passing of the 1950 Act.

Nurses Act 1950

This Act was highly significant in the history of nursing in Ireland for a number of reasons. Firstly, it created An Bord Altranais and dissolved the General Nursing Council and the Central Midwives Board. Secondly, it included a midwife in the definition of 'nurse' and including the practice of midwifery in the definition of 'nursing'.

In terms of this Act, the Board consisted of twenty-three members, thirteen of those being appointed by the Minister. The thirteen appointees included a master or assistant master of a maternity hospital, two doctors who trained nurses in training hospitals, one doctor with experience in mental nursing, a doctor representative, a medical officer of health, a person specially experienced in educational matters, a representative of councils of counties, and a representative of councils of county boroughs. Two appointees had to be registered nurses.

The balance of the membership of the Board, namely ten members, was elected. These ten people had to be nurses and were elected by nurses. What this meant was that at any time the Board would have a minimum of twelve nurses on the Board, which was one less than an outright majority. The other members were people associated with the practice of nursing or midwifery.

Of the ten nurses who were elected, one had to have a qualification or experience in public health nursing, two had to be qualified or experienced in midwifery, two had to be qualified or experienced in mental nursing, three of the nurses had to have experience in training nurses, one had to have experience in private nursing, and one had to be employed by a hospital, which was not a training hospital.

The Act also established a Midwives Committee, which was a committee of the Board, consisting of eight members. The Minister appointed three of these members (one doctor and two midwives), with the Board itself appointing the other five members (three being existing Board members – at least one of those being a midwife, and two doctors, one being involved in training and the other in obstetrics).

This Act also created a new Register of Nurses, which was maintained by the Board, and was divided into the divisions mentioned earlier, including a division for midwives. The Board could add or remove names from the Register, specify qualifications and examinations necessary for an Irish nurse (which would include recognition of foreign qualifications), and even provide scholarships to allow persons to study and train as nurses.

In hindsight, the significance of this Act cannot be limited to the establishment of the Nursing Board, which was essentially run by nurses for nurses, but in addition it must be remembered that it demarcated the specific divisions within the nursing profession. It brought the practice of midwifery into the profession of nursing, whereas previously midwives had been regarded as extraneous and somewhat 'foreign' to the practice of nursing. The midwives had lost their independent Board and any recommendations put forward by the midwives as a profession had to be put to An Bord Altranais for approval. Similarly, the midwife register was contained as a division within the Nursing Register. Finally, the Midwifery Committee was now essentially a committee of An Bord Altranais. Although the midwives' profession kept their independent training schools, the Nursing Board was empowered to approve them (and therefore also not approve them), again meaning a significant loss of power and independence previously enjoyed by the midwives.

Although this Act was repealed in its entirety by the 1985 Act, that 1985 Act owes much to the 1950 Act, which was a trendsetter in many respects.

Nurses Act 1961

This Act was an administrative Act, specifying voting procedures and eligibility to vote at the elections of members of the Board. The Act also repealed section 44 of the Midwives Act 1944. Section 44 provided for the issue and regulation of Midwives Badges by the now defunct Central Midwives Board, and accordingly this power now fell to An Bord Altranais.

The Nurses Act 1985

As a result of sustained pressure from within and outside the nursing profession, regarding the clear need to update and extend the training facilities for nurses along the lines being implemented in England, and as a result of the deliberations of the Working Party on General Nursing originally established in 1975, the Nurses Act 1985 was enacted.

The Preamble to the Act, which provides a guide as to the aims and objects of the Act, reads as follows:

> 'An Act to provide for the establishment of a board to be known as An Bord Altranais or, in the English language, The Nursing Board, which shall provide for the registration, control and education of nurses and to provide for other matters relating to the practice of nursing and the persons engaged in such practice and to provide for the repeal of the Nurses Acts, 1950 and 1961, and to provide for other matters connected with the matters aforesaid.'

If one were to be guided by the Preamble alone, one would be justified in believing that all the Act did was create the new An Bord Altranais. However, similar to its 1950 predecessor, this is only one aspect of the Act, and its impact on the structure and regulation of the nursing profession as a whole was enormous.

The Act is a large and comprehensive Act, which is structured as follows:

Part One of the Act is entitled 'Preliminary and General' and deals with the short title of the Act, and the very important Interpretation section (which gives specialised interpretations to some words and concepts in order to alert the reader that their meanings in the Act might be different from their ordinary or everyday meaning). Part One also contains details of the commencement and establishment of the Act, and the previous statutes that were repealed by this Act.

Part Two deals with the establishment and regulation of An Bord Altranais, which, as we have seen, constitutes a significant portion of this Act, but is not the only thing of importance governed by the Act. This section will be closely examined in the chapter dedicated to the workings of the Board.

Part Three of the Act deals with the maintenance of the Register of Nurses, which is divided up into its appropriate sections, determined by specialisation, including a section for midwives. The Register is maintained by the Nursing Board. One of the first tasks of the Board after its establishment was to establish and thereafter maintain the Register. There is also provision for the registration of professions ancillary to nursing.

Part Four deals with one of the most important functions carried out by the Board, and that is the education and training of nurses, and this will be considered in a later chapter.

Part Five of the Act deals with the question of Fitness to Practise and the fitness to practise hearing.

Part Six is the final part, and is entitled 'Miscellaneous' as it is essentially a section dedicated to tidying up little aspects of the Act that needed attention, a sort of 'housekeeping' part. Included in this Part are details of what happens to people who improperly call themselves nurses or hold themselves out as nurses, the reporting and advisory functions of the Board, including those concerning EU Directives relating to the profession of nursing in Europe, notification by a midwife to the Board that he or she intends to establish and practice as such in a specified area, and finally provision for the Board to retain the authority to punish offenders, rather than handing them over to governmental or justice officials.

The definitions' section

Before going on to examine the specific Parts of the Act, as mentioned above, it is necessary to have a close and careful look at the definitions' section (titled 'Interpretation'). The reason why it is important to look at this section in any statute is that certain words in a statute might be given a specialised meaning which is very different from the usual ordinary everyday use of the word. If the reader failed to read the definitions' section, and then used those words in their ordinary sense rather than in their newly defined sense, there is a good chance that the reader will misunderstand the statute, with sometimes disastrous results. Remember to always read the definitions' section carefully before reading any statute, it really is vitally important.

SECTION 2: Interpretation

'In this Act:

> "the Board" means An Bord Altranais or the Nursing Board established by this Act;
>
> "establishment day" means the day appointed to be the establishment day under section 4 of this Act;
>
> "Fitness to Practise Committee" means the committee established by the Board under section 13 (2) of this Act
>
> "the former Board" means An Bord Altranais established under the Nurses Act, 1950;
>
> "health board" means a health board established under the Health Act, 1970;
>
> "Member State" means a state, other than the State, which is a

member of the European Economic Communities;

"midwife" means a person whose name is entered in the midwives division of the register;

"the Minister" means the Minister for Health;

"nurse" means a woman or a man whose name is entered in the register and includes a midwife and "nursing" includes "midwifery";

"prescribed" means prescribed by rules made by the Board;

"the register" means the register of nurses established under section 27 of this Act;

"registered medical practitioner" means a person whose name is entered in the General Register of Medical Practitioners established under the Medical Practitioners Act, 1978;

"rules" means rules made under section 26 of this Act.'

The Interpretation or definitions' section is surprisingly small and simple, given the size and impact of the 1985 Act. Most of the definitions contained in the Interpretation section are straightforward and require very little comment.

The definition of 'nurse' now includes the words 'or a man', which emphasises that the ranks of nurses are made up of both men and women.

As previously mentioned, the midwife is now included in the definition of nurse, as the profession of midwifery is now a part of the nursing profession. Midwifery is now regarded as a specialisation, rather than a separate discipline or profession.

What the somewhat limited size and extent of the Interpretation section means is that most words in the Nurses Act 1985 must be given their ordinary everyday meaning. This is often desirable, as the statute can then be read by everybody, as opposed to being restricted to those with special skills. The practice of nursing is fundamentally important to the people of Ireland, and it is right that they should be able to understand the Act that governs this profession.

A Statutory Overview: Summary

1. In order to understand the current statute that governs the nursing profession, namely the Nurses Act 1985, it is important to know about the statutes that went before it, as the content of those statutes, and their success or failure, played an important part in determining the content of the 1985 Act.

2. At the beginning of the twentieth century, there was no statute dealing specifically with the nursing profession in Ireland, and the Irish nurse was treated, at least in the eyes of the law, as simply being governed by the same laws that governed nurses in England.

3. However, in 1931 the first statute that specifically applied to the profession in Ireland was enacted. This was the Midwives Act 1931, which was followed by the Midwives Act 1944; the Nurses Registration Act 1948; the Nurses Act 1950; and the Nurses Act 1961. The currently applicable statute, the Nurses Act 1985, has replaced all of those statutes, and has effectively brought the nursing and midwifery professions, and all ancillary professions, under the one umbrella body.

4. The Nurses Act 1985 is made up of six sections, and these sections are concerned with An Bord Altranais, the registration of nurses and the maintenance of the Register of Nurses, the education and training of nurses, and the fitness to practise as a nurse.

5. Useful websites:
    a. *British and Irish Legal Information Institute* (www.bailii.org).
    b. *Government of Ireland* (www.irlgov.ie).
    c. *Irish Statute Book 1922-2001* (www.irishstatutebook.ie).
    d. *Irish Medical Directory* (www.imd.ie).
    e. *Irish Medical Publications On Line* (www.imd.ie/pub.htm).

2

AN BORD ALTRANAIS

Learning Outcomes
At the completion of this chapter, the reader should know and understand the following:

- How the Nursing Board was established.
- That the Nursing Board is a juristic person and what that means.
- The composition of the membership of the Nursing Board.
- That the Nursing Board is authorised to establish committees and make rules for these committees.
- The circumstances in which the Nursing Board is authorised to charge fees.
- The registration process.
- The concept of a harmonisation directive and its effect in the European Union.

Important legal concepts and phrases that are crucial to an understanding of this chapter

An Bord Altranais (pronounced 'Anne Bored Ultranish') is the Irish name for the Nursing Board established by the Nurses Act 1985.

A juristic person with perpetual succession is a body or organisation created by law, with its own rights and duties that does not depend for its survival on the humans that make it up.

The European Union (EU) is a collection of countries on the continent of Europe that are joined in an attempt to break down economic barriers and promote a common policy in regard to movement of citizens from one country to another, to health and safety practices, to professional qualifications, to environmental policies, and so on. The most important legislation that governs the EU is the Treaty that is signed by all Member States.

The first Treaty signed by the six founding countries was in 1951. The most recent Treaty that has been signed is the Treaty of Nice. These

Treaties are known as 'primary legislation' in that they govern all the other laws, rules and regulations made by the EU. It is hoped that these Treaties will create a common market and a common union. One of the most important aims of the Treaties – monetary union – was achieved with the introduction of the Euro, which replaced the local currency of each Member State (apart from Britain which has held onto its own currency).

A Directive of the EU is what is known as 'secondary legislation' in that it is made by the EU in terms of the Treaty and must conform to the letter and spirit of the Treaty. They are used to ensure that Member States adapt their own laws to ensure uniform standards throughout the EU, but they allow the Member States (subject to limits) to choose how and when they will bring the Directive into force. They are used in areas (for example, professional qualifications and health and safety standards) where the continued orderly existence of the EU depends on the Member States having uniform policies and practices.

Introduction: The establishment of the Nursing Board

An Bord Altranais, the Nursing Board, is the body that regulates the nursing profession in the Republic of Ireland. It is established by the Nurses Act 1985. Section 6 of the Act is the specific section that establishes the Board.

SECTION 6: Establishment of An Bord Altranais
'(1) There shall, by virtue of this section, be established on the establishment day a body to be known as An Bord Altranais or, in the English language, as the Nursing Board (in this Act referred to as the Board) the general concern of which shall be to promote high standards of professional education and training and professional conduct among nurses, and which shall, in particular, fulfil the functions assigned to it by this Act.

(2) The Board shall be a body corporate with perpetual succession and power to sue and be sued in its corporate name and to acquire, hold and dispose of land.

(3) The Board may, subject to the provisions of this Act, regulate its own procedure.

(4) The Second Schedule to this Act shall apply to the Board.'

Commentary
Sub-section (1) sets out the main functions of the Board, which are to:

- promote high standards of education and training in the nursing profession (which would include the drawing up of syllabi and exit qualifications, and post-registration training),
- promote high standards of professional conduct among nurses (which would include questions of discipline and punishment related to the operation of the fitness to practise procedures),
- perform the other functions assigned to it by the Act, the most important being the maintenance of the Register of Nurses and the compliance with EU directives relating to nursing and midwifery.

Sub-section (2) creates what is known in law as a 'juristic person'.

All persons have what is known as 'legal subjectivity', which means that they are subjects of the law, and not objects of the law. The law exists for them, not they for the law. Therefore persons are regarded by the law as being the possessors of rights and duties. This capacity to be the possessor of rights and duties is called legal capacity. While not all persons have equal or complete legal capacity, (for example young children have limited capacity), a person cannot be without some form of legal subjectivity, as everybody has at least some basic rights.

However, although all persons have legal rights and duties, a person, in a legal sense anyway, is not always a human being. In other words, the subject recognised as a person by the law is not always flesh and blood.

It is necessary to distinguish between two classes of legal subjects. The first is that of human beings, and all human beings have the capacity to be the possessors of rights and duties and are therefore legal subjects.

Human beings belong to a class of persons termed 'natural persons' in order to distinguish them from the second class of persons known as 'juristic persons'.

Juristic persons are devices that, although they are not human beings, are still recognised by the law as legal subjects that have rights and duties. This does not mean that they are treated exactly like flesh and blood natural persons.

For the purpose of business and public necessity the law recognises a business entity or community or group of persons as having a legal personality, which in turn means that it can have rights and duties. The fact that this device can have rights and duties means that it can participate in administrative, political, economic and other activities, alongside other persons, in its own name.

These devices are called juristic persons because it is the law that gives them the status of persons (in certain respects at least – for example, juristic persons cannot marry and they cannot be assaulted). They are known as juristic persons, because in reality they are artificial persons created by the law.

Well-known examples from legal life around us will make this clear. A company is probably the best-known example of a juristic person; a university is another. Both consist of two or more persons or groups of persons - a company of its shareholders, and a university of its council, senate, convocation, principal, lecturers and students; but both are legal entities or persons in their own right, and legally separate from the people that make them up.

Therefore, ABC Company remains the same juristic person even though its shareholders change, and the Dublin City University remains the same legal subject from year to year. Both take part in juristic acts through their organs (the parts that make them up – just like the organs in a human body), for example a company through a director, and a university through its principal. If these organs buy some land, for instance, it is the company or the university that becomes the owner of that land, and not the director or the principal or even the shareholders of the company or the members of the university. Likewise, it is the company or the university that has the duty to pay the purchase price for that land, and not the individual person who acted on their behalf or the shareholders or the members.

By the same token, the death of a director, or a shareholder, or the principal, or one or more of the members, will not affect the continued existence of the company or the university. This is known as the principle of perpetual succession.

A company has perpetual succession as it continues to exist even though the individual members may change. This perpetual succession continues until the company is wound up or dissolved, even if all the original members of the company have changed or ceased to exist. As the law has created this artificial person, so the law gives it a life of its own, which is separate from the lives of the human beings that make it up.

Therefore, by creating the Nursing Board as a corporate body with perpetual succession, the Act is creating the Nursing Board as a juristic person. This means that the Nursing Board will continue to exist even though its members might change (after each election), or where a member might die or retire and be replaced. This is because the Nursing Board is regarded as a person in its own right, and does not depend for its continued existence on the human beings that serve on the Nursing Board. Human beings are necessary as the Nursing Board needs them to carry out its functions, as clearly artificial persons cannot do anything themselves.

The other important consequence of the Nursing Board being a juristic person is that it can buy and sell land and other property, in its own name, rather than in the name of the people that serve on the Board. This is very useful as if the land or property was in the names of the people that serve on the Board, it would mean that every time the people serving on the Board changed, all the documentation relating to the land and property would need to be altered and the new names inserted. In this way, there is only one name on the documents that record the ownership of the land and other property, and that is of the Nursing Board itself, as it is a recognised person capable of owning property.

Finally, because it is recognised as a person in the eyes of the law, the Nursing Board can sue, and be sued, in its own name. It is not necessary to sue all the human beings that serve on the Board.

Sub-section (3) provides that the Board can regulate its own procedure, subject to what the Act might instruct it to do. This means that the Board can develop its own practices and procedures, as long as these do not contravene anything in the Act. Schedule 2 to the Act is entitled *'Rules In Relation To Membership And Meetings Of An Bord Altranais (The Nursing Board)'*. It provides details of how the Board is to run its meetings and voting procedures, etc.

Section 7 of the Act dissolves the former Nursing Board, and transfers all the legal rights and duties, including land and property and contracts (including contracts of employment) etc. to the new Board created by this Act. This ensured the smooth continuing operation of the Board.

Section 8 provides that the Board shall have its own seal (essentially a badge or a coat of arms as it is sometimes called). When the Board issues a document, it must be stamped with the seal in order to be an official publication of the Board. This is to prevent just anybody issuing documents in the name of the Board, which would obviously be very confusing to the public.

Membership of the Nursing Board

SECTION 9: *Membership of Board*
'(1) The Board shall consist of 29 members appointed in the following manner, that is to say:
(a) five nurses resident in the State and who are engaged in training nurses of whom—
- (i) one shall represent nurses who are training nurses in general nursing,
- (ii) one shall represent nurses who are training nurses in paediatric nursing,
- (iii) one shall represent nurses who are training nurses in psychiatric nursing,
- (iv) one shall represent nurses who are training nurses in the care of mentally handicapped persons, and

(v) one shall represent nurses who are training nurses in midwifery,

elected by nurses;

(b) five nurses resident in the State and who are engaged in nursing administration of whom—
- (i) one shall represent nurses who are engaged in general nursing administration,
- (ii) one shall represent nurses who are engaged in the administration of public health nursing,
- (iii) one shall represent nurses who are engaged in the administration of psychiatric nursing,
- (iv) one shall represent nurses who are engaged in the administration of midwifery, and
- (v) one shall represent nurses who are engaged in the administration of nursing of mentally handicapped persons,

elected by nurses;

(c) seven nurses resident in the State who are engaged in clinical nursing practice of whom—
- (i) two shall represent nurses who are engaged in clinical practice in general nursing,
- (ii) two shall represent nurses who are engaged in clinical practice in psychiatric nursing,
- (iii) one shall represent nurses who are engaged in clinical practice in midwifery,
- (iv) one shall represent nurses who are engaged in clinical practice in public health nursing, and
- (v) one shall represent nurses who are engaged in clinical practice in the nursing of mentally handicapped persons,

elected by nurses;

(d) twelve persons appointed by the Minister, after consultation with such bodies or organisations as he considers suitable to advise him, of whom—
- (i) one shall be a registered medical practitioner engaged in the practice of medicine in a hospital approved of by the Board for the training of general nurses,
- (ii) one shall be a registered medical practitioner engaged in the practice of medicine in a hospital approved of by the Board for the training of psychiatric nurses,
- (iii) one shall be a registered medical practitioner engaged in the practice of obstetrics in a hospital approved of by the Board for the training of midwives,

(iv) one shall be a person representative of the management of health boards,
(v) one shall be a person representative of the management of hospitals, other than hospitals administered by health boards, two shall be persons representative of the Department of Health,
(vi) one shall be a person who is experienced in the field of education,
(vii) one shall be a person representative of third level educational establishments which are involved in the education and training of nurses, one shall be a nurse, and
(viii) two shall be persons representative of the interest of the general public.'

Commentary

The Nursing Board consists of twenty-nine members. Seventeen of these members, in other words a clear majority, are nurses elected by nurses. This is important as the Board is a body that governs the activities of the nursing profession, and it is only right and proper that the nurses can determine who is in control of the Board. The Minister appoints the other twelve members, and one of these must also be a nurse, which means that in total there are at least eighteen nurses on the Board.

The seventeen elected nursing representatives are drawn from the demarcated disciplines of general nursing, paediatric nursing, psychiatric nursing, 'mentally handicapped' nursing (an insulting phrase – preferably called intellectual disability nursing), and midwifery. In turn these disciplines are represented by representatives from the functional sections of training, general administration and clinical practice. Accordingly, the entire nursing profession is properly represented, ensuring that there is not a dominance of interest in favour of one discipline or one function within the profession.

The twelve appointees of the Minister ensure that the government, the medical profession, and the public are also represented on the Board. This is important for the legitimacy of the Board, otherwise a perception could be created that the Board was only there to serve the interests of nurses, to the detriment of anybody else.

It is interesting to note that the Act grants the Minister power to change these numbers if he or she so pleases. This grants the Minister considerable power, and it is hoped that this power, and any abuse of this power, will be kept firmly under control by the profession and the public. There is also the further safeguard that the Minister must place any regulations before both houses of the Oireachtas and both houses need to approve those regulations. As the Minister would need to pass a regulation if he or she wanted to change the composition of the Board, these changes would need to be justified to both houses before approval was granted. This should prevent any abuse of this power.

Section 10 provides that the Minister has to take all steps necessary for the appointment of (the twelve appointed) members to the new Board. Section 11 provides for the election of those (seventeen elected) members, including any qualifications necessary to be a member of the Board, and any qualification necessary to vote for the members of the Board. Essentially, the rules provide that a person may be a member of the Board for five years, and no person shall remain in office for more than two consecutive terms (i.e. no longer than ten years). In practice a nurse must simply be a registered nurse to qualify both for election and to vote. There is no qualifying period.

Committees of the Nursing Board

SECTION 13: *Committees of the Board*

'(1) The Board may, subject to the subsequent provisions of this section, from time to time establish committees to perform such, if any, functions of the Board as, in the opinion of the Board, may be better or more conveniently performed by a committee, and are assigned to a committee by the Board.

(2) In particular and without prejudice to the generality of subsection (1) of this section, the Board shall establish a committee in relation to its functions under Part V of this Act.

(3) A committee established under this section, other than the committee referred to in subsection (2) of this section may, if the Board thinks fit, include in its membership persons who are not members of the Board.

(4) The chairman of every committee established under this section shall be a member of the Board provided that in the case of the committee referred to in subsection (2) of this section the chairman shall be a member of the Board other than the President or the Vice-President of the Board.

(5) Every member of the committee established under subsection (2) of this section shall be a member of the Board.

(6) A majority of the members of the committee referred to in subsection (2) of this section shall be persons who have been appointed by election to the Board and at least one-third of the members of that committee shall be persons other than persons who have been appointed by election to the Board.

(7) The acts of a committee established under this section shall be subject to confirmation by the Board unless the Board, at any time,

dispenses with the necessity for such confirmation.
(8) The Board may, subject to the provisions of this Act, regulate the procedure of committees established under this section, but, subject to any such regulation, committees established under this section may regulate their own procedure.'

Commentary
Section 13 authorises the Board to form committees, which can consist of Board members and other people specially appointed onto these committees. The exception to this rule is the Fitness to Practise committee (sub-section (2)), which must consist of only Board members (sub-section (5)). In addition, the Fitness to Practise Committee must have as a majority of its members elected Board members, rather than appointed Board members. The appointed Board members must consist of at least one-third of the Fitness to Practise Committee. Put simply, at least one-half of the Fitness to Practise Committee must consist of elected Board members (who are themselves nurses), and at least one-third of the Fitness to Practise Committee must consist of appointed Board members. Finally, the chairperson of the Fitness to Practise Committee cannot be the Chairperson or Vice-Chairperson of the Board. These measures ensure the credibility and legitimacy of the Fitness to Practise Committee, as it is hopefully independent (and autonomous) of the executive of the Board.

The fact that the majority of persons on the Fitness to Practise Committee are nurses ensures that nurses are disciplining nurses. The appointed members add balance and therefore legitimacy to the functions of the Committee. They prevent anybody accusing the Committee of being self-serving in the sense that it might be argued that nurses would protect nurses and cover up any wrongful conduct.

Section 15 provides that if the Board fails or refuses or neglects to discharge a function that it is bound to perform in terms of the Act, the Minister can order the Board to do so and if the Board continues to fail or refuse or neglect to perform that function, the Minster can remove the Board from office. This rather drastic action must be approved by both houses of the Oireachtas and the order by the Minister can be annulled if the Oireachtas is not satisfied with the actions of the Minister. This is obviously a very drastic step and it is unlikely that such a thing would happen.

Section 16 provides for the appointment of a Chief Executive Officer ('CEO') and section 17 for the appointment of other officers and servants of the Board. These are essentially the bureaucratic support staff who ensure the smooth running of the Board.

Fees charged by the Nursing Board

SECTION 25: Fees
'The Board may charge such fees as may, from time to time, be determined by the Board, with the consent of the Minister, for:
(a) the registration of a person in the register,
(b) the retention of the name of a person in the register,
(c) the restoration in the register of the name of any person whose name has been erased or removed pursuant to the provisions of this Act from the register,
(d) the giving to any person of a certificate of registration,
(e) the registration of any candidate for nurse training in any register maintained by the Board,
(f) entry into any examination conducted by the Board,
(g) applications to undergo nurse training,
(h) any other service which the Board may, from time to time, provide.'

Commentary
The Board generates its own income by charging fees to nurses for the privilege of being registered as a nurse, to continue being registered as a nurse (a nurse will pay an annual retention fee in order to remain on the register), or to be re-registered as a nurse if for any reason the nurse's name was removed from the register. Other sources of income are fees paid for the certificate of registration, fees paid to be registered as a trainee nurse, examination fees, training fees and any other service for which the Board might decide to charge.

Section 39 of the Act authorises the Board to apply to the High Court for the removal of a nurse, from the Register, who has failed to pay the fee. On 14 July 2003, the Board issued a press release stating that it had made application to the High Court in terms of section 39 for the erasure of 3069 names from the Register of Nurses maintained by the Board for the non-payment of annual retention fees. The press release continued that the 'names erased are nurses who owe fees for two or more years'. Nurses are obliged to inform the Board of changes in their name or address and it would appear that a significant proportion of the names erased were nurses who had failed to notify the Board of their current address. The balance were nurses who are working abroad or deceased, as well as those who no longer wished to remain on the Register'.

Rules made by the Nursing Board

SECTION 26: Rules
'The Board may, with the approval of the Minister, make rules for the purpose of the operation of this Act and any such rules may, inter alia,

provide for the establishment, membership, functions and procedures of committees to assist the Board in carrying out its functions under this Act.'

Commentary
The Board is empowered to make rules regarding committees and their membership and functions. These rules must be approved by the Minister. The Code of Professional Conduct for each Nurse and Midwife (often called '*The Nurses Rules*') of January 1988 and again in April 2000 were created in terms of this power. The 2000 Rules are contained as an appendix at the end of this chapter.

Registration

One of the most important functions of An Bord Altranais is the registration of newly qualified nurses and the re-registration of existing nurses. There is also the question of recognition of nurses who have trained and qualified in countries other than Ireland.

Part Three of the Act deals with the question of registration. It covers aspects such as the registration of names in the Register of Nurses, the correction and updating of the Register, as well as the registration of those persons in professions which are regarded as ancillary to the nursing profession (sometimes called 'support staff' which is a somewhat derogatory term).

Section 27 places the duty of maintaining the Register of Nurses firmly in the lap of the Board, and confirms that the Register should be divided into the specified divisions, including a division for midwives. A nurse is under a duty to notify the Board of a change of address, so that the Register can be amended to show that change. When a nurse is placed on the Register, he or she must receive a certificate to that effect.

SECTION 28: *Registration in the register of nurses*
'(1) The Board shall, in accordance with rules, register in the register every person who satisfies the Board that he complies with the prescribed conditions for registration.
(2) The Board may register a person in more than one division of the register if such person applies and satisfies the prescribed conditions for registration in each such division.
(3) Every person whose name, at the date of the establishment of the register, is entered on the register of nurses maintained by the former Board pursuant to the Nurses Act, 1950, shall be registered in the register.
(4) Every person who is a national of a Member State and has been

awarded a qualification in nursing in a Member State which, pursuant to the provisions of any Directive adopted by the Council of the European Communities, the State is obliged to recognise, shall, on making an application in the form and manner specified in rules made by the Board, and on payment of such fee as may be so specified, be registered in the register.

(5) Nothing in this section shall operate to prevent the Board from refusing to register the name of any person, who is otherwise entitled to be registered, on the grounds of the unfitness of that person to engage in the practice of nursing.

(6) On making a decision pursuant to subsection (5) of this section, the Board shall forthwith send by pre-paid post to the person to whom the decision relates a notice in writing stating the decision, the date thereof and the reasons therefor.

(7) A person to whom a decision under subsection (5) of this section relates may, within the period of two months, beginning on the date of the decision, apply to the High Court for cancellation of the decision and, if such person so applies, the High Court, on the hearing of the application, may—
   (a) declare that it was proper for the Board to make the decision, or
   (b) cancel the decision and direct the Board to register the name of the person making the application, or
   (c) cancel the decision and—
       (i) direct the Board to make a new decision, or
       (ii) give such other directions to the Board as the Court thinks proper.'

Commentary

Section 28 provides that a nurse may be registered in more than one division. In other words, a nurse may be a registered nurse and a midwife, or a general practice nurse and a learning disability nurse, and these qualifications must be entered on the register in the appropriate divisions.

The Harmonisation Directives For European Nurses

Section 28(4) gives effect to the EEC (the European Union as it is called now) Directives No. 457 1977 (77/452) and No. 154 1980. This Directive provides that any Member State in the European Union must take the necessary steps to recognise nurses who have trained in any of the other Member States. This provision includes Ireland which joined the EEC (now the EU) in 1972, at the same time as the United Kingdom and Denmark. With the recent addition of the ten new states, there are now twenty-five states in the EU: Austria, Belgium, Denmark, Finland, France, Germany, Greece, Ireland, Italy, Luxembourg, Portugal, Spain, Sweden, The Netherlands, The United Kingdom, Cyprus, Czech Republic, Estonia, Hungary, Latvia, Lithuania, Malta, Poland, Slovakia and Slovenia. There are three further applicant countries, who are presently not members of the EU but are likely to become so in the not too distant future. These are Bulgaria, Romania and Turkey.

The specific provisions of European Union law (called Directives), and the administrative decisions putting in place structures to oversee and implement these directives (called Decisions) which impact on the nursing profession are as follows:

Directive 77/452/EEC concerning the mutual recognition of diplomas, certificates and other evidence of the formal qualifications of nurses responsible for general care, including measures to facilitate the effective exercise of this right of establishment and freedom to provide services.

Directive 77/453/EEC concerning the coordination of provisions laid down by Law, Regulation or Administrative Action in respect of the activities of nurses responsible for general care.

Decision 77/454/EEC setting up an Advisory Committee on Training in Nursing.

Decision 77/455/EEC amending Decision 75/365/EEC setting up a Committee of Senior Officials on Public Health.

Directive 81/1057/EEC supplementing Directives 75/362/EEC, 77/452/EEC, 78/686/EEC and 78/1026/EEC concerning the mutual recognition of diplomas, certificates and other evidence of the formal qualifications of doctors, nurses responsible for general care, dental practitioners and veterinary surgeons respectively, with regard to acquired rights.

Directive 89/594/EEC amending Directives 75/362/EEC, 77/452/EEC, 78/686/EEC, 78/1026/EEC and 80/154/EEC relating to the mutual recognition of diplomas, certificates and other evidence of formal qualifications as doctors, nurses responsible for general care, dental practitioners, veterinary surgeons and midwives, together with Directives 75/363/EEC, 78/1027/EEC and 80/155/EEC concerning the coordination of provisions laid down by Law, Regulation or Administrative Action relating to the activities of doctors, veterinary surgeons and midwives.

Directive 2001/19/EC amending Council Directives 77/452/EEC, 77/453/EEC, 78/686/EEC, 78/687/EEC, 78/1026/EEC, 78/1027/EEC, 80/154/EEC, 80/155/EEC, 85/384/EEC, 85/432/EEC, 85/433/EEC and 93/16/EEC.

It is beyond the scope of this work to study these provisions in any detail. It is important to notice, however, that the recognition of qualifications in other Member States is restricted to nurses in general care. The question of specialisation and divisions, including the profession of midwife, is still a long way from achieving uniformity in the various Member States. It is, however, encouraging to note that most Member States are now following the same route as regards specialisation.

A nurse must first train as a general nurse, and once completing the training as a general nurse, may then move on to a specialist field. This at least allows uniformity amongst the Member States, as it means that all nurses will be trained general nurses, irrespective of the nature of their subsequent speciality. This common denominator allows the Member States to recognise each others' general nurses, and in so doing encourage mobility of nurses who can move around the European Union to countries where they are needed.

In a nutshell, should a nurse wish to practise as a general nurse in another Member State, it would seem that this is now relatively easy to achieve. However, should a nurse wish to work abroad as a specialist nurse in another Member State, he or she is advised to contact the Nursing Board of that country in order to establish the employment opportunities available with regard to any specialisation.

The European Court of Justice (ECJ), on 14 September 2000 laid out some important guidelines concerning the question of the recognition of foreign qualifications by Member States. The decision of the ECJ was in Case C-238/98 *Hocsman v Ministre de l'emploi et de la solidarité*.

Facts
Hocsman had qualified as a doctor of medicine in Argentina. He acquired Spanish nationality and his Argentinean diploma was recognised as equivalent to a Spanish university degree. He was thus authorised to practise medicine in Spain, where he trained as a specialist. He was subsequently employed in various French hospitals and applied to practise medicine in France. The Ordre des Médecins refused to grant him authorisation on the grounds that his Argentine qualification could not be recognised.

Issue before the court
Does a Member State have the right to refuse to authorise a national of another Member State to practise medicine if the person concerned holds a diploma acquired in that other Member State and has been accorded equivalence for a diploma obtained in a non-member country?

Decision of the court
The Court ruled that 'the competent authorities of the Member State concerned must take into consideration all the diplomas ... of the person

concerned and his relevant experience, by comparing the specialised knowledge and abilities certified by those diplomas and that experience with the knowledge and qualifications required by the national rules.'

The Court ruled that all qualifications and experience must be taken into account, that is to say, both those acquired in another Member State and those acquired in a non-member country.

Commentary
It may therefore be concluded that access to a profession covered by a Harmonisation Directive cannot be refused on the grounds that the applicant does not have the actual diploma required by the Directive. The host Member State must in all cases compare the training acquired and the training required. The registering authorities must look at the content of the person's training and the sum of their experience, and compare these to the academic and practical content required of the EU health professional.

Although Mr Hocsman was a medical doctor, the same principles will apply to a nurse seeking work in the European Union. In brief, it is relevant content, consisting of skills, qualifications and experience, and not just the title, that will secure employment in the EU. In the next chapter, the four-year Irish Bachelor of Science in Nursing is compared with the EU requirements as laid down in the aforementioned Directives.

APPENDIX ONE

The Nurses' Rules 2000

The Code of Professional Conduct for each Nurse and Midwife: April 2000

Definition

'Patient' - the use of the word patient in the code is to be broadly interpreted as individuals or groups who have contact with the nurse in his/her professional capacity and does not necessarily denote or imply ill health.

'Nurse' - where used in the code, the word nurse shall have the meaning assigned to it in the Nurses Act 1985. The word 'nurse' means a person registered in the Live Register of Nurses as provided for in section 27 of the Nurses Act 1985 and includes a midwife and nursing includes midwifery.

An Bord Altranais is the statutory body which provides for the registration, control and education of nurses and for other matters relating to nurses and the practice of nursing. It sees its overall responsibility to be in the interest of the public.

The purpose of this code is to provide a framework to assist the nurse to make professional decisions, to carry out his/her responsibilities and to promote high standards of professional conduct.

This code provides guidelines. Specific issues will be considered, when they arise or may be the subject of interpretative statements to be issued from time to time by An Bord. An Bord shall take appropriate action as defined in Part V of the Nurses Act 1985 where nurses fail to meet the following requirements.

The nursing profession demands a high standard of professional behaviour from its members and each registered nurse is accountable for his or her practice.

The aim of the nursing profession is to give the highest standard of care possible to patients. Any circumstance which could place patients/clients in jeopardy or which militate against safe standards of practice should be made known to appropriate persons or authorities.

Information regarding a patient's history, treatment and state of health is privileged and confidential. It is accepted nursing practice that nursing care is communicated and recorded as part of the patient's care and treatment. Professional judgement and responsibility should be exercised in the sharing of such information with professional colleagues. The confidentiality of patient's records must be safeguarded. In certain circumstances, the nurse may be required by a court of law to divulge information held. A nurse called to give evidence in court should seek in advance legal and/or professional advice as to the response to be made if required by the court to divulge confidential information.

The nurse must uphold the trust of those who allow him/her privileged access to their property, home or workplace.

It is appropriate to highlight the potential dangers to confidentiality of computers and electronic processing in the field of health services administration.

It is necessary for patients to have appropriate information for making an informed judgement. Every effort should be made to ensure that a patient understands the nature and purpose of their care and treatment. In certain circumstances there may be a doubt whether certain information should be given to a patient and special care should be taken in such cases.

Any form of sexual advance to a patient with whom there exists a professional relationship will be regarded as professional misconduct.

Competence is the ability of the registered nurse or registered midwife to practice safely and effectively fulfilling his/her professional responsibility within his/her scope of practice.

In determining his/her scope of practice the nurse or midwife must make a judgement as to whether he/she is competent to carry out a particular role or function. The nurse or midwife must take measures to develop and maintain the competence necessary for professional practice.

The nurse or midwife must acknowledge any limitations of competence and refuse in such cases to accept delegated or assigned functions. If appropriate the nurse or midwife must take appropriate measures to gain competence in the particular area.

A nurse shall be entitled to make known at the earliest possible opportunity to an appropriate person or authority any conscientious objection which may be relevant to professional practice.

The nurse shares the responsibility of care with colleagues and must have regard to the workload of and the pressures on, professional colleagues and subordinates and take appropriate action if these are seen to be such as to constitute abuse of the individual practitioner and/or to jeopardise safe standards of practice.

Each nurse has a continuing responsibility to junior colleagues. He/she is obliged to transmit acquired professional knowledge, skills and attitudes both by word and example. The nurse must not delegate to junior colleagues tasks and responsibilities beyond their skill and experience.

The nurse is responsible for the overall care provided by students. The nurse's responsibility in transmitting knowledge, skills and attitudes and in maintaining standards of care extends to student nurses wherever their learning activity occurs.

The nurse shall work in close co-operation with members of the health professions and others in promoting community and national efforts to meet the health needs of the public.

The nurse must at all times maintain the principle that every effort should be made to preserve human life, both born and unborn. When death is imminent, care should be taken to ensure that the patient dies with dignity.

When making public statements, the nurse shall make it clear whether he/she is acting in a personal capacity or on behalf of the profession.

The nurse should avoid the use of professional qualifications in the promotion of commercial products in order not to compromise the independence of professional judgement.

The nurse should not accept any gifts or favours from patients/relatives which could reasonably be interpreted as seeking to exert undue influence or to obtain preferential treatment.

The nurse must at all times take reasonable precautions to ensure that from the point of view of his/her health he/she is competent to carry out his/her duties. Abuse of alcohol or other drugs adversely affects that competence.

In taking part in research, the principles of confidentiality and the provision of appropriate information to enable an informed judgement to be made by the patient, must be safeguarded. The nurse has an obligation to ascertain that the research is sanctioned by the appropriate body and to ensure that the rights of the patient are protected at all times. The nurse should be aware of ethical policies and procedures in his/her area of practice.

An Bord Altranais: Summary

1. An Bord Altranais, or The Nursing Board, is created by the Nurses Act 1985 and is an organisation specifically set up to regulate the nursing profession in the Republic of Ireland.

2. The Nursing Board is a juristic person. This means it has rights and duties, and is capable of owing land and property. It has perpetual succession, which means it continues to exist in its own name even though the human beings that make up the Board might die or be replaced in elections. It can also sue or be sued in its own name.

3. The most important functions of The Nursing Board are:
   a. To register nurses and maintain the Register of Nurses.
   b. To control the education and training of nurses and the post-training of nurses in specialist fields.
   c. To provide for the discipline and if necessary punishment of nurses, by holding a Fitness to Practise Hearing.
   d. To ensure that Ireland complies with its obligations as a Member State of the European Union as regards the recognition of qualifications of nurses who have trained outside Ireland but in the European Union.

4. Useful websites:
   a. *An Bord Altranais* (http://www.nursingboard.ie).
   b. *European Union* (http://europa.eu.int).

3
THE EDUCATION OF NURSES IN IRELAND

> **Learning Outcomes**
> **At the completion of this chapter, the reader should know and understand the following:**
> - The specific powers of An Bord Altranais with regard to the education and training of nurses in Ireland.
> - The replacement of the Diploma in Nursing with the four-year Bachelor of Science in Nursing.
> - The EU requirements in regard to theoretical and clinical training.

Introduction

Part Four of the Nurses Act 1985 deals with the education and training of nurses in Ireland, which is controlled and regulated by An Bord Altranais.

The Nursing Board shall either provide or make provision for training courses and examinations, including approval of lecturers, the conditions of admission to examinations, and the granting of certificates to people taking the courses and passing the examinations. These training courses and examinations can be both for trainee nurses (section 31) and already qualified nurses (section 32), in other words qualification and post-qualification courses. Section 33 authorises the Board to hold examinations and appoint examiners who are suitably qualified to examine the candidates writing these examinations.

Section 34 authorises the Board to approve an institution or hospital as a place of training for nursing or trainee nurses. Section 36 stipulates that the Board must reassess these training hospitals and other training institutions at least every five years.

Section 36 also provides that the Board must reassess the training courses and examinations, both pre- and post-registration, at least once every five years.

Finally, section 37 places a duty on the Nursing Board to ensure compliance with the minimum standards specified by the Council of European Communities. In other words, the Board will not only assess the qualifications of nurses who have been educated and trained outside

Ireland should they wish to practise in Ireland, but the Board must also ensure that Irish nurses are sufficiently qualified to work elsewhere in the European Union.

The Evolution of nurses' education in Ireland

During the previous decade the changes in the education of nurses in Ireland have been remarkable. In 1995 the traditional apprenticeship model of nurse training was replaced by the registration/diploma programmes, commencing on a pilot basis in University College Hospital, Galway, in association with the National University of Ireland. Over the next three years, this programme of education became known as the 'Galway Model' and extended to all schools of nursing involved with pre-registration education of nurses. The introduction of the diploma model meant that links were forged between schools of nursing and third-level institutes, with the curriculum consisting of both theoretical and clinical placement components.

However, problems soon arose with the diploma programme, particularly concerning the difficulties involved with the unrealistic requirement that all of the biological and social sciences had to be taught in the first year of the programme.

As a result of the guidelines contained in the document produced by The Commission on Nursing (Government of Ireland (1998) *Report of the Commission on Nursing: A Blueprint for the Future,* Dublin: Stationery Office, 1998), it was decided that in order to meet the increasing complexity of nursing, coupled with rapid technological advancement, a four-year degree in nursing would become the standard programme for nursing education in Ireland. These four-year degree programmes would be offered in general, psychiatric and mental handicap nursing.

The universities offering nursing degrees are as follows:
National University of Ireland and constituent colleges,
University of Dublin Trinity College,
Dublin City University,
University of Limerick.

The following Institutes of Technology were included in the scheme (in addition to the universities that already offered a degree programme):
Athlone Institute of Technology,
Dundalk Institute of Technology,
Galway-Mayo Institute of Technology,
Letterkenny Institute of Technology,
Institute of Technology, Tralee,
Waterford Institute of Technology.

The course in general nursing trains nurses to take care of the total nursing of the patient, whereas psychiatric nursing involves caring for persons exhibiting abnormal behaviour, usually as a result of a personality or emotional disorder, and finally nurses trained in mental handicap nursing will strive to develop the inherent qualities and capabilities of the intellectually disabled, to allow those patients to take their rightful place in the world.

The Bachelor of Science in Nursing is a four-year programme consisting of sixty-eight weeks' theory and eighty weeks' clinical practice. The programme complies with the abovementioned sections of the Nurses Act 1985, with the Requirements and Standards for Nurse Registration Education Programme (An Bord Altranais (2000) *Requirements and Standards for Nurse Registration Education Programmes*, Dublin: An Bord Altranais 2000), Marks and Standards (National Council for Educational Awards (2001) *Examinations: Marks and Standards*, Dublin: NCEA 2001) and EU Directive requirements, as mentioned in the previous chapter.

Two-thirds of the theoretical content of the programme is devoted to Nursing Studies, one-sixth to Biological Sciences and one-sixth to Social Sciences.

In compliance with the EU Directive, the student nurse must receive 4600 hours of theoretical and clinical instruction, where theoretical instruction must account for not less than one-third of the programme (in other words, at least 1533 hours) whilst clinical instruction must account for no less than one-half of the programme (in other words, at least 2300 hours).

The requirements for the Irish four-year nursing degree course are set out in *Requirements and Standards for Nurse Registration Education Programmes* (Dublin: An Bord Altranais: page 22) and are as follows:

Theoretical instruction (which includes self-directed study and examinations): 1740 hours over 58 weeks;
Clinical instruction: 2646 hours over 74 weeks;
Discretionary hours (which must be accounted for in the Curriculum Document): 390 hours over 12 weeks;
TOTAL HOURS: 4776 HOURS OVER 144 WEEKS.

It is clear that the four-year degree programme offered to Irish nurses comfortably exceeds the minimum requirements laid down by the EU directives, and will qualify the Irish nurse to practice as a general nurse anywhere in the EU.

Education of nurses: Summary

1. The Nursing Board is responsible for the education and training of nurses in Ireland.
2. The education of nurses in Ireland has undergone a radical transformation in a relatively short period, with the initial apprenticeship system being replaced first by the diploma and currently the four-year degree.
3. The four-year degree is streamed into three disciplines, namely general nursing, psychiatric nursing and mental handicap nursing.
4. The EU Directive that governs the training requirements for nurses in the EU stipulates that a nurse must have a total of 4600 hours of training, with at least one-third of those hours (at least 1533 hours), being devoted to theoretical instruction and at least one-half of those hours (at least 2300 hours) being devoted to clinical instruction.
5. The current four-year degree offered at specified Irish third-level institutions comfortably exceeds the minimum requirements as laid down by the EU.
6. Useful websites:
    a. *National Implementation Committee* (www.nursing-nic.ie).
    b. *Health Research Board* (www.hrb.ie).
    c. *An Bord Altranais* (www.nursingboard.ie).

4
THE FITNESS TO PRACTISE INQUIRY

> *Learning Outcomes*
> **At the completion of this chapter, the reader should know and understand the following:**
> ▸ A nurse can be removed from the Register of Nurses for either misconduct or incapacity.
> ▸ Where a nurse is removed for either misconduct or incapacity this can only be done following a Fitness to Practise Inquiry.
> ▸ An internal disciplinary body is governed by administrative law and the principles of natural justice.
> ▸ A nurse can challenge any decision made by the Inquiry and this challenge will be heard by the High Court.

Important legal concepts and phrases that are crucial to an understanding of this chapter

'Ultra vires' ('outside the law') is used to describe the actions of an individual or body of persons whose powers and authority are created by a statute (called an enabling Act) but who purport to exercise powers that either were not given to them by the Act, or exceed the powers given to them by the Act.

'Audi alteram partem' ('hear the other side') means that for every version there is an opposing version, and a court or tribunal or disciplinary hearing must ensure that both sides are heard. In practical terms it means that everybody is entitled to speak in his or her defence.

'Nemo judex in sua causa' ('nobody must be a judge in his own court') means that the person or people who sit in judgment of other people must be independent of any of the participants in that hearing or trial and must also have no interest in the outcome of the hearing or trial.

Introduction

Part Four of the Nurses Act 1985 is entitled 'Fitness to Practise', and details the disciplinary powers of the Nursing Board, and more specifically, the workings of the Fitness to Practise Committee, the structure of which was examined in Chapter Two.

A nurse can be removed from the Register of Nurses for misconduct or incapacity. It is impossible to precisely define misconduct in the nursing sense, but clearly a starting point would be the Nurses' Rules, which are an appendix to Chapter Two.

Most professions, for example doctors, lawyers and accountants, have a watchdog body that regulates and disciplines the profession from within. These professional bodies are often criticised in that they are seen to protect their profession at the cost of the complainant. Whilst this might sometimes be true, most of the criticisms arise from members of the public who do not necessarily understand the workings of these bodies and their powers in contrast to courts of law.

Ultra vires and the principles of natural justice

An internal disciplinary body is governed by what is often known as administrative law. The most important principles that need to be remembered when looking at administrative law are the principle of *ultra vires* and the principles of natural justice.

As the powers of an administrative tribunal or disciplinary body are usually created by statute, in this case the Nurses Act 1985, it is important that the powers the disciplinary body exercises are actually bestowed (given) to that body by the Act. If the body does something that is not provided for by the empowering statute, it has acted outside of the powers given to it by the Act. The body will then have acted *ultra vires*, which means 'outside the law'.

In other words, the Fitness to Practise Committee must and can only do what the Nurses Act 1985 allows it to do, and nothing more. If the Committee disciplined a nurse in circumstances that were not covered by the Nurses Act 1985, or punished the nurse with a punishment that was not allowed by the Act, that discipline or punishment would be *ultra vires* and would have no legal effect. The nurse could challenge the decision of the Committee before the High Court, through a process known as judicial review.

Once it had reviewed the decision and actions of the Committee, if the High Court was satisfied that the Committee was not authorised by the Nurses Act 1985 to do what it did, the High Court would declare the actions of the Committee to be *ultra vires*. This would mean that the High Court would reverse that decision and declare it null and void.

The rules of natural justice are rules entrenched in our common law. They may be excluded by statute, but this is rare.

The first important principle of the rules of natural justice is *audi alteram partem* (which literally means 'hear the other side'), and which, in the context of disciplinary hearings, means that anyone whose rights, privileges and liberties are affected by the action of an administrative authority, must be given a chance to be heard on the matter.

The second important principle of natural justice that is applicable to disciplinary hearings is *nemo judex in sua causa* (no-one may be a judge in his own cause).

The first principle, of *audi alteram partem*, means that everyone is entitled to speak in his or her defence. This would include the right, where applicable, to bring forward evidence and witnesses in his or her defence, to inspect and challenge the evidence brought against him or her, and question the witnesses who testify against him or her.

If the High Court found that a nurse accused of misconduct was in some way prevented from carrying out a proper defence, it could declare the finding of the hearing null and void (which means that the law says it never existed). So for example, in the decision of *K. v An Bord Altranais* [1990] I.R. 396, the nurse was not given details of the evidence that was to be led against her at the hearing, and this caused the inquiry to be fatally defective.

What this means is that the charge sheet, detailing the complaints against the nurse, and all the statements from people required to give evidence at the hearing, must be furnished to the nurse before the hearing, usually even before a date is set for the hearing.

In addition, a nurse is entitled to be represented at the hearing.

The second principle, of *nemo judex in sua causa*, means that the person or people who sit on the disciplinary hearing must be independent of both sides and have no interest in the outcome of the hearing. This second requirement is sometimes quite difficult to satisfy when you consider that the Fitness to Practise Committee is composed mostly of nurses sitting in judgment of nurses, but what the principle would mean is that those people who are sitting on the Committee must be completely fair and impartial to the person who has been accused of misconduct. If a person on the Fitness to Practise Committee is unable to be impartial to a person appearing before that Committee (they might know the person well or might have had a previous unpleasant experience with the person), they must excuse themselves and take no part in the disciplinary hearing.

Again, if the High Court found that a person on the Committee was biased or prejudiced against a particular person appearing before that Committee, the decision of the Committee could be declared null and void.

With those principles in mind, it is necessary to examine the provisions of Part Four of the Nurses Act 1985.

The procedure to be followed in a Fitness to Practise Inquiry

SECTION 38: Inquiry by the Fitness to Practise Committee into the conduct of a nurse.

'(1)　The Board or any person may apply to the Fitness to Practise Committee for an inquiry into the fitness of a nurse to practise nursing on the grounds of—
   (a)　alleged professional misconduct, or
   (b)　alleged unfitness to engage in such practice by reason of physical or mental disability,
   and the application shall, subject to the provisions of this Act, be considered by the Fitness to Practise Committee.

(2)　Where an application is made under this section and the Fitness to Practise Committee, after consideration of the application, is of opinion that there is not sufficient cause to warrant the holding of an inquiry, it shall so inform the Board and the Board, having considered the matter, may decide that no further action shall be taken in relation to the matter and shall so inform the Committee and the applicant, or it may direct the Committee to hold an inquiry into the matter in accordance with the provisions of this section.

(3)　Where an application for an inquiry is made under this section and the Fitness to Practise Committee, after consideration of the application, is either of opinion that there is a prima facie case for holding the inquiry or has been given a direction by the Board pursuant to subsection (2) of this section to hold the inquiry, the following shall have effect—
   (a)　the Committee shall proceed to hold the inquiry,
   (b)　the Chief Executive Officer, or any other person with the leave of the Fitness to Practise Committee, shall present to the Committee the evidence of alleged professional misconduct or unfitness to practise by reason of physical or mental disability, as the case may be,
   (c)　on completion of the inquiry, the Fitness to Practise Committee shall embody its findings in a report to the Board specifying therein the nature of the application and the evidence laid before it and any other matters in relation to the nurse which it may think fit to report including its opinion, having regard to the contents of the report, as to—
      (i)　the alleged professional misconduct of the nurse, or
      (ii)　the fitness or otherwise of that nurse to engage in the practice of nursing by reason of alleged physical or mental disability,
   as the case may be.

(4) When it is proposed to hold an inquiry under subsection (3) of this section the person who is the subject of the inquiry shall be given notice in writing by the Chief Executive Officer sent by pre-paid post to the address of that person as stated in the register of the nature of the evidence proposed to be considered at the inquiry and that person and any person representing him shall be given the opportunity of being present at the hearing.

(5) The findings of the Fitness to Practise Committee on any matter referred to it and the decision of the Board on any report made to it by the Fitness to Practise Committee shall not be made public without the consent of the person who has been the subject of the inquiry before the Fitness to Practise Committee unless such person has been found, as a result of such inquiry, to be—
   (a) guilty of professional misconduct, or
   (b) unfit to engage in the practice of nursing because of physical or mental disability,
as the case may be.

(6) The Fitness to Practise Committee shall for the purpose of an inquiry held under subsection (3) of this section have the powers, rights and privileges vested in the High Court or a judge thereof on the hearing of an action in respect of—
   (a) the enforcement of the attendance of witnesses and their examination on oath or otherwise, and
   (b) the compelling of the production of documents,
   and a summons signed by the Chairman of the Committee or by such other member of the Committee as may be authorised by the Committee for that purpose may be substituted for and shall be equivalent to any formal procedure capable of being issued in an action for enforcing the attendance of witnesses and compelling the production of documents.

(7) Where—
   (a) a person on being duly summoned to attend before the Fitness to Practise Committee makes default in attending, or
   (b) a person, being in attendance as a witness before the Fitness to Practise Committee, refuses to take an oath lawfully required by the Fitness to Practise Committee to be taken, or to produce any document in his power or control lawfully required by the Fitness to Practise Committee to be produced by him or to answer any question to which the Fitness to Practise Committee may lawfully require an answer, or
   (c) a person, being in attendance before the Fitness to Practise Committee, does anything, which, if the Fitness to Practise

Committee were a court of law having power to commit for contempt, would be contempt of court,
such person shall be guilty of an offence and shall be liable on summary conviction to a fine not exceeding £1,000.
(8) A witness before the Fitness to Practise Committee shall be entitled to the same immunities and privileges as if he were a witness before the High Court.'

Commentary
Section 38 is a vitally important section as it lays down the entire procedure to be followed when a complaint is made concerning a nurse's conduct or capacity, which raises questions about that nurse's fitness to practise. It is for that reason that the entire section has been reproduced for the reader to carefully study.

First, it is important to realise that a complaint against a nurse can be made by 'any person', which would often be a member of the public (including visitors and relatives of patients), but could be a fellow nurse, a patient, any other health professional, or perhaps even a lawyer acting on behalf of an unhappy patient.

Second, it is important to note that the complaints are not restricted to misconduct on the part of nurses, but this section will also apply where it is alleged that a nurse is incapacitated from fulfilling his or her functions and duties by reason of a physical or mental disability.

What happens once a complaint is received is essentially a two-step procedure. The Committee must first consider the merits of the complaint, and whether the nurse in question has a case to answer. If the Committee feels that there is no substance to a complaint, or that the actions of the nurse were so minor that any disciplinary action would be excessive, the matter should end there and then, and the complainant sent packing. However, the Committee does not take this decision on its own, but rather makes a report to the Board with its recommendation. After considering the recommendation, the Board can either agree that the matter be closed, or disagree and insist that a disciplinary hearing be held. It is highly unlikely that the Board would ever refuse to follow the Committee's recommendation.

Where the Committee (and/or the Board) feels that there is some merit in the complaint, and that the nurse has a case to answer, they will proceed to the second stage of the proceedings, namely holding the disciplinary hearing itself. This disciplinary hearing is called an 'inquiry' in the Act.

The procedure that used to be adopted by the Fitness to Practise Committee was that the first stage of the process was essentially an internal matter dealt with by the Committee. The nurse, who was the subject of the complaint, had very little to do with the matter at that stage, and often was not even notified of the complaint until the Committee had decided whether to pursue or discard the matter.

This procedure would seem to be supported by section 38 (2), which provides that the nurse in question need only be notified by the Board once it has decided whether to proceed with the complaint or not.

The Supreme Court has criticised this approach in two decisions involving the same person, a midwife named O'Ceallaigh, with the one decision looking at the section 38 procedures and the second decision looking at the section 44 proceedings (which will be looked at later in this chapter).

The decision that examined the section 38 procedure was *O'Ceallaigh v An Bord Altranais* (unreported, Supreme Court, 17 May 2000).

Facts
The applicant was a registered nurse practising as a midwife. Four complaints were made against her in respect of her conduct during a number of difficult labours, in one of which the baby had died. The complaints alleged misconduct in that it was claimed that the applicant had practised dangerous methods.

The applicant was notified of the first complaint, where she was asked to respond, but she was never informed about the other three complaints. After deciding that there was a case to answer in respect of the first complaint, the Fitness to Practise Committee decided that the other three complaints should be heard at the same time.

The applicant said that this was unfair as she had not been given a chance to respond to the other three complaints before the Committee had decided to send them onto a disciplinary hearing.

Issue before the court
Was it necessary to inform the nurse of the complaints and allow her to respond at the stage where the Committee had to decide whether to pursue the matter or was it only necessary to inform the nurse of the complaints when it was decided to proceed with the disciplinary inquiry?

Decision of the court
The Supreme Court decided that there was no express provision in section 38 for either the Board or the Committee to notify the nurse, who is the subject of the complaint, before making a decision whether to establish an inquiry in terms of section 38. However, the Supreme Court held that, despite the wording of section 38(2), there was a duty to notify the nurse at that stage so that the nurse could respond to the complaint before the decision was taken whether or not to establish an inquiry.

The Supreme Court said that neither the Committee nor the Board could be said to be exercising its power lawfully and fairly without the nurse being informed of the complaint and the Committee and/or the Board having sight of any response to the complaint that the nurse might make, before the Committee and/or the Board decided whether or not to proceed with the inquiry.

Commentary
This decision of the Supreme Court is very important as it means that a nurse would have an opportunity to stop the matter going any further if he or she could produce evidence at the preliminary stage to show that the complaint had absolutely no merit. Without being given this opportunity, the nurse would have to go through an excruciating wait whilst an enquiry was set up.

Therefore, the decision of the Supreme Court must be supported as being fair to the nurse who is the subject of the complaint. It will also force the Committee and the Board to get a move on with the formalities and procedures if they want to take any action against a nurse. When one considers that Ms O'Ceallaigh was suspended for over two years as a result of those complaints, it is easy to see how prejudicial that first stage decision could be to a nurse, and it is only proper that the nurse should be able to respond to the complaint as soon as possible.

Erasure or suspension of a nurse from the Register of Nurses

SECTION 39: Erasure or suspension of registration from register for professional misconduct, unfitness to practise or failure to pay retention fee

'(1) Where a nurse—
  (a) has been found, by the Fitness to Practise Committee, on the basis of an inquiry and report pursuant to section 38 of this Act, to be guilty of professional misconduct or to be unfit to engage in the practice of nursing because of physical or mental disability, or
  (b) has failed to pay a retention fee charged by the Board after the Board had, not less than two months previously by notice in writing sent by pre-paid post to the person, at his address as stated in the register, requested payment of the fee on more than one occasion,
  the Board may decide that the name of such person should be erased from the register or that, during a period of specified duration, registration of the person's name in the register should not have effect.

(2) On making a decision under this section, the Board shall forthwith send by pre-paid post to the person to whom the decision relates, at his address as stated in the register, a notice in writing stating the decision, the date thereof and the reasons therefor.

(3) A person to whom a decision under this section relates may, within the period of 21 days, beginning on the date of the decision, apply to the High Court for cancellation of the decision and if such person so applies—

  (a) the High Court, on the hearing of the application, may—
    (i) cancel the decision, or
    (ii) declare that it was proper for the Board to make a decision under this section in relation to such person and either (as the Court may consider proper) direct the Board to erase such person's name from the register or direct that during a specified period (beginning not earlier than 7 days after the decision of the Court) registration of the person's name in the register shall not have effect, or
    (iii) give such other directions to the Board as the Court thinks proper,

  (b) if at any time the Board satisfies the High Court that such person has delayed unduly in proceeding with the application, the High Court shall, unless it sees good reason to the contrary, declare that it was proper for the Board to make a decision under this section in relation to such person and either (as the Court may consider proper) direct the Board to erase the person's name from the register or direct that during a specified period (beginning not earlier than 7 days after the decision of the Court) registration of the person's name in the register shall not have effect,

  (c) the High Court may direct how the costs of the application are to be borne.

(4) Where a person to whom a decision of the Board under this section relates does not, within the period of 21 days beginning on the date of the decision, apply to the High Court for cancellation of the decision, the Board may apply ex parte to the High Court for confirmation of the decision and, if the Board so applies, the High Court, on the hearing of the application shall, unless it sees good reason to the contrary, declare accordingly and either (as the Court may consider proper) direct the Board to erase the name of such person from the register or direct that during a specified period (beginning not earlier than 7 days after the decision of the Court) registration of the person's name in the register shall not have effect.

(5) The decision of the High Court on an application under this section

shall be final, save that, by leave of that Court or the Supreme Court, an appeal, by the Board or the person concerned, from the decision shall lie to the Supreme Court on a specified question of law.

(6)
(a) On erasing the name of a person from the register under this section, the Board shall forthwith send by pre-paid post to such person, at his address as stated in the register, notice in writing of the erasure.

(b) Where a direction is given under this section that during a specified period registration of the name of a person in the register shall not have effect, the Board shall, before the commencement of that period, send by pre-paid post to such person, at his address as stated in the register, notice in writing of such direction.

(7) The name of any person which has been erased from the register under this section may at any time be restored to that register by direction of the Board but not otherwise, and when a person's name is so restored to that register, the Board may attach to the restoration such conditions (including the payment of a fee not exceeding the fee which would be payable by such person for registration if he was then being registered for the first time) as the Board thinks fit.

(8) Where the registration of a person in the register has ceased to have effect under this section for a period of specified duration, the Board may, if it so thinks fit, on application made to it by such person, by direction terminate the suspension.

(9) On the hearing of an application under this section, the High Court may, if it thinks proper to do so, admit and have regard to evidence of any person of standing in the nursing profession as to what is professional misconduct.'

Commentary
If the Nursing Board finds that a person is unfit to practise, either because of misconduct or incapacity, the Board can do one of two things in terms of this section. It can remove the nurse from the Register of Nurses altogether (which is called 'erasure' in the section), or it can suspend that nurse from practising as a nurse for a certain period. We shall see that the Board has other options when it comes to sanctioning nurses. These further options are provided in later sections.

The Board must inform the nurse of this decision in writing and this written decision may be delivered to the nurse by post. The nurse has twenty-one days from the date of the decision to challenge that decision before the High Court, as a matter of judicial review. It is important to note that the twenty-one day time limit starts to run from the day of the decision, and not from the day that the letter was received by the nurse. A nurse can only pray that there is no postal strike when he or she is waiting for the outcome of an inquiry.

If the nurse does appeal to the High Court, these applications are usually heard 'on the papers', which means that the court does not hear the witnesses again, but only considers written arguments and evidence presented to it. A nurse proceeds with her application for an appeal by using a special summons and an affidavit, which is sworn evidence in a document, and will set out the reasons of the nurse for challenging the decision of the Nursing Board. The Board will reply to these written representations in its own affidavit.

Where there are extraordinary circumstances, for example where a witness was not available at the hearing, or where there is a dispute about whether a witness was telling the truth, the High Court can order a full rehearing of the matter. At this rehearing the witnesses will again give their evidence, but this time it will be in court. This is what happened in the case of *K. v An Bord Altranais* [1990] I.R. 396.

If a nurse does not apply to the High Court, nor gives any intention that he or she will challenge the decision of the Board, the Board is entitled to do so itself, and can ask the High Court to confirm its decision. If the Board does make this application it must show that the nurse had an opportunity to be heard, that the finding of the Board was correct and equitable, and that the Board is seeking to enforce what is an appropriate punishment.

On reviewing the decision of the Committee and/or the Board, the High Court can do one of three things: It can agree with the decision and confirm it; it can disagree with the decision and cancel it; or it can change the decision for one it decides is more appropriate.

The nurse could be given leave to appeal the decision of the High Court to the Supreme Court, but only on a point of law. In other words, if the nurse was arguing that the High Court's interpretation of the Act or the common law was wrong, this could be the basis of an appeal. The nurse cannot appeal the decision just because he or she does not agree with the decision.

Sanctions other than erasure or suspension

SECTION 40: *Attaching of conditions to retention on register*
'(1) The Board, following an inquiry and report by the Fitness to Practise Committee pursuant to section 38 of this Act, may decide to attach such conditions as it thinks fit to the retention in the register of a person whose name is entered in the register.
(2) On making a decision under this section, the Board shall forthwith send by pre-paid post to the person to whom the decision relates, at

his address as stated in the register, a notice in writing stating the decision, the date thereof and the reasons therefor.

(3) A person to whom a decision under this section relates may, within the period of 21 days beginning on the date of the decision, apply to the High Court for cancellation of the decision and if he so applies—
   (a) the High Court, on the hearing of the application, may—
      (i) cancel the decision, or
      (ii) declare that it was proper for the Board to make a decision under this section in relation to such person and either (as the Court may consider proper) direct the Board to attach such conditions as the Court thinks fit to the retention of the name of such person in the register, or
      (iii) give such other directions to the Board as the Court thinks proper,
   (b) if at any time the Board satisfies the High Court that such person has delayed unduly in proceeding with the application, the High Court shall, unless it sees good reason to the contrary, declare that it was proper for the Board to make a decision under this section in relation to such person and (as the Court may consider proper) direct the Board to attach such conditions as the Court may specify to the retention of the name of such person in the register,
   (c) the High Court may direct how the costs of the application are to be borne.

(4) Where a person to whom a decision of the Board under this section relates does not within the period of 21 days beginning on the date of the decision, apply to the High Court for cancellation of the decision, the Board may apply ex parte to the High Court for confirmation of the decision and, if the Board so applies, the High Court, on the hearing of the application shall, unless it sees good reason to the contrary, declare accordingly and (as the Court may consider proper) direct the Board to attach such conditions as the Court may specify to the retention of the name of such person on the register.

(5) The decision of the High Court on an application under this section shall be final save that, by leave of that Court or the Supreme Court, an appeal by the Board or the person concerned from the decision shall lie to the Supreme Court on a specified question of law.

(6) On attaching conditions under this section to the retention of the name of a person on the register, the Board shall forthwith send by pre-paid post to such person, at his address as stated in the register, notice in writing of the conditions.

(7) The Board may at any time remove in whole or in part the conditions attached to the retention of the name of any person on the register.'

Commentary
Where the Board decided that, in the circumstances, a removal or suspension from the Register of Nurses would not be appropriate on the facts of the proven complaint, it can allow the nurse to continue to practise, but place conditions or restrictions on the nurse's freedom to practise. For example, a nurse might be prohibited from doing certain tasks, or practising outside a certain area.

If the nurse is unhappy with this decision, the same procedures apply as were described in relation to the previous section of the Act, namely to bring the matter before the High Court.

Actions in lieu of sanctions

SECTION 41: Powers of Board to advise, admonish, etc
'(1) The Board, following an inquiry and report by the Fitness to Practise Committee pursuant to section 38 of this Act into the conduct of a person whose name is entered in the register may, on receipt of the report of the Committee, if it so thinks fit, advise, admonish or censure such person in relation to his professional conduct.
(2) The powers conferred by subsection (1) of this section may be exercised either in addition to or in substitution for any of the powers conferred by sections 39, 40 and 42 of this Act.'

Commentary
If the Board decided that removal, suspension or restriction would not be appropriate on the proved facts of the complaint, it can advise, admonish or censure a nurse, which essentially amounts to an official (and therefore recorded) scolding.

Interestingly enough, the section does not provide that the nurse can challenge the censure in the High Court. However, if the nurse can show that the censure will have a serious and damaging impact on his or her future career, it must be argued that the failure of the legislature to provide for a remedy in the High Court cannot be said to disqualify the nurse from challenging the censure in the High Court. Such an approach, of not allowing a challenge to the punishment, would be seen as an attack on established equitable principles, and it is doubtful that the High Court would allow its inherent powers to be removed.

Section 42, not surprisingly, provides that a nurse can be removed from the Register if convicted in the Republic of an indictable (a criminal offence that is serious enough to warrant a jury). If the nurse is convicted in another country of an offence that would be an indictable offence in the Republic, that offence shall have the same effect, and the nurse can be removed from the Register.

Again, the nurse can challenge this decision in the High Court, and the same procedures apply as in sections 39 and 40.

Immediate suspension of nurse pending the Fitness to Practise Inquiry

SECTION 44: *Application by Board for order suspending registration*
'(1) Whenever the Board is satisfied that it is in the public interest so to do, the Board may apply to the High Court for an order in relation to any person registered in the register that, during the period specified in the order, registration of that person's name in the register shall not have effect.
(2) An application under this section may be made in a summary manner and shall be heard otherwise than in public.
(3) The High Court may make, in any application under this section, such interim or interlocutory order (if any) as it considers appropriate.'

Commentary
In addition to section 38, section 44 is the other critical section in Part Four.

Section 44 authorises the Nursing Board to apply to the High Court, before or even during the inquiry, to remove a nurse's name from the Register. This is clearly a serious step, as in so doing it prevents the nurse from practising and therefore from earning a living. The Board must show the court that it would be in the interest of the public to have the nurse's name removed from the Register, in order to stop that nurse practising.

Sub-section (2) means that the Nursing Board can approach the High Court on an urgent *ex parte* application, which is an application to the court by the Nursing Board in the absence of the nurse against whom the complaint was made. This means that the Nursing Board can approach the High Court, without any notice to the nurse that it intends applying to the High Court, for his or her removal from the Register. This application can be heard *in camera*, which means that no members of the general public are allowed to be present when the application is argued before the judge.

Sub-section (3) gives the High Court a very wide discretion in deciding what would be the appropriate thing to do on the facts presented to it.

These are called injunction proceedings as they stop the nurse from practising. They are granted in urgent and serious circumstances where a disciplinary hearing could not act soon enough to prevent harm to the public. In other words, as a person is always presumed innocent until proven guilty, there would need to be clear evidence that the nurse must be stopped immediately, as he or she presents a danger to the public.

An injunction hearing is usually a two-stage procedure. As the court might only hear the version of the applicant before it grants the injunction, this first injunction is called an interim injunction, and is really seen as a temporary or stop-gap measure, until the court can hear full arguments from both sides. When the court grants an interim injunction, it will often set down what is known as a return day, which is the date that both parties will have an opportunity to argue the matter fully and at that stage the court can either make the injunction permanent or it can refuse to grant any further relief and the interim junction will simply fall away. If the court does not do so, either the Board or the nurse can apply for a return day, which ensures that the matter will be resolved and not drag on forever.

Nurse O'Ceallaigh, the midwife we spoke about earlier, was also injuncted (prevented by an injunction) from practising as a midwife, as the Board made a successful application to the High Court for an injunction against her, even before the section 38 hearing started.

This so-called interim injunction prevented Nurse O'Ceallaigh from practising for two years. When the Board approached the High Court two years later and asked the court to make the injunction a permanent injunction, this application was refused. The court said that the Board should have familiarised itself with the current facts of the case before making the application for a permanent order, as a lot of things could change in two years.

The Nursing Board appealed this decision to the Supreme Court, and argued that it was not obliged to reassess the facts before it applied for a permanent injunction, as long as it could show that it was in the public interest to prevent Nurse O'Ceallaigh from practising at the time of the first application.

The Supreme Court pointed out that a court might not grant the permanent injunction if it was clear things had changed considerably since granting the interim injunction. Accordingly, the Nursing Board must keep up to date with developments so that it can properly decide whether it is worthwhile asking for the injunction to be made final.

On the facts, the Supreme Court agreed with the High Court that the injunction should not be renewed or finalised, as the circumstances had changed considerably over the intervening two years.

The Supreme Court criticised the Nursing Board for dragging the matter on for two years, and pointed out that the section 44 proceedings were designed to provide speedy relief to the Board whilst the complaints against the nurse were investigated. It was not meant to be used to punish the nurse for two years.

Denham J. made this point forcefully when she said in her judgment:

> 'The section does not anticipate a situation where an application made in 1997 is heard in 1999. It anticipates a situation where an application is heard and determined within a reasonable time. If there has been considerable delay and a developing situation and facts, depending on the circumstances, there may be a responsibility on a Board to meet a changing situation with fresh evidence.'

(*An Bord Altranais v O'Ceallaigh*, unreported, Supreme Court, 17 May 2000.)

The Supreme Court did not go so far as to say that section 44 imposed a duty on the Nursing Board to determine how the situation had changed between the situation at the time of the interim injunction and the time of the full hearing, but it made it clear that the court would be reluctant to act on old information.

In practice this should force the Nursing Board to complete the disciplinary hearing as soon as possible, and to keep itself up to date with developments between the dates of the first and second hearings.

Other sections contained in Part Four of the Nurses Act:

Section 45 provides that anything that is said or done at the inquiry cannot be used in a defamation action.

Section 46 places a duty on the Nursing Board to inform the Minister (and the nurse's employer where this is a different person) of the outcome of the inquiry.

Section 47 authorises the Board to reinstate a nurse onto the Nurses' Register where that nurse's name was deleted from the Register as a result of non-payment of fees. The section is clear that this is the only reason the Board can use to reinstate a nurse on the Register. In other words, this section does not cover the situation where a nurse was removed for misconduct or incapacity, but only where the nurse was removed for not paying the annual fee.

Fitness to Practise Hearing: Summary

1. A nurse can be removed or suspended from the Register of Nurses for misconduct or incapacity.
2. If the Nursing Board decides that removal ('erasure') or suspension is too harsh a punishment in the circumstances, the nurse can be restricted or censured.
3. These punishments can only be imposed on a nurse after an inquiry finds him or her guilty of misconduct or incapacitated by reason of physical or mental disability.
4. Section 38 of the Nurses Act 1985 sets out the procedure for the Fitness to Practise Inquiry. Section 44 sets out the procedure where the Board can injunct (legally prevent) a nurse from practising as a nurse before and during the inquiry.
5. This inquiry must obey the principles of natural justice and the nurse must be given a proper opportunity to defend himself or herself against any complaints, and the nurse is entitled to expect that the Fitness to Practise Inquiry will be carried out by neutral and impartial people.
6. Section 38 provides for a two-step procedure. The first stage is where the Committee decides whether there is any substance to the complaints made against a nurse. If the Committee or the Board decide that the complaints are serious enough to justify an inquiry, the inquiry will be set up. The nurse must be given a chance to respond to the complaints at the beginning of the first stage, before a decision is made whether or not to proceed with the inquiry.
7. A nurse is entitled to appeal the decision of the Committee and the Board to the High Court.
8. The High Court can disagree with the finding of the Committee and/or the Board and reverse the decision, or it can agree with, and confirm, the decision, or it can substitute its own decision.
9. It is possible to appeal the decision of the High Court to the Supreme Court, but only on very narrow grounds.
10. Useful websites:
    a. **Irish Student Law Review**
       (http://www.islr.ie/Reviews/2000/Review0087.html).
    b. **Ann Kelly Support Page**
       (http://ireland.iol.ie/~raydj/Ann/entry.htm).

PART TWO

CIVIL LIABILITY

5
INTRODUCTION TO TORT LAW

> **Learning Outcomes**
> **At the completion of this chapter, the reader should know and understand the following:**
> - What a tort is.
> - What is meant by 'tort law' and where tort law fits into the overall scheme of things.
> - What is meant by the concept of 'liability'.
> - The general defences to tort, which are defences that can be used to defend against any claim brought in tort.

Important legal concepts and phrases that are crucial to an understanding of this chapter

Plaintiff and defendant
The plaintiff is the person who begins the court proceedings in a civil trial, and is usually the person who has been hurt or suffered damages. The defendant is the person who is being accused of wrongdoing, and who is being sued for damages.

Duty of care
A duty of care is owed by one person (the defendant) to another (the plaintiff) by reason of a prior relationship which is based on care, or if one person (the defendant) can reasonably foresee (contemplate) that his or her actions will cause harm to another person (the plaintiff) or their property, that person has a duty of care to take reasonable steps to avoid, or at least minimise, that harm.

Liability
Any legal obligation can generally be described as a liability. It could be a debt or a promise to do something. When a person is 'liable' for a debt or wrongful act it means that they are the person responsible for paying the debt or compensating the wrongful act. A person who owes another person a duty of care, and does not reasonably fulfil that duty of care, will be liable in tort to that injured person. Essentially that person will be legally in debt to the other person.

Actionable

If a plaintiff is entitled to sue a defendant because of the conduct of the defendant, that conduct is described as being actionable, which means it can support or justify an action in a court of law. To put it another way - a person can be sued in a court of law if their conduct is actionable.

Immunity

Being exempt from some liability to which others are subject. A person who is immune from action cannot be sued, either at all or for certain actions.

Causation

A defendant in an action in tort is liable only if the chain of causation between that defendant and the plaintiff, or more specifically the defendant's actions and the plaintiff's damages, is unbroken. There must be a clear link of cause and effect between the wrongful action and the damages caused.

Simple causation problems are solved by the 'but for' test (would the damage have occurred but for the defendant's tort?), but this test is inadequate for cases of concurrent (where two or more wrongful actions happen at the same time and it is not possible to establish who actually caused the harm) or cumulative causes (where the acts of two or more independent tortfeasors would each have been sufficient to produce the damage).

Matters get even more complicated when the courts introduce policy questions into the calculation. In other words, rather than ask 'can the defendant's actions be seen as the cause of the plaintiff's damage?' the courts ask 'should the defendant's actions be seen as the cause of the plaintiff's damage?'.

'Novus Actus Interveniens'

'A new act intervening'. A defence in an action in tort where it is claimed that the defendant is not liable for the damage done to the plaintiff, if the chain of causation between the defendant's act or omission is broken by the intervention of a third party. Where the chain of causation is broken by the actions of a third party, the damage caused is described as being too remote. In other words, there is no direct link of cause and effect between the wrongful action and the damage.

For example, the defendant negligently runs over the plaintiff's foot with his motor vehicle, and the plaintiff's foot is bruised. There is a clear link between the negligent driving and the bruise on the foot – no problems there.

The defendant drives the plaintiff to the hospital. The surgeon decides that an operation is necessary (this is later shown to be a faulty diagnosis). As a result of the surgeon's negligence the artery in the foot is severed, causing paralysis and necrosis. The foot is eventually amputated as a result of these complications. The plaintiff sues the driver for the loss of his foot (as opposed to the bruising of his foot).

The court would need to consider whether the negligent surgery was an intervening act. The defendant driver would argue that it was not his driving that caused the loss of the foot, but rather the surgeon's misdiagnosis and subsequent negligence. The plaintiff will argue that if it was not for the defendant's negligent driving, he would not have needed the surgery in the first place. The court will have to decide, using the test of causation, whether the defendant is liable for the plaintiff's damages.

Consent
To allow or to agree to allow a specific thing to happen.

Introduction: What is a tort?

Tort is a word used to describe a wrong committed by one person against another person, causing injury or damage to that person, which entitles that injured person to be compensated by the person who committed the wrong.

Every person is expected to go about their business without injuring others. When they do injure somebody, either because they meant to do so (intentionally) or because they were careless in what they were doing (negligence), they can be required by a court to pay money (damages) to the injured party so that, ultimately, they will also suffer from their conduct. Like criminal law, tort law also serves as a deterrent by sending a message to the community as to how people are expected to behave.

Students are often puzzled at the strangeness of the word 'tort', which is clearly foreign. The word originally comes from the Latin word *tortus*, which meant 'wrong' (it also meant 'twisted'). In French, tort means 'a wrong'.

Tort law is often described as the civil equivalent of criminal law, and as a working definition it is as good a place to start as any. It must be realised that one wrongful act can lead to both criminal and civil liability. For example, if a person negligently drives through a red traffic light and crashes into an oncoming car, the driver can be charged in the criminal court with dangerous driving. At the same time the driver can be sued in the civil court for negligence arising from the damage caused to the other car and for the personal injuries suffered by the driver and passengers of the other vehicle. Although there was only one crash, there will be two trials in different courts with different consequences. Essentially criminal law punishes the wrongdoer, whilst civil law compensates the victim. Tort law is part of the civil law.

There are numerous specific torts including assault, battery, negligence, products liability, and intentional infliction of emotional distress. Torts fall into three general categories: intentional torts (e.g., intentionally hitting a person); negligent torts (e.g., causing an accident by failing to obey traffic rules); and strict liability torts (e.g., liability for making and selling defective products).

In summary therefore, a tort is a civil wrong for which the normal remedy is an action for unliquidated damages, which means that the amount of money that will be awarded to the injured party must be assessed and decided by the court, and not by the parties themselves.

Not all actions which result in damage are actionable. To be actionable some right recognised and protected by law must be breached (broken). Where harm results without the violation of a recognised legal right, the injured party is left without a remedy. Examples would be a trader ruined by the legitimate competition of rival traders, or a petrol station that loses business when the local authority reroutes the highway resulting in a loss of traffic passing the station.

The person who commits a tort is known as a tortfeasor (wrongdoer), who is the defendant in court. Tort is concerned with physical injury (but including certain forms of psychiatric injury) and economic loss (including damaged reputation). The key issue is that of liability: in other words, was the defendant responsible for the plaintiff's loss. If so, the court must decide what compensation should be awarded.

In criminal law, it is vital to show the requisite mental element or *mens rea* (guilty mind), which means that a person must know what they are doing is a crime. In tort, the absence of a malicious motive will not make an otherwise unlawful act lawful. Similarly, the presence of a malicious motive will not normally make an otherwise lawful act unlawful. When speaking of intention in tort, as a general rule it is enough to show that the defendant intended the act or omission that injured the plaintiff, but it is not necessary to show that the defendant intended to injure the plaintiff. So for example, if a nurse lifted a patient out of bed intentionally, and hurt that patient's back, the nurse could be liable as he or she intended to lift the patient out of the bed, and it was the lifting that led to the injury. It does not matter that the nurse did not intend to hurt the patient – it is enough to show that the nurse intended to lift the patient out of the bed.

While each individual tort has its own rules governing liability, in general a plaintiff must prove that the defendant has infringed a right of the plaintiff which is recognised by law and some damage was caused to the plaintiff by the tortious act. However, in some special cases a plaintiff need not prove that there was any damage or loss - merely that their legal right was infringed. These are called torts actionable *per se*, such as trespass or libel, where the wrongful act is penalised, rather than the consequences.

General Defences in Tort

There are a number of general defences, which can be raised to answer most actions in tort. There are other special defences which can be raised in reply to particular torts and those will be considered at the appropriate time when considering the specific tort. General defences are:
- Inevitable accident.
- Necessity.
- Statutory authority.
- Consent of plaintiff.

Inevitable accident

Where the consequences of an action are neither foreseen nor intended, and which could not have been avoided by any reasonable care exercised by the defendant, the defendant can use the defence of inevitable accident (in other words, no matter what the defendant did or did not do, the accident would have happened anyway).

An 'Act of God' is a special form of inevitable accident, as it occurs when damage is caused by the happening of natural causes, which a reasonable person could not have foreseen or guarded against. For example, a house owner sues the city council for the damages caused to his home by floods, on the basis that the city council had a duty of care to provide decent storm drains. The city council might argue that even if they had installed the biggest and best storm drains available, the floods were so severe that the plaintiff's house would have been flooded in any event.

A medical example would be where a patient suffers a massive heart attack during a routine operation, and it is shown that the patient suffered from congenital heart disease and the attack was not foreseeable and nothing could have saved him.

Necessity

Where the defendant deliberately commits a tort against a person in order to prevent or avoid some greater harm where there is no reasonable alternative. For example, the pulling of a person from the river, usually a trespass against the person, in order to prevent that person drowning. Another example would be the entering of a person's house, usually a trespass onto property, in order to stop a fire in that house. This defence is saying that it was necessary to commit a smaller evil in order to prevent a greater evil, usually where that greater evil will result in death or harm that cannot be repaired.

A medical example would be emergency CPR (heavy blows to the chest – a serious battery) being administered to an unconscious crash victim with cardiac arrest.

Statutory authority
Where a statute affords a defence for conduct, which is otherwise actionable in tort. In other words, the statute authorises you to commit what would usually be a tort. It will of course depend on the wording and interpretation of the statute in question as to whether it does provide a defence to an action for tort.

In general, where a person is acting in terms of a statute, that person will be immune from liability for any torts committed as long as that person does not act negligently or in bad faith. For example, a detective enters a person's house under the authority of a valid search warrant, and whilst searching the house negligently (or maliciously) smashes an expensive crystal vase. The homeowner cannot sue the detective for trespass, as the search warrant authorises the detective to trespass. However, the homeowner could legitimately claim damages for the loss of the vase, as there was nothing in the search warrant that would allow that action to go unpunished.

A medical example would be where a statute places a duty on a doctor or a nurse to notify the authorities if a patient has a notifiable disease. If the patient was to sue for breach of confidentiality, the nurse or doctor could rely on the defence of statutory authority, as the statute ordered them to breach patient confidentiality.

Consent of plaintiff
To be an effective defence, the consent of the plaintiff to the act in question must be free (voluntary), full (with proper understanding) and unfettered (not modified in any way). Mere knowledge of the risk is not sufficient, the plaintiff must understand exactly what it is that they are consenting to. So for example, a cancer patient cannot be said to have consented to a course of chemotherapy unless they understand the nature and severity of the side effects of that treatment.

Consent is the most common defence to tort and is really an essential ingredient of our everyday life. Imagine if you could sue somebody for bumping you in a queue, for innocently touching you on a bus, for cutting your hair in a barbershop, or for tattooing you with a design that you chose.

Without you consenting to these people doing these things, these actions would all be torts, some of them quite serious. You have consented to these people doing these things to you, which makes everyday life a lot easier.

A party who agrees to run the risk of injury from a specific source of danger, usually negligence, is said to have voluntarily assumed the risk (which the law describes as the defence of *volenti non fit inuria*). For example, a sport photographer taking close up action pictures in a rugby match or in a show jumping arena is voluntarily assuming the risk that he or she will be bowled over by a speeding player or bumped into by a horse. This can raise interesting questions in the hospital scenario – when a patient agrees to be admitted to a public ward, does that patient consent to contracting a disease from another patient, or witnessing some distressing scenes of sick and suffering people, just by being admitted into a public ward?

An Introduction to Tort Law: Summary

1. Tort is a word used to describe a wrong committed by one person against another person, causing injury or damage to that person, which entitles that person to be compensated by the person who committed the wrong.
2. Tort law complements the criminal law. One wrongful action by a person can result in that person being charged under the criminal law and sued under the tort law. The criminal law is essentially concerned with punishing the wrongdoer, whilst tort law is essentially concerned with compensating the victim.
3. Torts fall into three general categories: intentional torts, negligent torts and strict liability torts.
4. While each individual tort has its own rules governing liability, in general a plaintiff must prove that the defendant has infringed a right of the plaintiff which is recognised by law, and that some damage was caused to the plaintiff by the tortious act.
5. In some special cases a plaintiff need not prove that they suffered any damage or loss – merely that their legal right was infringed. These are called torts actionable *per se*, such as trespass or libel.
6. There are a number of general defences that can be raised to answer most actions in tort. These are the defences of inevitable accident; necessity; statutory authority; and consent of plaintiff.
7. Useful websites:
    a. ***Irish Student Law Review*** (http://www.islr.ie).
    b. ***British and Irish Legal Information Institute*** (www.bailii.org).

6

PATIENT AUTONOMY AND THE TORT OF TRESPASS TO THE PERSON

> **Learning Outcomes**
> **At the completion of this chapter, the reader should know and understand the following:**
>
> ▸ The concept of patient autonomy.
> ▸ The torts of assault, battery and false imprisonment.
> ▸ The defences of consent, self-defence, lawful authority and necessity.

Important concepts and phrases that are crucial to an understanding of this chapter

Autonomy
A state of personal independence often referred to as self-reliant or self-sufficient. When speaking about patient autonomy we mean the right of patients to make decisions about their medical care without their health care provider trying to influence their decision. Whilst the concept of patient autonomy does allow for health care providers to educate the patient, it does not allow the health care provider to make the decisions for the patient.

Paternalism
Treating or governing people in a 'fatherly' manner, by providing for their perceived needs without giving them rights or responsibilities or the right to decide what their needs are.

Subjective
Something that originates in, or takes place in, a person's mind rather than being created in the external world. A concept or statement is subjective when it is created by a person's own consciousness or when an existing concept or statement is modified by one's own views and bias. (e.g. 'Everybody loves chocolate').

Objective
The opposite of subjective. Something that has actual existence in reality

and is not influenced by emotions or personal prejudices, and is usually based on observable events or phenomena. (e.g. 'The sun rises in the morning').

Fraud
Conduct which is deceitful and which aims to manipulate another person to give something of value by telling untruths or repeating something that is known to be untrue, or concealing a fact from the innocent person which may have saved that person from being cheated.

Duress
Where a person is forced to act, or is prevented from acting, according to their free will, by the threats or force of another.

Illegality
An act that breaks the law.

Introduction – the concept of patient autonomy

The relationship between patient and health professional is inherently unequal. This inequality is due to a variety of reasons, including unequal access to knowledge and information, the fact that the patient is often in a state of physical or mental weakness, and the natural feelings of dependency that are always present in the treatment relationship.

Although the inequality in power is far more obvious when looking at the relationship between doctor and patient, it can be said that the nurse also has status, knowledge and experience and often appears quite formidable to the patient. The patient on the other hand is vulnerable, dependant and in relative ignorance. Of course the characteristics of this relationship are found in other professions, for example the relationship of lawyer and client. However, as the medical relationship often involves questions of life and death, privacy and bodily integrity, and moral and ethical dilemmas, the law has devoted particular emphasis to it.

Again, although these questions become far more serious when considering the relationship between doctor and patient, nurses are increasingly being given more authority and responsibility, and it is therefore necessary to recognise that these questions of power and inequality need to at least be recognised by the nursing profession. In addition, the nurse is often called upon to be a patient advocate, caught in the middle of a 'power struggle' between the doctor and the patient, and therefore the nurse must be aware of the dynamics of this power relationship, and the manner in which the law attempts to deal with it.

The law has attempted to correct this power imbalance by developing the concept of patient autonomy, which has been described in a number of ways, including the right of self-governance, or the right of self-determination. Essentially the law is concerned with giving the patient a voice that can be heard and respected, as opposed to just being ignored.

The most important weapon provided to the patient is the power to consent, or refuse, any medical treatment.

The legal right of the patient to consent to, and also refuse, medical treatment is grounded in the Irish Constitution. Article 40.3 1 provides as follows:

> 'The State guarantees in its laws to respect, and, as far as practicable, by its laws to defend and vindicate the personal rights of the citizen.'

The personal rights of the citizen to consent to, or refuse, medical treatment as a fundamental personal right is constitutionally protected, provided that the citizen has sufficient mental (intellectual) capacity, sufficient and up-to-date information and freedom of choice (voluntariness). It is no longer permissible to apply the paternalistic practices that were the norm not that long ago.

The State has a constitutional duty to pass laws, or change existing law, to ensure that the patient is free and empowered to properly consent, or refuse, medical treatment.

Of course this emphasis on the polar opposites of paternalism and patient autonomy tends to conceal the practical reality of medical treatment – the concept of collaborative decision-making. Rather than looking at medical law as controlling these two opposing forces – nurse/doctor versus patient, we should rather be looking at what is often termed 'a therapeutic alliance', which means that the health professional and the patient will consult and agree on what is best for the patient. This sense of shared power will be far more beneficial to the healing process than a situation where the patient is continuously fighting for independence against a health professional who is continuously trying to impose his or her will on the patient.

This would be the ideal situation. Unfortunately, the health profession tends to dictate and decide for the patient, rather than advise and facilitate with the patient. This is not because doctors and nurses are domineering bullies or know-it-alls. As resources become scarcer and numbers heavier, most doctors simply do not have the time to listen to their patients, and cannot enter into mutually beneficial consultations. This is where the role of the nurse should assume greater importance – as doctors are put under increasing pressure, it must become the task of the nurse to listen to patients and convey their sentiments to the doctor, so that the doctor can consider the thoughts and feelings of the patient.

Presently, it would seem that our nurses are under similar pressures, and are not able to stop and listen as much as they would like.

At the moment the law does stand as a referee between two opposing forces, rather than acting as a facilitator between two collaborating forces. By affording the nurse an opportunity to learn the law, we will hopefully also be affording the nurse the opportunity to become a valuable facilitator in the therapeutic process.

The 'doctrine' of informed consent

The concept of informed consent is based on the principle of patient autonomy – it is really the practical application of this principle. The patient must be in a position to make an educated decision as an expression of free will.

Consent is one of the common defences. In other words, it is a defence to every tort (within the limits of public decency) that the plaintiff consented to the actions of the defendant.

The doctrine of informed consent is an area supposedly unique to medical law, and we will study it in detail later. This claim of uniqueness is an oversimplification as essentially the 'doctrine' is really a specialised form of the defence of consent, and the phrase 'informed consent' is imported from American law, which has not always made it popular with Irish or English courts.

What can be said about this 'doctrine' is that it has developed through the law of tort, where consent is recognised as a general defence to all torts. More specifically, it is an accepted defence to the tort of trespass against the person.

What this means is that to be able to fully understand the doctrine of informed consent, the reader needs to first be familiar with the basics of the tort of trespass to the person, and the defences (of which consent is one) available to a person who is sued for trespass to the person.

The tort of trespass

The tort of trespass is probably the oldest tort known to our law, and a defendant can trespass on a plaintiff's land (which is probably the most well-known form of trespass), or the defendant can trespass against a plaintiff's goods, or finally, the defendant can trespass against a plaintiff's body, which is the type of trespass examined here.

The tort of trespass to the person means direct and intentional acts of interference by the defendant with the person of the plaintiff, and can consist of three acts: assault, battery and false imprisonment.

All three of these torts have common characteristics, which are as follows:

The act that is the cause of the complaint must have been a voluntary act by the defendant. In other words, the defendant must have been in conscious control of his or her actions when performing the wrongful or unlawful act that is the cause of the complaint. For example, you are on a ladder hammering nails into a wall. There is a loud bang and you drop the hammer in fright. The hammer falls on the head of a passer-by. You could argue that your action was not voluntary, as you did not let the hammer go as an act of conscious control.

The act, which is the cause of complaint, must be intentional. Unlike the criminal law, it is not necessary to show that the defendant intended to injure the plaintiff. When speaking about intention in tort, it is meant that it is necessary to prove that the defendant intended to commit the act that caused the plaintiff's injury (as opposed to intending to cause the injury itself) – in other words, it is always necessary to be in conscious control.

The plaintiff need not prove that he or she has suffered injury or damages, in the sense of physical or emotional damage, or financial loss. The tort of trespass is known as a tort actionable *per se*. This concept was discussed earlier, and means that the wrongful conduct is regarded as being so serious on its own that it must be penalised, even where damages might have been minimal or even non-existent.

The tort of assault
Assault is the threat of, or attempt to apply, force to another that puts that other person in reasonable apprehension that they are about to be hurt. In other words, when faced with the conduct of the defendant, an ordinary person would think: 'Uh oh, I'm in for it now!' The shaking of a fist in front of a person's face or the pointing of a loaded gun are assaults, whether or not they are accompanied by threatening words or other gestures.

Assault would seem to consist of a mental element – the plaintiff was of the view that the defendant was about to hurt him or her. Accordingly, this would appear to be a subjective wrong, as it relies on the mind-set of the victim.

This is not the case. The test is the same as used in all areas of tort law, namely what would the reasonable person do or think in that situation – in other words, an objective test is used. Would a reasonable person, when confronted with the threatening gestures or words of the defendant, have felt that he or she was about to be hurt? That is the essence of the tort of assault – the reasonable apprehension of the use of immediate violence.

So, if a person said to you over the telephone: 'If I was in the same room as you, I'd give you the hiding of your life!', that can never be an assault, as the defendant has stated that he is powerless to harm you – he is somewhere else. On the other hand, if a person said over the telephone: 'There is a bomb in the building, set to go off in a minute', that could very well be an assault, as the receiver of the telephone call would reasonably apprehend that he or she was about to be killed or seriously injured in less than a minute's time.

It is doubtful whether a nurse, or any health professional for that matter, would ever find himself or herself being sued for assault arising out of their professional duties, unless the patient could show that they were in reasonable apprehension of 'violence' by reason of the nurse's words or actions. For example: 'If you sit still for a minute, I can inject you with this "flu vaccine"', would be an assault if the patient had not consented to the injection and was in reasonable apprehension of having a hypodermic needle plunged into his or her arm.

The tort of battery

Battery is the touching of another person, directly or indirectly, however slightly, without the consent of the person being touched. Touching, prodding or rubbing another person, without consent, are examples of direct battery. Spraying water or detergent over another person, or tipping a bed causing the person to fall out, are examples of indirect battery. To be successful in an action for battery the plaintiff does not need to prove physical injury. It is sufficient to prove unauthorised contact, which is really touching without permission.

Once again, the unlawful or wrongful act must have been voluntary on the part of the defendant. In other words, the defendant must be in conscious control when committing the act that is the cause of the complaint.

Force is not essential. For example, an uninvited kiss or gentle stroking is a battery. It also explains why it is not necessary for the plaintiff to suffer physical harm or injury, as what is being penalised is the conduct, rather than the consequences of that conduct.

The fact that battery can extend to anything which is attached to the plaintiff's body and is practically identified with the plaintiff's body means that it is possible to have indirect battery, as it is not necessary to have direct physical contact between the person of the plaintiff and the person of the defendant.

So just as assault could be generally described as the mental component of trespass to the person, so battery could be generally described as the physical component, as it consists of unauthorised touching of the plaintiff's body or person.

Clearly the touching of a patient by a nurse without the consent of that patient is a battery. Some would argue that the touching would be a battery only if done with hostile intent. So for example, if a nurse administered treatment to a patient in order to make that patient feel more comfortable, some would argue that this is not a battery, despite the lack of consent. This is a dangerous approach to adopt in the field of medicine, as it takes for granted that the patient wanted to feel 'comfortable' in the first place (whatever that might mean), and also presupposes that the patient shares a similar concept, with the nurse, of what it means 'to feel comfortable'.

The modern law has effectively done away with the idea that there must be a hostile intent for there to be battery. The only ingredient necessary for a battery is the unauthorised touching – the intention or motive behind that touch might be grounds for a defence to the battery, but it does not change the fact that a battery has occurred.

The tort of false imprisonment

False imprisonment is the unlawful and total restraint of the personal liberty of another. This can be physical bondage, whether by manacles or in a cell, or mental bondage, which is achieved by the defendant acting in such a way that the plaintiff knows or reasonably thinks that he or she must not move.

The essential element is the unlawful detention of a person, or the unlawful restraint of his or her liberty. It is not necessary that there be violence or forcible detention. The person does not even have to be aware at the time that he or she is imprisoned. There must, however, be a total restraint of the liberty of a person. It is not false imprisonment to block a person's way forcing them to walk around you, although it may be a nuisance.

Again, it is hardly likely that a nurse will ever face a claim of unlawful imprisonment, unless they are in the habit of strapping patients to beds or locking them in the toilet. A nurse might look sternly at a patient, who is in the habit of wandering the corridors, and say: 'Don't move!', but this would not constitute false imprisonment, as the patient can move if he wants to, and would be aware of this. It is in any event quite lawful in the circumstances to prevent a patient wandering around the hospital.

Assault, battery and unlawful imprisonment can also be criminal offences, and this area of law is governed by a statute known as the Non-Fatal Offences Against the Person Act 1997, which will be closely examined in the criminal law section.

Defences to the Tort of Trespass Against the Person

Consent
A person impliedly consents to ordinary social contact, for example being

jostled or bumped in a queue, or having their hand shaken. It is clear that contact sports like rugby would not be possible if there was not some form of consent to touching.

Consent may also be expressly given, for example having your haircut or a tooth extracted. Where consent is pleaded, it must be shown that the terms of the consent were not exceeded. For example, consenting to take part in a game of rugby is not consent to being battered. If a rugby player broke the rules and whilst breaking the rules hurt another player, that would be a battery, as the other player did not consent to the guilty player breaking the rules. Your consent to physical contact extends only to physical contact within the rules of the game in which you participate. The consent must be genuine, and consent obtained by fraud, duress or illegality is not a defence to trespass.

This is clearly the most important defence available to the nurse when accused of trespass to the patient's person, and is the basis of the doctrine of informed consent.

Self-defence

The defence of person or property is a defence to trespass. To repel force with force is lawful provided that no unnecessary force was used. How much force and of what kind is considered reasonable in the circumstances is a question of fact for the court to decide. Resistance must not exceed the bounds of defence and prevention. What this means is that the amount and kind of force used in defence must be equivalent and similar to the force used in the attack. To use a crude example, you would not use a handgun to defend yourself from a slap, but a hard shove or even a punch (if the attacker kept coming at you) would probably be within the limits of self-defence.

Hopefully a nurse would never have to rely on this defence.

Lawful authority

There are many laws which permit public officials, usually the Gardaí Síochána, to detain or arrest people, and these laws, as long as the official does not abuse the power conferred, will be a defence to an action for trespass. Similarly, health professionals often act in terms of a statute when treating a patient without consent – for example, taking blood samples from a person arrested for driving under the influence of alcohol.

Necessity

Where it is necessary to commit one evil (the tort complained of) in order to avoid a greater evil happening to the injured party, the act of committing the original lesser evil is justified (for example, grabbing somebody by the hair in order to save them from drowning).

The defence of necessity is the legal basis of emergency medicine. In situations of emergency (for example, an unconscious patient is bleeding to death), if a health professional was to wait for the consent of a patient the harm or damage will occur and might be irreparable. Consequently, the nurse or doctor performs the treatment without consent (the lesser evil) in order to avoid irreparable damage or death (the greater evil).

The life-saving treatment was performed without consent, and is therefore a battery. The defence to that is necessity – the battery was necessary in order to save the patient's life, in circumstances where the wishes of the patient could not be obtained.

Clearly if the patient is conscious and mentally competent, and instructs the nurse or doctor not to administer any treatment, that wish must be respected, and there is no defence of necessity available in those circumstances. The defence of necessity is only available where it is not possible to obtain the patient's consent (or refusal) to treatment.

Autonomy and Trespass to the Person: Summary

1. The tort of trespass can be broken down into the three categories of trespass to land, trespass to goods, and trespass to the person.
2. In turn, trespass to the person can be broken down into assault, battery and false imprisonment.
3. Medical treatment without consent is battery.
4. The recognition of patient autonomy means that a patient has the right to accept (consent) or refuse treatment.
5. Consent is a recognised defence to the tort of battery. The so-called doctrine of informed consent is essentially a modified form of the defence of consent to battery.
6. Necessity is another recognised defence to the tort of battery. The practice of emergency medicine is based on the defence of necessity.
7. Finally, lawful authority is also a recognised defence to the tort of battery. An example would be the taking of a blood sample from an intoxicated driver.
8. Useful websites:
    a. *Oasis* (http://www.oasis.govie/health).
    b. *Worcester VTS* (http://www.text.worcestervts.co.uk/index.htm).
    c. *Canadian Medical Association Journal* (http://www.cmaj.ca/).

7
INFORMED CONSENT TO MEDICAL TREATMENT

> **Learning Outcomes**
> **At the completion of this chapter, the reader should know and understand the following:**
>
> ▸ Why and when a health professional can be sued for battery.
> ▸ What is meant by consent, and more importantly, what is meant by informed consent to medical treatment.
> ▸ What is meant by the duty to explain, and how this duty affects both doctors and nurses.
> ▸ The role that the nurse can perform to ensure that a patient fully understands the nature and the risks of any proposed treatment.
> ▸ The three elements of informed consent to medical treatment.

Important concepts and phrases that are crucial to an understanding of this chapter

Capacity
In the general sense capacity means the power of receiving and holding ideas. In the legal sense capacity means one's ability or authority to perform certain acts that have specific legal consequences.

Disclosure
To reveal or uncover or to make something known that was previously unknown. In the legal sense it means to allow access to previously unknown information.

Voluntary
Freely, acting by one's own choice or decision, and without duress or coercion.

Introduction

The acts of assault and battery constitute the tort of trespass to the person and are actionable *per se*, which means that no proof of damage to the patient is necessary.

When members of the medical profession carry out treatment on patients, they must have the patient's consent to do so, otherwise the treatment could be regarded as battery.

In an early American decision, *Schonloendorff v Society of the New York Hospital* 501 NE 92(1914), Cordoza J. provided a very useful summary of the law relating to consent to medical treatment, which still holds true today:

> '... every human being of adult years and sound mind has a right to determine what shall be done with his own body; and a surgeon who performs an operation without his patient's consent commits an assault, for which he is liable in damages. However, this cannot be taken beyond the compass of its words to support an action of battery where there has been consent to the very surgical procedure carried out upon a patient but there has been a breach of the duty of disclosure of attendant risks. In my opinion, actions of battery in respect of surgical or other medical treatment should be confined to cases where surgery or treatment has been performed or given to which there has been no consent at all or where, emergency situation aside, surgery or treatment has been performed or given beyond that to which there was no consent.'

The phrase 'informed consent' is an American phrase which has been imported into Irish and English law, and which sits rather uneasily in our law. It has been criticised as having no real place in our law, and whilst there is merit in these arguments, it is nonetheless a useful phrase as it is clearly self-explanatory and therefore reminds those in the health profession that a patient must be properly informed before consent to treatment is sought.

The duty to explain

The modern law relating to consent places a duty on the medical professional to clearly and properly explain the risks of the proposed medical treatment, in order to obtain what is known as informed consent.

It is this duty to fully explain the risks (and not just the benefits) of the proposed medical treatment that turns this duty into a specialised form of consent. What is meant by informed consent is that the patient consents on the basis that he or she understands what it is that is being consented to, as it can hardly be argued that a patient is operating on an informed basis if he or she is aware of the nature of the proposed treatment, but is not aware of the risks. It is difficult to talk of a patient consenting to chemotherapy for example, if the patient has not been informed of the many and damaging side effects caused by such treatment, for example the loss of hair, nausea and general physical weakness.

Where consent has been obtained from the patient to perform the treatment in question, the English courts have held that there can never be a battery, as there is consent to the act. However, should a doctor fail to warn or advise the patient about the probable consequences of the treatment, including the usual risks that are part and parcel of the suggested treatment, that doctor has not discharged his or her professional duty of care, and will be liable in negligence, as he or she has not placed the patient in a position to properly understand the consequences of the proposed treatment.

In other words, the English position is that there is battery if there is no consent at all, and there is negligence if there is consent, but that consent is based on ignorance as a result of the treatment not being properly and fully explained to the patient.

Battery or negligence?

It is interesting to note that the American courts have since gone further than their English counterparts. A number of American decisions have held that there is a battery where the patient has consented to a treatment but that consent was not informed consent. This is contrary to English decisions, and although the Irish courts have not conclusively decided the question, it is likely that they will follow the English example.

The American approach holds great benefits for the patient, for the simple reason that if a patient has an action in battery, that plaintiff/patient does not need to prove causation (which is always a stumbling block). In addition, the defendant, rather than the plaintiff, needs to prove that there was real (i.e. informed) consent to the treatment. On the other hand, if the plaintiff sues for negligence, it is the plaintiff (the patient) who must prove all four elements of the tort of negligence.

The American approach was rejected in the leading English decision of *Sidaway v Governors of Bethlehem Royal Hospital* [1985] 1 All E.R. 821, and the Court of Appeal went so far as to say that the doctrine of informed consent had no place in English law, as it would damage the relationship between the doctor and patient, as most patients preferred to place themselves in the hands of their doctors. The *Sidaway* decision will be examined more closely in the chapter on disclosure.

In *Walsh v Family Planning Services* [1992] 1 I.R. 496, the patient consented to a vasectomy operation, and the surgeon was identified. The operation was extensively performed ('assisted') by another surgeon under the supervision of the original surgeon. The patient was conscious during the operation, which was conducted under local anaesthetic, and did not complain about this. The High Court held that a 'technical assault' had been committed on the grounds that the patient had not consented to somebody else performing the procedure and accordingly there was no consent at all. The Supreme Court disagreed with this analysis and, following the English reasoning, held that the patient had given his consent to the procedure on the basis that it would be carried out by a person with the requisite skill and competence (as opposed to a specific surgeon), and the operation had been performed on that basis.

When considering this decision, one could argue that the fact that the patient was conscious and aware that the other surgeon was performing the operation saved the day for the hospital. However, the Supreme Court seemed to go further than that, and effectively followed the lead of the English courts.

Accordingly, in English (and it would seem Irish) law, the failure to properly inform a patient can only lead to an action in negligence, but not in battery.

Whether this approach is justifiable is the subject of another debate. What it does mean is that the nurse bears a heavy responsibility, albeit ethical as opposed to strictly legal, of making sure that the patient understands the explanation given by the doctor. Although the patient's choice is usually limited to accepting or rejecting the proposed treatment, at least that patient should know the benefits and the risks associated with the proposed treatment. Although our courts have not gone as far as the American courts, the law does not say that the patient must be kept in the dark about everything.

The role of the nurse in ensuring informed consent

It is the duty of the doctor to explain the benefits and risks of the proposed treatment, and therefore a nurse might be of the opinion that such matters fall outside his or her responsibility. However, it often falls on the nurse, as an advocate of the patient, to ensure that the patient did in fact understand the explanation given by the doctor. If the nurse is in any doubt as to whether the patient did fully understand, and appreciate, the nature and consequences of the proposed treatment, the nurse's duty of care to the patient demands that the nurse brings this to the attention of the doctor, with a recommendation that the doctor go through the treatment or procedure with the patient again.

As the nurse often has more contact with the patient on a daily and more intimate basis, the nurse would most often be in the best position to assess the capacity of the patient to understand the explanation given by the doctor. If the nurse is in any doubt as to the intellectual capacity of the patient to understand the explanation, the nurse is under a duty to bring this to the attention of the doctor, and ask the doctor to explain the nature and consequences of the treatment again to the patient, but this time in language that the patient can understand.

Consent and informed consent

In other words, there are two steps in ensuring informed consent: Firstly, there must be general consent to the touching involved in any medical treatment or even diagnosis. Secondly, there must be informed consent to the specific treatment that is proposed for the patient. This can only happen as a result of the medical professional properly informing the patient of the nature of the treatment and the proposed outcome, the consequences of the treatment, and the attendant risks of that treatment, in such a way that the patient properly understands the explanation.

If the medical professional fails to obtain consent *per se*, there is battery, and if the medical professional fails to properly inform the patient about the proposed treatment, there is negligence.

The three requirements for informed consent

In summary therefore, in order for there to be a valid consent from the patient, three factors must exist:

- The patient must have the capacity to consent. What this means is that the patient must have sufficient mental faculties to appreciate the nature and consequences of his or her actions and the nature and consequences of the treatment in question;
- the nature and consequences of the treatment must be fully disclosed to the patient. This includes the risks usually associated with such treatment, often called 'material risks';
- the patient must give the consent voluntarily.

These three essential ingredients of informed consent – capacity, disclosure and voluntariness – will be examined in detail in later chapters.

Conclusion

If a patient is to be informed, then he or she must be capable of understanding the nature of his or her current medical condition in terms and language that can be understood by a person of average education and with no medical knowledge. The patient must similarly be able to understand, again in basic accessible terms, the nature, scope and significance of any proposed treatment, procedure or intervention. The health professional must explain the aims of the treatment, any discomfort, side effects, or foreseeable risks and complications. Choices of treatment must be offered and explained, when applicable. The patient must always be aware of his or her right of choice between types of treatment, and between treatment and no treatment. The right and capacity to refuse medical treatment is as important as the right and capacity to consent to treatment.

Despite English decisions like *Sidaway* it must be argued that no longer can we rely on the 'reasonable doctor' test in deciding whether there has been sufficient disclosure of information. The test should be that of the 'reasonable patient', and what that patient would consider important and material in the circumstances. This proposed swing to the patient's viewpoint would mean that general and approved practice in the health professions would need to be considered in combination with the rights of the patient, rather than in a medico-technical vacuum. The Irish courts have not always followed their English counterparts, particularly in areas concerning civil liberties, and it is to be hoped that a more patient-oriented approach will be adopted by our Supreme Court. As will be seen later, there is a High Court decision that adopts this approach.

Whatever happens in our courts, the nurse has an important role to play as the patient's advocate, in ensuring that the explanation that is given to the patient is understood by the patient.

What we can be certain of is that where there is no consent at all, there will be a battery. This principle is established in Irish law and has been confirmed by the Supreme Court on more than one occasion. Perhaps the most emphatic of these was in the decision of *In the matter of a Ward of Court (withholding medical treatment)* No. 2 [1996] 2 I.R. 79, where at page 156, Denham J. stated:

> 'Consent
> Medical treatment may not be given to an adult person of full capacity without his or her consent. There are a few rare exceptions to this e.g., in regard to contagious diseases or in a medical emergency where the patient is unable to communicate. This right arises out of civil, criminal and constitutional law. If medical treatment is given without consent it may be trespass against the person in civil law, a battery in criminal law, and a breach of the individual's constitutional rights. The consent which is given by an adult of full capacity, is a matter of choice. It is not necessarily a decision based on medical considerations. Thus, medical treatment may be refused for other than medical reasons, or reasons most citizens would regard as rational, but the person of full age and capacity may make the decision for their own reasons.'

Although it would seem that the 'doctrine of informed consent' has no place in our law of battery, it clearly has an important place in our law of negligence, which will be examined in detail in later chapters.

Informed Consent: Summary

1. Consent to treatment must always be obtained from a patient, as treatment without consent is battery.
2. American law states that medical treatment without informed consent is battery. This approach holds great benefits for the plaintiff patient.
3. English law has refused to follow this reasoning and has held that a failure to properly explain the nature, benefit and risks of proposed treatment can be the basis for an action in negligence, but never in battery.
4. It is likely that Irish law will follow the English law, but our courts have not yet considered this specific issue.
5. The nurse has an important role to play in assuring that a patient understands and appreciates the doctor's explanation.
6. For there to be a genuine consent to medical treatment, the patient must have the capacity to consent, the nature, benefits and risks of the proposed treatment must be disclosed and explained to the patient, and the patient must be allowed to make a choice without any pressure or coercion from the health professional.
7. Useful websites:
    a. *Irish Health* (http://www.irishhealth.com).
    b. *International Centre for Nursing Ethics* (http://www.freedomtocare.org/iane.htm).
    c. *British Medical Journal* (http://bmj.bmjjournals.com).
    d. *E-medicine* (http://www.emedicine.com).
    e. *American Medical Association* (http://ama-assn.org).

8
CAPACITY OF THE PATIENT TO GIVE INFORMED CONSENT

Learning Outcomes
At the completion of this chapter, the reader should know and understand the following:

- What is meant by capacity in the legal sense.
- That the capacity to consent to medical treatment includes the capacity to refuse medical treatment.
- That once it is established that a patient has the capacity to consent to, or refuse, medical treatment, the decision of the patient must be respected.

Important concepts and phrases that are crucial to an understanding of this chapter

Deemed
To regard as something. In law, when something is deemed to mean or represent something, it is taken as the truth or fact until there is proof that it is not the truth or is not a fact. So, for example, a person is deemed innocent until proven guilty, a person is deemed sane until shown to be insane.

Presumption
The law accepts certain things at face value until there is evidence to show differently. A presumption means that something is deemed to be the truth or a fact until the contrary is proved. So the presumption of innocence means that a person charged with a crime is deemed to be innocent until the State proves, beyond a reasonable doubt, that he or she is guilty.

Child
From a legal point of view, a child is a human being who is unmarried, has never married, and is under the chronological (calendar) age of eighteen years.

Introduction

The capacity of a person can be described as the ability of a person to do something. Capacity in the legal sense can be described as relative capacity in that a person's capacity or competency is always measured in terms of their ability to do a specific thing. For example, we say a person has testamentary capacity if we are satisfied that he or she can understand the necessary duties and obligations and legal consequences involved in the making of a will. We say that a person has the capacity to enter into a marriage (a 'marital capacity' if you like) if that person can understand the nature and consequences of the marriage ceremony. We say that a person has the capacity to consent to medical treatment if that person can understand the need for the treatment, the consequences and risks of the treatment, and what would happen if they refused that treatment.

The fact that a person has the capacity to perform one type of legal act does not automatically mean that they have the capacity to perform all sorts of other legal acts. Their capacity must be measured at the time in relation to that specific act. The converse is also true – the fact that a person is found to be incapacitated to do a certain legal act, does not disqualify him or her from doing any other legal acts. Each situation is regarded separately.

For example, an elderly man sits his family down at the dinner table. He describes to them what it is that he owns in terms of property and valuables and money. He proceeds to carefully explain that he has made a will and he tells each and every family member present what he or she has been left in the will, and why they have been left such a thing. The man (called the 'testator') appears perfectly lucid and calm. He explains that he does not have long to go on this Earth and he understands that his will shall become operative on his death. However, every now and then he looks at an empty corner in the room and has a discussion with the corner concerning the decisions he has made. When his family ask what he is doing, he explains that he is talking to a recently deceased friend of his, who acts as his advisor.

Assuming that they are unhappy with the distribution of his property, as soon as the man dies the family will challenge his will, on the basis that he was clearly having delusions or hallucinations at the time he wrote out his will. Despite that, the court will not necessarily declare the will invalid, as the court might reason that the man knew exactly what he was doing, and what the consequences of his actions were, and the fact that he thought he was talking to a ghost did not impact on his capacity to make and understand the will. In other words, the court might accept that the testator had testamentary capacity. His capacity is measured in relation to the legal act of making a will and his belief in ghosts does not necessarily make his will invalid.

Capacity to consent to medical treatment

One of the factors that has to be determined in deciding whether the patient consented to the treatment, is whether the patient had the capacity to consent to medical treatment.

A person is deemed to have the capacity to give true consent when that person is of adult years (over the age of eighteen years) and possessed of a sound mind.

It must be realised that the age or status of a person is only a starting point when assessing legal capacity. Being a child or suffering from a mental disability does not necessarily mean that a person lacks capacity to make decisions about treatment, just as being over eighteen years of age does not automatically mean that you have the capacity to consent to medical treatment. What the age of a person means is that presumptions are created – so a person over the age of eighteen is presumed to be capable of consent, until the evidence clearly shows and it becomes a matter of fact that he or she lacks capacity.

In other words, the question of capacity is a question of fact in every case and requires that the patient is able to understand what is involved in the decision to be taken. With children, the issue will frequently be a developmental one, namely whether the patient has acquired sufficient maturity and intelligence to understand what is involved.

In adults, the issue may be the same but usually it will not be. The law will not question the degree of intelligence or education of an adult. In most instances the issue with adults will be whether the patient's diagnosed and documented mental disability or disorder is such that he or she has lost the capacity to consent or refuse medical treatment. Where the disability or disorder is particularly severe, the patient may never have acquired the capacity to consent, and would have beeen incapacitated from birth (an autistic child, for example).

A patient may have the capacity to make some but not all treatment decisions. This would depend on the complexity of the treatment or procedure, and similarly the complexity of the explanation by the health professional concerning the consequences and side effects of such treatment or procedure. For example, a child can consent to having a plaster placed on a graze, but is not sufficiently intellectually developed to consent to heart surgery or chemotherapy.

In other words, a patient's capacity must be assessed in light of the decision the patient is being asked to make, hence the phrase 'relative capacity'.

The greater the patient's capacity to comprehend the issues involved and make a decision after considering the issues, the greater will be the duty on the health professional to disclose relevant information about the proposed treatment.

Although it may be argued that the lesser the capacity of the patient to understand, the lesser the extent of the duty to inform, it would seem to be a preferable approach that the health professional should perhaps spend a little more time and effort in ensuring that there is proper consent from a person with some form of intellectual disability. Use of appropriate language, and aids such as drawings, pictures, even dolls or puppets, could all be used in achieving proper understanding and true consent.

The nature and complexity of the explanation must cater to the intellectual capacity of the patient. However, a perceived lack of 'intelligence' must not be a licence for paternalism. Again, there is opportunity for the nurse, as the patient's advocate, to thoroughly brief the doctor about the patient and the patient's level of understanding and perhaps even suggest a preferred form of communication if such form has been successful in the past (for example, explaining with pictures or the use of certain fictional characters).

Capacity to refuse medical treatment

The health professional is trained and essentially indoctrinated that the primary objective is to save life. Patients might not always share this view. They might regard no life as being preferable to what they perceive to be an 'inferior life', particularly in circumstances where they excelled in that former lifestyle.

Consider a scenario where a nineteen-year-old youth injures his foot in a motorcycle accident. The foot is treated but complications arise and the foot becomes gangrenous. The consulting surgeon informs the young man that it will be necessary to amputate. However, the young man in question has already represented Ireland in soccer at the under-19 level and has realistic aspirations of becoming a professional soccer player. He informs the surgeon that he would rather die than lose his foot. In this scenario the youth is over eighteen years old and therefore is an adult. He appears to be fully competent to make his own decisions – in other words, he has the intellectual capacity to know what the surgeon wants to do, to consider the implications of not following the surgeon's advice, and to make a final decision to refuse to follow that advice. He would certainly convince the surgeon that he understood the decision made.

Whilst we might not agree with, or understand, the young man's decision, that is not a legally valid reason to ignore his refusal to have the treatment prescribed, in this case an amputation. He is entitled to refuse medical treatment, for whatever reason he chooses, be it good, bad or indifferent. In fact, he is not obliged to give any reason at all, he can just outright refuse medical treatment, and there is very little that anybody can do about it.

Recognising that a patient has the right of self-determination, which includes the right to refuse life-saving treatment, is very difficult for health professionals (and the relatives of the patient) as it runs against the core of their training.

Only in situations where there is clear evidence that the patient lacks the intellectual capacity to make that decision could the surgeon approach the court to override that patient's refusal of treatment, in the best interests of the patient.

The fact that the treatment might be the best thing, in the objective sense, for that patient is not a defence to an action for battery, if the patient has sufficient capacity to refuse medical treatment.

'Do Not Resuscitate' (DNR) Orders

In an age where, allegedly, the autonomy of the patient is being given priority, it is surprising how little legislation and guidelines exist regarding the question of DNR Orders.

DNR orders usually arise in relation to the question of whether to apply CPR (cardio-pulmonary resuscitation) to a patient who is suffering a heart attack.

Irish law is silent about DNR orders. There is no statute on the subject. There are no national guidelines about DNR orders.

If one applies the general principles relating to consent to the question of DNR orders, the following conclusions can be reached:
- The Irish Supreme Court has recognised that a patient has the right to refuse medical treatment, even where this refusal would lead to that patient's death (*In the Matter of a Ward of Court* [1995] 2 I.L.R.M. 401).
- If a patient specifically instructed the hospital and the professional staff that he or she did not want to be resuscitated if he or she suffered a heart attack, this would be an advance directive.
- There is no specific Irish law on advance directives, and it is debateable whether these would be recognised by Irish courts.
- What this means is that the ultimate decision on whether to resuscitate is left up to the health professional who first arrives at the scene.

It is important for Ireland to formulate national guidelines on DNR Orders. In the United Kingdom, although there is no statute that governs the question of DNR Orders, there is a set of very good and clear Guidelines that have been drawn up by the British Medical Association and the Royal College of Nursing to deal with DNR decisions. These Guidelines allow doctors and nurses to assess whether CPR would be appropriate in the circumstances, taking into account factors like the patient's condition and the likelihood of the CPR being successful and, even where the patient's heart might be started again, whether the resultant brain damage is such that the patient's length and quality of life is likely to be unacceptable to the patient if the patient had been given the choice.

The Guidelines recognise that the nurse often has the most important role to play in DNR decisions, as it is often the nurse who is first to arrive at the scene, and it is the nurse who must decide whether to commence CPR or call a crash team. Again, it would also be the nurse who would have the greatest insight into the wishes of the patient, given that the nurse would likely have had more contact with the patient than any other health professional involved in the decision.

In Ireland, the lack of law or guidelines on the subject does not necessarily mean that DNR Orders do not exist. It is hardly a secret that DNR Orders are made in our hospitals. These orders are usually made after the medical team treating the patient have fully consulted with the patient (if possible) and the patient's family to be certain that everyone supports the principle that CPR should not be attempted if the patient suffers from cardiac arrest. It is also advisable that the nursing staff be consulted, as they are on the 'front-line' as it were.

The lack of a statute or guidelines makes nurses extremely vulnerable concerning the carrying out of a DNR Order. Nurses are well advised to obtain the written consent of the patient regarding the implementation of a DNR Order, and to properly document this in the patient's medical file. Although this will not necessarily be a legal defence to any subsequent proceedings, it is the best defence in the circumstances.

Ireland would do well to look to the American state of New York, which passed a statute in 1988 that provides that CPR must be administered unless medically futile. The express exception to this is where the patient had made a DNR Order after being informed about his or her diagnosis and prognosis, the risks and benefits of CPR being administered in his or her particular condition, and the meaning and implication of a DNR Order.

If the patient wishes to make a DNR Order, this must be done before two witnesses, with one of those witnesses being the hospital doctor.

If the patient is not in a fit state to consent or refuse, the statute allows the attending doctor to implement a DNR Order if CPR would cause the patient severe and immediate injury (or again, where CPR would be futile). A second doctor must confirm this, and if the patient is a ward of court or under the legal guardianship of another, the consent of that person or body must be obtained.

The DNR Order must be reviewed on a weekly basis. The statute grants immunity to the health professional who complies with a DNR Order.

There is clearly an urgent need for the Irish authorities to consider statutory regulation of DNR Orders, perhaps along the lines of the New York statute described above. The uncertainty that surrounds these not only means that the practice in hospitals around the country is not uniform, but that health professionals are expected to make extremely difficult decisions in circumstances where they might be legally vulnerable.

Capacity to Give Informed Consent: Summary

1. Capacity is the ability or authority to do something.
2. In legal terms capacity is a relative concept, as a person's legal capacity is measured in relation to a specific task performed at a specific time.
3. As a task becomes more complex and challenging, so the demands on a person's capacity will increase.
4. As the nature and consequences of medical treatment become more complex, there is a greater duty on a health professional to clearly explain the nature and consequences of that treatment.
5. Similarly there is a duty on the health professional to explain to the patient in language and concepts that the particular patient can understand.
6. An adult person is presumed to have capacity until the contrary is proved.
7. The capacity to consent to medical treatment includes the capacity to refuse treatment.
8. A health professional must respect the wishes of a patient, as long as that patient has the capacity to accept or refuse medical treatment.
9. Useful websites:
    a. *Resuscitation Council (UK)* (www.resus.org.uk/).
    b. *Guild of Catholic Doctors* (http://www.catholicdoctors.org.uk/Submissions/BMA_Withdrawing_Rx.htm).
    c. *European Resuscitation Council* (*http://www.erc.edu/*).
    d. *Irish Health* (http://www.irishhealth.com/).

9
THE MENTALLY INCAPACITATED ADULT PATIENT

> **Learning Outcomes**
> **At the completion of this chapter, the reader should know and understand the following:**
> - The differences between the medical and legal approach to the question of capacity.
> - The notion of relative capacity and its application to adult patients with either an intellectual disability or a psychiatric illness.
> - How one determines whether a person suffering from an intellectual disability has the capacity to consent to, or refuse, medical treatment.
> - The issues surrounding the question of who can consent to medical treatment on behalf of an incapacitated patient.

Important concepts and phrases that are crucial to an understanding of this chapter

Injunction
An order of the court directing a party to an action to do something (mandatory injunction) or refrain from doing something (prohibitory injunction).

Person under disability
A person who lacks legal capacity, which is the legal ability to do something. The law assumes that an adult can make decisions and sign legal documents and enter into contracts. This includes things like signing tenancy agreements, taking out insurance policies or credit, getting married or giving consent to medical treatment.

Some people are not able to make decisions for themselves – especially important legal decisions – because they lack understanding and awareness of what they are doing and the consequences. Such people are said to have 'legal incapacity' or to be *incapax*. This can affect people with learning disabilities or with other intellectual impairments like dementia, head injury or mental illness.

Introduction

The situation of the mentally incapacitated adult presents two immediate problems in our law: Firstly, how is one to decide whether a patient is mentally incapacitated, and secondly, if mental incapacity is established, who is authorised to consent on that patient's behalf?

Lawyers and doctors have a different approach to capacity

Dealing with the first problem – how can a patient be identified as being mentally incapacitated to the extent that he or she is unable to give informed consent to medical treatment?

What makes the legal concept of consent so tricky is that it is not decided on the same lines as the medico-psychological tests for insanity.

The law is not necessarily concerned about whether a patient thinks that there are little people at the end of the garden, but rather whether the person can understand the nature and consequences of the proposed treatment, and in the light of that understanding, make a decision whether to have that treatment or not.

In other words, despite that person suffering from a mental illness, they might have what the law calls 'lucid intervals', during which time they are as competent as the next person to make legally binding decisions, or their illness might be such that it does not affect the patient's ability to make decisions about medical treatment.

The medical profession would use what is often called 'a status approach' – which is essentially a 'label and be done with it' approach – if a person is diagnosed as suffering from a severe mental disorder or even where a person is intellectually disabled, the status approach assumes that the patient is incompetent to make any decisions, and it would be up to the patient to show otherwise. On the other hand, the 'competence approach', or as it has been named in this chapter, the 'relative capacity' approach, starts on the basis that everybody is treated equally and it is determined, with reference to the task at hand, whether that patient is competent to perform the task asked of him or her.

The fact that a patient suffers from some mental disability does not automatically disqualify the patient from giving consent, or refusing treatment. Where it is clear that the patient fully understands the nature and consequences of the proposed treatment, the health professional would be acting reasonably in accepting the consent of the patient. Of course, the health professional should be absolutely certain in his or her mind that the patient is giving informed consent, knowing the background of the patient.

A case in point would be a patient who is a diagnosed schizophrenic. It is widely accepted that persons suffering from this mental disability (which often appears to the layperson as a convenient umbrella term covering a very wide range of mental illnesses) often have 'lucid intervals', in other words episodes of absolute clarity. In addition, although the schizophrenic might be incompetent in other areas, for example driving a car, he or she might be perfectly competent and lucid on the subject of personal health, and could even possess expertise on the subject. What this means is that the fact that the patient is a diagnosed schizophrenic does not automatically disqualify him or her from giving consent, or alternatively, refusing to give consent. What is important to decide is whether the patient is without capacity at the relevant time (of making the decision) on the matter in question, namely whether he or she is unable by reason of intellectual disability to make a reasoned decision on the matter in question.

In the matter of C (an adult)(refusal of medical treatment) F.D. [1994] 1 All E.R. 819, was an important English decision, which has subsequently provided valuable guidelines in determining the capacity of a person who has been medically diagnosed as being mentally ill or intellectually disabled. It can also be used to support arguments for the use of the competence approach, rather than the status approach.

Facts
A patient diagnosed as a paranoid schizophrenic was advised to have an amputation below the knee of a grossly infected (gangrenous) lower leg in order to save his life. The patient responded that he would 'rather die with two feet than live with one'. He refused to give consent to the amputation. The hospital indicated to the patient that they intended to override his refusal and allow a surgeon to perform the amputation, as they did not believe that the patient had the necessary mental capacity to make an informed decision on the amputation. The patient asked the High Court to grant an injunction against the hospital, preventing the amputation from taking place.

Issue before the court
Did the patient have the necessary capacity to make the decision to keep his leg, even if this might result in his death, and bearing in mind that he was a diagnosed paranoid schizophrenic?

Decision of the court
The court stated that three questions needed to be asked in determining the mental capacity of a patient to consent to, or refuse, treatment: Could the patient comprehend and retain the necessary information, was he able to believe it; and finally, was he able to weigh the information, balancing risks and needs, so as to arrive at a choice?

The court held that despite being diagnosed as a paranoid schizophrenic, the patient did have the necessary mental capacity to refuse to give consent to the amputation and an injunction was issued forbidding the amputation.

Commentary
Is the patient able to comprehend and retain the necessary information?
In other words, did the mental illness complained of prevent the patient from storing information in order to mull over that information before making a decision. Certain mental illnesses, like Alzheimer's disease, attack the memory directly, and the nature of the disease and its direct impact on the memory need to be carefully considered.

Is the patient able to believe the information given to him or her?
If the patient cannot take the health professional seriously, or if they think that the health professional is part of a greater conspiracy against them, then clearly the patient will not believe the information being given by that health professional. The fact that a person is diagnosed as a paranoid schizophrenic is clearly important when considering this second requirement. Again, the prudent health professional will not merely rely on the diagnosis, but will rather question the patient on why the medical advice is being refused. If the patient replies that the doctor is 'one of them' or words to that effect, the health professional has grounds to believe that the patient fails on this second leg of the capacity test.

Is the patient able to consider and weigh the information, including the balancing the risks against the advantages and needs, and finally arrive at a decision?
The final test involves an assessment of the patient's cognitive abilities to understand and assess the medical advice, including both 'pros and cons', and thereafter make a considered decision. In other words, the 'brain power' and relative intelligence of the patient will need to be assessed, in relation to the nature and complexity of the medical advice presented. So a person with a learning disability might succeed on the first two legs of the test, but not be able to assess or analyse the information sufficiently to make an informed decision, and so could fail on the last leg.

The *In the matter of C* decision can be criticised as being somewhat vague in stating the standard to be imposed on health professionals to firstly assess competence and thereafter assess understanding – in other words, questions one and three are somewhat open-ended and broadly phrased.

On the other hand, it does provide a very useful framework and could be used as a reference in creating some sort of formalised questionnaire that could be used by health boards in establishing the competence of patients with a history of mental illness or intellectual disability.

Finally, health professionals should be cautious in taking silence to be consent where the patient is known to have a history of mental illness.

Whilst the health profession seems very quick to challenge the competence of a mentally ill patient when that patient refuses to give consent to treatment, they are slow to closely question the patient's competence when consent is given, or is taken to be given. If it can be shown that the reasonable health professional should not have regarded the patient's behaviour as indicating consent in the circumstances, it will be held that there was no informed consent. In America, this would lead to an action in battery, but in England (and probably Ireland) it is likely that the doctor will be held negligent for not properly ascertaining the wishes of the patient.

At the end of the day, irrespective of whether the health professionals in question agree with the patient's decision, if they are reasonably of the impression that he or she has sufficient capacity to make the decision to refuse the treatment, they must respect that wish.

The role of the nurse

The relevance for nurses of the law of consent with regard to patients with an intellectual disability, is that these patients really do need an advocate to speak for them, as they are often severely challenged when it comes to understanding the implications of consenting to, or refusing, treatment. Doctors might not have the time, or might not have enough contact with the patient to realise that the patient is struggling to understand. The nurse is in a position to know that patient more intimately, and should speak up if not convinced that the patient understands the explanation given or choices offered by the doctor.

It also happens that the patient does not want to know the details, and would rather the doctor 'get on with it', as explanations often scare the patient who must now deal with affairs they would rather leave to the doctor. In this case a well-meaning doctor trying to explain the proposed treatment in detail might be causing acute distress to the patient. The nurse would know of the patient's desire to be kept in the dark and could inform the doctor of the patient's fears, thus allowing the doctor to adopt an appropriate style when explaining the treatment to the patient. Knowledge of the law on capacity and consent should give the nurse the confidence to play this role.

Specific incapacity

We have seen that patients with a diagnosed mental illness or intellectual disability might have the capacity to consent to, or refuse, medical treatment. On the other hand, the decisions of seemingly rational people (without a history or diagnosis of mental illness or intellectual disability) might be of such a nature as to cause the law to regard them as mentally incapacitated to make a decision regarding a specific form of treatment.

The English decision of *In the matter of MB* [1997] 2 F.L.R. 426, is a good example of a seemingly rational person suffering from a specific phobia.

Facts
A pregnant woman suffered from needle phobia and refused to have an epidural that would precede a Caesarean section. The surgeon overrode the refusal of the mother and the epidural was administered and the operation was performed successfully.

Issue before the court
Was the surgeon justified in ignoring the patient's refusal to have an epidural or was the patient a victim of an unjustified assault and battery?

Decision of the court
The English High Court held that her needle phobia rendered her mentally incapacitated to take the decision not to have an epidural. The matter went on appeal and the English Court of Appeal confirmed the reasoning of the High Court, but emphasised that if the mother had been legally competent, she could have refused the operation.

Commentary
The court, using very similar principles as laid down in the earlier case of *In the matter of C*, held that a person lacks the capacity if some impairment or disturbance of mental functioning renders the person unable to make a decision whether to consent to or to refuse treatment. That inability will occur when the patient is unable to comprehend and retain the information so as to consider and evaluate the likely consequences of accepting or refusing the treatment in question.

A distinction must also be drawn between patients who are partially incapacitated by their mental illness or intellectual disability, and those patients who suffer from a serious and permanent illness or disability that incapacitates them from making legally binding decisions. This distinction was clearly drawn in the English case of *In the matter of F (Mental patient: Sterilisation)* [1989] 2 All E.R. 545.

Facts
An adult, but intellectually disabled female patient, had formed a sexual relationship with an intellectually disabled male patient. The hospital authorities were certain that she would not be able to cope with pregnancy and motherhood, and rather than take a chance with contraception, they sought permission to have her sterilised.

Issue before the court
Was the patient incapable of deciding whether to be sterilised or not, and could the hospital act without her consent, but in her best interests?

Decision of the court
The court used the opportunity to formulate important principles when deciding on the question of consent in relation to the intellectually disabled patient:

> 'But where the state of affairs is permanent or semi-permanent, as may be so in the case of a mentally disordered person, there is no point in waiting to obtain the patient's consent. The need to care for him is obvious; and the doctor must then act in the best interests of his patient just as if he had received the patient's consent to do so. Were this not so, much useful treatment and care could, in theory at least, be denied to the unfortunate.
>
> ...
>
> In the case of routine treatment of mentally disordered persons, there should be little difficulty in applying this principle. In the case of more serious treatment, I recognise that its application may create problems for the medical profession; however, in making decisions about treatment, the doctor must act in accordance with a responsible and competent body of relevant professional opinion...'.

Commentary
Although the 'best interests' test might be regarded as overly paternalistic, there seems to be no viable alternative when considering the intellectually disabled or mentally ill patient, as it is difficult to speak of true autonomy, which is the basis of the patient orientated approach. At the same time, it would seem to leave the way open for courts to impose their own views as to what is in the best interests of the patient.

In addition, it is sometimes evident that whilst claiming to act in the best interests of the patient, the health professional is acting in the best interests of the carer, with the emphasis being to make the carer's life a little easier rather than the patient's. This is a difficult problem, as the people caring for the intellectually disabled patient also have rights, specifically rights to self-determination and autonomy. Questions become difficult when the rights and aspirations of the carer are in conflict with the rights of the patient.

One way of dealing with this conflict is to focus solely on the rights of the patient to the exclusion of all else. This has led to the courts using what is called the 'welfare principle', where the court will base its decision purely on the welfare of the patient. This was the approach adopted in the English case of *In the matter of B. (a minor) (Wardship: Sterilisation)*[1990] 2 A.C. 1, a case decided by the House of Lords, where the facts were very similar to *In the matter of F*. In this case the House of Lords granted the application to sterilise the patient, a seventeen-year old girl with profound intellectually disability. The court rejecting the argument that non-consensual sterilisation would be a violation of the patient's right to reproduce, as the patient was incapable of understanding the connection between intercourse and pregnancy, and similarly would not comprehend the birth process and the need to care for her child. To talk about the right to reproduce in circumstances such as this was 'wholly to part company with reality'. The court also rejected that its decision had to be influenced by the interests of the carers.

Whilst we might applaud the championing of the rights of the intellectually disabled patient, we must also recognise the realities of caring for patients with profound intellectual disabilities. It is often an exhausting, stressful and unrewarding job, and health professionals who are involved in this sort of work need to be extremely dedicated and deserve all the support they can get. At the same time, to be declared legally incompetent effectively leaves you at the mercy of those looking after you, and as the court is the one to declare the patient legally incapacitated or incompetent, so the court has a duty to ensure that the rights of the patient are protected. It is a very difficult situation indeed.

It is perhaps due to the uneasiness this causes that the court will always presume a patient to be sane and competent until it is conclusively shown otherwise, as the consequences of being declared legally incompetent are severe. In addition, the situation needs to be extreme before an incapacitated patient can be treated without consent, and the best interests test should be practiced only in an emergency, or when it is not possible to obtain consent through other methods, or where the court itself has granted consent. These aspects are discussed next.

Who decides for the incapacitated patient?

There is a widespread misconception that family or relatives must always be consulted and the ultimate decision left to them with regard to a patient who does not have the capacity to decide whether to accept medical treatment.

This is simply not true, and breaches the principles of confidentiality and autonomy. An adult person is not entitled, by reason only of blood or marriage, to consent on behalf of another adult. In order to consent on behalf of another adult, the person seeking to supply the consent must be authorised by law to supply that consent. The fact that one is a relative by marriage or a member of the family does not, by itself, confer any authority on a person to consent on behalf of another person.

Where the doctor or nurse needs to treat a patient who does not have the capacity to consent to treatment, there are two alternatives:

Firstly, there could be a reliance on the defence of necessity. In other words, if the situation was, or became, an emergency where the incapacitated patient needed to be treated in order to avoid death or permanent and serious damage.

Secondly, and alternatively, an application can be made to establish the individual as a Ward of Court, which will appoint the President of the High Court or the Circuit Court as the patient's guardian, able to make choices on his or her behalf (usually on the advice of a wardship committee). The court will always regard the patient's best interests as the most important consideration when making decisions about his or her treatment. This is often problematic as it is not always clear what the best interests of the patient might be, and there could be differing opinions as to what constitutes the best interests of the patient, and whether the proposed treatment is in the best interests of the patient.

Unfortunately this procedure is complicated and expensive, and generally is only justified from a financial point of view when there are substantial assets involved. Accordingly, most people who cannot make decisions for themselves are in a sort of legal limbo, as they do not have legally recognised representatives acting on their behalf. It is for this reason that it is such a common practice for health professionals to seek consent from family members concerning proposed medical treatment. From a strict legal point of view, these family members have no right to consent on behalf of the patient, but from a practical point of view, the health professional has no option.

The leading Irish case dealing with issues of consenting to treatment, or in this case to the withdrawal of treatment, on behalf of an intellectually disabled patient, is *In the matter of a Ward of Court* [1995] 2 I.L.R.M. 401.

Facts
The patient was a middle-aged woman in a near persistent vegetative state (PVS). A wardship committee had been established, and at the time of the decision consisted of the patient's mother. The committee and other family members wanted life support to be withdrawn from the patient, so

as to allow her to die naturally. The life support consisted of medical treatment, and nutrition by way of a tube surgically implanted in the patient's stomach. The clinic that treated the patient was ethically opposed to allowing the patient to die.

Issue to be decided
Whether life support could be withdrawn.

Decision of the court
The majority of the Supreme Court held that the right to life guaranteed by the Constitution necessarily implied that a person had the right to die a natural and dignified death, which would include the right to refuse to have a life artificially prolonged. The rights of privacy and bodily dignity allow a patient to refuse medical treatment, even where that medical treatment might be the difference between life and death.

Where the patient was not competent to decide to refuse medical treatment, the question was whether the court was entitled to make that decision for her. The Supreme Court decided that it was entitled to make that decision, by virtue of the *parens patriae* power (which is essentially a paternalistic power), which was originally held by the Lord Chancellor of Ireland over people without legal capacity, and had since been transferred to the High Court by statute.

By a majority decision of four judges to one the Supreme Court decided that it could take the decision, on behalf of the patient, to terminate life support. The four judges all gave slightly different reasons for their decision, but as a common denominator, all four judges used a form of the best interests of the patient test, as did the High Court before it.

Commentary
As previously mentioned, one of the criticisms of the best interest of the patient test is that it depends on the subjective views and values of the person deciding what constitutes the patient's best interests, which in turn leads to uncertainty and the lack of clear guidelines.

Be that as it may, four out of five judges decided that it was in the patient's best interest to withdraw life support.

Although this decision involved the withdrawal of treatment, rather than the provision of treatment, the principles are the same. It would seem therefore that the best interests of the patient test is the dominant position in Ireland as regards the provision or withdrawal of medical treatment from patients who cannot consent to, or refuse, medical treatment, by reason of intellectual disability.

Again, it is important that nurses are aware of the law regarding incapacitated patients, as it is these patients who are the most vulnerable, and need somebody to represent their interests. A nurse is in a position to stop unauthorised treatment of a mentally incapacitated patient, after personally determining whether that patient is in fact incapacitated. This could help prevent the practice of declaring competent patients to be incompetent. The nurse can also assist incompetent patients and ensure that it is the patient's best interests that are being safeguarded, and not somebody else's interests at the expense of the patient.

The Incapacitated Adult: Summary

1. A patient suffering from an intellectual disability might still have capacity to consent to medical treatment, depending on the nature and extent of that disability.
2. A health professional must ascertain the capacity of a patient to consent to, or refuse medical treatment by determining whether the patient has the cognitive abilities to remember and therefore consider the medical treatment in question, whether the patient believes the description and advice given by that health professional, and whether the patient has the intellectual capacity to balance the benefits against the risks of the proposed treatment.
3. The presence or absence of the capacity to consent is a question of fact, which is decided on legal principles, as opposed to medical principles.
4. Where a patient is found to be intellectually disabled to such an extent that they lack any capacity to consent to, or refuse, medical treatment, the health professional can treat that person where treatment must be rendered as an emergency to avoid death or permanent damage, or where a superior court authorises that treatment, or where a wardship committee (appointed by the court) authorises the treatment.
5. In cases where a court is asked to authorise treatment on an incapacitated patient, the court will decide what is in the best interests of the patient.
6. Useful websites:
    a. *National Disability Authority* (http://www.nda.ie/).
    b. *Mental Health Ireland* (http://www.mentalhealthireland.ie).
    c. *Comhairle Health* (http://cidb.ie).

10

THE CONSENT OF PARENTS TO THE MEDICAL TREATMENT OF THEIR CHILD

> **Learning Outcomes**
> At the completion of this chapter, the reader should know and understand the following:
> - The legal definition of 'a minor'.
> - What a minor is allowed to do in law.
> - The specific issues surrounding the question of a minor consenting to, or refusing, medical treatment.
> - The similarities and differences of the English and Irish law regarding the question of parental consent and medical treatment of minors.

Important concepts and phrases that are crucial to an understanding of this chapter

Contract
An agreement with legal consequences, which can either be in words and/or in writing, or even created by the behaviour of the parties to the agreement.

Void
A contract is void when it never existed in the eyes of the law. So for example, a contract to supply a certain quantity of illegal drugs or arms is void as it was never capable of being legally recognised or enforced.

Voidable
A voidable contract, on the other hand, is a contract that can be enforced if the law agrees to recognise it and if one or both of the parties wish it to continue. A minor, for example, may enter into a contract for the sale and delivery of luxury items. As these are not necessaries, the minor can reject the contract and a court will not force the minor to pay for those luxury items, as the shopkeeper should not have entered into the contract in the first place. On the other hand, if the shopkeeper refuses to deliver the luxury goods to the minor because he is a minor, and the minor has already paid for those goods, the court will force the shopkeeper to

honour his side of the contract or at the very least return the money. In other words, a voidable contract is a contract that is capable of either being recognised and enforced, or abandoned and not enforced.

Guardian ad litem
A court appointed lawyer who acts on behalf of a person who does not have the capacity to represent him- or herself. This ensures that the incapacitated person has somebody speaking on their behalf and supporting their rights in court.

Express
An express term is a provision or clause in a contract that is specifically talked about and agreed between the parties to that contract.

Implied
An implied term in a contract is a provision or clause in a contract not specifically considered and agreed upon by the parties, but the nature of the contract means that it must be included in the contract. For example, in a contract for health services the parties do not have to expressly agree that the health professional shall practice a duty of care, as this is taken as a given. In other words, the duty of care is implied in every contract for health care.

Paramount
The most important or the most powerful.

Introduction

A minor is a natural (flesh and blood) unmarried person of either gender below the age of eighteen years, by virtue of the Age of Majority Act 1985. There is a similar definition in the Child Care Act 1990 when defining a 'child'.

If we begin the difficult question of consent to medical treatment of minors by analysing the relationship between the health professional and the patient on a purely contractual basis, then it is recognised that a minor can enter into certain contractual relationships.

A minor may enter binding contracts for necessary goods and services, and beneficial contracts of employment or apprenticeship.

'Necessary goods' or 'necessaries' are defined as goods suitable to the condition of life of the particular minor and to their actual requirements at the time of sale and delivery. In other words, the court will study the economic and financial background and standard of living of the child at the time of purchase, and decide whether, in the circumstances, it was appropriate and necessary for the minor to have those goods. The goods (or services) must, therefore, satisfy a double test of suitability and need if they are to be regarded by the law as necessaries.

The test in each case is what is reasonable for that particular minor, and it is the seller who needs to prove (should the contract be challenged as voidable) that the goods or services in question are necessary goods.

Necessaries do not include goods with which the minor is already well supplied, and so does not require more (as a matter of necessity in any event). Minors are accordingly not liable for payment where they already had sufficient supplies of that product, even where the trader or seller did not know this.

A contract for medical treatment falls within the definition of a beneficial contract for services, which means that a minor can enter into a binding contract without parental assistance. It can be argued therefore, at least at common law, that the consent of the child patient should be obtained where the consent of the child is meaningful, in other words, where the child has the intellectual capacity to understand the nature and the consequences of the proposed treatment.

This position more accurately summarises the English law than it does the Irish law.

The English position

In England it has been held that minors may give valid consent if they fully comprehend the nature and consequences of the proposed medical treatment, without requiring parental consent. What is critical in these cases is whether the child has sufficient understanding and intelligence to appreciate the nature and the consequences of the proposed treatment. In other words, does the child have the competence to give informed consent?

The leading case in England in this regard is *Gillick v West Norfolk and Wisbech Area Health Authority* [1985] 3 All E.R. 402.

Facts
The Health Authority issued a circular saying that doctors could prescribe contraceptives to a girl under the age of sixteen without the consent of the parents of the girl if the doctor acted in good faith to protect the girl against the harmful effects of sexual intercourse. The plaintiff, a mother of five daughters, asked the Health Authority to give her an assurance that contraceptive advice would not be given to any of her daughters without her consent. The health authority would not give the plaintiff this assurance. The plaintiff brought an action against the health authority seeking a declaration that if the Health Authority gave her daughters contraceptive advice this would be unlawful and wrong, would adversely affect the welfare of her children, her right as a parent and her ability to

properly perform her duties as a parent. She asked the court to declare that nobody should be allowed to give any contraceptive advice or treatment to any of her children below the age of sixteen without her consent.

Issue before the court
Should the practice of giving contraceptive advice to minors without the knowledge or consent of the parents or guardians be allowed?

Decision of the court
The dispute went all the way to the highest court in the United Kingdom, the House of Lords, who decided, on a split decision of three to two, that in exceptional circumstances a doctor could provide contraceptive advice and treatment to a girl under 16 without a parent's consent.

The House of Lords (Lord Fraser) described these exceptional circumstances as follows:
- Although the girl was under the age of 16, she would understand the advice of the doctor.
- The doctor was not able to persuade the girl to inform her parents, or allow him to inform her parents, that she was seeking contraceptive advice.
- The girl was very likely to have sexual intercourse, with or without contraceptives.
- Unless the girl received contraceptive advice or treatment, her physical and/or mental health would suffer.
- The best interests of the girl required the doctor to give her contraceptive advice and/or treatment without parental consent.

Commentary
These guidelines leave many questions unanswered. Do they only affect contraceptives or can they be used for other forms of medical treatment? What efforts, if any, should be made by the child to get the consent of the parents? Should the parents be informed (after the fact) that treatment has been given to their child? Does this also mean that competent minors under the age of sixteen can refuse medical treatment?

A criticism of the *Gillick* case is that it has not given the child the autonomy of decision making at all. Rather than shift the decision-making capacity from the parent to the child, it has shifted the decision-making capacity from the parent to the doctor.

There have been a number of cases decided since the *Gillick* case and it would seem that its impact on English law has not been as widespread as was forecast at the time. Courts have paid what can be seen as lip service to the question of autonomy of a competent child patient. In cases where the decision of the child (usually to refuse treatment) would lead to ghastly consequences, the courts have overruled the child's wishes on the basis of that child's 'best interests'. This would not happen to the adult patient, who can choose to die a horrible death if he or she so wishes. It would seem that the English position is that a mature and competent child can decide whether to receive or refuse medical treatment as long as that decision is one with which the courts agree. It could be argued that the mature minor patient has no autonomy in the proper sense.

The Irish position

When considering the question of parents refusing to consent to medical treatment of their children, the courts in Ireland are likely to overrule the wishes of the minor, but perhaps for different reasons than those of the English courts since *Gillick*.

It is questionable whether a similar decision to *Gillick* would, or could, be reached by an Irish court, by virtue of Articles 41 and 42 of the Constitution:

> 'THE FAMILY
> ARTICLE 41
> 1. 1° The State recognises the Family as the natural primary and fundamental unit group of Society, and as a moral institution possessing inalienable and imprescriptible rights, antecedent and superior to all positive law.
> 1.2° The State, therefore, guarantees to protect the Family in its constitution and authority, as the necessary basis of social order and as indispensable to the welfare of the Nation and the State.
>
> EDUCATION
> ARTICLE 42
> 1   The State acknowledges that the primary and natural educator of the child is the Family and guarantees to respect the inalienable right and duty of parents to provide, according to their means, for the religious and moral, intellectual, physical and social education of their children.
>
> 2   Parents shall be free to provide this education in their homes or in private schools or in schools recognised or established by the State.
>
> 3. 1° The State shall not oblige parents in violation of their conscience and lawful preference to send their children to

schools established by the State, or to any particular type of school designated by the State.

3.2° The State shall, however, as guardian of the common good, require in view of actual conditions that the children receive a certain minimum education, moral, intellectual and social.

4 The State shall provide for free primary education and shall endeavour to supplement and give reasonable aid to private and corporate educational initiative, and, when the public good requires it, provide other educational facilities or institutions with due regard, however, for the rights of parents, especially in the matter of religious and moral formation.

5 In exceptional cases, where the parents for physical or moral reasons fail in their duty towards their children, the State as guardian of the common good, by appropriate means shall endeavour to supply the place of the parents, but always with due regard for the natural and imprescriptible rights of the child.'

Commentary

From a reading of these two articles, it would seem that the Constitution is based on the belief that children are not capable of autonomy or self-determination before they are adults, and are accordingly bound by the wishes of their parents, as long as the parents are not failing in their duty of care towards their children.

The Irish courts, by virtue of Articles 41 and 42, have refused to follow the international trend of overruling the wishes of the parents where these wishes are considered to be contrary to the best interests of the child, unless in 'exceptional cases, where the parents for physical or moral reasons fail in their duty towards their children.' (Article 42.5), in which event the child would become a ward of court, and the court would be a 'substitute parent'. In cases where the child was not a ward of the court, and there was no evidence suggesting that the parents were not fit parents, the court would be slow to interfere with the parental refusal to consent to medical treatment.

This was graphically illustrated in the Supreme Court case of the *North Western Health Board v HW and CW* (unreported, Supreme Court, 8 November 2001).

Facts

The Health Board sought an injunction authorising it to conduct a blood test on the defendant's child. The test was described as a 'pinprick' and would be used to avoid a number of serious illnesses, but the parents refused to allow the child to be pierced, and rather offered urine samples for testing instead of blood. It was not contested that the overwhelming medical opinion was that the test was of a minor nature, and very safe, and that the illnesses (phenylketonuria, maple syrup disease, galactosaemia and hypothyroidism) they sought to protect against were serious and could result in brain damage.

Decision of the Court

A majority of the court (four judges to one) held that by virtue of Articles 41 and 42, the refusal of the parents should not be overruled.

As was held by Denham J. (and effectively echoed by the rest of the majority judges):

> 'A constitutional test has to be applied. In this case the test involves the weighing of all the circumstances, including parental responsibility, parental decisions, the child's personal rights, and the rights of all persons involved to and in the family, to determine in these circumstances what is in the best interests of the child. A factor in these circumstances is the medical advice which will carry weight but which must be balanced (in this case) against the parental decision and the rights of the child and the rights of all to and in the family to achieve a decision in the child's best interests.
>
> ...
>
> The Constitution recognises the family as the fundamental unit group of our society. Even when, as here, it is alleged that parents have failed in their duty to the child and the State endeavours to supply the place of parents it does so with due regard to the rights of the child. The rights of the child encompass the panoply of constitutional rights which include personal rights to life and bodily integrity. However, in addition the child has a right to and in his family. When assessing the welfare of a child – the fundamental concept when analysing the position of a child – complex social, political, educational and health rights of the child in and to his family are important. The bonds which bind a child in a family are strong. However, any intervention by the courts in the delicate filigree of relationships within the family has profound effects. The State (which includes the legislative, the executive and the courts) should not intervene so as to weaken or threaten these bonds unless there are exceptional circumstances. Exceptional circumstances will depend on the facts of a case; they include an immediate threat to the health or life of the child.
>
> ...
>
> In relation to the child, the fundamental principle is the welfare of the child. The welfare of the child includes religious, moral,

intellectual, physical and social welfare. These elements must be analysed in light of the facts relating to the child and the family in issue. The court has a constitutional duty to protect the life or health of the child from serious threat and the court has a constitutional duty to protect the family. A just and constitutional balance has to be sought.'

Commentary

One immediate comment can be made on this case. The Irish courts always speak about balancing the rights of the parents, the child and the State in deciding these difficult questions. This is simply not the case, as the child never gets a word in. The balancing is essentially between the interests of the parents and the State, with the child being lost in the mix.

What is needed in these cases is for a separate lawyer to be appointed to act for the child (known as a 'guardian *ad litem*') and so force the court to consider things from a child's point of view. What child would refuse to donate a tiny drop of blood if it was properly explained that this would avoid the risk of some very serious illnesses? The court did not consider the argument from the perspective of the child, and therefore to talk of the 'child's best interests' is misleading.

It would seem that unless the Constitution is amended to give children express rights that are paramount and therefore more important than family rights, which is highly unlikely, the Irish courts have two options in order to properly protect the rights of children in Ireland. They can be more creative when interpreting the phrase 'in exceptional cases' found in Article 42.5 and use this wider interpretation to limit parental power over their children, or they can restrictively interpret the definition of 'child' to mean only those minors who are clearly incapacitated to take their own decisions (in other words, follow the *Gillick* approach). Until they do this, to speak of the child's best interests when these interests clash with the wishes of the parents is to pay lip service and nothing more – much like the English courts are doing.

Statutory progress in Ireland

There has been some progress made in Ireland on the question of children being able to consent to medical treatment. The Non-Fatal Offences Against the Person Act 1997 states in section 23:

'(1) The consent of a minor who has attained the age of 16 years to any surgical, medical or dental treatment which, in the absence of consent, would constitute a trespass to his or her person, shall be as effective as it would be if he or she were of full age; and where a minor has by virtue of this section given an effective consent to any treatment it shall not be necessary to obtain any consent for it from his or her parent or guardian.

(2) In this section "surgical, medical or dental treatment" includes any procedure undertaken for the purposes of diagnosis, and this section applies to any procedure (including, in particular, the administration of an anaesthetic) which is ancillary to any treatment as it applies to that treatment.

Nothing in this section shall be construed as making ineffective any consent which would have been effective if this section had not been enacted.'

Commentary

Although the definition of an adult is a person over the age of eighteen years, section 23 allows a sixteen-year old to consent to surgical, medical or dental treatment.

At the same time, this provision leaves many questions unanswered. The Act defines competency purely on age and not in terms of the person's capacity to understand the nature and consequences of the medical treatment. It does not deal with the question of mature and competent children under the age of sixteen, and in the absence of the Irish equivalent of the *Gillick* decision, it would seem that children under the age of sixteen would always need to involve their parents when seeking medical treatment or advice. The specific question of the provision of contraceptives and contraceptive advice is not covered, and given the controversial history surrounding the question of the supply of contraceptives and contraceptive advice in this country, it remains to be seen whether the Irish courts would be willing to include contraceptive advice and supply under the broad heading of 'medical treatment'. There is similarly confusion as to whether the right to consent to treatment includes the right to confidentiality, or whether parents could argue that the failure to inform them of their child's consent to treatment, and subsequent treatment, was an unconstitutional invasion of their parental rights.

Finally, it is not clear whether the right of a sixteen-year old to consent to treatment includes the right to refuse treatment, even where that refusal might lead to death, and whether the Irish judges would follow their English counterparts and effectively reject the ability of minors to refuse medical treatment.

The role of the nurse

It is clear that the issues surrounding consent to medical treatment on minors in Ireland are very confused, and confusing, and are not likely to become clearer in the foreseeable future. While this might not directly impact on nurses, as it is usually the Health Board or the doctor who must make the decision whether to treat a child, a nurse will often be the one to first meet the child, and often will be the one to take the child to one side and attempt to explain the very complicated situation. For this reason it is important that nurses properly understand the difficult issues involved.

Parental Consent to Treatment of Minors: Summary

1. A minor is a human being under the age of eighteen years who has never married.
2. A minor has limited contractual capacity and the law allows a minor to contract for necessaries, which would seem to include necessary and beneficial medical treatment.
3. The English law, since the *Gillick* case, would seem to recognise the right of the mature and competent minor patient to consent to medical treatment without the assistance of his or her parents. In cases where a child refuses medical treatment however, the courts are quick to overrule that refusal if they decide such a refusal is against the best interests of the child.
4. The Irish courts have not followed the example set by the English courts, as the Irish Constitution protects the rights of the family and parents before the interests of the child. Where parents refuse to consent to medical treatment, even where this would seem to be against the best interests of the child, the Irish courts have held that the parents have the constitutional right to do so, unless the refusal was such that it meant that the parents were unfit parents. This is a matter of degree, rather than principle.
5. The Non-Fatal Offences Against the Person Act allows a sixteen-year old patient to consent to surgical, medical and dental treatment, but this provision leaves many questions unanswered.
6. Useful websites:
    a. *Youth Ireland* (http://www.youth.ie).
    b. *Flesh and Bones* (http://www.fleshandbones.com).
    c. *Oasis* (http://www.oasis.govie/health).

11

FULL AND PROPER DISCLOSURE TO THE PATIENT

> **Learning Outcomes**
> At the completion of this chapter, the reader should know and understand the following:
>
> ▸ The complex legal and ethical issues surrounding the question of disclosure.
> ▸ The different approaches taken by American, English and Irish courts to the question of disclosure.
> ▸ The Irish approach to disclosure, which involves a distinction between elective and non-elective (therapeutic) procedures.
> ▸ The qualified adoption of the reasonable patient test in Irish law.

Important concepts and phrases that are crucial to an understanding of this chapter

Binding and persuasive judgments
In a legal system where there is no single, codified (written down) system of law in place, past judgments are a very important tool for predicting the decision of the court in a new legal dispute. In deciding a new case, a judge will consider and be guided by previous decisions of other courts. The *ratio decidendi* (which means 'the reason for the decision') is the guiding principle to be taken from a case, as it was on the basis of that principle that the dispute before that court was decided. The *obiter dictum* (the 'excess words') are that part of a judgment which were not necessary for the final decision and do not have to be followed by another court.

This system of courts following previous judgments is known as judicial precedent. Not only does this system of judicial precedent allow predictions to be made, but it also ensures that there is continuity in judgments, which in turn means certainty in the law. It is important for the law to be certain, so that at any given time a person knows what is allowed and what is not, what is possible and what is not, and so on.

The courts stand in a structure known as a hierarchy. What this means is that the most powerful court is at the top of the pile, and the least powerful court is at the bottom of the pile.

The higher the court, the more universally followed will be the decision. A superior court may overrule or replace a judgment of a lower court. Courts of equal standing will usually follow each other's judgments, but do not have to do so. A lower court must follow the decisions of a higher court.

A binding precedent is a decision which a court must follow. A decision of a superior court is binding on a lower court. A persuasive precedent is a decision, which the court may follow but is not obliged to follow if it does not agree with the decision. A decision of a lower or equal court or foreign court will be persuasive only.

A court may 'distinguish' a previous *ratio decidendi* from the case before it if the court decides that the factual or legal differences between the two cases are sufficient to justify not following the earlier decision. The distinguishing of the present case from an earlier case allows a different legal principle to be formulated.

The hierarchy of the courts in Ireland is as follows:

Supreme Court
▼
The Court of Criminal Appeal
▼
High Court
▼
The Circuit Court
▼
The District Court

The highest court in Ireland is the Supreme Court, and decisions of the Supreme Court bind all other courts in the country. The Supreme Court has said that it does not have to follow its own decisions if there are compelling reasons that require the law to change. This would usually be where the political and social nature of the Irish society has changed to such an extent that a judgment made, for example in 1980, is no longer relevant to the Irish society of 2005 – for example, changing attitudes to contraception, single mothers, divorce and cohabitation might make early decisions on these subjects irrelevant for the modern society.

Privilege
In law privilege means a number of things, depending on the area of law under consideration. In the law of evidence, privileged evidence is not allowed to be heard or produced in court. In the law of defamation, if a person defames somebody during a privileged occasion, that person

cannot be sued (for example, during a debate in the Oireachtas). Essentially therefore, if something is privileged it means it cannot be used as evidence in court.

Introduction

The law about disclosure can be stated in a straightforward manner: The nature and the consequences of the proposed treatment must be fully disclosed to the patient, as the patient cannot consent to a procedure or treatment that he or she does not properly understand.

This unfortunately is a lot more complicated than it sounds. The most obvious difficulty is who decides what is important and needs to be disclosed – the doctor or the patient? If the patient must decide what is important, how is the doctor to know what the patient regards as important? If the doctor is to decide, does this not mean that the doctor can withhold information that the patient might regard as crucial?

The second problem with this principle is what 'understanding' on the part of the patient means? Doctors and nurses receive extensive training in areas like biology, physiology and the related sciences, so that they can understand the complicated functions of the human body. If a patient has not received this training, how can that patient properly understand the illness or injury and the proposed treatment?

A third problem with this principle concerns what is known as 'the inquisitive patient'. This is the patient who is genuinely interested in the proposed treatment and asks a lot of questions about some quite technical and complex issues, often as a result of doing some reading and research before coming into hospital. How far does the health professional need to go in answering these questions?

These are all difficult issues, and the question of disclosure raises a number of legal dilemmas, with the courts in different countries answering it in different ways.

Perhaps the most well-known case on this subject is the American case of *Canterbury v Spence* 464 F 2d 772(1972).

Facts
A nineteen-year-old patient was suffering shoulder pains and the suspected cause of this was a ruptured disc. The surgeon recommended the surgical removal of the bony arches of the vertebrae to expose the spinal cord. As this sounded hazardous, the patient's mother asked if it was dangerous. The surgeon replied that the procedure was not 'any more serious than any other spinal operation'. The mother consented.

The operation was performed, apparently successfully, and whilst the patient was recovering, he fell out of bed, and was paralysed from the waist down. Further surgery was recommended and the mother again consented. The second operation regained some of the muscle control but for all intents and purposes the patient remained paralysed from the waist down.

Issue before the court
Should the surgeon have warned the mother that there was a risk of paralysis? The surgeon argued that the risk of paralysis was about one per cent and all this warning would have done is frighten the patient away from undergoing necessary surgery.

Decision of the court
The court rejected the notion that the surgeon should decide how much to tell the patient, based on professional custom and practice. It held that the court would decide how much should have been disclosed to the patient to allow the patient to make an informed decision. The court held that a doctor should disclose all material risks that would influence the decision of a reasonable patient. By material risks is meant risks to which a reasonable patient would attach significance.

Commentary
While this case must be applauded as an important step forward in patient rights, it has been argued that this places the doctor in a difficult position, as the doctor is expected to know what a 'reasonable patient' would consider a significant risk. This might not be as big a problem as it first appears, and can usually be determined on the basis of common sense. The gap between the 'reasonable doctor' and the 'reasonable patient' is not as wide as some think.

Some would argue that many patients would rather not be told anything as what they do not know cannot scare them – an 'ignorance is bliss' approach. This might sometimes be true, but it places the doctor in a vulnerable position if the patient later complains that he or she was told nothing at all. The doctor would be well advised to gently but firmly insist on explaining the nature and aims of the treatment, and discuss the probable outcomes including the material risks, in a calm and sensible manner. Unless the patient sits with hands over ears and head between the knees, he or she will soon be drawn into the conversation. A nurse would have an important role to play, as he or she could know the patient more intimately than the doctor, and would be an important emotional support to the patient.

The leading case in the United Kingdom dealing with the issue of disclosure is *Sidaway v Board of Governors of Bethlehem Royal Hospital* [1985] A.C. 871.

Facts
The patient suffered from persistent neck and shoulder pain. The surgeon advised surgery on her spinal column. It was accepted in evidence that the surgeon had warned her of the possibility of disturbing a nerve root and the possible consequences, but he did not mention the possibility of damage to the spinal cord itself, even though he would be operating within three millimetres of it. The surgeon did not tell her of this danger, as the risk of damage to the spinal cord was less than one per cent. However, if the spinal cord was damaged, the consequences could be very severe.

The patient consented to the operation, and it was accepted that the operation was performed with care and skill. However, her spinal cord was damaged, and she was severely disabled. She sued on the basis that she had not been properly informed of the dangers inherent in the operation.

Issue before the court
Should the surgeon have told the patient about the very small risk of the spinal cord being damaged, where that damage could have severe consequences?

Decision of the court
The House of Lords did not follow the principles of *Canterbury v Spence* (that the court should decide whether the patient would have considered the risk as being material) and held that the profession should decide what was acceptable disclosure in the circumstances ('a practice accepted as proper by a responsible body of opinion' – this is known as the *Bolam* test and will be further discussed under the heading of negligence).

Commentary
The English courts have rejected the American approach, and have held that the doctor can decide just how much to tell the patient, based on accepted practice in the medical profession. In essence, the court does not decide, but is guided by the practice of the medical profession.

This approach has been criticised as it places too much power in the hands of the medical practitioner, none in the patient's, and very little in the court's. This could lead to all sorts of questionable practices, which would have to be accepted as long as they were endorsed by the medical profession.

It would seem that the recent judicial trend in many countries is to move away from the *Sidaway* approach in favour of the 'prudent patient' test. This is in accordance with the recognition by the courts that the practice of informed consent is there for the benefit of the patient, and not for the benefit of the health professional.

Lord Scarman best describes this approach in his dissenting judgment in the *Sidaway* decision:

> 'English law must recognise a duty of the doctor to warn his patient of risk inherent in the treatment which he is proposing, and especially so if the treatment be surgery. The critical limitation is that the duty is confined to material risk. The test of materiality is whether in the circumstances of the particular case the court is satisfied that a reasonable person in the patient's position would be likely to attach significance to the risk. Even if the risk is material, the doctor will not be liable if on a reasonable assessment of his patient's condition he takes the view that a warning would be detrimental to his patient's health.'

In other words the test is not what would the reasonable doctor think was important information when talking to a patient, but rather what would the reasonable patient think to be significant in deciding whether to undertake the treatment or not. This is a patient orientated test, and has been followed in a number of jurisdictions around the world, including the USA, Australia, Canada and South Africa.

The Irish position – elective and non-elective (therapeutic) treatment

It remained to be seen how the Irish courts would deal with the question. Would they follow the patient-oriented approach of the Americans, or the doctor-oriented approach of the English?

One of the earliest Supreme Court cases to deal with the question of disclosure was *Daniels v Heskin* [1954] I.R. 73, although it must be pointed out that this case did not involve questions of consent prior to treatment, but rather what constitutes proper disclosure during treatment that goes awry.

Facts

The patient gave birth at her home, assisted by a midwife. The following day a doctor visited her at home in order to insert stitches in her perineum. During the stitching process, the needle broke. The doctor completed the stitching (hopefully with a new needle) but did not find the broken point of the previous needle. At the time the doctor did not tell the patient about the broken needle and the fact that it was still in her, as he thought this would cause her unnecessary distress. The patient subsequently had to undergo an operation to remove the offending needle point.

Issue before the court
Should the doctor have told the patient about the broken needle and offered to remove it?

Decision of the court
The court found that it was not negligent of the doctor to fail to remove the broken needle point before completing the stitching, and his failure to disclose this to the patient was reasonable in the circumstances. The court held as follows:

> 'I cannot admit any abstract duty to tell patients what is the matter with them, or, in particular, to say that a needle has been left in their tissue. All depends on the circumstances – the character of the patient, her health, her social position, her intelligence, the nature of the tissue in which the needle was embedded.
> ...
> In the present case the patient was passing through a post-partum period in which the possibility of nervous or mental disturbance is notorious...'.

Commentary
It is doubtful whether such a paternalistic approach would be condoned in these times. The practice and law of medicine has moved on a lot since that decision was made. It must be said that the formula proposed by the learned judge could be adapted to a patient-orientated approach, but patients must be given a lot more credit as regards their intelligence and indeed their mettle.

A better approach is found in a subsequent Irish case of *Walsh v Family Planning Services Ltd* [1992] 1 I.R. 496 where Finlay C.J. considered the guidelines laid down in *Daniels v Heskin* but declared them difficult to understand, and laid down a far more direct formula, namely that to 'supply the patient with the material facts is so obviously necessary to an informed choice on the part of the patient that no reasonably prudent doctor would fail to make it'.

Facts
The patient had a vasectomy operation. This was categorised by the court as an elective procedure, as it was not performed to save life or avoid permanent and serious injury, but was rather for prophylactic purposes. The patient thereafter suffered from extreme pain in the testicles caused by 'an exceptionally rare and not properly accounted for consequence of vasectomy operations' called orchialgia.

Issue before the court
Should the surgeon have warned the patient about the danger of orchialgia, seeing as this was a very rare consequence of a vasectomy?

Decision of the court
The Supreme Court held that there was an obligation on the doctor to inform the patient of this condition, even if it was rare:

> 'On the evidence and in the circumstances of the case there was an obligation on the defendants to warn the plaintiff of the possible consequences of any condition such as orchialgia notwithstanding the rarity of its incidence, particularly since the operation was elective, rather than under any compulsion and the Court would not disturb on appeal the trial judge's determination that a warning had been given and that it had been sufficient.'

On the evidence the Supreme Court was satisfied that the doctor had in fact warned the patient about the danger of suffering testicular pain after the procedure, although she had pointed out that its incidence was extremely rare. Accordingly, the doctor had made full and proper disclosure.

Commentary
The Irish courts have adopted a different approach to the English courts, by retaining the right to challenge established medical opinion, where it would seem that this established medical opinion is clearly faulty. This important distinction will be examined in the chapters on negligence. In addition to that, it might be argued that the *Walsh* case has gone further in its definition of attendant risks than other common law jurisdictions, by including rare conditions within the scope of foreseeable consequences.

The Supreme Court adopted a rather unique approach by distinguishing between elective and non-elective procedures. The court held that where the procedure was non-elective (in other words necessary to avoid permanent damage or death), the duty to inform might not be as extensive as when the procedure was elective. Chief Justice Finlay explained this distinction as follows:

> 'There is, of course, where it is possible to do so, a clear obligation on a medical practitioner carrying out or arranging for the carrying out of an operation, to inform the patient of any possible harmful consequence arising from the operation, so as to permit the patient to give an informed consent to subjecting himself to the operation

concerned. I am also satisfied that the extent of this obligation must, as a matter of common sense, vary with what may be described as the elective nature of the surgery concerned. The obligation to give a warning of the possible harmful consequences of a surgical procedure which could be said to be elective may be more stringent and onerous.'

The logic of this distinction is that in cases where the treatment is necessary to avoid death or permanent serious injury, the patient does not really have much choice but to agree to the treatment, and in those cases disclosure might not make much of a difference. On the other hand, where the patient chooses to undergo treatment, which is not necessary to save life or limb, the patient should be fully informed before finally going ahead with the treatment or procedure.

What is also important is that in an elective procedure the doctor or surgeon is not required to do the usual weighing up of the risks involved in not having the operation as opposed to the risks involved in having the operation. The patient has made the choice to have the operation, and in so doing has taken that decision away from the medical practitioner.

This procedure in question, a vasectomy, was an elective procedure, as the patient would have been perfectly healthy without it, and therefore there was a more onerous duty on the surgeon or doctor to explain and discuss risks and complications normally associated with a vasectomy. On the facts the court was satisfied that the surgeon had done so.

The obvious problem with this distinction between elective and non-elective procedures is that the distinction is not always clear, as the Supreme Court would have us believe. The vasectomy is a popular choice amongst the Irish courts as being a prime example of an elective procedure, but what if a patient wanted a vasectomy because he already had two children suffering from severe intellectual disability, which seemed to be genetic, and he did not want any more children, or if his wife could not risk another pregnancy because of severe complications in her previous pregnancy? Would a vasectomy in that context still be regarded as elective?

The practical answer to this problem is that the doctor and nurse, when dealing with the patient, must fully explore the reasons why the patient is requesting the treatment or procedure, and if in any doubt, should choose to disclose risks rather than conceal them. The nurse, as the person who would have more frequent contact with the patient, is in an ideal position to properly explore the reasons for a patient choosing to undergo a specific treatment or procedure, and could thereafter fully brief the doctor or surgeon about the reasons given by the patient.

A more recent Irish case which looked at these issues was *Geoghegan v Harris* [2000] 3 I.R. 536.

Facts

The patient underwent a dental implant procedure. As a result of a bone graft, which was taken from his chin in the course of the procedure, the patient suffered damage to the incisive nerve at the front of his chin, which, from the time of the procedure, left him with a condition of severe pain at the mid line of his chin known as chronic neuropathic pain. It was accepted by both plaintiff and defendant that the bone graft, rather than the insertion of the dental implants, was the cause of this chronic pain. The patient sued the surgeon for failing to disclose to him in advance of the operation that there was a risk that he might suffer this chronic pain as a consequence of the procedure. The defendant surgeon argued that the risk of this occurring was less than one percent and he did not think it necessary to disclose this risk. The plaintiff responded to this argument by stating that he would not have consented to the operation if he had known of the risk, however small.

Issue before the court

Should the defendant have disclosed the risk of the pain, despite the improbability of it occurring?

Decision of the court

The court adopted the position that is more commonly used in deciding causation in negligence cases, and held that the plaintiff was required to show the court that he would not have consented to the procedure if the risk had been disclosed. The court accepted that the patient had been very eager to proceed with the implant and it was not convinced that the patient would not have proceeded if told of the risk. The plaintiff therefore failed in his claim. The court explained its position as follows:

> 'The application of the reasonable patient test seems more logical in respect of disclosure. This would establish the proposition that, as a general principle, the patient has the right to know and the practitioner a duty to advise of all material risks associated with a proposed form of treatment. The Court must ultimately decide what is material. 'Materiality' includes consideration of both (a) the severity of the consequences and (b) statistical frequency of the risk. That both are critical is obvious because a risk may have serious consequences and yet historically or predictably be so rare as not to be regarded as significant by many people. For example, a tourist might be deterred from visiting a country where there had been an earthquake causing loss of life, but if told the event happened fifty years ago without repetition since, he might well wonder why his travel agent caused him unnecessary worry by mentioning it at all.

The reasonable man, entitled as he must be to full information of material risks, does not have impossible expectations nor does he seek to impose impossible standards. He does not invoke only the wisdom of hindsight if things go wrong. He must be taken as needing medical practitioners to deliver on their medical expertise without excessive restraint or gross limitation on their ability to do so.

...

It is a very easy thing for a disappointed patient to say, in the aftermath of a procedure, as Mr Geoghegan has done, that he would not have undergone the operation had he been warned of the particular risk which came to pass. There may be many instances where the only evidence available to a Court is that of the patient and/or a spouse, one or both of whom may be prejudiced by bitterness and the wisdom of hindsight. It is a most unsatisfactory backdrop to the task which the Court must face in these cases.'

Commentary

The court adopted the objective reasonable patient test, along the lines of the American case of *Canterbury v Spence*. At the same time, the court attempted to solve the problems inherent in the *Canterbury v Spence* approach by adopting what is essentially a causation test. What this means is that it is not enough to show that the medical practitioner did not disclose the risk, but the plaintiff needs to go further and show that he would not have agreed to the procedure if he had known of the risk. It is not enough to just assert this – as it is clear that by suing the doctor you are asserting this – you must prove on a balance of probabilities that you would not have agreed to the procedure if the risk had been disclosed.

The decision is to be welcomed in that it clearly establishes a duty on the doctor to disclose material risks (in elective treatment) and therefore also establishes the right of the patient to choose whether to proceed with treatment only when in full knowledge of the material risks. At the same time the decision seems to place a great burden on the patient to prove that he or she would not have agreed to the procedure if the risk had been disclosed. This might be a difficult requirement, and in practice the court will probably be led by the magnitude of the risk. If a patient is told that there is a less than one percent chance of the harm occurring, it is likely that this will not cause the reasonable or average patient to refuse the treatment. On the other hand, where the risk is described as being a real possibility, many patients might have second thoughts. Of course the most problematic situations are where the risk is very small, but the consequences are drastic. The courts might have difficulty in deciding these cases.

The court also made it clear that it would take evidence concerning the events leading up to the consent being given, including more subjective factors, like the patient's behaviour and prior statements, and in that way attempt to assess the state of mind of the patient and his or her eagerness to have the treatment or procedure. After looking at this big picture, the court would be in a better position to decide whether a disclosure of the risk would have caused the patient to change his or her mind.

It must be noted that *Geoghegan v Harris* is a High Court decision, and therefore is not a binding precedent on the Supreme Court, but is of persuasive value only. This means that *Walsh* is still the leading Irish decision on the question of disclosure of material risk. However, *Geoghegan v Harris* is such a well-balanced and carefully considered decision, which reviews all the Irish decisions (including *Walsh*) on the question of disclosure, that it must be regarded as a highly persuasive decision which is likely to be followed by the Supreme Court if a similar issue is ever considered by that court.

How do health professionals know what the patient wants to know about?

The approach adopted by the English courts has been criticised as being overly paternalistic, as doctors can decide on their own what to tell and what not to tell the patient about proposed treatment. At the same time, the notion of informed consent along the lines of American law is often criticised as being impractical and idealistic as doctors cannot guess what it is that patients want to know about or what they would consider important. In the modern world of medicine, where doctors are often rushed off their feet and never have the opportunity to get to know their patients very well, this is a credible argument.

The Irish courts have adopted a position somewhere in the middle of this. If we consider the decisions of *Walsh* and *Geoghegan*, it can be said that the Irish law on disclosure says that the patient has the right to know all material risks, particularly if the procedure is elective as opposed to therapeutic, but at the same time the patient must show that consent would have been withdrawn or withheld if he or she was told of the particular risk that subsequently materialised.

The practical implications of the law relating to disclosure

What does this mean in practice? Firstly, health professionals should realise that patients are usually ordinary people, and they want to know the things that ordinary people want to know. These would run along the lines of:
- What are the chances of success?

- Are there any serious risks involved?
- Are there any alternatives?
- Is it going to be very expensive?
- Have you done many of these before?
- Does it have to be done now or can I think about it a little longer?
- Do you think it is necessary?
- Can you think of anybody else that I should talk to?

These questions can be answered in ordinary everyday language, as they are ordinary everyday questions. If a doctor trained himself or herself to contemplate and prepare the answers to these questions before doing rounds, it might be possible to put a lot of patients at ease in a relatively short time, rather than attempting to either avoid the whole process or being evasive in answering questions.

People who claim that the concept of informed consent is idealistic and impractical are assuming that a patient wants to know everything about anything. This is not true and the practice of informing patients should not be dismissed on that false premise.

Secondly, the nurse can play an important role in this question and answer exercise by finding out the questions beforehand. Through frequent contact with the patient, the nurse could soon discover the questions the patient would like to ask but has not, could not, or will not. Again, rather than go through the time-consuming process of getting over these hurdles, a doctor who has been briefed in advance could answer these questions in a considerably shorter period.

Thirdly, doctors need to keep careful notes detailing consultations with patients and should record the questions asked by a patient and record the patient's responses to the answers given to these questions and other information relating to risks. Nurses would do well in keeping a similar record of the questions asked by the patient. Not only could they thereafter hand these questions over to the doctor or surgeon, as an aid in assisting that medical practitioner in properly informing the patient, but this would also ensure that the nurse has an independent record of the patient's questions and concerns, as this could be crucial evidence if the matter went to court.

Informed consent is really a fancy name for honest-to-goodness communication, and one does not need the law to make that possible. It is a practical matter concerning more common sense than anything.

The benefits of disclosure are not only for the patient

We have already seen that if a health professional obtains the consent of the patient, an action for battery cannot lie against that professional if the operation is not a success. However, full disclosure further protects the professional, as the patient is the one who makes the choice of treatment after being properly informed. Accordingly, if the operation is not a success, the patient is responsible for the decision, and cannot argue that he or she would have chosen another procedure. In fact, they did choose that procedure, and only after being properly briefed. The law will never allow unjustified wisdom after the event where the patient was properly involved in the decision leading to that event.

What this means is that if a professional performs his or her job competently and to the required standard of care, after answering the types of questions previously discussed, that professional is effectively immune from being found liable under tort. In addition are the obvious therapeutic advantages of joint decision making.

Accordingly, the nurse can be seen as a 'doctor advocate' as well, in that the nurse should facilitate the process leading to the disclosure to the patient.

Conclusion – disclosure is about empowerment

It must be realised that more often than not the patient is going to consent to the procedure, as they would not be in the hospital in the first place if they were opposed to having treatment. Proper disclosure is not about getting the patient to agree to a treatment or a procedure in instances where the patient would usually refuse. Proper disclosure is about giving the patient more autonomy – if the patient is aware of the attendant risks that patient might ask for a second opinion, or might employ the services of a more experienced or skilled surgeon, which is the patient's way of attempting to minimise those risks. If the patient did not know about the risks, these options would not be available. Therefore disclosure is about autonomy and empowerment, rather than about changing one's mind.

Doctors often argue that they did not tell the patient about the risks as this would have frightened the patient away, thus preventing that patient from receiving necessary treatment. This is paternalism, as it assumes that the patient will flee at the first sign of danger, which is often not the case. The patient has often already been through that internal conflict before admitting himself or herself to hospital, and it is unlikely that, when told of a risk with a less than one percent chance of occurring, the patient will have a change of heart.

If the practice of disclosure becomes an established part of a health professional's mode of operation, it has benefits for both patient and health professional, and indeed for the health service as a whole. As previously discussed, the nurse has a crucial role in ensuring its successful implementation.

Postscript – 'therapeutic privilege'

What is meant by the term 'therapeutic privilege'? The issue of therapeutic privilege was considered in *Canterbury v Spence* where it was stated that where the patient is likely to become so distraught by the disclosure of medical information, and that this distress will cause the patient to become incapable of making an informed decision, that information may be kept from the patient by the doctor.

In *Sidaway* the practice was accepted as being necessary in certain situations, but the court stressed that the burden of proof was on the doctor to show that concealment was necessary and justified:

> 'There is a need that the doctor should have the opportunity of proving that he reasonably believed that disclosure of the risk would be damaging to his patient or contrary to his best interests.'

This approach can be criticised for a number of reasons. Firstly, it is formulated very widely – 'best interests of the patient' can be interpreted in a number of ways. Would it not be better to restrict its application to instances of clearly foreseeable harm or damage to the patient? If not, it would be possible for doctors to use the 'privilege' to avoid telling patients about the risks on the basis that they think it is in the patient's best interests to have the treatment. This is why most of the problems arise, as doctors think that a patient will necessarily refuse the treatment when told of the risks. As has been argued before, this is probably far from the truth. Secondly, when it was used in *Canterbury v Spence* the court was dealing with the concept as a capacity issue. In other words, the doctor can withhold information only where the patient's capacity to make an informed decision would be lost if the risk was made known to the patient. This is a far narrower test than the 'best interests' test.

The notion of 'therapeutic privilege' can be condemned as being paternalistic in the extreme. The example usually given to justify therapeutic privilege is when a person has a terminal illness and the relatives have asked that the patient is not informed. This situation is fraught with both ethical and legal problems. From an ethical point of view, it is insulting and demeaning to a patient that he or she is considered incapable of handling the news of imminent death. Very often it is the relatives who seek to protect themselves from having to confront the truth, rather than concern for the patient. From a legal point of view, it means that confidentiality has been breached, as the relatives should only be told the condition of the patient with the consent of that patient. As the patient has been kept in the dark, clearly he or she could not have consented to the disclosure being made to the relatives or family.

Remember that privileged information is that information which a person can prevent from being led as evidence in court, or in tort it means that a person cannot be sued for defaming somebody on certain privileged occasions. It is therefore somewhat puzzling that 'therapeutic privilege' has nothing to do with either of those things, and it is not clear why it has been called a 'privilege' at all. The 'privilege' belongs to the doctor, as it is the doctor that claims he or she cannot be forced to disclose bad news.

Nurses and therapeutic privilege

Nurses often find themselves in impossible positions in such situations. They are obliged (usually under threat of disciplinary proceedings) to obey the doctor's instructions not to inform the patient of his or her condition, and yet at the same time their daily contact with the patient in question might force them to lie if asked a direct question.

The nurse in such a position must obey the doctor's instruction, and if the patient does ask a direct question, the nurse should summon the doctor immediately, and allow him or her to respond to the patient's questions. The fact that the nurse evades the question and summons the doctor should be enough to tell the patient that something is not right, in any event, and the doctor is certain to face a barrage of questions. This of course assumes that the doctor is available to respond to the nurse's call.

Nurses would do well in informing doctors that the concept of therapeutic privilege is riddled with ethical and legal problems, and that doctors would be well advised to avoid such a practice. Recent experiences with AIDS patients have shown that patients often adopt a positive attitude once told of their illness (sometimes leading to miraculously long lives), as the uncertainty was more crippling than the truth.

The concept of therapeutic privilege does not seem to have gained a foothold in Irish law, and it is unlikely that any court in this day and age would accept it, at least not in such wide terminology as the court in *Sidaway*.

Full and Proper Disclosure: Summary

1. The patient-orientated approach to disclosure is based on what the patient thinks is a material risk. This can place the medical practitioner in an impossible position as he or she is expected to know what a patient would consider important.
2. The doctor-orientated approach to disclosure is based on what the medical profession as a whole thinks should have been disclosed. This can lead to paternalism and excludes the patient from the

decision-making process, itself an important aspect of the therapeutic process. It also means that the courts must surrender to the opinions of the medical profession.
3. The Irish courts have attempted to steer a middle course between these two extremes. It is the court and not the medical profession or the patient that must ultimately decide whether there was sufficient disclosure.
4. Although the Irish courts have used an approach that is similar to the reasonable patient test, the important difference is that the patient must show that he or she would not have consented to the treatment or procedure if he or she was aware of the risk in question. This causative requirement lessens the burden placed on the medical practitioner by the patient-orientated approach, but at the same time makes it clear that the patient must be properly informed of all material risks.
5. Useful websites:
    a. *Medical Council of Ireland* (http://www.medicalcouncil.ie).
    b. *British Medical Journal* (http://www.bmj.com).
    c. *General Medical Council* (http://www.gmc-uk.org).

12
VOLUNTARY CONSENT

> **Learning Outcomes**
> **At the completion of this chapter, the reader should know and understand the following:**
> - The legal concept of voluntariness.
> - Informed consent relies on more than a supply of sufficient information.
> - The patient must be given the freedom to decide.
> - Education of the patient is an essential prerequisite to voluntariness.

Important concepts and phrases that are crucial to an understanding of this chapter

Coercion
Where the threat of harm is used by one person to control the actions or decisions of another.

Persuasion
Where a person is convinced by another, usually through a process of reasoning, to do or not to do a certain thing.

Manipulation
Where information is given to a person in such a way that the presentation and selected content of that information will influence the person's decision.

Education
The development of a person's character and intellectual powers, coupled with an ideally unlimited access to information, so as to enable that person to make an informed choice as an exercise of free will.

Vitiate
To nullify, to make something invalid.

Introduction

If a patient was given sufficient information to enable them to make an informed decision concerning the acceptance or refusal of medical treatment, this would be meaningless if the patient was not allowed the freedom to make up his or her own mind on the matter.

While cases of involuntary or forced treatment are obviously outside the bounds of what is accepted as consensual treatment, the question of consent to treatment in a formalised institution such as a hospital, and the corresponding question whether patients are properly advised of their right to refuse treatment, are thorny issues with no clear answers. The fine line between a person in a position of authority and power advising a patient as opposed to instructing a patient, is not always that easy to distinguish. In addition, the manner in which advice and information is presented can have profound influences on a patient, and the question of manipulation of evidence and emotions is again a very complex and difficult issue.

The notion of voluntariness

Voluntariness as a concept is often difficult to explain, as it is usually defined in relation to the absence of other factors. In other words, a person's conduct is regarded as voluntary where there is an absence of coercion or duress or control.

Duress and undue influence are very similar concepts and are really separated by degree rather than by meaning. Duress involves the threat of bodily injury or violence (in other words, a physical threat) whereas undue influence involves psychological pressure or even blackmail (an emotional threat). It is sometimes difficult to distinguish between the two, and therefore for the purposes of this chapter they will be considered together, although examples of duress and undue influence in the health care context are thankfully rare. As there are no reported decisions concerning duress and undue influence in the health care sector, it is necessary to look elsewhere in our law in an effort to properly understand these concepts.

An area where duress and undue influence are often considered is the law of marriage, and more specifically, the law of nullity, where the allegation is made that a valid marriage was never entered into because of some vitiating factor. The most obvious example of a marriage under duress is the so-called 'shotgun marriage', but the examples in the reported cases are usually a little more sophisticated than a gun in the ear.

The leading Irish case in this area is the Supreme Court decision of *N (otherwise K) v K* [1986] 6 I.L.R.M. 75

Facts
The nineteen-year-old bride claimed that her father had forced her to marry when it was discovered that she was pregnant. Her evidence was that her father had given her the option of marriage or an abortion.

Issue before the court
Was the choice of marriage or abortion a real choice or did the bride feel that she had no choice but to marry?

Decision of the court
The Supreme Court held that consent to marriage must be a full and free exercise of the independent will of the parties. Consent must be real, and not just apparent. The Supreme Court held that it did not matter whether the external pressure was proper or improper, legal or illegal, what was important was that the pressure was enough to remove the free exercise of will.

McCarthy J. defined this consent as:

> 'a true voluntary consent based upon adequate knowledge and freed from vitiating factors commonly described as undue influence or duress, particularly those emanating from third parties.'

The marriage was annulled.

Commentary
On a reading of the judgment, it is important to notice that the Supreme Court adopted a subjective approach to the question of voluntary consent. Did the person in question feel that they had the freedom of choice? This would have important implications for the question of patient consent, as although the test for disclosure is essentially an objective test ('the reasonable patient' or in England 'the reasonable doctor'), it might be argued that the test for voluntariness should be a subjective test – did the patient feel that he or she had the right to refuse treatment or demand alternative treatment?

Of course, like in all subjective tests, the court will not just take the word of the patient as the absolute truth, the judge will look at the behaviour of the patient at the time of consent, and will hear evidence as to what the patient said or asked at the time that consent was sought. The court will try and determine the state of mind of the patient by the way he or she was acting at the time. What is important, however, is that the court will be looking at the question from the patient's point of view when deciding whether there was an exercise of free will by the patient.

When health professionals speak to patients in order to obtain consent, the phrasing of advice and the tenor of questions and answers very often create the impression that the only possible option available to the patient is to consent to the treatment offered. It might sometimes happen that alternative treatments are offered, but here the patient would be made to think that it was imperative to choose one. It would very seldom occur in practice that a health professional offered a patient the choice of refusal.

If one were to adopt a truly subjective test on the issue of voluntariness, the health professional should be careful to explain the options available, including the right to refuse any treatment and the probable consequences of that refusal. If a patient is not offered all the available options, it can hardly be said to be a subjective test of voluntariness, as the patient is not given the freedom of choice – at the most the patient has a restricted choice, and in many instances, no choice at all.

The scenario that the nurse is likely to encounter is the terminally ill or elderly patient who wants to 'go home to die', rather than spending the last days in a hospital ward in a strange bed surrounded by strangers. If the principle of voluntariness was upheld, that patient should be allowed to leave immediately, assuming that they did not pose any danger to society, for example if they were suffering from a notifiable or contagious disease. How many times is this allowed to happen? Not very often – the patient is more often than not kept in the hospital, on increased medication, until all resistance expires.

It is in situations like this that the nurse can truly be a patient advocate. A doctor cannot lawfully order a patient to remain in hospital if that patient wants to leave, unless that patient is incapacitated to make that decision, or if the patient poses some threat to society. The competent patient who wants to leave and go home should be allowed to do so, and the nurse should inform the patient of that right.

The other potentially relevant case involving marriage and true consent is the Supreme Court decision in *B v O'R* [1991] 1 I.R. 289.

Facts
The wife as a young girl was raised in an orphanage until the age of fifteen, when she left, immature and naïve. She had sexual intercourse with a twenty-six-year old man and fell pregnant. When her parents discovered her pregnancy they sent her back to the orphanage. The sister in charge of the orphanage contacted the man and arranged for them to be married. The girl took part in the marriage ceremony but the evidence was that she was in a dazed state at the time and did not truly comprehend what was going on.

Issue before the court
Although nobody had forced the girl to marry (as in the previous case), could it be said that she had voluntarily consented to the marriage?

Decision of the court
The Supreme Court found that the pressure to marry had not come from a person but was rather created by the situation in which the girl found herself. This pressure of circumstance was enough to rob the girl of her capacity to consent as it was not possible in those circumstances for the girl to exercise free will.

Commentary
Once again a subjective test was used, and in addition it was recognised that the pressure can be created by events or by a situation: it does not need to come from another person.

This again might be relevant to the question of a patient voluntarily consenting to treatment in an institutionalised setting. Patients in a hospital might get used to the idea of people telling them what to do – when to wake up, when to eat, what to eat, when to take their medicine, when to take a bath, and so on. The patient in that frame of mind might not realise that he or she is being offered a choice, as they are so used to doing as they are told.

Once again the nurse has a crucial role to play in ensuring that the patient is aware that consent to treatment involves choice, and that this choice should include alternative treatments or no treatment at all.

Education is a crucial element of free choice

It is necessary to distinguish between education and undue influence. Doctors and even nurses might routinely recommend certain types of treatment or procedures to patients. What is important is how these recommendations are phrased, so that once again, the patient is fully aware that what is being suggested is one of a number of choices, including the right to refuse treatment altogether. If the patient is not properly informed about all the choices available, in other words educated, it cannot be said that the patient has the freedom of choice.

As has been mentioned in an earlier chapter, doctors and nurses are trained to save lives or at least to make people's lives more comfortable. It goes against all their training to allow a person to die. However, the concept of informed consent and the element of voluntariness would be meaningless if that right to refuse treatment was not recognised and respected. The doctor and nurse can provide the patient with choice, they can educate the patient about the choices, but they cannot make the choices. That must be left to the patient.

Voluntariness: Summary

1. Voluntariness is a state of mind. The patient must feel that he or she can exercise free will.
2. Duress and undue influence can both rob a patient of his or her free will.
3. Although duress will usually come from another person, and is not likely to occur in the healthcare context (at least where consent is required); undue influence can come from a person or a situation.
4. An institutionalised setting like a hospital can create an environment where a patient might become unconscious of the fact that he or she has the right of free will. It is the duty of the health professional, in particular the nurse, to remind the patient of this right to free will.
5. The education of the patient is an important part of voluntariness. The patient cannot be said to exercise free will if that will is curtailed by the choices on offer.
6. Advice should never go further than a reasoned recommendation. The patient must make the final choice.
7. The freedom to consent to medical treatment includes the freedom to refuse treatment or choose an alternative treatment.
8. Useful web site:
NHS National Electronic Library for Health
(http://www.nelh.nhs.uk).

13

EMERGENCY TREATMENT

> **Learning Outcomes**
> At the completion of this chapter, the reader should know and understand the following:
> - Informed consent should always be sought and obtained from a patient.
> - One of the exceptions to this rule is the emergency situation where it is not possible to obtain consent before treatment is administered.
> - The very limited circumstances where the defence of necessity can be pleaded when it comes to medical treatment.

Introduction – the defence of necessity

You will hopefully remember the discussion in an earlier chapter about the defence of necessity, which is known as a general defence in tort as it can be raised as a defence to a claim based on any tort.

To recap: The defendant deliberately commits a tort against a person in order to prevent or avoid some greater harm where there is no reasonable alternative. This defence claims that it was necessary to commit a lesser evil in order to prevent a greater evil, usually where that greater evil will result in death or harm that cannot be repaired.

Emergency treatment

At first it was argued that emergency medical treatment was based on implied consent. In other words, it was argued that if the patient was able to respond to the question: 'Should I try and save your life?' the obvious response would be 'Yes, please!'

This argument has been abandoned in favour of the more logical basis of the defence of necessity. The health professional can not wait for the patient to give consent, as the time lost in waiting could be the difference between life or death or at least the avoiding of permanent damage to the patient.

In order to successfully defend a claim of battery, the health professional would need to show a number of things:
1. The health professional would need to show that the treatment was

in fact necessary as opposed to being convenient. In other words, the treatment must be medically necessary as an objective fact.
2. The health professional would need to show that the treatment that was carried out was no more than was necessary in the circumstances to save the life of the patient or prevent permanent damage. The health professional is not allowed to perform other treatments at the same time because it is convenient to do so.
3. The health professional would need to show that it was not reasonably possible to obtain consent from the patient.
4. The health professional would also need to show that he or she was not reasonably aware of any prior objection by the patient to the treatment in question (often called an 'advance directive').

A Canadian case that dealt with this situation was *Malette v Shulman* (1990) 67 D.L.R. (4th) 321.

Facts
The plaintiff was severely injured in a car crash and was rushed to the casualty section, where she arrived unconscious. The attending doctor ordered a blood transfusion, but a card was discovered on the patient's person, which informed the reader that she was a Jehovah's Witness and that under no circumstances was she to receive a blood transfusion.

The doctor ordered that the blood transfusion go ahead. The plaintiff recovered, and on learning of the blood transfusion sued for battery.

Issue before the court
Did the doctor's duty to save life justify the fact that the advance directive of the patient was ignored?

Decision of the court
The court held that the doctor's decision to ignore the advance directive of the patient amounted to battery on his part, notwithstanding the emergency situation.

> 'On the facts of the present case, Dr Shulman was clearly faced with an emergency. He had an unconscious, critically ill patient on his hands who, in his opinion, needed blood transfusions to save her life and preserve her health. If there were no Jehovah's Witness card, he undoubtedly would have been entitled to administer blood transfusions as part of the emergency treatment and could not have been held liable for so doing. In those circumstances, he would have had no indication that the transfusions would have been refused had the patient then been able to make her wishes known and,

accordingly, no reason to expect that, as a reasonable person, she would not consent to the transfusions.

However, to change the facts, if Mrs Malette, before passing into unconsciousness, had expressly instructed Dr Shulman, in terms comparable to those set forth on the card, that her religious convictions as a Jehovah's Witness were such that she was not to be given a blood transfusion under any circumstances and that she fully realised the implications of this position, the doctor would have been confronted with an obviously different situation. Here, the patient, anticipating an emergency in which she might be unable to make decisions about her health care contemporaneous with the emergency, has given explicit instructions that blood transfusions constitute an unacceptable medical intervention and are not to be administered to her. Once the emergency arises, is the doctor nonetheless entitled to administer transfusions on the basis of his honest belief that they are needed to save his patient's life?

The answer, in my opinion, is clearly no. A doctor is not free to disregard a patient's advance instructions any more than he would be free to disregard instructions given at the time of the emergency.'

Commentary

The defence of necessity is only available in situations where the patient has not given prior instructions and at the time is not capable of giving consent to the medical treatment. The health professional cannot rely on the defence of necessity where that professional is aware that the patient has already refused treatment whilst capable of doing so. If that were the case, it would be very easy to wait until a patient lost consciousness and then administer emergency treatment contrary to prior instructions.

While there have not been similar decisions in Ireland, the principles of Irish law regarding treatment to consent have been clearly spelt out, and there is no reason to suppose that the Irish courts would come to a different conclusion.

Emergency Treatment: Summary

1. Emergency treatment relies on the defence of necessity.
2. It must be shown that the treatment was necessary to save life or limb. Treatment carried out because it was convenient to do so will not be covered by this defence.
3. The defence can only be used in circumstances where the patient has not given prior instructions and where it is not possible to wait for the patient to give consent.
4. The treatment that is given must be just enough to enable the patient to live another day or avoid permanent and serious damage, and thereafter to make his or her wishes known.
5. If a health professional is aware that the patient has stated that he or she does not consent to treatment, it is not permissible to wait for that patient to lose consciousness and thereafter to proceed on the basis of emergency. The prior directive of the patient must be honoured and obeyed.
6. Useful websites:
    a. *Looksmart* (http://www.findarticles.com/p/articles/).
    b. *Murdoch University Electronic Journal of Law (Australia)* (http://www.murdoch.edu.au/elaw).
    c. *Priory Lodge Education Ltd* (http://www.priory.com/ethics.htm).

14

NEGLIGENCE — AN INTRODUCTION

> **Learning Outcomes**
> **At the completion of this chapter, the reader should know and understand the following:**
> - The basic principles governing the law of negligence.
> - The elements that need to be proven by the patient claiming negligence.
> - The concepts of the burden of proof and the balance of probabilities.
> - The doctrine of *res ipsa loquitur*.

Important concepts and phrases that are crucial to an understanding of this chapter

Litigant
A person taking part in a trial at court. Therefore both the plaintiff and defendant are litigants as they are involved in litigation.

Probable
Something that is expected to happen or is likely to prove true.

Introduction

When a health provider or health professional is careless it does not automatically follow that he or she will be liable in negligence. Negligence has a very specific technical meaning and does not mean the same thing as carelessness.

A person is negligent in a legal sense when their actions (or lack of action in circumstances where they should have acted) fall short of what is determined as acceptable behaviour, and as a result of that action (or inaction) a person is harmed in some way.

The elements of negligence

The four elements in the tort of negligence are as follows:
- A duty of care;
- a failure to conform to the required standard of care;

- actual loss or damage to the interests of the plaintiff (the patient);
- a sufficiently close causal connection between the conduct of the defendant and the resulting injury to the patient.

These elements will be closely examined in chapters Fifteen-Eighteen.

The patient must prove

For the tort of battery the patient need only prove unauthorised touching. Thereafter it is up to the health professional to prove consent.

In an action for negligence, however, the patient must prove all four elements of negligence in order to succeed in a negligence action. Three out of four elements is not enough – the plaintiff must prove all four elements, in the correct order, to be successful in an action for negligence.

For this reason, many commentators argue for the approach that says where there is no informed consent there should be an action in battery available to the patient. As has been pointed out however, the approach of the English (and probably Irish) courts has been that where there is consent, albeit not informed consent, there can only be an action in negligence available to the patient. As a result most actions brought by patients against hospitals or health professionals are based on negligence, and therefore the duty is on the patient to prove his or her case.

For that reason it is necessary that the reader have an understanding of some basic concepts in the law of evidence, before we move on and consider the specific elements making up an action in negligence.

The burden of proof and the civil standard of proof

The degree of proof required by the civil standard is easier to express in words than the criminal standard, because it involves a comparative rather than a quantitative test. On the whole it is not difficult to say that one thing is more probable than another, although it may be impossible to say how much more probable. The civil standard, or 'balance of probabilities', has been formulated by a great English judge, Lord Denning, as follows:

> 'It must carry a reasonable degree of probability but not so high as is required in a criminal case. If the evidence is such that the tribunal can say 'we think it more probable than not', the burden is discharged, but if the probabilities are equal it is not.' (*Miller v Pensions* [1947] 2 All E.R. 372 at 374.)

Courts in civil trials often speak of a 'balance' of probabilities, but the metaphor must be treated with care. The idea this image suggests is that the party bearing the onus has to put sufficient evidence into the pan of the scales to make it outweigh the other. What is weighed in the 'balance' is not quantities of evidence but the probabilities arising from that evidence and all the circumstances of the case.

For example: Six people are driving in a car. They have recently left a pub after drinking a large amount of stout. They are all drunk, including the driver. A collision occurs and a pedestrian is injured. There is only one independent eyewitness to the accident who testifies that the pedestrian was walking in obedience to the 'green man' at the traffic light intersection. However, all six people in the car, including the driver, testify that the traffic light was green and the pedestrian light was the 'red man'.

If one were to use the scales simply as a measuring device, six would outweigh one every time. However, if the judge takes into account the high levels of alcohol coursing through the veins of those six witnesses, and the fact that they are biased, the more probable version is that of the independent eyewitness, who has nothing to gain by lying. Accordingly, one outweighs six. The inherent probabilities of the competing evidence are what tip the scales, rather than the amount or volume of the evidence. Quality is more important than quantity.

To put it simply, it is the person with the best evidence that wins a civil case, not the person with the most witnesses or the most evidence.

What this means in the area of medical litigation is that the hospital or health professional might admit that they do not know what went wrong and they have no explanation for the damages suffered by the patient. This does not mean that the patient will win the case, as it is not the hospital or health professional that needs to discharge the onus or legal burden of proof. It is the patient who needs to show that the hospital or health professional was negligent. This is often a difficult thing to do.

Res Ipsa Loquitur

In some cases the law presumes that the defendant has been negligent when he or she has sole control of the cause of the incident and because the incident could not normally have happened without some element of negligence. In such a case the doctrine of *res ipsa loquitur* ('the facts speak for themselves') is applied.

Note, however, that this is only an evidential presumption, it does not win the case. The defendant can still lead evidence which provides another plausible reason for the accident or incident in question.

In the case of *Scott v London and St. Katherine Docks Co.* [1865] 3 H. & C. 569 at 722 the court described the principle as follows:

> '(There) must be reasonable evidence of negligence. But where the thing is shown to be under the management of the defendant or his

servants, and the accident is such as in the ordinary circumstances does not happen if those who have the management use proper care. It affords reasonable evidence, in the absence of explanation by the defendants, that the accident arose from want of care.'

Since the *St Catherine Docks* case, the English courts have been more willing to apply the doctrine than many other legal systems. This does not mean that all the plaintiff has to do is make a bare allegation and thereafter rely on the doctrine. The plaintiff must show that:
- The damage occurred in an unexplained way,
- that it would not have occurred in the ordinary course of events without there being some form of negligence,
- that circumstances point to the liability of the defendant as opposed to any other person, and
- that the incident or factor that caused the damage was within the control of the defendant.

Once the plaintiff has established the requirements, the defendant is then called upon to offer a reasonable explanation for the damage. This does not mean that the defendant must disprove the allegation of negligence. The defendant must merely offer another non-tortuous reason for the damage which is just as likely to have caused it. To do this the defendant must lead evidence to show either that the damage could have occurred without any negligence, or if there was negligence, that the negligence was not of its doing.

In other words, the defendant has to displace the inference raised by the plaintiff. If the defendant cannot do so, the plaintiff will be well on the way to proving his or her case.

The Supreme Court of Ireland ruled in the case of *Lindsay v Mid-Western Health Board* [1993] 2 I.R. 147 that where a person entered hospital for a routine medical procedure and was administered an anaesthetic and subsequently failed to regain consciousness, the principle of *res ipsa loquitur* applied. The defendants, however, rebutted the presumption of negligence by showing that all reasonable care and precautions were taken in the administration of the anaesthetic. Accordingly, the evidential burden moved back to the plaintiff to prove negligence in the usual way on a balance of probabilities.

What was important about this case was that the Supreme Court confirmed that the doctrine was still applicable in Irish law at a time when many countries (for example Canada and Australia) are moving away from the doctrine.

Negligence and Proof: Summary

1. In order to succeed in an action for negligence the patient needs to prove all four elements of negligence.
2. The four elements of negligence are:
   a. A duty of care.
   b. The standard of care.
   c. Damages.
   d. Causation.
3. As an action for negligence is an action based on tort, the case will be heard in the civil court.
4. This means is that the patient must prove his or her case on a balance of probabilities.
5. The balance of probabilities is a qualitative test, rather than a quantitative test; the person with the most evidence will not necessarily win. It is the person with the best evidence (the most probable evidence) that will win a civil case.
6. The doctrine of *res ipsa loquitur* can assist a patient who is pursuing a claim of medical negligence. A presumption of negligence will arise if the plaintiff can show that the defendant was in control of the events leading to the damage and that it is reasonable to assume negligence when considering the particular facts at hand.
7. Useful websites:
   a. *Irish Medical News* (http://www.irishmedicalnews.ie).
   b. *Consilio* (http://www.spr-consilio.com).
   c. *David Evans* (http://www.davidevans-law.co.uk/index.htm).
   d. *Medical Litigation* (http://www.medneg.com).

15

A DUTY OF CARE

> **Learning Outcomes**
> At the completion of this chapter, the reader should know and understand the following:
> ▸ When a duty of care arises or exists between parties.
> ▸ The application of these principles in a health care context.

Important legal concepts and phrases that are crucial to an understanding of this chapter

Omission
The failure to do something in circumstances where a reasonable person would have acted.

Introduction

As a rule, there is no general duty of care. For example, a man on his way to the pub notices a young child struggling in a shallow river. There is a very real danger that the child will drown. The man does not fancy getting his shoes wet, and is eager for that first pint, and so continues on his way. The child drowns. Whilst the man may burn in Hell, he cannot be held legally liable for his action, or in this case his inaction or omission. He had no duty of care towards that child, given that he did not cause the child to fall in the river in the first place. As long as you were not the creator of the harm, there is no duty of care on you to save others from the harm.

Essentially there are two methods to determine whether a duty of care exists.

The first is to determine whether there was a pre-existing relationship between the plaintiff and defendant, and that the relationship was based on a duty of care. This is particularly appropriate in cases of so-called professional negligence, which is the focus of this study.

The second is to apply what is called the 'neighbour principle'. It was recognised by the courts that there might not be a pre-existing relationship between a wrongdoer and the victim of that wrongdoing, and that it was necessary to extend the law of negligence to include actions between strangers. The neighbour principle provides that reasonable care must be taken to avoid acts or omissions that can reasonably be foreseen as likely to injure a 'neighbour'. In this case the neighbour is not necessarily the person who lives next door to you, but rather your neighbour in the wider sense of the word – a person so closely and directly affected by your act or omission, which forms the conduct complained of, that when you performed that conduct you ought to have reasonably contemplated or foreseen that your conduct might cause harm or damage to that person.

The case that is credited with creating the neighbour principle is the English decision of *Donoghue v Stevenson* [1932] A.C. 562.

Facts
The plaintiff's friend purchased a bottle of ginger beer from a retailer and gave it to the plaintiff to drink. The glass of the bottle was opaque. The plaintiff drank some of the ginger beer straight from the bottle and thereafter poured the remainder into a glass. The remains of a small partially decomposed snail were discovered. She sued for damages, primarily for emotional shock.

Issue to be decided by the court
Did the defendant, the manufacturer of the ginger beer, owe the plaintiff a duty of care, given that there was no prior relationship between them, as the plaintiff had not purchased the ginger beer, and therefore the plaintiff and defendant were strangers?

Decision of the court
The Court of Appeal of England decided that a duty of care did exist between the manufacturer of the ginger beer and the plaintiff, the customer.

Commentary
In essence, what the Court of Appeal held was that it was not necessary to show that there was an existing relationship between the plaintiff and defendant to prove a duty of care. All that had to be shown was that the defendant should have foreseen that its actions could cause harm to the plaintiff and taken steps to avoid that harm. It did not matter that the plaintiff who was in danger of being harmed was a stranger. That plaintiff became your 'neighbour' if you could foresee that your actions might cause him or her harm.

This principle became known as the neighbour principle because of the following portion of the judgement delivered by Lord Atkin:

'The rule that you are to love your neighbour becomes, in law, you must not injure your neighbour; and the lawyer's question who is my neighbour? receives a restricted reply. You must take reasonable care to avoid acts or omissions which you can reasonably foresee would be likely to injure your neighbour. Who then, in law, is my neighbour? The answer seems to be persons who are so closely and directly affected by my act that I ought reasonably to have them in contemplation as being so affected when I am directing my mind to the acts or omissions which are called in question.'

In other words, if a person at the time of doing something (or not doing something they should be doing) should foresee that what they are doing might harm somebody, they must take steps to avoid that harm. Their failure to take those reasonable steps to avoid the foreseeable harm amounts to negligent conduct.

For example, a farmer is hunting rabbits in a field. The field is bordered on the one side by the national highway. The farmer has his back to the highway. Out of the corner of his eye the farmer sees a rabbit running for its life in the direction of the highway. As the farmer swings his shotgun around to take a shot, he should be thinking: 'Hang about, if I miss the rabbit I might hit a vehicle on the highway'. As a result of this little voice in his head, the reasonable farmer doesn't take the shot, the rabbit lives to see another day, and the drivers on the highway are safe, for the time being. The unreasonable or negligent farmer takes the shot at the fleeing rabbit, misses the rabbit (which lives to see another day) but hits a vehicle on the highway. The fact that the farmer does not know the driver of the vehicle is of no consequence, that driver has become the farmer's 'neighbour' by virtue of the farmer foreseeing that he might cause the driver harm if he takes the shot. If the farmer proceeds to take the shot despite the foreseeable consequences, he is negligent.

We can apply these principlees to aa mediacl scenario: A heavily intoxicated man staggers into the back entrance of a hospital in the early hours of the morning, collapses on his back, and some time later chokes and dies on his own vomit.

In this scenario the court would need to determine whether the man could be regarded as a patient of the hospital and consequently whether the hospital owed that patient a duty of care. It is doubtful that a relationship was formed when the drunk staggered onto the premises. The court's decision would largely depend on whether it could be said that such a situation was reasonably foreseeable, and whether the hospital should have ensured that the back entrance was closed and locked, forcing people to approach the front of the hospital where they would be noticed by the night staff.

The duty of care since Donoghue v Stevenson

The courts have often held that Lord Atkin in *Donoghue v Stevenson* was stating a principle, and that principle needs to be kept up to date as society changes and the public expect different things. In other words, the courts could introduce matters of policy into the investigation when deciding if a duty of care exists in a particular situation.

What this means is that the modern notion of the duty of care does not rest on one magic formula, as there are a number of possible approaches. Society is always changing, as are the expectations of the public. It is no longer possible to say that any one thing would decide whether there was a duty of care. It would seem that to establish a duty of care, the plaintiff must show that either:

1. There is a direct precedent, or a very similar precedent, where a duty of care had been imposed. In other words, a previous binding decision of the court where the facts of that case are identical or very similar to the facts of the present case, in which event the court would follow the earlier decision if appropriate; or
2. Where there is no earlier case that has similar facts, and the court is faced with a new and unique situation, and needs to decide on its own whether a duty of care exists, the court should apply three criteria, which must all be satisfied, to determine whether a duty of care exists:
   - The damage must be foreseeable;
   - there must be a sufficiently proximate or close relationship between the parties;
   - it must be fair, just and reasonable for the court to impose a duty of care in the light of policy considerations with which the court is concerned.

These principles often need to be applied in the so-called 'Good Samaritan' cases. For example, a nurse drives past a motor vehicle accident and stops to see whether he can help. The nurse is legally entitled to continue past as there is no general duty of care to strangers, and he was not the cause of the accident. He does the 'decent thing' and stops. Unfortunately, the nurse is negligent in his treatment of the injured driver and the driver suffers further injury. Should the nurse be held liable for the driver's increased injuries caused by the nurse's negligence?

As previously mentioned, there is no legal duty to volunteer help. There must be a pre-existing duty. The nurse in this scenario is not legally obliged to stop and assist. Of course the nurse might be under an ethical or professional duty to stop and assist, and it is likely that a nurse who failed to stop and render assistance at a crash site could face disciplinary measures if this conduct was noticed and reported, but there is no duty imposed by law.

There is no mention that the driver is an existing patient of the nurse, and even if he was, it is debatable whether that existing relationship would impose a duty on the nurse to stop in this unrelated incident. Similarly, the nurse was not the cause of the accident and therefore has not committed any unlawful or wrongful conduct that might give rise to the neighbour principle.

However, once the nurse stops and says something like, 'I'm a nurse, tell me what's wrong and I'll help', a relationship is formed and a duty of care is established. In addition, by actually treating the driver, the nurse is bringing the neighbour principle into play, as he must foresee the probable consequences of his conduct, namely that if he is negligent in his treatment of the driver, the chances are high that the injuries will be aggravated.

The extent of a duty of care is always tempered by policy considerations

As mentioned at the beginning of this section, negligence is a legal concept and the fact that a nurse makes a mistake does not necessarily mean that the nurse will be judged to be at fault and negligent. If, for example, the situation was an emergency and the nurse needed to act immediately without time for consideration, the court would take that circumstance into account, and decide what would have been the appropriate standard of care in the circumstances. A balance needs to be struck between the magnitude of the risk and the burden imposed on the defendant to do the right thing.

Even where the risk is foreseeable, the court will not always find that it was negligent not to take steps to avoid the risk. Precautions need only be taken against harm or damage that is reasonably likely to happen. If any person, including a health professional, had to take precautions against every risk which he or she can foresee, life would be impossible and nothing would ever get done, as we would all be too busy taking precautions.

In deciding whether a reasonable person would have taken precautions against a foreseeable risk, or if precautions were taken, whether those precautions were reasonable in the circumstances, the court will consider a number of factors:

- **The foreseeability of harm.** As is clear by now, this is the principal test in negligence, and the courts always emphasise the importance of the concept of foreseeability of harm.
- **The magnitude of the risk.** What is the likelihood of the risk

happening? Is it remote or so improbable that it can be ignored and no precautions taken? Or is it highly likely making precautions an absolute necessity? Or, as is more likely, is it somewhere between these two extremes? The defendant must properly assess the risk, and act accordingly. The more serious the consequences, the greater the care that needs to be taken.

- **The burden of taking precautions.** If the effort and cost involved in taking precautions to avoid the harm far outweigh the chances that the harm or damage will ever happen, it is not reasonable to expect a person to take those precautions. In other words, a court will ask questions such as the cost of taking precautions and how practical it was to take them.

  To use an example to illustrate the previous two concepts. If the chances of a nurse suffering a needlestick (or 'sharps') injury are very high, the nurse should be provided with adequate protective gloves, which are relatively cheap and easy to provide, as the possible consequences of a needlestick injury where there is infected blood are very serious, and possibly fatal. On the other hand, if the nurse has nothing to do with needles or infected blood, the provision of even cheap gloves might be seen as an unnecessary extravagance where the money could be used somewhere else.

- **The utility (usefulness) of the defendant's conduct.** If the defendant was involved in a service to the public interest, the court might give the defendant some leeway in assessing his or her conduct. This will often apply when a health professional is performing emergency treatment, or voluntary work, when practicalities determine it necessary to cut corners.

- **Finally, the court will often look at what is common or established practice in determining the reasonableness of the defendant's conduct.** As we will see in the next section, in the field of medicine this often causes problems of its own, as there are often differing opinions as to what good practice is and what a reasonable standard of care is.

The duty of care is determined on the basis of knowledge available at the time of the incident under consideration

It is important to remember to judge a person according to knowledge available at the time. To judge somebody with knowledge of hindsight, in other words knowledge only discovered after the accident in question, is unfair. A clinical negligence case that illustrates these concepts is the English decision of *Roe v Ministry of Health and Others; Woolley v Same* [1954] 2 Q.B. 66.

Facts
Roe and Woolley were the two plaintiffs who entered hospital to undergo minor surgery, and after the operation they were both paralysed from the waist down. A spinal anaesthetic, nupercaine, was commonly used at the time. As there was a risk of the needle becoming infected during the loading of the syringe from the ampoule, the ampoules of nupercaine were kept in a disinfectant called phenol. This was a common and established practice at the time. Unbeknown to the hospital, the ampoules of nupercaine developed microscopic cracks through which the phenol seeped, and mixed with the nupercaine. Phenol is a form of carbolic acid, and when the contaminated nupercaine was injected into the spines of the plaintiffs, the acid corroded all the nerve endings in the spine that controlled the lower part of their bodies.

Issue to be decided by the court
Had the hospital failed in its duty of care to the patients?

Decision of the court
The court found that neither the hospital nor the anaesthetist could reasonably have known about the cracks in the ampoules, which were not visible when inspected by the naked eye. The danger or risk was not reasonably foreseeable.

Commentary
After this tragic accident there were publications that were issued, warning about the danger of this practice of keeping ampoules in phenol. In other words, the knowledge of that particular danger was now out in the public domain. After that warning, the danger was now foreseeable by the reasonable medical professional, who needs to keep up to date about developments such as this. However, at the time of the accident, the risk was not foreseeable, as it was not reasonably possible for the defendants to know about the danger.

The wisdom of hindsight is an easy discipline, and not much use to anybody. The courts recognise this, particularly in the area of medicine, where health professionals are taking hard decisions about things that directly affect the quality of a patient's life, and often mean the difference between life and death for that patient.

What this means, however, is that the health professional needs to be aware of current developments in medicine and other healthcare issues. This obviously leads to the question: What is meant by reasonable updating? In other words, while it is accepted that a reasonable health professional is expected to keep up to date with developments in medical science, what does this mean in practice? A very useful case, which dealt squarely with this question, was another English decision, *Crawford v Board of Governors of Charing Cross Hospital,* (*The Times*, 8 December 1953.

Facts
The plaintiff was admitted into the defendant hospital for an operation to remove his bladder. The plaintiff was given a blood transfusion into his left arm, which was extended outward for that purpose. After the operation the plaintiff's left arm was paralysed.

Issue to be decided by the court
Was the paralysis caused by the negligence of the hospital? Evidence was led by the plaintiff that an article had appeared six months previously in *The Lancet* (a leading English medical journal) warning of the dangers of brachial palsy when the arm was kept in such an extended position. The anaesthetist in charge at the operation in question had not read the article. The trial court found for the plaintiff and the defendant hospital appealed that decision.

Decision of the court
The Court of Appeal allowed the hospital's appeal (it reversed the decision of the trial court) and found that the anaesthetist was not negligent. In his judgment, Lord Denning stated the following helpful guideline:

> 'It would, I think, be putting too high a burden on a medical man to say that he has to read every article appearing in the current medical press and it would be quite wrong to suggest that a medical man is negligent because he does not at once put into operation the suggestions which some contributor or other might make in a medical journal. The time may come in a particular case when a new recommendation may be so well proved and so well known, and so well accepted that it should be adopted, but this was not so in this particular case.'

Commentary
The *Crawford* case was decided in 1953 and, although the principles remain the same today, the practice has changed considerably. The health professional now has access to major electronic libraries, to databases and the Internet. There are both public and private organisations that make it their business to disseminate information about new procedures, new technology, new treatments and medicines, and so on.

What this means is that society expects more from the health professional, and the reasonable health professional would not be able to adopt a head-in-the-sand approach to medical technology and innovation. The modern health professional is expected to be aware and 'up-to-speed' on new developments, and to use these new methods and techniques once they are recognised by the health profession as 'well proved, well known, and well accepted'.

Reasonable updating may include keeping abreast in developments occurring in related fields of health care

An interesting case which dealt with the issue of research and reasonable updating was another English decision, *Shakoor (Administratix of the Estate of Shakoor (deceased)) v Situ (t/a Eternal Health Company)* [2000] 4 All E.R. 181.

Facts
Mr Shakoor was troubled by multiple benign lipomata. A lipoma is a collection of fatty tissue lying just below the surface of the skin. A benign lipoma does not constitute any risk to health. In 'conventional' medicine there is no known treatment other than removal by surgery. Mr Shakoor was not keen on the surgery alternative, and decided to pursue the route of 'alternative medicine'. The defendant, a practitioner of Chinese herbal medicine, was not a registered doctor, and did not claim to be. He was qualified in Chinese herbal medicine, and the patient had approached him on that basis.

The defendant prescribed to the patient a course of herbal remedy, which consisted of dried herbs which were boiled and the resulting liquid consumed. The patient consumed this on at least nine occasions. Thereafter the patient grew seriously ill and died. It was accepted that the herbal remedy had caused acute liver failure, the cause of death.

Evidence was led that this reaction to the herbs was rare and 'idiosyncratic' (peculiar to a specific person). Evidence was also led that there were writings in journals of 'conventional' medicine warning about the ingestion of such herbs as being the likely cause of liver failure. The defendant admitted that he did not read journals devoted to conventional medicine, and his own studies and reading had not alerted him to this danger. He had regarded the herbs as being completely safe.

The issue before the court
In deciding on the question of negligence, should the defendant be judged by the standards of the reasonable practitioner of Chinese herbal medicine, or according to the standards applicable to the practitioner of 'orthodox or conventional Western medicine'?

DUTY OF CARE 149

The decision of the court
The court held that the defendant could not be judged against the standards of orthodox health care as he had not claimed to be such and his patient had chosen to reject the orthodox approach. However, the alternative practitioner could not just be judged against his own standards of alternative medicine. It must be recognised that the alternative practitioner is practising alongside the area of orthodox medicine, and the alternative practitioner needed to recognise that fact – he was not practising in a vacuum. If somebody did not respond well to alternative medicine, they might return to orthodox treatment, or they might receive both alternative and orthodox treatment at the same time. What this meant was that the alternative practitioner needed to stay updated about any possible risks that had been identified by conventional medicine in relation to the products offered by the alternative profession.

The defendant was found not negligent in this case on these facts, as his equivalent in the profession of orthodox medicine was the ordinary careful General Practitioner (GP), and a GP would not be found negligent if he had failed to notice the letters and warnings relied upon by the plaintiff. The court held that even if a GP had seen these warnings, the reasonable GP would not necessarily have decided that the herbal remedy was too hazardous to prescribe as the letters were not in agreement and did not paint a consistent picture of serious risk. Evidence was led and accepted by the court that there were many conventional medicines, for example antibiotics, which posed a far greater risk of liver damage than the herbs in question. Accordingly the defendant had acted in accordance with the standard of care appropriate to traditional Chinese herbal medicine and was not in breach of his duty of care to the deceased. The court said the following:

> 'The issues in this case do not raise a question relating to competence in diagnosis and so I do not express a view on that aspect. But where, as here, a practitioner chooses to prescribe a remedy, be it chemical or herbal, for internal consumption it seems to me that a number of implications do follow. First of all, the practitioner has to recognise that he is holding himself out as competent to practise within a system of law and medicine which will review the standard of care he has given to a patient. Secondly, where he prescribes a remedy which is taken by a patient it is not enough to say that the remedy is traditional and believed not to be harmful, he has a duty to ensure that the remedy is not actually or potentially harmful. Thirdly, he must recognise the probability that any person suffering an adverse reaction to such a remedy is quite likely to find his way into an orthodox hospital and the incident

may well be 'written up' in one or other of the orthodox medical journals. An alternative practitioner who prescribes a remedy must take steps to satisfy himself that there has not been any adverse report in such journals on the remedy which ought to affect the use he makes of it. That is not to say that he must take a range of publications himself. It should be enough if he subscribes to an 'association' which arranges to search the relevant literature and promptly report any material publication to him. The relevant literature will be that which would be taken by an orthodox practitioner practising at the level of speciality at which the alternative practitioner holds himself out. If he does not subscribe to such an association the practitioner will not have discharged his duty to inform himself properly and may act at his peril.'

Commentary

Although the defendant was judged according to the standards of a reasonable 'alternative' practitioner (thus bringing some subjectivity into an essentially objective test) the court also used the standard of the reasonable GP (an objective test) to assess the conduct of the defendant, including the fact that even alternative practitioners are duty bound to keep up to date with current writings, including conventional writings where these warn of potential hazards regarding treatment or medicines used in the alternative profession.

While there must be an element of subjectivity in assessing the conduct of a health professional, at the same time it is necessary for the law to impose some minimum level of care that everybody must fulfil.

Duty of Care: Summary

1. Negligence does not mean the same as carelessness.
2. Negligence is a legal concept with a technical meaning.
3. There can only be a finding of negligence if the defendant (the health professional) owes the plaintiff (the patient) a duty of care.
4. A duty of care is created either as a result of a prior relationship involving a duty of care, or by reason of the neighbour principle.
5. The neighbour principle states that if, at the time of doing something wrongful, the defendant could or should reasonably foresee that the wrongful act would cause harm to the plaintiff, the defendant owes the plaintiff a duty of care to take steps to avoid that harm or damage.
6. Although foreseeability is the most important concept in determining whether a duty of care existed and accordingly whether

the defendant was negligent, it is not the only factor that the court will consider.
7. The court, after deciding that the risk of harm or damage was foreseeable, will thereafter consider whether a reasonable person would have taken precautions against that risk after considering the magnitude of the risk and the burden of taking precautions against that risk, against the background of what was regarded as good or common practice at the time, given the state of current knowledge.
8. Useful website:
Unison (http://www.unison.org.uk/acrobat/13038.pdf).

16

THE STANDARD OF CARE

> *Learning Outcomes*
> At the completion of this chapter, the reader should know and understand the following:
>
> ▸ The concept of 'the reasonable person', and its health care equivalents: 'the reasonable professional', 'the reasonable doctor' and 'the reasonable nurse'.
> ▸ How the courts decide what is reasonable in the circumstances.

Important concepts and phrases that are crucial to an understanding of this chapter

Vicarious liability
Where one person is held liable for the actions of another person. For example, an employer might be held liable for the acts of an employee if that employee was acting in the course and scope of his employment.

Introduction

If we recognise that a duty of care is owed by one person to another person, the next question that we need to ask is just how good must that care be? This measure of care is called 'the standard of care'.

The usual standard of care recognised by the law is that of the reasonable person.

In the case of *Kirby v Burke* [1944] I.R. 207, which is the Irish case that accepted the principles of *Donoghue v Stevenson* into Irish law, the test in regard to a reasonable person was stated as follows:

> 'The foundation of liability at common law for tort is blameworthiness as determined by the average standards of the community; a man fails at his peril to conform to these standards. Therefore, while loss from an accident generally lies where it falls, a defendant cannot plead an accident if, treated as a man of ordinary intelligence and foresight, he ought to have foreseen the danger which caused injury to his plaintiff.'

The 'reasonable person' is really a fictitious person who represents a standard of conduct that must be regarded as a goal to be worked toward. It is an objective standard or measurement of conduct, against which the actual conduct of the defendant is compared.

A reasonable person is expected to know the facts of common experience (for example, looking before stepping off the pavement onto the road), and the laws of nature (for example, not going into a field where there is a bull, as bulls don't take kindly to people coming into their field).

A reasonable person is expected to know and appreciate his or her personal limitations and act accordingly (for example, not using a chainsaw, without proper instruction). This would include physical disabilities (for example, a sight-disabled person must not drive a car).

The reasonable person in the healthcare services

It could be argued that things are, however, a little different when deciding on the standard of care expected of the reasonable doctor or nurse. As a professional, he or she should be judged according to the standard of the reasonable health professional. In other words, a reasonable nurse or doctor must practice the degree of skill that a member of the public would expect from a person in his or her position as a skilled nurse or doctor.

O'Donovan v Cork County Council [1967] I.R. 173 is an Irish case, which deals with these issues.

Facts
A county surgeon was employed by the hospital to head the surgery division. He was telephoned for advice by a house surgeon employed by the hospital. The county surgeon authorised the house surgeon to operate on the patient, for the removal of his appendix. The house surgeon performed the operation, and a general anaesthetic was administered by the hospital anaesthetist.

At the end of the operation, as the house surgeon was about to close, he noticed that the wound was seeping and he was unable to stop the bleeding. He again telephoned the county surgeon who immediately drove to the hospital to assist. At the time that the county surgeon arrived, the patient developed ether convulsions, a rare condition.

The county surgeon closed the patient's wound and instructed the anaesthetist to cut the supply of ether and increase the supply of oxygen, in an attempt to stop the convulsions. The anaesthetist did not administer a relaxant drug, an accepted part of treating ether convulsions, because he did not think of doing so. The convulsions continued and the patient died.

A jury found that the county surgeon and the anaesthetist had been negligent, and that the hospital as their employer was vicariously liable. The jury found that the house surgeon had not been negligent. The finding was appealed to the Supreme Court.

The issue before the court
Was the finding of negligence against the county surgeon and the anaesthetist correct and justified in law?

The decision of the court
The Supreme Court found that the county surgeon was not negligent. There was no evidence that the county surgeon had acted negligently in allowing the house surgeon to perform the operation, as he himself was not available to perform the operation. In allowing the house surgeon to perform the operation, he had followed a general and approved practice that was not shown to have been inherently defective.

The court held that the anaesthetist owed a duty to the patient to know how to deal with the condition of ether convulsions if they occurred. Although the condition was rare, it was still a foreseeable risk when ether was used. In the absence of evidence that the procedure adopted by the anaesthetist was a general and accepted procedure, the fact that some expert witnesses were of the opinion that the conduct of the anaesthetist was in conformity with their idea of competence and skill, did not exclude the jury from deciding whether the anaesthetist had been negligent in the circumstances. The court held:

> 'On the evidence, in my view, it could not be held on this aspect of the case that the practice, if common practice it be, to so permit a house surgeon of Dr O'Donnell's qualifications and experience and one who had the full confidence of his senior surgeon, has any inherent defects which ought to be obvious to any person giving the matter due consideration. There was evidence that it is a practice and an accepted practice and in the result there is no evidence to the contrary. Challenge, unsupported by evidence, is not sufficient to put the matter in issue. A medical practitioner cannot be held negligent if he follows general and approved practice in the situation with which he is faced: see *Daniel and Heskin (1)* and the cases cited therein.
>
> That proposition is not, however, without qualification. If there is a common practice which has inherent defects, which ought to be obvious to any person giving the matter due consideration, the fact that it is shown to have been widely and generally adopted over a period of time does not make the practice any the less negligent.

Neglect of duty does not cease by repetition to be neglect of duty. Furthermore, if there be a dispute of fact as to whether or not a particular practice is a general and approved practice, it is a matter for the jury to determine whether or not the impugned treatment is general and approved practice. In such circumstances a jury would be told that if they find that there is such a general and approved practice they must acquit the practitioner where there is not the qualification that I have referred to above.

If some witnesses say that a particular practice is a general and approved one and other medical witnesses deny that, then it is an issue of fact to be determined as any other issue of fact. This particular issue cannot be withdrawn from a jury merely because the practice finds support among some medical witnesses if there be others who deny the fact that it is a general and approved practice.'

Commentary
The approach of the Irish courts at the time was an important departure from the traditional approach to the question of the professional standard of care as held by the English courts. The English approach was to find that a health professional cannot be found negligent for using a particular procedure or following a particular practice if it could be shown that such a practice or procedure is used by a responsible body of health professionals. The fact that there was another body that takes a contrary view, or that the accepted procedure had obvious defects, was not by itself indicative of negligence. As previously mentioned, the English approach effectively leaves the decision in the hands of the medical profession, rather than the courts.

The prime example of the English approach is the case of *Bolam v Frien Barnet Hospital Management Committee* [1957] 1 W.L.R. 582.

Facts
The plaintiff consented to electro-convulsive therapy but was not warned of the risk of fracture involved in the procedure. There was evidence that the risk of fracture was very small, about one-hundredth of one per cent. On the second occasion when the treatment was given to the plaintiff in the defendants' hospital he sustained fractures. No relaxant drugs or manual control (save for support of the lower jaw) were used, but a male nurse stood on each side of the treatment couch throughout the treatment. The use of relaxant drugs would have excluded the risk of fracture. Among those skilled in the profession and experienced in this form of therapy, however, there were two bodies of opinion, one which (since 1953) favoured the use of relaxant drugs or manual control as a general practice, and the other thinking that the use of these drugs was

attended by mortality risks, confined the use of relaxant drugs to cases where there were particular reasons for their use, as opposed to being used as a general prophylactic.

The plaintiff's case was such a case where there were particular reasons for their use. Similarly there were two bodies of professional opinion on the question of whether, if relaxant drugs were not used, manual control should be used. In addition, different views were held among the profession on the question of whether a patient should be expressly warned about risk of fracture before being treated, or should be left to inquire what the risk was; as there was conflicting evidence whether such an explanation would cause the patient to change his or her mind about having the treatment.

The plaintiff sued the defendants for negligence in the administration of the treatment, namely that they did not use relaxant drugs or some form of manual control, and failed to warn him of the risk involved before the treatment was given.

The issue before the court
Were the defendants negligent in failing to take account of an opposite or contrary view to the approach they took?

The decision of the court
In the summing-up, the judge directed the jury that a doctor is not negligent if he is acting in accordance with a practice accepted as proper by a responsible body of medical professionals skilled in that particular art, despite there being a body of such opinion that takes a contrary view.

> 'In an ordinary case it is generally said, that you judge that by the action of the man in the street. He is the ordinary man. In one case it has been said that you judge it by the conduct of the man on the top of a Clapham omnibus. He is the ordinary man. But where you get a situation which involves the use of some special skill or competence, then the test whether there has been negligence or not is not the test of the man on the top of a Clapham omnibus, because he has not got this special skill. The test is the standard of the ordinary skilled man exercising and professing to have that special skill. A man need not possess the highest expert skill at the risk of being found negligent. It is well established law that it is sufficient if he exercises the ordinary skill of an ordinary competent man exercising that particular art. I do not think that I quarrel much with any of the submissions in law which have been put before you by counsel. Counsel for the plaintiff put it in this way, that in the case of a medical man negligence means failure to act in accordance with the standards of reasonably

competent medical men at the time. That is a perfectly accurate statement, as long as it is remembered that there may be one or more perfectly proper standards; and if a medical man conforms with one of those proper standards then he is not negligent.'

The jury found that the defendants were not negligent.

Commentary

This approach has been criticised as it means that medical negligence cases become a battle of the experts, and the court must follow what the experts decide. It is argued that as long as a defendant can show that there is a considerable body of opinion favouring the treatment that he or she chose to use, there can never be a finding of negligence. This would save a medical professional from liability even where the practice was clearly defective or where there was a new and improved treatment, as long as the defendant could show that there was still a following that supported the old inferior treatment. It was this approach that the Irish courts avoided.

This alternative approach was confirmed by the Supreme Court of Ireland in the case of *William Dunne (an infant suing by his mother and next friend Catherine Dunne) v The National Maternity Hospital and Reginald Jackson* [1989] I.R. 91.

Facts

The plaintiff's mother was expecting twins, a fact known to Dr Jackson, her doctor, the second defendant. The mother started to experience labour pains at 9.00 a.m. and entered hospital at 11.15 a.m. Dr Jackson was not at the hospital but was informed of progress by telephone. Dr Jackson was informed when the mother's membranes were punctured, when he was informed that the doctor who had punctured the membranes had discovered a foetal heartbeat, and that the mother had dilated to two centimetres. Dr Jackson knew that the practice at the hospital was to only ascertain one foetal heartbeat but he did not direct that the second heartbeat be ascertained and monitored.

At 2.00 p.m. the Sister had telephoned Dr Jackson and expressed concern at the very slow labour progress, and reported that the mother had dilated to only three centimetres. Dr Jackson directed that the mother be walked up and down the corridor to speed up the labour. This was done from 2.00 until 4.00 p.m. The Sister telephoned to report that there had been no progress despite these measures. Dr Jackson directed that the mother be put on an oxytocin drip and she was examined by the assistant master at 4.20 p.m. The mother was now dilated to five centimetres, but her labour progress was poor and her membranes had resealed. The

Assistant Master again punctured the membranes, discontinued the oxytocin drip, and performed a foetal blood test on the plaintiff, which gave a normal result. The Assistant Master thereafter attached a monitor to the plaintiff. At 5.15 p.m., the plaintiff was born and Dr. Jackson arrived within minutes at the hospital. The plaintiff's twin brother was stillborn at 5.30 p.m.

It was determined that the plaintiff had suffered severe and irreversible brain damage rendering him a spastic quadriplegic with severe mental disability.

At the trial the expert witnesses for the plaintiff testified that if the foetal heart monitor had been applied earlier, it would have become obvious that the plaintiff was in severe distress and he could have been delivered by Caesarean section, which would have avoided the injury. The plaintiff's witnesses further testified that as it was known that there were twins, it was not sufficient to just identify one heartbeat, and monitors should have been attached to both babies. The witnesses for the defendants however contradicted this evidence and testified that the brain damage to the plaintiff was the result of a massive twin-to-twin blood transfusion some twelve to twenty-four hours before the plaintiff's birth and before the commencement of labour.

They further testified that the practice of identifying one foetal heartbeat only was established practice, as attempts to identify and monitor the second foetal heartbeat were notoriously unreliable. After considering the evidence before them, the jury found that the plaintiff's brain injury had occurred during his mother's labour and could have been avoided by an earlier Caesarean delivery. They found both defendants negligent for not monitoring both foetal heartbeats.

This finding of the jury was taken on appeal to the Supreme Court.

Issues the court had to decide
Whether the trial judge was wrong in directing the jury to consider the evidence of all the witnesses in deciding whether as a matter of fact Dr Jackson was negligent and whether the hospital was vicariously liable for the negligence of its employee, or whether the case should have been dismissed simply on the basis that there was a considerable body of opinion favouring the course of treatment conducted by Dr Jackson.

Decision of the court
The Supreme Court held that in considering whether a health professional's diagnosis and treatment were negligent, a finding of negligence would be made only if it was shown that no practitioner of equal status and skill, acting with ordinary care, would have done the same. A deviation from a general and approved practice will not be

negligent unless no doctor of equal status and skill, acting with ordinary care, would have done the same. It is not a defence for a doctor to claim that he followed an established practice of conduct, if the practice has inherent defects that should be obvious to any person who carefully considered the procedure. Where there is an honest difference of opinion between two doctors as to which is the better procedure or treatment to follow, this difference of opinion does not provide any ground for leaving a question to the jury as to whether the defendant who has followed one course rather than the other has been negligent.

It is not for the judge or jury to decide which of the two courses was better, but rather whether the course that was followed complied with the careful conduct of a medical practitioner of like specialisation and skill as that of the defendant. Where there is a dispute of fact as to whether the practice in question is or is not general or approved, that question must be left for the decision of the jury. Finally, that for a practice (be it treatment or diagnosis) to be regarded as 'general and approved' it does not have to be followed by everybody but must be an approved procedure which is followed by a substantial number of reputable practitioners holding the relevant specialist or general qualifications. The court explained these principles as follows:

> 'In order to fully understand these principles and their application to any particular set of facts, it is, I believe, helpful to set out certain broad parameters which would appear to underline their establishment. The development of medical science and the supreme importance of that development to humanity makes it particularly undesirable and inconsistent with the common good that doctors should be obliged to carry out their professional duties under frequent threat of unsustainable legal claims. The complete dependence of patients on the skill and care of their medical attendants and the gravity from their point of view of a failure in such care, makes it undesirable and unjustifiable to accept as a matter of law a lax or permissive standard of care for the purpose of assessing what is and is not medical negligence. In developing the legal principles outlined and in applying them to the facts of each individual case, the courts must constantly seek to give equal regard to both of these considerations.'

Commentary
What the Supreme Court was doing was taking the decision away from the expert witnesses, and back to where that power of decision belongs, with the court itself. At the end of the day a judgment of court is a legal decision, not a medical decision.

The difference in approach between the Irish and English courts was a significant one at the time of this decision. However, it can be said that the English courts have slowly moved to a similar position. It must also be pointed out that the English courts have never said that a practice will be accepted as an approved practice if it is clearly defective or recognised as outmoded – if it was such it would never be accepted by a 'responsible body of men'. Refer to the quote from *Bolam*'s case where the judge says that in his judgment. In any event, it would seem that the English courts are also beginning to move away from the battle of the experts approach. Consider the case of *Bolitho (Administratix of the Estate of Bolitho (Deceased) v City and Hackney Health Authority* [1997] 4 All E.R. 771, a decision by the House of Lords, the highest court in the United Kingdom.

Facts
A two-year-old boy was admitted to hospital suffering from respiratory problems. The boy had been previously treated at the hospital for croup. On the following day he suffered two short episodes at 12.40 p.m. and 2.00 p.m., during which he turned white and clearly had difficulty breathing. A doctor was called who examined the boy after the 12.40 pm episode. That doctor delegated to another doctor the task of returning to check on the boy if further difficulties were experienced. Despite the 2.00 p.m. attack, the boy was not checked on by either doctor. After both attacks the boy returned to a stable state. At 2.30 p.m., the boy suffered total respiratory failure and a cardiac arrest, resulting in severe brain damage. He subsequently died.

The defendant hospital accepted that the first doctor had acted in breach of her duty of care to the boy but argued that the cardiac arrest would not have been avoided if the second doctor or some other suitable deputy had attended earlier than 2.30 p.m. It was accepted by the court that intubation (inserting a breathing tube) so as to provide an airway would have made sure that respiratory failure did not lead to cardiac arrest and that such intubation would have had to have been carried out before the final episode.

The judge found that the views of the expert witnesses for the plaintiff and defendant, though diametrically opposed, both represented a responsible body of professional opinion. He therefore held that the first doctor, if she had attended and not intubated, would have come up to a proper level of skill and competence according to the standard represented by the views of the expert witness and that it had not been proved that the admitted breach of duty by the defendants had caused the injury which occurred to the boy. The plaintiff's case was dismissed. The Court of Appeal also dismissed an appeal by the plaintiff (the dead boy's mother) and she appealed to the House of Lords.

THE STANDARD OF CARE 161

Issue before the court
Was it enough for the first doctor to show that her actions were supported by a number of expert witnesses, despite the fact that her actions were opposed by another body of experts?

Finding of the court
A doctor could be liable for negligence in respect of diagnosis and treatment despite a body of professional opinion justifying his or her conduct where the judge was not satisfied that the view held by the experts was reasonable or responsible. In the vast majority of cases the fact that distinguished experts in the field were of a particular opinion would demonstrate the reasonableness of that opinion. However, in a rare case, if it could be demonstrated that the professional opinion was not capable of withstanding logical analysis, the judge would be entitled to hold that the body of opinion was not reasonable or responsible.

On the evidence before it the House of Lords held that the present case did not fit into such a category. Although the judge had recognised that there was merit in the plaintiff's argument that the boy should have been intubated, he could not find that the opposite evidence of the defendant's witnesses was unreasonable or illogical. Therefore the House of Lords upheld the judgment of the trial court and the plaintiff's appeal was dismissed. The court held:

> 'Mr Brennan ... submitted that the judge had wrongly treated the *Bolam* test as requiring him to accept the views of one truthful body of expert professional advice, even though he was unpersuaded of its logical force. He submitted that the judge was wrong in law in adopting that approach and that ultimately it was for the court, not for medical opinion, to decide what was the standard of care required of a professional in the circumstances of each particular case.

> My Lords, I agree with these submissions to the extent that, in my view, the court is not bound to hold that a defendant doctor escapes liability for negligent treatment or diagnosis just because he leads evidence from a number of medical experts who are genuinely of opinion that the defendant's treatment or diagnosis accorded with sound medical practice. In *Bolam*'s case [1957] 2 All ER 118 at 122,[1957] 1 WLR 583 at 587 McNair J. stated that the defendant had to have acted in accordance with the practice accepted as proper by a "*responsible* body of medical men"(my emphasis). Later he referred to "a standard of practice recognised as proper by a competent *reasonable* body of opinion"(see [1957] 2 All ER 118 at

122,[1957] 1 WLR 583 at 588; my emphasis). Again, in the passage, which I have cited from *Maynard*'s case, Lord Scarman refers to a "respectable" body of professional opinion. The use of these adjectives—responsible, reasonable and respectable—all show that the court has to be satisfied that the exponents of the body of opinion relied on can demonstrate that such opinion has a logical basis. In particular, in cases involving, as they so often do, the weighing of risks against benefits, the judge before accepting a body of opinion as being responsible, reasonable or respectable, will need to be satisfied that, in forming their views, the experts have directed their minds to the question of comparative risks and benefits and have reached a defensible conclusion on the matter.

...

These decisions demonstrate that in cases of diagnosis and treatment there are cases where, despite a body of professional opinion sanctioning the defendant's conduct, the defendant can properly be held liable for negligence.'

Commentary

Although on the facts the dead boy's mother lost her case, and it was found that the defendant hospital was not negligent, the principle emerging from the case is very important. It says quite clearly that the courts will not necessarily accept that a medical professional has not been negligent because there is a body of opinion that says as much. The court will critically analyse this body of opinion before accepting it as a valid defence. This is what the Irish Supreme Court seems to be saying in that much earlier decision of *O'Donovan* and then later in the *Dunne* decision.

This is accepted practice in other areas of law, where it is recognised that an expert witness is giving an opinion, as opposed to factual evidence, and therefore this opinion can be rejected by the judge if considered illogical or fanciful. It would seem that the medical profession is finally being treated like other professions with regard to expert witnesses.

There is another consequence of this approach. If the conduct of the defendant must be shown to be logical and reasonable, it does not follow that simply to fail to follow the accepted practice is in itself evidence of negligence, since there might be very strong reasons for the defendant not to follow standard procedure in that case. Where a decision has been made carefully and with great consideration, seems reasonable and logical and is supported by substantial professional opinion, even if not everyone would have followed the same practice, it is doubtful that the court would find negligence. There must be room for difference in opinion, as long as that opinion was reasonable in the circumstances.

What the House of Lords, and by implication the Supreme Court of Ireland, is saying, is that they will only be guided by professional opinion, where that opinion is shown to be reasonable and logical in the circumstances. Similarly, where a health professional makes a decision and is able to show that the decision made, given the factual background to the decision, was reasonable and logical, it is doubtful that the court will make a finding of negligence, even where the decision made flew in the face of established opinion. This is how a science develops and progresses, by testing the 'tried and trusted'.

For example, there is growing controversy about the effect of the three-in-one mumps/rubella/measles vaccination on young children, with a portion of the medical community arguing that there are strong indications that this vaccination might lead to serious immuno-deficient diseases, including autism. It can be said that the majority of the health profession rejects this view, but this alternative view does have a lot of support in the community.

If a medical practitioner, or health authority, refused to vaccinate any more children as a result of these concerns, and some of those children subsequently died from one of those diseases, the health authority or medical practitioner might argue, and would need to show, that there was some logical and reasonable basis for their belief in the danger of such vaccinations, and that this danger outweighed the danger of contracting the disease with the resulting consequences.

So, too, will the 'established practice' defence fail if a reasonable person should have spotted an inherent defect in that established practice, if he or she had bothered to properly examine that practice. A good example of this approach being adopted by the Irish courts is the case of *Collins v Mid-Western Health Board* [2000] 2 I.R. 154.

Facts
On 20 February 1991 the deceased complained of a headache and visited Dr C at his surgery, which was close to the deceased's home. He was diagnosed as having a head cold and sore throat ('upper respiratory tract infection') and told to go home and sleep. His condition worsened, but Dr C maintained his original diagnosis and said that the 'flu' had to take its course.

On 25 February, the deceased was no better and his wife telephoned Dr C, who came around to the house and examined the deceased. His diagnosis was that the headaches were caused by sinus congestion, and he suggested that the deceased have a blood test as there were signs of increased cholesterol. On 28 February the deceased gave blood at Dr C's surgery and on 5 March was informed that the test was normal. The deceased did not improve and on 17 March the deceased's wife (the plaintiff) telephoned the clinic, but Dr C was not present.

A locum, Dr B was present, and he examined the deceased the following day and suggested a CT scan. On 20 March the deceased was brought to the outpatient's department of the hospital where he was examined by Dr N, who decided that the deceased needed further tests and should see a specialist. The deceased was sent home. The deceased's wife contacted Dr B, who telephoned Dr N to seek his assurance that the deceased would be admitted to the hospital. He could not get this assurance. As this haggling was going on, events took over as the deceased suffered an attack on 22 March and he was admitted as an emergency patient as his condition was serious. A lumbar puncture and a CT scan revealed that the deceased had suffered a subarachnoid haemorrhage. The deceased was transferred to Cork Hospital under the care of Mr. M, a consultant neurosurgeon. A further CT scan was done which confirmed the results of the first scan. At this stage the deceased was unconscious with no hope of recovery, and he died on 27 March.

Issues before the court
Was Dr C negligent at the consultation on 20 February and in his subsequent failure to refer the deceased to a specialist? Did the hospital breach its duty of care in not admitting the deceased? Was the hospital negligent in its treatment of the deceased after he was admitted on 22 March?

Decision of the court
What Dr C did not determine was that the patient had suffered a sudden and extremely severe headache while at work. The patient had not volunteered this information as it was some time later that he had come to the surgery. With regard to the first question, the court asked whether a reasonable GP would have limited his questions to confirming what the patient had already told him, or whether the reasonable GP would have been put on guard by the circumstances of the visit, namely that it was after hours, that the deceased's wife had telephoned prior to the deceased arriving and described him as 'bad' and remarked that he did not usually go to doctors.

Should Dr C have relied on the history that the patient supplied or should Dr C have made sure that he took down a full and proper history of the patient? The court found that in the circumstances a reasonable doctor would have been put on his guard, particularly by the telephone call and the information that the patient did not usually go to doctors, and he should have been looking for more than a mild infection, and the failure to ask the necessary questions about the onset of the patient's headache was negligent.

For the same reasons, Dr C was negligent in not referring the patient to a specialist after his second consultation. Again he failed to ask the proper questions, particularly as on this occasion the deceased complained of a headache, and no 'flu symptoms were present. Again, the deceased's wife had telephoned and described the patient as 'bad', and this should have put him on his guard. With regard to the third question, the court found the hospital negligent on the basis of the system that they used, namely giving a junior doctor the absolute authority to refuse admission. He should have been compelled to seek the advice of a medical team before taking such a momentous decision, but the hospital system did not require him to do so, indeed encouraged him not to do so.

The court held:

'It seems to me that any system which gives absolute authority to a junior doctor is inadvisable. By its very nature the position of a senior house officer is one where the holder is learning his profession. He must meet from time to time cases with which he is not familiar and in which he would welcome the opinion of a senior. If he is given absolute authority there is a danger that he may miss things which his seniors would not. I do not seek to impose greater liability on hospitals than is necessary. House officers should not be required to look over their shoulders on every occasion that a patient is brought to casualty. An absolute authority is inadvisable. It is a matter for the hospital authorities themselves to indicate a scheme to provide under what circumstances a house officer would be required to seek the advice of somebody more senior. In the present case, a member of the medical team might well have taken a different view.

It seems to me that the problem really arose from the system which gave Dr. Nur such an absolute authority to refuse admission. All the indications were that he ought to have referred the deceased to the medical team having regard in particular to the letter from Dr. O'Brien. In my view he was wrong not to do so. He was, in effect, ignoring Dr. O'Brien's concerns and treating the case as calling solely for his own diagnosis.

Perhaps he felt himself bound by the system in which case it is the authors of the system who must take the blame. In either case, there was breach of the duty of care for which the first-named defendant is liable.'

Commentary
What was defective was the system preceding admission, and the hospital (and the defendant health authority) should have recognised these defects

and remedied them. The fact that such an admission procedure was common practice was not a sufficient defence, as it was clear to the reasonable person that the admission procedure was defective.

Summary of the principles as laid down by the Irish courts

In applying these principles, it can be said that in most circumstances the medical practitioner will be expected to follow the standards laid down by the profession or the local policy of his or her employer, but there may be exceptional circumstances where it is justifiable not to follow the accepted practice. If that practitioner takes reasonable care having due regard to the then professional opinion on the matter, there cannot be a finding of negligence.

In summary then:
- There is no breach of the standard of care if the practitioner has acted in accordance with the practice accepted as proper by a responsible body of professional skill in that particular practice, and this practice was appropriate (in other words, reasonable and logical) in the circumstances of the case.
- There is no breach of the standard of care if there is no acceptable body of opinion covering the situation at hand, but what the practitioner did was considered reasonable and logical in all the circumstances.
- There is no breach of the standard of care if the practitioner did not follow the accepted practice, but his or her actions were reasonable and logical in all the circumstances and would be supported by competent professional opinion.
- On the question of foreseeability, the law recognises that precautions can only be taken against reasonably known risks. If a risk is not known at the time, precautions cannot be taken against an unforeseeable possibility. However, once that risk is known, the standard of care increases, as now the defendant is expected to know of the risk.
- Both doctors and nurses must ensure that they are always aware of standing instructions and accepted Codes of Practice, as these often contain the latest information on accepted procedure. A failure to follow a standing instruction or Code of Practice, without some exceptional justification, would usually mean negligence.

Are nurses 'professionals' in assessing the reasonable standard of care?

There is one other point to clear up with regard to the standard of care, specifically with regard to nurses. When speaking about the standard of care expected of health professionals, we are clearly referring to the profession of medicine, and the standard of care expected of a professional in that field. In this work, the term 'health professional' has been used to include both doctors and nurses, and indeed could be used to include dentists and psychiatrists.

Profession is defined by the Oxford Dictionary as 'vocation, calling, especially one that involves some branch of learning or science' (*The Concise Oxford Dictionary of Current English*, 5th edition, Oxford University Press, 1964).

Nursing is clearly a vocation, and one is only recognised as a qualified and registered nurse when one has completed an arduous course of theoretical learning and practical training.

However, an Irish decision is often used as authority for the proposition that nursing is not to be regarded as a profession for the purposes of establishing professional negligence. This decision is *Kelly v St. Laurence's Hospital* [1989] I.L.R.M. 437.

Facts
Kelly was admitted to the defendant hospital diagnosed with epilepsy. He had been acting rather strangely and the reason for his admission to the hospital was to determine whether this behaviour was as a result of epilepsy or as a result of schizophrenia. Kelly was taken off all medication as a necessary prerequisite to his diagnosis. Some nights after his admission, Kelly left the ward, climbed onto a windowsill in a nearby toilet, and fell some twenty feet into a yard below, severely injuring himself. The jury found that the hospital was negligent in allowing the patient to go to the toilet unaccompanied, given his history. The hospital appealed this decision, saying that there was no evidence of negligence.

Issue before the court
Was the accident reasonably foreseeable?

Decision of the court
The court dismissed the appeal (it found against the hospital) and held that the duty of care owed to the patient was for the hospital to take reasonable care to avoid permitting him to be exposed to injury that a reasonable person ought to foresee.

The parts of the reported judgement which form the basis of the proposition that nurses are not to be regarded as professionals for the purpose of establishing clinical negligence, are the following:

Finlay C.J. said:

'I am satisfied, however, that as appears from the form of the question left to the jury, the propriety of which is not challenged, that this is more precisely a case where the issue is one of nursing care and attention than it is of one where the allegation of negligence is to be categorised as negligence in medical treatment. Undoubtedly, the extent and nature of the care and attention which a reasonably careful hospital would have afforded to the plaintiff whilst he was an in-patient there on 15 July 1981 and in particular, of course, the question as to whether a reasonably careful hospital staff would have arranged for a person to attend him when he left the ward in the middle of the night to go to the toilet, depends to a very large extent on the foreseeability from a medical point of view of the risk that the plaintiff would, if allowed to go unattended to the toilet in the middle of the night, injure himself in some way.

That does not, however, seem to me to make this a case solely to be tested by the standards which have been accepted by the courts with regard to allegations of negligence in treatment afforded to their patients by professional medical people.'

And Walsh J. added to that:

'What was in issue in this case was not a question of medical negligence in the strict sense as arose in the case of *O'Donovan v Cork County Council*. What was in issue was the adequacy of the system and of care for the plaintiff by the hospital authorities while he was in their hospital. There is no question of any allegation of negligence against the consultant who treated the plaintiff while he was in hospital. It is also clear from the evidence given by the consultant that he, in effect, was distancing himself from any responsibility for the way the nurses in question and the rest of the nursing staff carried out their duties, and, as he pointed out in his evidence, in effect, that it was up to them to know their patient and to give him the care appropriate to his condition and his case history and, above all, appropriate to the reason why he was in the ward in question.'

Commentary

It is doubtful whether these portions of the judgement can be used as authority for the proposition that nurses are not to be regarded as 'professionals' for the purpose of assessing whether there has been professional negligence. What the judges are saying is that doctors and nurses, whilst both health professionals, have different qualifications and different duties, and hence the duty of care is different.

In effect this is the subjective element that is used in an otherwise objective test, for example in the *Shakoor* case, where the defendant was assessed as a reasonable alternative practitioner, rather than as a conventional practitioner. So too, a nurse will be assessed against the standard of a reasonable skilled nurse, and a doctor against the standard of a reasonable skilled doctor. This is hardly a ground for saying that a nurse is not a professional whilst a doctor is. It is rather saying that their professions are different and therefore their duties of care are different.

What the law says is that if a person claims to have a particular skill or qualification, they will be assessed against the standard of a reasonable person possessing such a skill or qualification. Whether they are part of a profession or not is really neither here nor there.

This is not a new concept. Even within the ranks of doctors the courts have assessed the duty of care in relation to the post held by the specific doctor under consideration. Consider the English decision of *Wilsher v Essex Area Health Authority* [1987] Q.B. 730.

Facts
A premature baby was admitted to a specialist neo-natal unit. The medical staff failed to notice that the baby was receiving too much oxygen. The medical staff in question consisted of a junior doctor, who made the mistake of inserting the catheter into the baby's vein instead of its artery. Thereafter the Senior Registrar (who was in effective supervision of the junior doctor) made the same error. As a result the baby was given excessive oxygen and went blind. The doctors were held to be negligent. The defendants appealed on the basis that they had exercised a duty of care to be expected of a junior doctor in the circumstances.

Issue before the court
What standard of care had to be used in assessing the conduct of the defendants, given that they differed in experience and qualification?

Decision of the court
The Court of Appeal held that they had to be judged according to their posts in the unit. In determining the standard required in a particular post, expert evidence of the proper practice in that post had to be led. There was no reason why, in certain circumstances, a health authority could not be directly liable to a plaintiff if it failed to provide sufficient or properly qualified and competent medical staff for the unit. There was no concept of 'team negligence', in the sense that each individual member of the team was required to observe the standards demanded of the unit as a whole, because it could not be right, for example, to expose a student nurse to an action for negligence for her failure to possess the experience

of a consultant. The court held:

> 'I ...recognise that a young hospital doctor who must get onto the wards in order to qualify without necessarily being able to decide what kind of patient he is going to meet is not in the same position as another professional man who has a real choice whether or not to practice in a particular field. Nevertheless, I cannot accept that there should be a special rule for doctors in public hospitals; I emphasise *public*, since presumably those employed in private hospitals would be in a different category. Doctors are not the only people who gain their experience, not only from lectures or from watching others perform, but from tackling live clients or customers, and no case was cited to us which suggested that any such variable duty of care was imposed on others in a similar position. To my mind, it would be a false step to subordinate the legitimate expectation of the patient that he will receive from each person concerned with his care a degree of skill appropriate to the task which he undertakes to an understandable wish to minimise the psychological and financial pressures on hard-pressed young doctors.
>
> For my part, I prefer the third of the propositions which have been canvassed. This relates the duty of care, not to the individual, but to the post which he occupies. I would differentiate 'post' from 'rank' or 'status'. In a case such as the present, the standard is not just that of the averagely competent and well-informed junior houseman (or whatever the position of the doctor) but of such a person who fills a post in a unit offering a highly specialised service. But, even so, it must be recognised that different posts make different demands. If it is borne in mind that the structure of hospital medicine envisages that the lower ranks will be occupied by those of whom it would be wrong to expect too much, the risk of abuse by litigious patients can be mitigated, if not entirely eliminated.'

Commentary

If a person fills a post in a hospital then that person will be judged according to the skills that are expected of a person holding that post. The same is true of nurses – they will be judged according to the level of skill expected of a reasonable nurse in that particular position, be that a junior nurse or theatre sister.

Care must be taken in assessing the standard expected of a professional and must take into account the skills he or she claims to hold and not demand unrealistic standards of skill and knowledge. A general practitioner consulted by a patient complaining of stomach ache is not expected to have the same level of knowledge and expertise as a consultant gastro-enterologist, but as a reasonable general practitioner he or she should know when it is time to refer the patient to the specialist consultant. Similarly, a nurse who is a specialist theatre sister will be assessed against that standard, as will a nurse who is a specialist Accident and Emergency nurse. They are all professionals; they just have different qualifications and responsibilities.

To argue that nurses are not professionals and therefore cannot be tested in terms of 'professional negligence standards' misses the point. A nurse is a person who claims to have special qualifications and skills not possessed by an ordinary person. As such, the nurse's performance will be judged. Labels will not change that fact.

Standard of Care : Summary

1. The common law general standard of care is described as the standard of care expected of the 'ordinary reasonable person'.
2. This is an objective test and represents a goal to be worked toward.
3. A person holding themselves out to the public as having specific skills or qualities, or belonging to a particular profession, must exercise the standard of care that a reasonable member of the public is entitled to expect from somebody with those qualifications or belonging to that profession.
4. A nurse is expected to exercise the skills of a reasonable qualified nurse, a General Practitioner is expected to exercise the skills of a reasonable qualified GP, and a specialist practitioner is expected to exercise the skills of a reasonable specialist in his or her field.
5. The actions of a health professional will be judged according to the standards accepted at the time of the conduct leading to the action. The court will not practice wisdom in hindsight.
6. In Ireland, a doctor or nurse will be negligent if no health professional of equal status and skill, acting with ordinary care, would have done the same.
7. It is not a defence for a doctor or nurse to argue that he or she followed an established practice, if the practice has inherent defects that should be obvious to any person giving due and proper consideration to the matter.
8. Useful websites:
a. *Irish Nurses Organisation* (http://www.ino.ie/).
b. *Nurses Info.* (http://www.nurses.info/).
c. *Nursing Standard* (http://www.nursing-standard.co.uk).

17

DAMAGES

> **Learning Outcomes**
> **At the completion of this chapter, the reader should know and understand the following:**
> - The reasoning behind the award of damages.
> - The difference between liquidated and unliquidated damages.
> - How the courts decide what damages to award.

Important concepts and phrases that are crucial to an understanding of this chapter

Actuary
A person who is an expert in the theory and practice of statistics, particularly those statistics relating to mortality (the length of your lifetime), sickness, retirement and unemployment. An actuary can calculate the amount of money you will need to continue your lifestyle as it is at the moment, and this will allow you to make financial plans for the future.

Adversarial
The Irish legal system is essentially adversarial, which means it is characterised by its confrontational nature, where parties directly oppose each other, and there is a 'winner' and a 'loser', with the judge acting as a referee rather than as a facilitator. An alternative to the adversarial system is what is known as the inquisitorial system, where the proceedings are conducted by the judge in the form of an investigation, rather than a direct contest. France is a good example of a country that practices an inquisitorial system in many of its courts.

Introduction

In essence, when one speaks about damages in medical law, and in the law of tort in general, one is talking about compensation, which in turn means money.

The question of damages is a controversial one. Many would argue that money can never undo the wrong suffered by a patient at the hands of a health care professional. Others argue that the lure of money often causes patients to sue health care professionals for the wrong reasons.

Neither of these arguments is totally right or totally wrong. For both parties litigation is a highly stressful business. It is very difficult for a court to deal with the hurt and anger felt by wronged patients in any other way but to compensate them. By their very nature and function courts are not equipped to offer solace or holistic healing, and they do not pretend to do so.

At the same time, it must be recognised that money awards can lead to greed and less than honourable behaviour on the part of some patients, who can pressurise a health professional merely by threatening to sue, or 'go public'. This is turn causes the health professional to practice safe or defensive medicine, and to take out very expensive insurance policies, with these expenses being passed on to the patient in the form of high fees.

No-fault compensation

A possible solution to the problems associated with fault liability and medical malpractice litigation is the concept of no-fault compensation where the patient does not need to show that a health professional or hospital is at fault. What the plaintiff needs to show is that he or she suffered damages as a result of medical treatment. In other words, causation must be established but not fault.

Two countries that have introduced no-fault compensations systems are New Zealand and Sweden.

In New Zealand, the Accident Compensation Act 1972 abolished claims for damages based on tort and replaced them with a scheme providing benefits for accident victims without the need to prove fault. The scheme is financed by the public through three funds:
- The Earners' Fund that provides compensation for work related injuries. This Fund is financed by a levy imposed on employers and the self-employed.
- The Motor Vehicle Fund, which provides compensation for injuries arising from motor vehicle accidents, and is financed by a levy imposed on motor vehicle owners.
- The Supplementary Fund provides compensation for all other victims suffering personal injury, and this would include medical accident victims. It is financed by the State through taxes.

Although causation must still be proven there is a lot more flexibility compared to claims based on tort. There is nobody at fault, and therefore no need to consider the rights of the tortfeasor when deciding on liability. Decisions are based more on equity than on strict principle or precedent.

Sweden has the Patient Insurance Scheme (PIS), which provides no fault compensation for victims of medical accidents. The Scheme is not statute based but is essentially a product of free enterprise, with cover being provided by a consortium of private insurers on payment of a very cheap annual premium.

The PIS covers five types of injuries under the heading of medical accident, and these are treatment injuries, diagnostic injuries, accidental injuries, infection injuries (where the infection occurred whilst receiving medical treatment or care) and injuries arising from a faulty diagnosis. It does not cover minor injuries, which are defined as injuries which need less than thirty days sick leave or ten or less days in hospital. Similarly, the PIS does not cover unavoidable complications, injuries involving life-sustaining or emergency treatment, psychological injuries, and drug injuries (which are covered by a separate scheme funded by drug manufacturers).

Again, the patient would need to prove causation and that their injuries fell within one of the recognised categories as described above. It is not necessary to prove fault or to prove that any particular party was at fault.

These systems have been criticised, as they can be very lengthy procedures with the delays adding to the stress felt by the patient. In addition, the specified categories of injuries can be restrictive. There are also other alternatives available, for example arbitration.

Ireland does have what is known as the Personal Injuries Assessment Board (PIAB). This Board deals with employment liability, road traffic, public liability and civil personal injury actions. However, medical negligence claims have been expressly excluded from its jurisdiction.

A new Civil Liability and Courts Bill 2004 attempts to keep a record and cross-reference personal injury claims, in an attempt to prevent abuse by 'career claimants'. The Bill also seeks to limit the time period in which a patient must lodge a claim, with the probable time period being set at two years.

The fact of the matter is that Ireland has a very successful no-fault scheme on its doorstep in an EU country, and pressure needs to be brought on the government by the health services and professions to take a closer look at setting up a similar system in Ireland, or perhaps a scheme could be created in the EU as a whole, as clearly the present adversarial court system does not serve the interests of either the patient or the health professional.

In the section on employment law, some consideration will be given to the scheme known as the Clinical Indemnity Scheme, which is based on a health agency admitting vicarious liability for its employees for damages arising during 'professional medical services'. This is not a 'no-fault' scheme, but rather seeks to minimise the parties involved in litigation by reducing the defendant to one, namely the health agency.

The calculation or computation of damages

The plaintiff's claim for damages is assessed under the following headings:

Medical expenses
These include the cost of the hospital bills, doctor's fees, medications, the cost of rehabilitation training and any miscellaneous medical costs. They are known as special damages and can be calculated in exact amounts.

Loss of wages
This type of damages would include loss of wages both in the past and in the future, if the plaintiff is unable to go back to work, either in his or her previous job or at all. These damages are often assessed or computed by an actuary, who is called as an expert witness.

In practice, these figures are often agreed beforehand and are not challenged in court. This is as a result of the difference between liquidated damages and unliquidated damages. Liquidated damages are damages that can be calculated exactly, and therefore can be agreed between the parties to a dispute. If they do come to an agreement on a specific figure, then all that needs to be done is for the parties to inform the court what that agreed figure is. Unliquidated damages are not capable of exact calculation (and are sometimes referred to as 'thumb-suck damages' for obvious reasons). Where the parties cannot agree on a sum, or where it is not possible to calculate an exact sum, it is the task of the court to decide on a figure.

As a general rule special damages (for example, medical expenses, loss of wages) are liquidated damages, and general damages (for example, pain and suffering) are unliquidated damages.

Pain and suffering
The plaintiff is paid general damages for pain and suffering to the date of his or her court hearing and for any future pain and suffering or for any loss of amenity, which he or she suffers. These are called general damages as it is impossible to calculate an exact figure, and the court decides this amount.

Put simply, special damages are where the amount of money is capable of being accurately calculated, whereas general damages are a discretionary amount to be decided by the court.

An illustrative case heard by the High Court of Ireland is *Cody v Hurley*, (unreported, High Court, 20 January 1999).

176 NURSING LAW FOR IRISH STUDENTS

Facts
In this case, the plaintiff had suffered pain in her knee as an eleven-year-old. She sought treatment for the pain and subsequently had to undergo five years of hospitalisation, operations and pain because of a misdiagnosis. At the time of the court case she walked with a gross limp and suffered more or less continuous back pain.

The court said the plaintiff's condition could probably have been corrected within a short time if it had been correctly diagnosed in the first place, thus avoiding lengthy and unpleasant treatment and preventing the type of disability from which she now suffered.

She had endured appalling pain, suffering and loss during a very important part of her life, and her disabilities and hospitalisation had had a devastating effect on her.

The issue before the court
What type of damages should be awarded to the plaintiff, and how much in monetary terms?

The decision of the court
The plaintiff was awarded £190,000 general damages and £391,000 special damages. The headings under which the court awarded damages were as follows:

'DAMAGES
Damages have been claimed under a number of headings, many of which are in fact agreed. I propose to list all the damages which I am awarding, but I think it is only necessary to comment where there has been some measure of disagreement. The items of damage are as follows:-
   1. Medical expenses to date including accommodation for the Plaintiffs mother at Crumlin Hospital. This has been agreed at £18,648.00.
   2. The net cost of an extension built on to the Plaintiffs parents' house this is also agreed at £2.500.00
   3. Compensation for the Plaintiffs parents for caring for her to date (£61,898.00).
   4. The Plaintiffs parents' transport costs (£7,500.00).
   5. Future care (£16,200).
   6. Post operative care (£5,718).
   7. Future care for the remainder of her life.
      As I have said I do not accept that the Plaintiff will require to be cared for in this sense as I believe she will be quite independent. This is particularly so as I am awarding her

damages which allow for some home help and for child minding, and I think this should be sufficient to cover her needs.
8. Child minders (£44,800).
9. Motor car (£15,500).
10. Computer (£1,500).
11. Heating (£2,400).
12. Television and video (£994).
13. Cost of activities of daily living (£47,809).
14. Other expenses as set out in Ms. Barnes report – I accept the figure of £22,095.
15. Transport (£27,933).
16. Support services – I accept the figure of £489.
17. Cost of future arthrodesis – I will award her £17,136 as calculated by Mr. Delaney.
18. Future loss of earnings (£390,975).

GENERAL DAMAGES
I fully accept that there must be a limit to the amount of general damages which can be awarded. However, in assessing such damages the Court has to take into account the particular circumstances of each case, and while the Plaintiff in the present case will be able to lead an independent life, although a limited one, she has had to endure appalling pain and suffering and loss during a very important part of her life. While I think that she will probably adapt better to her situation in the future, particularly if there is some improvement in her condition, she can never relive her childhood and teenage years. I would propose to assess damages on the basis that the maximum figure referred to by the Supreme Court should now be in the region of £250,000 and I would award the Plaintiff £120,000 for pain and suffering to date and £70,000 for pain and suffering in the future making in all £190,000 general damages.'

Commentary
As can be seen, the court must attempt to predict the future and make provision for what the plaintiff will need for the rest of his or her life. This is an extremely complex task and the court is guided by experts like actuaries who are qualified to make these calculations. When it comes to general damages, however, which cannot be calculated, the court will look at previous decisions, taking into account factors like inflation and the increased cost of living.

Damages awarded in tort are often referred to as 'negative *interesse*' damages, as they seek to place the patient in the position he or she was before the tort occurred, in other words the damages attempt to turn back the time, hence the 'negative' label. These are contrasted with contractual damages which are a form of 'positive *interesse*' damages which seek to place the plaintiff in the position he or she would have been had the contract been properly performed, in other words forward in time.

Damages: Summary

1. Damages are a financial award made by a court to one of the parties to an action as part of the judgment of that court.
2. Damages in tort are seen as compensation for the harm or damages suffered by that party, and are paid to the injured party by the wrongdoer party (sometimes called the 'tortfeasor').
3. Damages either attempt to reverse the damage done by attempting to place the injured person in the position they were before the harm occurred to them, or alternatively they attempt to place the injured party in the position they would have been if the legal duty that was owed to them had in fact been performed.
4. There are essentially three types of damages, namely financial damages ('out of pocket loss'), physical damages and emotional or psychological damages.
5. Damages are also divided into special damages, which are damages capable of precise calculation, and general damages, which amount is decided at the discretion of the court.
6. In medical negligence cases, the most common damages are medical expenses and loss of wages, which are special damages, and pain and suffering, which is a general damage.
7. Useful websites:
    a. *RTE Health* (http://www.rte.ie/health).
    b. *McCann FitzGerald* (http://www.mccannfitzgerald.ie).
    c. *Irish Medical News* (http://www.irishmedicalnews.ie).

18

CAUSATION

> **Learning Outcomes**
> At the completion of this chapter, the reader should know and understand the following:
> ▸ The importance of the link between the action of the defendant and the damage caused to the plaintiff.
> ▸ The difference between factual causation and legal causation.
> ▸ The policy factors that are taken into account by the courts when deciding questions of causation.
> ▸ The importance of the concept of foreseeability when deciding on questions of causation.

Introduction

Unlike battery, negligence is not actionable *per se*, which means that the plaintiff must suffer injury or damage as a matter of fact. In other words, the plaintiff needs to prove that he or she has suffered actual injury or damage.

The plaintiff (the patient) needs to show that there is a causal link between the harm suffered by the patient and the failure of the defendant (the health service provider) to follow the approved practice or procedure.

Picture in your mind a chain connecting the act or omission of the defendant to the harm or injury caused to the plaintiff. If that chain is unbroken, causation is established.

Actual causation and legal causation

There are essentially two tests for causation: the actual causation test (often called factual causation or cause in fact) and the legal causation test (often called proximate cause). One must not read this to mean that the actual causation test does not involve questions of law. This would not be an accurate description of the actual causation test, which is a question of both law and fact, as is the legal causation test. These two tests are not mutually exclusive of each other, but should rather be seen as complementing each other.

The actual cause or factual test is the easier of the two to understand and apply. It relies on evidence of fact, and essentially it asks one question: was the defendant's negligent act the factual cause of the plaintiff's harm?

The cause of the damage must be relevant to the enquiry. The lawyer must consider only those causes to which legal responsibility may be attached. For example, if a football coach pushes his players too hard so that one of them suffers from exhaustion which causes him to go home early in the rush hour traffic. In that traffic he has an accident, as a result of his own negligence, which renders him unconscious. Whilst being carried to the ambulance a saline drip is inserted into his artery rather than his vein, the lawyer will need to sort the relevant from the irrelevant, or remote, the lawyer must not only decide whether those causes are legally relevant, but also needs to decide whether the authors of those causes can be held legally responsible or liable.

The 'but for' test in factual causation

The traditional approach to the factual causation test is to use the 'but for' test. But for the defendant doing what he or she did, would the harm have occurred?

An English decision which clearly illustrates this approach in the clinical field is *Barnett v Chelsea Kensington Management Committee* [1968] 1 All E.R. 1068.

Facts
The deceased drank a cup of tea and felt ill. He went to hospital where he was treated by a nurse who consulted with a doctor over the telephone. After being treated, the deceased left the hospital. He died soon thereafter. It was discovered that the cup of tea had contained arsenic and the deceased had died of arsenic poisoning. Evidence was given and accepted by the Court that cases of arsenic poisoning were rare, and even if the deceased had been admitted to the hospital and treated, there was little or no chance that an effective antidote would have been administered to him in time to save his life.

Issue before the court
Was the doctor negligent in not physically examining the patient instead of consulting over the telephone, and if so, was the hospital liable for the harm suffered by the plaintiff, the deceased's widow, arising from his death?

Decision of the court
The court found that the doctor had indeed been negligent in not seeing the deceased patient personally. However, the court went on to find that

the deceased was in any event doomed to die, and the fact that the doctor did not see him personally did not cause his death, and therefore the harm was not but for the doctor's negligence – there was no causal link.

The Irish case that adopted the reasoning of the *Barnett* decision was *Kenny v O'Rourke* [1972] I.R. 339.

Facts
The plaintiff fell off a ladder and was seriously injured. Evidence was led that the ladder was defective. This evidence was countered by evidence for the defendant that the plaintiff was leaning too far out on the ladder and this caused the ladder to topple.

Issue before the court
Should the defendant be held liable for supplying a defective ladder, where it would seem that the conduct of the plaintiff, rather than the defective ladder, was the ultimate cause of the injury?

Decision of the court
On the evidence the injury was due to the plaintiff's leaning too far over rather than the defective ladder. By using the 'but for' test it could not be said that but for the defect in the ladder the plaintiff would not have been injured.

Commentary
Although the 'but for' test is appealing in its logic and simplicity, the mechanical and unfeeling nature of the test can lead to difficulties. Decisions by the court based on this test might be regarded as unfair by the ordinary person, particularly in circumstances where that ordinary person thinks that the health professional should be held liable. For example, if the average person was asked about the arsenic tea case, his or her response would be along the lines that the doctor did not do his job properly and should be punished. Similarly, a fair-minded person would not support the idea that somebody should be allowed to get away with supplying defective ladders.

That, however, is not the law of tort. In a case like *Barnett*'s case the doctor is not liable in tort for the patient's death. He might get his come-uppance in a disciplinary hearing for letting down the values of his profession, but he is not legally liable for the death of the patient – it was the arsenic that killed him. In other words, the relevant cause of the harm was the drinking of the arsenic in the tea, and the doctor's negligence is regarded as remote – it is simply too far removed from the damage.

The 'but for' test is open to further criticism as it struggles to determine causation where there are successive (one after another), simultaneous (at the same time) or uncertain causes of harm. Its real value lies in situations where the cause of the loss or damage is easily identifiable. However, problems are caused where the facts before the court are not clear enough to show a connection between the damage caused and the conduct of the defendant.

The Civil Liability Act 1961

The Civil Liability Act 1961 was passed to remedy some of the shortfalls of the factual test, and the Act has established another legal action known as 'concurrent liability'.

A concurrent wrongdoer is a person, who is responsible along with another or others for the damage or injury caused to the plaintiff, but it is not possible, as a matter of fact, to determine exactly who did what and who is responsible. The Act says that in these circumstances the wrongdoers are jointly liable for that damage.

A person might become a concurrent wrongdoer in a number of ways:

Vicarious liability

This occurs where a person is legally responsible for the actions of another. It most often occurs in the area of employment law, where an employer is held liable for the actions of an employee. It is a very important basis of liability in the area of medical or clinical negligence, as the wrongdoer is often an employee of a hospital or health board.

Breach of a joint duty

Where two or more persons are under a joint duty of care, it is not necessary to show which of those persons breached the duty. The fact of its breach is sufficient. Again, this has particular significance in the area of medical or clinical negligence where procedures are often lengthy and complicated and involve numerous personnel.

Conspiracy or concerted action

A conspiracy or concerted action towards a common end, or alternatively, where the acts are independent but cause the same damage. The same principle would apply as covered in the previous point.

To use an example to illustrate the above scenarios. A surgeon is operating to remove the tonsils of the patient and negligently severs an artery, causing a huge and rapid loss of blood. The theatre sister receives such a shock at this river of blood that she injects a large amount of oxygen into the patient's vein, causing a fatal embolism.

If one were to use the 'but for' test, it could be argued that both surgeon and theatre sister would not be liable, as it would not be possible to determine who actually killed the patient. If they were employees of the hospital, however, the hospital would be vicariously liable for the actions of both. Similarly, under the second principle they could both be held to have breached their respective duty of care towards the patient, and therefore would be jointly liable. Finally, whether their actions were regarded as independent or in concert, they could be held jointly liable in terms of the third principle.

These developments are crucial in the area of medical malpractice law, as it means that in cases where a patient cannot pinpoint the exact or relevant cause of damage amongst a number of potential causes, it will not necessarily mean that the plaintiff must lose the case.

Another interesting approach to (and perhaps rejection of) the 'but for' test in medical negligence occurred in the previously discussed case of *Bolitho (Administratrix of the estate of Bolitho (deceased)) v City and Hackney Health Authority* [1997] 4 All E.R. 771

Facts
A two-year-old boy was admitted to hospital suffering from respiratory problems. The boy had been previously treated at the hospital for croup. On the following day he suffered two short episodes at 12.40 p.m. and 2.00 p.m., during which he turned white and clearly had difficulty breathing. A doctor was called who examined the boy after the 12.40 p.m. episode. That doctor delegated to another doctor the task of returning to check on the boy if further difficulties were experienced. Despite the 2.00 p.m. attack, the boy was not checked on by either doctor. After both attacks, the boy returned to a stable state. At 2.30 p.m. the boy suffered total respiratory failure and a cardiac arrest, resulting in severe brain damage. He subsequently died.

On the question of causation, the first doctor argued that even if she had seen the child she would not have intubated because it was not the proper procedure, therefore her alleged negligence was not the cause of the child's death.

Issue before the court
Should the first doctor be held liable for not checking on the boy, even if it could not be shown that he would have died but for her checking up on him?

Decision of the court
The House of Lords held (distinguishing the *Bolam* test of causation and effectively overruling the very unpopular *Wilsher v Essex Health Authority* judgment) that the plaintiff could prove causation if it was proved that the defendant would have intubated if she had attended, or that she should have intubated if she had attended because she had a duty to do so and a failure to do so would have been negligent.

Commentary
This is a clear departure from the narrow limitations of the factual 'but for' test, as the policy question becomes all important, namely, if the health professional had done what he or she should have done, would the damage have occurred?

A more recent English case considering the law of causation is *Fairchild v Glenhaven Funeral Services Limited and others* [2002] 2 All. E.R. 305, a decision of the House of Lords.

Facts
The plaintiffs were employees of the defendants. The plaintiffs had developed the cancer mesothelioma following negligent exposure to asbestos fibre during the course and scope of their employment with the defendants, who had employed the various plaintiffs at different times and for different periods of service. It was accepted that both employers, the defendants, had allowed the plaintiffs to inhale excessive quantities of asbestos dust, and as such, the defendants had breached the duty of care owed by every employer to its employees.

Issue before the court
It was not scientifically possible to isolate during which period of service the employees had contracted the cancer and therefore it was argued by the defendants that the plaintiffs could not succeed, as they could not prove which employer was responsible.

Decision of the court
The House of Lords held that the 'but for' test was inadequate in these circumstances. The House of Lords held that the object of the law of tort was to compensate victims of wrongful acts, and the courts were there to define cases in which the law could hold one party liable to compensate another, as a matter of fairness. To allow technicalities to prevent fairness was not justice.

Both employers were held liable to compensate the plaintiffs, their former employees.

Commentary
Technicality must not stand in the way of justice and fairness. The law is a living thing, and must be adapted to meet modern notions of equity.

As previously mentioned, one of the primary functions of law is to provide certainty. The law must be certain and definite so as to allow citizens to plan their lives in the knowledge that the law will protect them and they in turn will not contravene the law. It is clear that when courts introduce policy into judicial decisions, this element of certainty takes a back seat, as it is the particular circumstances that cause the court to come to the decision it does, and to break with tradition and legal precedent.

On the other hand, the public would not support a system of law that handed out unfair results by inappropriately following earlier decisions. The courts recognise that for the law to remain legitimate in the eyes of the people it governs, it must grow and adapt to a changing society. This judgement is clearly an example of that, where a strict adherence to the 'but for' test would have resulted in an unjust decision.

Whether this new approach to multiple or alternate causes of injury would make a dramatic difference to medical law is debatable. In Ireland the defendant is usually a hospital or health board being sued on the basis of vicarious liability as the employer of the medical team that treated the patient at the time that he or she suffered injury. In this situation the Civil Liability Act would come into play, and it would not be necessary for the plaintiff to prove which of the medical professionals on the team actually caused the injury. The fact that they were all employees of the same employer would be sufficient to ground an action against the employer as the principal defendant.

Where a patient is treated by a team of private practitioners, however, the new approaches might be significant. For example, if it was held that both the anaesthetist and surgeon were negligent during an operation, but it was impossible to determine who dealt the 'killer blow', the court could use the new approach to ensure that both professionals did not escape liability entirely on the basis that they each blamed the other.

Another approach that has found favour in the High Court of Ireland is what is known as the 'material and substantial factor test' which is very similar to tests used by the House of Lords (in *McGhee v National Coal Board* [1972] 3 All E.R. 1008, for example), and is essentially a recognition that policy needs to play a large part in determining questions of causation. Legalism must give way to pragmatism.

The High Court decision is *Superquinn Limited v Bray Urban District Council and others* [1998] 3 I.R. 542.

The facts
The plaintiff owned a supermarket at Castle Street, Bray, County Wicklow. As a result of a violent storm, locally known as 'Hurricane Charlie', the River Dargle overflowed its banks and caused extensive damage to the goods in the supermarket. The defendant was carrying out drainage construction works in the area prior to the storm and the plaintiff alleged that the damage was caused or at least worsened by the manner in which the drainage construction works were being carried out just before the storm.

Issue before the court
Were the defendants (the Council and the contractors) negligent?

Decision of the court
The plaintiff's claim failed with the court finding that the defendants were not negligent. However, in its reasoning the High Court seemed to accept that a new approach to causation was necessary.

> 'It seems to me that …if it could be established that there were two causes of the damage to the plaintiff's property, the wrongdoing of the defendant and *vis major*, there should be an apportionment so that the defendant should only be liable for the damage attributable to its wrongdoing. The head-note in the report bears out this interpretation. Interpreted thus, the decision does not give rise to any conceptual difficulties in this post Civil Liability Act era.
> …
> Mr. Prendiville's observations, in my view, are the most reliable record we have of what happened on the night and I accept Professor Cunnane's analysis of those observations as to the significance of the breach in the flooding of the Little Bray area. In my view, it has not been demonstrated that water flowing through the breach was a material element or a significant factor in the flooding of the Plaintiff's premises. In relation to the afflux at the bridge, whatever the correct measurement of the afflux, in my view, the Plaintiff has not established that the drainage construction works, rather than natural processes, were a material element or a substantial factor in creating it.'

Commentary
The High Court seems to accept that the test for causation is the 'material element' or 'substantial factor' test, in other words the material and substantial factor test. This again could be significant in the area of clinical negligence, as it is clearly an expansion of the traditional 'but for' test. For example, where it can be shown that the medical practitioner's negligence significantly decreased the patient's chances of survival (as opposed to directly causing his death), this would allow the court to find that the increased risk to the patient was a substantial factor or material element in causing his death. In other words, the substantial contribution test, which is traditionally used in the assessment of damages, could now be used in deciding questions of causation.

This approach can also lead to controversy. If we recall the case of the cup of poisoned tea, where the court held that although the doctor was negligent, the deceased would have died in any event. That was really a question of the state of medical technology at the time. What if the argument was lead at a time that there was a cure for arsenic poisoning, as long as it was implemented immediately? Could it be argued that although the doctor did not poison the tea, his failure to be at the clinic when the patient presented with arsenic poisoning was a material contribution to his death, in that the deceased might not have died as quickly or might even have been saved?

These new tests might muddy the waters slightly and instil a slight sense of panic in the lives of lawyers, who enjoy life when it is orderly and predictable. However, it can also be argued that the end justifies the means, namely that victims receive compensation in instances where previously they might have not been awarded damages because of a legal technicality.

At the same time a word of caution must be sounded, and that is that these alternative tests for causation should not be applied in every instance where the traditional 'but for' test causes a plaintiff difficulty in discharging the onus. The law must be developed cautiously and with equitable principles, rather than a flawed product of knee-jerk decisions.

Legal causation or proximate cause

Even where the plaintiff proves factual causation, it cannot be guaranteed that he or she will win the case, as the court might still find that the defendant's action or omission was not the legal cause of the injury to the plaintiff.

Essentially this comes down to the court deciding, as a matter of policy, that the defendant should not be liable, despite factually causing the harm.

The most important factor in the test for legal causation is foreseeability. If the reasonable person in the shoes of the defendant could not have foreseen that his or her actions or omissions could cause the harm suffered by the plaintiff, the defendant will escape liability. Therefore even where, as a matter of fact, the defendant has caused the plaintiff's injury, if that injury was not foreseeable at the time of acting, the defendant will escape liability.

Another test used in deciding legal causation is the intervening act, the *novus actus interveniens*, where that intervening act breaks the chain of causation between the plaintiff's injury and the defendant's action by replacing the defendant's act as the sole cause of the plaintiff's harm. We discussed this concept earlier (see chapter 5: Introduction to Tort) when talking about the motorist who ran over the pedestrian's foot, and the negligent surgeon who finally caused the pedestrian to lose his foot. The motorist would argue that the negligent surgery was an intervening act that broke the chain between him and the pedestrian. The court would need to decide as a matter of policy whether this argument should succeed.

An Irish decision that demonstrates the principle of *novus actus interveniens* is *Conole v Redbank Oyster Company* [1976] I.R. 191, a Supreme Court decision.

Facts
The defendant knew that a boat was not safe, as it had failed to pass its water fitness tests. Orders were issued by the defendant that the boat be tied up and its use was forbidden. One of the defendant's employees ignored this instruction and took the boat out, with fifty children on board. The boat sank with loss of life.

Issue before the court
Was the defendant liable for the injury caused by their defective boat?

Decision of the court
The Supreme Court held that the cause of the injuries was the decision of the employee to take the boat out after the defects were discovered. This reckless decision of the employee broke the causal link between the negligence of the defendant as the controller/owner of the defective boat and the injury.

The Supreme Court (Henchy J.) held as follows:

> 'Assuming that Fairway were negligent in sending forth an unseaworthy boat, reliance on this negligence must, on the authorities, be confined to those whom Fairway ought reasonably to have foreseen as likely to be injured by it. Furthermore, the negligence must be such as to have caused a defect which was unknown to such persons. If the defect becomes patent to the person ultimately injured and he chooses to ignore it and subjects the person ultimately injured to that known risk, the person who originally put forth the article is not liable to the person injured. In such circumstances the nexus of cause and effect, in terms of the law of tort, has been sundered as far as the injured person is concerned.'

Commentary
This judgment illustrates the importance of having a clear picture in your mind of the chain that links the damage or injury on the one end, to the wrongful act of the defendant on the other. If that chain is broken by an intervening act, the court may find that causation has not been proved, and that the defendant is not liable. Note that the court may, rather than must, make this decision, as ultimately the decision will be largely determined by policy and foreseeability.

As a general rule the courts are quite reluctant to uphold this defence and will usually hold that where the original wrongdoer could or should have foreseen the intervening act, this cannot be a defence to their own wrongful actions. The courts will also reject the defence where the defendant is the cause of the intervening act.

A question of policy

When considering legal causation, the breadth of the factors that the court might take into consideration is too wide for the scope of this book, but essentially the questions of policy are the same or very similar to the questions that the court might ask in deciding foreseeability in the duty of care inquiry. The court, in addition to deciding on foreseeability, will consider factors like the magnitude of the risk, the burden of taking precautions, the utility (usefulness) of the defendant's conduct, and what is common or established practice in determining the reasonableness of the defendant's conduct.

These policy factors become very important in the context of health care where there are often budgetary and other restraints which do not make it possible for a health board or hospital to take every precaution. Even in instances where it can be shown that there is a factual link between the actions of the health service provider and the harm caused to a patient, the court might find as a matter of policy that the health service provider could not have reasonably prevented the harm.

The thin skull rule (the 'eggshell skull' rule)

In essence, this rule says that you take your defendant or claimant as you find him or her. If your patient has certain characteristics or a constitution that aggravates the original harm, you are liable for that increased damage, despite the fact that you could not foresee it. What is important is that you could foresee the original harm, which thereafter becomes worse due to the patient's make-up.

It is for this reason that hospitals have extensive questionnaires for their patients to complete on admission, in an attempt to discover these hidden characteristics.

The rule can, however, have harsh effects, particularly in the area of psychological damage. An Irish example is the decision in *McCarthy v Murphy* [1998] I.E.H.C. 23.

Facts
As a result of the defendant's negligence his car collided with the plaintiff's stationary car. The accident was not serious as the impact was slight. The plaintiff suffered minor whiplash. However, due to an existing

psychological condition, the plaintiff developed a serious depressive reaction.

Issue before the court
If it was accepted that the defendant should have foreseen that the plaintiff might suffer whiplash as a result of his negligent driving, could the defendant be held liable for the resulting injury arising from that whiplash, namely the depressive reaction?

Decision of the court
The Supreme Court applied the thin skull or eggshell skull rule and found that the defendant was liable for the depressive reaction.

> 'It was argued on behalf of the Defendant that he was only liable for injury which was of a type which was reasonably foreseeable, and that it was not foreseeable that any form of psychological injury would occur as a result of a very minor traffic accident such as in this case. The Defendant accepts the principles of the eggshell skull cases, but seeks to distinguish this case by saying that, while it could be foreseen that even a minor accident could cause physical damage such as a soft tissue injury, it was not reasonably foreseeable that that in turn would lead to a depressive condition.
>
> I do not think I can accept that argument.
> ...
> I am of the view, on the medical evidence, that the immediate cause of the Plaintiff's depression was the soft tissue injury which she suffered in the accident. Of course the Defendant could not have anticipated that she was a person with a pre-disposition to depression, but he could have reasonably foreseen a soft tissue injury, and that being so, he is liable for damage which flows from that injury, as he has to take the Plaintiff as he finds her.'

Commentary
This approach has been criticised by those who argue that it is an exception to the test of foreseeability. Others argue that this approach is a variety of the test of foreseeability, and is therefore justified, as what must be foreseeable is the original harm, and not the extent of the harm. Therefore they argue that where the extent of the harm is increased by a person's personal characteristics that is not an exception to the foreseeability rule, as the rule has never been that you must be able to foresee the extent of the damage, but only the nature of the damage itself.

Causation: Summary

1. In order to successfully prosecute a claim for negligence, the plaintiff must demonstrate, as a matter of fact, that there is a causal connection or 'chain' between the plaintiff's damage and the defendant's conduct.
2. The traditional common law test for causation is known as the 'but for' test and goes along the lines of 'but for the defendant's conduct, would the plaintiff have suffered harm?'
3. This is often referred to as the 'factual causation' test.
4. This test is very effective when the facts are clear and easy to establish, but fails where the cause of the damage cannot be adequately or accurately ascertained, usually due to the fact that science or technology is not yet sufficiently advanced to pinpoint a cause of the damage.
5. This is especially true in the field of medicine.
6. The courts have held that the 'but for' test is the first stage in establishing causation, and in special circumstances the courts can depart from this test. These departures are often called the tests for 'legal causation', and are essentially based on public policy considerations.
7. This terminology might be more confusing than helpful as it suggests that the first is a test of fact only and the second a question of legal policy. This is not the case and the two tests should rather be seen as complementing one another.
8. One of the more significant departures in our modern law of causation is the use of the 'material contribution' test where the court will hold that the element of causation is satisfied if it can be shown that the defendant's conduct was a material and substantial contribution to the plaintiff's damages.
9. The other departure in this area is for the courts to use the traditional test of foreseeability but hold that what must be reasonably foreseeable is the damage itself, as opposed to the events or conduct leading to the damage, or even the extent of the damage.

19

THE LEGAL DUTY OF CONFIDENTIALITY

> **Learning Outcomes**
> **At the completion of this chapter, the reader should know and understand the following:**
>
> ▸ The principle of confidentiality is based on a number of factors and policies.
> ▸ The idea behind the concept of a 'doctrine' of confidentiality, which arises from a variety of sources.

Important concepts and phrases that are crucial to an understanding of this chapter

Equity
Equity means fairness. In the legal sense equity has always been seen as a system that coexists with and supplements the common law, particularly where the common law 'falls behind the times'. Courts have the power to use the principles of equity to reach a fair decision, where a strict interpretation of the common law would result in unjustifiable unfairness.

Impart
To give, to hand over, to communicate. A person imparts information when they reveal something to another person.

Introduction

Confidentiality can be defined as the principle of receiving information in the course of a professional relationship, where that information is given by or about an identifiable individual under conditions of secrecy, and that information is kept secure and secret from others.

When admitting, or consulting with, a patient, the health agency or health professional will collect information from the patient. Most of that information will relate to the illness that is the focus of the treatment, and much of this information would fall under the categories of 'secret' or 'sensitive' or 'downright embarrassing'.

It is difficult for a patient to reveal some of this information, for obvious reasons. However, a patient is prepared to suffer the embarrassment and indignity because the patient knows that he or she can only be cured if all problems are revealed. Perhaps more importantly in many cases, the patient is confident that the secrets revealed will go no further than the four walls of the surgery or consulting room.

If the patient did not have that confidence and trust in the health professional, he or she would not reveal any embarrassing or sensitive information. This would hamper the health professional, and would usually result in a sub-standard diagnosis and treatment. What this means is that confidentiality is necessary to make the healthcare system work.

The law must ensure that the patient's act of faith in the health professional is rewarded and protected. One of the most important legal obligations owed by the health professional to the patient is the protection of confidences revealed by the patient to that health professional. The general principle is that the duty of confidence is breached when the health professional uses confidential information, directly or indirectly obtained from the patient, without the express or implied consent of that patient.

The duty of confidentiality is owed to all patients, including mature and immature minors, and adults who lack the capacity to take decisions. The duty endures beyond the individual's death.

The doctrine of confidentiality

Lawyers often speak about the 'Doctrine of Confidentiality'. This is in recognition of the fact that there is no specific law of confidentiality as such, but rather that a duty of confidentiality arises from a number of areas of law and equity. The concept of a doctrine is therefore an attempt to bring these various sources and principles together.

This doctrine arises from a number of sources:

From the duty of care in negligence
Clearly a health professional owes a duty of care not to disclose confidential information about a patient where it is foreseeable that such disclosure will cause harm to the patient.

From the implied duties under the health professional-patient contract
The obligation of confidentiality may be an express or implied term of the contract between the health professional and the patient. By implied is meant that although neither party wrote it down or said so in as many words, they both recognise and agree on the need for confidentiality.

Therefore, even in cases where there is no written contract or where a written contract does not expressly provide for confidentiality in so many words, there is always an implied term in any contract for health care that the health professional will obey the health profession's code of ethics which prohibit disclosure of confidential information except in specific circumstances. This ethical duty becomes part of the contract and is therefore enforceable in a court of law.

From the duty to keep confidential any information that has been passed on in confidence

An ethical duty is imposed on the health professional to respect patient confidentiality by reason of the relationship of trust. Although this is an ethical duty, it has been recognised and enforced by the courts, and therefore has the status of a legal rule.

In the High Court decision of *House of Spring Gardens v Point Blank Ltd.* [1984] I.R. 611, the court held that an action for breach of confidence could be brought if the following requirements were satisfied:

(a) An obligation of confidence, with respect to information that has been communicated, must exist within the relationship between the parties;

(b) the information communicated must be properly regarded as confidential;

(c) the recipient must have breached the duty to act in good faith. In other words, the medical professional must have used the information for a purpose for which it was not imparted, and this use of the information must be to the detriment of the patient.

The third requirement could be seen as an excuse for paternalism, as a health professional could argue that disclosure was in the best interests of the patient (for example, revealing the diagnosis and prognosis to family members in order to encourage their support for the patient). It is hoped that this argument no longer holds credibility in the present state of health care.

From requirements by professional registration bodies

Professional bodies usually have a Code of Conduct, which must be respected and followed by their registered members as part of the professional conduct expected of health professionals. For example, An Bord Altranais has a Code of Conduct for nurses, which expressly mentions the importance of confidentiality.

From a moral duty of confidentiality

The Hippocratic Oath contains the following duty of confidence:

> '... whatever in connection with my professional practice, or not in connection with it, I see or hear, in the life of men, which ought not

to be spoken of abroad, I will not divulge, as reckoning that all such must be kept secret.'

This Oath is confirmed in the 1947 Declaration of Geneva.

From statutory duties
There are a number of statutes that impose a duty of confidentiality or penalise a breach of confidentiality. For example, the Data Protection Act 1988 imposes a duty of confidentiality on data controllers, who are often health professionals in the sphere of medical data, like hospital records or patient records.

From the constitutional rights of confidentiality, privacy and dignity
There is no express right to privacy in the Irish Constitution. An unenumerated right is a right that the Constitution does not expressly mention in so many words, but the courts have interpreted the Constitution as granting and protecting that right. An example of such an unenumerated right is the right to marital privacy, as confirmed in *McGee v Attorney-General* [1974] I.R. 284. It could be argued that the State is under an obligation to safeguard the confidentiality, privacy and dignity of its citizens. In *Kennedy v Ireland* [1987] I.R. 587, the Supreme Court recognised a right to privacy.

From European law
Article 8 of the European Convention of Human Rights states that everyone has the right to be given respect for his or her private and family life, home and correspondence. Ireland signed the Convention in Rome on 4 November 1950 and ratified it in 1953. The Convention came into force on 3 September 1953. The provisions of the Convention are only enforceable in an Irish court when its provisions are passed as a statute by the Oireachtas. The European Convention of Human Rights Act 2003 has established the Convention as part of Irish law, subject to the Constitution. This means that the provisions of the Convention are now enforceable in an Irish court.

In *Z v Finland* (1988) 25 E.H.R.R. 371, the European Court of Human Rights stated that:

> 'The protection of personal data, not least medical data, is of fundamental importance to a person's enjoyment of his or her right to respect for private and family life as guaranteed by Article 8 of the Convention. ... Without such protection, those in need of medical assistance may be deterred from revealing such information of a personal and intimate nature as may be necessary in order to receive

appropriate treatment and, even, from seeking such assistance, thereby endangering their own health and in the case of transmissible diseases, that of the community.'

A true mixture

Some or all of these sources and elements of confidentiality are present when a health professional receives confidential information from a patient, and they will also be called into action when a health professional discloses confidential information received from a patient.

Although a reading of the many judicial decisions on the subject show that the courts have relied on the law of contract, tort and property, and the principles of equity and public policy, in effect the duty of confidentiality is a unique concept that covers all of these areas and calls all of them into play.

It is accordingly clear that the doctrine of confidentiality is indeed just that, as it cannot be regarded as arising from one area of law or from one identifiable legal duty. As Denning M.R. stated in the English case of *Seager v Copydex* [1967] 2 All E.R. 415:

> 'The law on this subject does not depend on any implied contract. It depends on the broad principle of equity that he who has received information in confidence shall not take unfair advantage of it. He must not make use of it to the prejudice of him who gave it, without obtaining his consent.'

These varied sources of the doctrine also create one of its most perplexing problems. The main difficulty concerning the law of medical confidentiality is that there is no specific statute governing the health professional's duty of confidence, nor is there any one legal basis for the duty of confidence. The whole question of confidentiality is governed by codes of professional conduct and the common-law doctrine of confidentiality.

This can create 'grey areas' where nobody is certain which area of law, if any, applies to the situation under consideration.

Guidance from judgments

There have been many attempts by the judiciary to define what is meant by the phrase 'confidential information'. What is clear is that information is only subject to an obligation of confidence when it is communicated in circumstances of confidence. The person we use to decide whether information was imparted in circumstances of confidence is our old friend, the reasonable person.

In the decision of *Co-Co Engineering v AN Clark (Engineers) [1969] R.P.C. 41*, the court suggested that:

> 'It seems to me that if the circumstances are such that any reasonable man standing in the shoes of the recipient of the information would have realised on reasonable grounds the information was being given to him in confidence, then this would suffice to impose upon him the equitable obligation of confidence.'

The same judge (Megarry V.C.) gave a more comprehensive definition of what constituted confidential information in a later case, *Thomas Marshall Ltd v Guinle* [1979] 1 Ch. 227:

> 'First, that the information must be information the release of which the owner believes would be injurious to him or of advantage to his rivals or others. Second, the owner must believe the information is confidential or secret. Third, the owner's belief under these headings must be reasonable. Fourth, the information must be judged in the light of usage and practices in the particular industry concerned.'

Patients have a right to expect that identifiable information about themselves provided or discovered in the course of their health care will not be shared with other people without their knowledge and consent. The disclosure of identifiable information without the patient's consent to someone who did not previously, and legitimately, know its content breaches confidentiality.

Therefore it is clearly reasonable that a patient expects such confidential medical information not to be released, where the release of such information can harm the patient's prospects or personal life.

Finally, it is clear, as previously mentioned, that the question of confidentiality is heavily regulated by the profession itself.

Accordingly, when considering the status of confidential medical information, the definition as proposed by Megarry V.C. is appropriate.

An objective or a subjective test?

What is not necessarily clear from the court's treatment of confidential material is whether the test is wholly objective, as is suggested by the use of the reasonable person test, or whether it can be argued that information is confidential purely on the basis that there is an expectation of confidence from the particular patient in question.

The objective test is the more practical of the two, as the information must be shown to have the basic attribute of inaccessibility to others. For example, in the English case of *Franklin v Giddins* [1978] Qd. R. 72, where the defendant stole cuttings from the plaintiff's secretly grafted fruit trees, the court held that this action had breached an obligation of confidence as the make-up of the trees was a 'trade secret'.

Whilst the second test, namely the patient's expectation of privacy, might seem to be a subjective test, and therefore difficult to define with any accuracy, it might be argued that this test can be similarly objectified, by asking the question whether the patient's expectation of privacy was reasonable in the circumstances.

In the Irish case of *Annie Cook v Thomas Carroll* [1945] I.R. 515, which is famous for establishing the principle of sacerdotal privilege (privileged communications between priest and parishioner), the principles established by this decision can be applied to the healthcare relationship.

Facts
The plaintiff took an action against the alleged seducer of her pregnant daughter. The girl and boy in question had been interviewed by the parish priest but he refused to testify about his conversation with the defendant.

Issue before the court
Could the priest be forced to reveal the nature and content of the conversation that he had with the defendant?

Decision of the court
The court held that the conversation between the priest and the defendant was privileged. The court held that the test as to whether a relationship of confidence exists was as follows (quoting Wigmore, a very famous legal philosopher and scholar):

> '... four fundamental conditions may be predicated as necessary to the establishment of a privilege against the disclosure of communications between persons standing in a given relation:
> The communications must originate in a confidence that they will not be disclosed.
> This element of confidentiality must be essential to the full and satisfactory maintenance of the relation.
> The relation must be one which in the opinion of the community ought to be sedulously fostered.
> The injury which would inure to the relation by the disclosure of the communication must be greater than the benefit thereby gained for the correct disposal of litigation.'

Commentary

The concept of evidential privilege was spoken about earlier. It means that if something is privileged, a party (to whom that privilege belongs) can prevent it from being used as evidence in court. For example, communications between a lawyer and client are privileged, and the lawyer and the client cannot be forced to reveal the nature and content of these communications. The client can voluntarily reveal the nature and content of these communications, but the lawyer must refuse until the client instructs otherwise.

Although these four requirements are necessary for the finding of evidential privilege, it has not been suggested that health professionals should enjoy the same absolute privilege as is enjoyed by lawyers. On the other hand, it is clear that the communications between a health professional and patient should enjoy a special status, as it could be argued that these communications do meet the abovementioned criteria.

If we go through the requirements one by one and attempt to phrase them in slightly more accessible English, the following can be deduced:

'The communications must originate in a confidence that they will not be disclosed.'
What this means is that the person who is revealing the confidential information is doing so because he or she believes that what is said will not be repeated to anybody, at least not without permission. This is clearly true of a patient confiding to a health professional.

'This element of confidentiality must be essential to the full and satisfactory maintenance of the relation.'
The principle of confidentiality must be necessary for the relationship, and the system as a whole, to be successful. This is clearly true of the relationship between health professional and patient, and the health care system as a whole.

'The relation must be one which in the opinion of the community ought to be sedulously fostered.'
The public must believe that confidentiality is essential for the success of the health care system. Again, this is clearly true, as people would stop seeking health care if they thought their secrets were to become public knowledge.

'The injury which would inure to the relation by the disclosure of the communication must be greater than the benefit thereby gained for the correct disposal of litigation.'
This is the balancing act that will be discussed in detail later. The courts

must balance the interests of society in knowing the confidential information, versus the interests of society in preserving patient confidentiality. If the former outweighs the latter, that information can be revealed.

Some commentators and courts have called the relationship between the health professional and patient a fiduciary relationship, which means a relationship based on trust and honest dealing. This classification of the relationship has not enjoyed the support of all courts however, as we will see later.

The function of the courts in enforcing the duty of confidentiality

As the duty of confidentiality in the healthcare context is mainly a moral or ethical obligation, it is governed by Codes of Conduct, for both doctors and nurses, and these are in turn enforced by the courts.

The court is being asked to enforce a moral or ethical obligation by legal sanction. It goes further than that, however, as it is recognised that the good practice of medicine and healthcare cannot be carried out without the patient being absolutely certain that confidential information will remain that way. As was argued at the beginning of this chapter, if the patient cannot be sure of that confidence, he or she will not speak freely to the health professional which will mean that the health professional will not be in a position to make a full and proper diagnosis, which could mean inadequate or unsuitable treatment. This was the basis of the court's reasoning in the *X v Y* case, which is discussed later.

In the end, the effect of these different and varied sources of the law of confidentiality means that there are no fixed rules to determine in what conditions information is to be protected as confidential and in what circumstances it does not deserve such protection. The question must be approached in a practical manner, asking whether disclosure would seek to avoid the mischief of patients losing faith in the health profession, but within the bigger context of what is good for society at large. Clearly these two goals more often than not are in agreement with one another, but in instances where they are not, the court is asked to act as referee between two conflicting interests. These interests are the public's right to know versus the patient's right to confidentiality, which is an essential part of any successful health care system.

Therefore, a patient's right to privacy is not absolute. Occasions arise where confidentiality must be breached to protect the greater interest of society.

In the decision of *Kennedy v Ireland* [1987] I.R. 587, the Supreme Court noted that the right to privacy was not absolute:

'It is not an unqualified right. Its exercise may be restricted by the constitutional rights of others, or by the requirements of the common good ... in certain circumstances the exigencies of the common good may require and justify ... intrusion and interference'.

Nevertheless, recognition of the importance of confidentiality should not cause both professionals and patients to lose sight of the ultimate and most important goal, which is the delivery of appropriate and effective medical or health care. Whilst confidentiality can certainly ensure this goal, it must never be used as an excuse to sacrifice this goal.

As a concluding remark, the essential elements of the law of confidentiality are conveniently summarised by Lord Goff, in the case of *A.G. v Guardian Newspapers* (No.2)[1990] A.C. 109:

'I start with the broad general principle (which I do not intend in any way to be definitive) that a duty of confidence arises when confidential information comes to the knowledge of a person (the confidant) in circumstances where he has notice, or is held to have agreed, that the information is confidential, with the effect that it would be just in all the circumstances that he should be precluded from disclosing the information to others.

...

(In addition to) this broad principle, there are three limiting principles to which I wish to refer. The first limiting principle (which is rather an expression of the scope of the duty) ... is that the principle of confidentiality only applies to information to the extent that it is confidential. In particular, once it has entered into what is usually called the public domain (which means no more than that the information in question is so generally accessible that, in all the circumstances, it cannot be regarded as confidential) then, as a general rule, the principle of confidentiality can have no application to it

...

The second limiting principle is that the duty of confidence applies neither to useless information, nor to trivia.

...

The third limiting principle is of far greater importance. It is that, although the basis of the law's protection of confidence is that there is a public interest that confidences should be preserved and protected by the law, nevertheless that public interest may be outweighed by some other countervailing public interest which favours disclosure.'

Conclusion

As is clear from this quotation, it is sometimes easier to define confidentiality by stating what it is not, rather than what it is. However, it can be said that the health professional's duty of confidence arises both from the quality of the information given by the patient and from the circumstances in which it was obtained by the health professional. As both of these elements would be sufficient in themselves to ensure confidentiality, it could be said that the health professional's duty of confidentiality is 'doubly certain'.

This assumes that both elements always co-exist, and clearly this is not always the case. Information which does not demand confidence by its nature might be given in circumstances of confidence. For example, non-medical information, like details of the patient's adulterous conduct, which is given during a consultation. Conversely, information of a clearly confidential nature might be given in circumstances where confidentiality was not ensured. For example, medical information, like the patient's HIV status, imparted on a golf course or in a pub.

Either the nature of the information given or the circumstances in which it was given will cause that information to be categorised as confidential. Only one of these conditions needs to be present, it is not necessary that both conditions be present before information is confidential.

Doctrine of Confidentiality: Summary

1. The efficiency and effectiveness, perhaps the survival, of any health care system is dependant on the practice of confidentiality. A health professional cannot properly diagnose and treat sickness unless the patient discloses all symptoms, and the patient will only disclose these if he or she is certain that they will not be revealed to anybody without consent.
2. The doctrine of confidentiality relies for its creation on many sources, both legal and ethical, and it can be argued it has developed into a class of its own.
3. Information is only subject to an obligation of confidence when it is communicated in confidence, or it is confidential by its very nature.
4. Medical information is confidential if:
    a. The patient reasonably believes its release would be harmful to his or her interests.
    b. The patient reasonably believes that the information is confidential or secret.
    c. The medical or health profession would recognise the information as confidential.

5. Any confidential information, including medical information, is worthy of legal protection if:
   a. The information was communicated between parties on the basis that it would not be disclosed.
   b. The relationship between the parties is based on mutual trust and confidentiality.
   c. The relationship and the confidentiality of that relationship must be respected and valued by society as being necessary for the overall good of society.
   d. The benefit to the public of keeping the information in question confidential must outweigh the benefit of the public knowing that information.
6. The nature of the relationship between the health professional and the patient would seem to satisfy these criteria.
7. Useful websites:
   a. *Oasis*
      (http://www.oasis.gov.ie/health/access_to_medical_records.html).
   b. *Omni*
      (http://omni.ac.uk/browse/mesh/detail/C0009669L0009669.html).

20

PERSONAL HEALTH INFORMATION

> *Learning Outcomes*
> **At the completion of this chapter, the reader should know and understand the following:**
>
> ▸ The meaning of personal health information.
> ▸ The concepts of aggregated and anonymous data.
> ▸ A breach of confidentiality only occurs if the identity of the patient is revealed.

Important concepts and phrases that are crucial to an understanding of this chapter

Aggregated data
Aggregated means to collect together, to unite. Therefore aggregated data is information that somebody has purposely collected together or compiled, usually in order to analyse that data. Statistics would be a form of aggregated data.

Utilitarianism
A doctrine that is closely associated with the teachings of Jeremy Bentham and John Stuart Mill. Its basic premise was that everything that is done must be done in order to promote the greatest happiness of the greatest number, even where this action might not be seen as inherently moral or pure and might discriminate against the individual. A great deal of law conforms to the utilitarian principle, as it is usually trying to achieve what is good for society at large, even where this might leave an occasional individual unhappy.

Introduction

Personal health information is any information relating to the physical or mental health of any patient, from which that patient can be identified. Such information may be contained in diagrams or illustrations, videos, tape recordings, computer files, registers and manual records, or it may reside in the health professional's memory. Wherever it may be, it is worthy of protection.

Information that is not clinical, such as a patient's registration details or address, for example, is also confidential and patients should be made aware of any potential uses of information beyond their own health care, like research or marketing.

Personal health information and confidentiality

It was in the English case of *X v Y and others* [1988] 2 All E.R. 648 that the doctrine of confidentiality was held to apply to personal medical information.

Facts
Two doctors practicing in the NHS were HIV positive, and continued to practice. A Sunday newspaper threatened to reveal this information and publish the names of the doctors on the grounds of public interest.

Issue to be decided by the court
What was more important, the public's right to know, or the patients' right to confidentiality?

Decision of the court
The court granted an injunction against the newspaper preventing it from publishing the story. The reason for the court's decision was that it was in the public interest that people with HIV come forward and present themselves for treatment. If HIV positive patients thought that there was a risk that their identities would be revealed through publication, they would not present themselves for treatment, driving the disease underground, and this would be a health care disaster.

The court was emphatic in its ruling that personal clinical information stored in a patient's medical records was afforded legal protection on the grounds of being confidential information.

> 'On the one hand, there are the public interests in having a free press and an informed public debate; on the other, it is in the public interest that actual or potential AIDS sufferers should be able to resort to hospitals without fear of this being revealed, that those owing duties of confidence in their employment should be loyal and should not disclose confidential matters and that, prima facie, no one should be allowed to use information extracted in breach of confidence from hospital records even if disclosure of the particular information may not give rise to immediately apparent harm.
> ...
> I keep in the forefront of my mind the very important public interest in freedom of the press. And I accept that there is some public interest in knowing that which the defendants seek to publish (in

whichever version). But in my judgment those public interests are substantially outweighed when measured against the public interests in relation to loyalty and confidentiality both generally and with particular reference to AIDS patients' hospital records. There has been no misconduct by the plaintiffs. The records of hospital patients, particularly those suffering from this appalling condition should, in my judgment, be as confidential as the courts can properly keep them ...'.

Commentary
The decision that faces a court in confidentiality disputes is usually the question: What is of most benefit to society at large? Is it in the interests of society to reveal the information, despite the prejudice to the individual concerned, or is it in the interest of society to keep the information concealed? It would seem that in most cases of this nature, given that confidentiality is seen as an essential requirement of any healthcare system, the courts will choose secrecy over disclosure. This is not always the case however, as we will see in *Egdell*'s case. Each decision is dependant on the specific facts at hand. What can be said is that where they conflict, the interests of the individual patient will necessarily take second place to the interests of the greater society. This is an essentially utilitarian approach – the greatest happiness of the greatest number is more important than the happiness of the individual patient.

Permissible use of anonymous data
Information, which does not allow the patient to be identified, is not legally problematic. Data, which has been stripped of any personal or identifiable characteristics, can still be useful and effective for many health service or research purposes instead of identifiable data. It is good practice to use non-identifiable information wherever possible. Use of minimal data identifying the patient's county, gender and year of birth is acceptable for administrative or research purposes. There seems to be no legitimate basis on which a researcher would need more than that, in any event.

It is often the case that information that would appear to be anonymous can be used to identify patients when used in combination with other seemingly anonymous information. Combinations of partial identifiers like initials, date of birth, gender, occupation, county or geographical area, diagnosis and date of admission, for example, can reliably identify many individuals, and it must never be assumed that information containing any combination of such details is truly anonymous. Aggregating data, in other words reducing it to bare statistics, will often serve to make it truly anonymous.

The other danger about information that first appears anonymous is that what is anonymous to a certain segment of the population might not be anonymous to other segments of the population who have access to additional means of identification. For example, information identified by a number is identifiable to those people who have access to a database of those numbers. With the introduction of electronic records, there is really no way to avoid this disclosure to a lot of people. Disclosures of information should involve the minimum exposure necessary to achieve the objective. Wherever possible, anonymous or aggregated data should be used in preference to identifiable information in an attempt to minimise exposure leading to identification.

An interesting decision which raised the question as to what exactly constituted anonymous data was the English case of *R v Department of Health, ex parte Source Informatics Ltd* [2000] 1 All E.R. 785.

Facts
Source Informatics attempted to persuade doctors and pharmacists to disclose prescription information, to enable the company to track prescription patterns and patient behaviour. The disclosure of this information by the health professionals concerned would not have revealed the identity of their patients. The Department of Health advised these doctors and pharmacists that such disclosure would constitute a breach of duty of confidence owed to patients.

Issue to be decided by the court
The court was asked to decide whether the disclosure of anonymous information by doctors and pharmacists could be a breach of confidence.

Decision of the court
The Court of Appeal reversed the finding of the trial court and held that in a case involving personal confidences, the disclosure of information by the confidant would not be a breach of confidence provided that the confider's identity was protected. In such a case, the law was concerned only to protect the confider's privacy, and it was immaterial that the disclosed information was not in the public domain. In this case the patient did not own the prescription form or the information it contained, and he therefore had no right to control its use provided that his privacy was not put at risk. The court held that:

> 'But that gives the patient no property in the information and no right to control its use provided only and always that his privacy is not put at risk. I referred earlier to Mr Sales' plea for respect for 'the patient's autonomy'. At first blush the submission is a beguiling one.

My difficulty with it, however, is in understanding how the patient's autonomy is compromised by Source's scheme. If, as I conclude, his only legitimate interest is in the protection of his privacy and if that is safeguarded, I fail to see how his will could be thought thwarted or his personal integrity undermined. By the same token that, in a case concerning government information, "the principle of confidentiality can have no application to it ... once it has entered ... the public domain" (per Lord Goff), so too in a case involving personal confidences I would hold by analogy that the confidence is not breached where the confider's identity is protected.'

Commentary

If data is made truly anonymous, there can be no breach of confidentiality, as what is being kept confidential is the identity of the patient and the privacy attached to that confidentiality. If the identity of the patient cannot be discovered, there can never be a breach of confidentiality.

At the same time, if information has already entered 'the public domain', the question of confidentiality disappears, as the information is public and that is that.

Personal Health Information: Summary

1. Personal health information is the medical details of a patient that can be used to identify the patient.
2. Whenever possible, information about patients should be made anonymous, particularly when it is used for purposes other than the immediate care of the patient, for example research or marketing.
3. Health professionals must be aware that information that seems to be anonymous can be combined with other seemingly anonymous information in order to identify a patient.
4. It can never be a breach of confidentiality to release truly anonymous ('aggregated') medical data, as what is being protected is the identity of the patient, which is the guarantee of privacy.
5. The courts often have to perform a balancing exercise between the right to confidentiality and its importance to a properly functioning health care system, on the one hand, and the right of the public to know about things that affect them, on the other hand.
6. Useful websites:
    a. *Department of Health Information* (http://www.doh.ie/hinfo/).
    b. *EU Information* (http://europa.eu.int/information_society/qualif/health/index_en.htm).
    c. *International Medical Informatics Association* (http://www.chirad.info/imiaoswg/).

21
PERMITTED DISCLOSURE OF CONFIDENTIAL INFORMATION

> *Learning Outcomes*
> **At the completion of this chapter, the reader should know and understand the following:**
> - Unauthorised disclosure of personal health information is only a breach of confidentiality where the recipient had no previous knowledge of that information.
> - Unauthorised disclosure of personal health information to other health professionals is justified in limited circumstances.
> - Any disclosure to other health professionals must be done on a 'need to know' basis.

Introduction

Confidentiality can only be breached when the recipient of the information learns something that was previously unknown to him or her. This explains why an often-used defence to an action for breach of confidentiality is that the information was already in 'the public domain'. You might remember that this was an argument that was (unsuccessfully) used in the *Source Informatics* case about doctors and pharmacists releasing anonymous information.

It is not a breach of confidentiality to discuss the medical implications of general information, where the recipient already knows that information. For example, where relatives are already aware of a patient's condition or diagnosis, an explanation of the possible options for that patient does not breach confidentiality. However, revealing the patient's views on those choices would be a breach of confidentiality.

Sharing information with patients about their own health and treatment is an essential part of good practice.

Disclosure to other health professionals

Disclosure is the revealing of identifiable health information to anyone other than the patient. Many would assume that sharing patient information with other health professionals who have professional obligations of confidentiality neither counts as a disclosure nor requires consent. This is not necessarily correct. It would be improper, for example, for a patient's previous doctor to have access to the record made after that doctor ceased to have care of that patient.

The exchange of identifiable information between health professionals caring for a patient, unless the patient has expressly prohibited it, is permitted. This does not mean that such data can be routinely circulated to others simply because they are members of the 'healthcare family'. Only people tending to a specific patient at any particular time should have access to the records of that patient. Within all health care establishments, procedures should be in place to allow necessary access to identifiable data for the provision of care. However, these same procedures must prevent unrestricted access.

People who are in administrative functions, as opposed to the health professionals actually tending to a patient, should not have routine access to identifiable data and should normally use anonymous data.

Patients should be made aware that health teams need to share essential, relevant information in order to ensure that the safety and effectiveness of treatment is maximised. The sharing of identifiable data on 'a need to know' basis should be limited to those who have a clear need to know about the patient as part of their role in providing care for that patient at the time of disclosure.

There has been considerable debate about how this works in practice, and there is agreement that an overriding concern is for appropriate and effective care to be delivered to the individual patient. As previously stressed, the need for confidentiality must not prevent the patient from receiving the best available treatment. In the hospital context, for example, all health professionals directly involved in a patient's care should have access to the patient's record (unless the patient has expressly prohibited this). Wider disclosure, however, to people who may be only loosely associated with care, for example, to volunteer helpers or people gaining work experience, requires specific patient consent.

The question of professionals who are not doctors or nurses but are clearly involved in the health care system as employees of a Health Board, for example social workers or social carers, is a problematic one. The better practice would be to obtain specific consent from the patient to release confidential information to these professionals on a need-to-know basis.

The confidentiality owed to a deceased person is sometimes overlooked. Professional codes state that obligations of confidentiality extend beyond a patient's death although certain statutes permit limited disclosure.

Confidentiality in the workplace

Confidentiality arises in a hospital between matron, sister, sister tutor, staff nurse and student, patient and doctor and any para-medical staff or members of the medical team. For example, reports concerning a nurse's progress, performance or conduct that arise during the course of training or employment, are private and confidential.

Confidentiality is usually an express term of any contract of employment, but in any event confidentiality is always implied in every contract of employment, as it is a common law duty owed by every employee to his or her employer.

For example, in the case of a nurse, a breach of confidentiality is regarded as a serious breach of the nurse's code of conduct, and will result in an enquiry being held by An Bord Altranais into the fitness of the nurse to practice.

When a breach of confidentiality occurs, the duty of care owed to the patient is breached, and the patient is entitled to damages caused to him or her and to the members of his or her family. Either the hospital as employer or the health professional in his or her personal capacity would be liable for those damages, and this would depend on whether the health professional was acting inside or outside the scope of his or her employment at the time that the breach occurred.

Another difficult area facing health professionals is where they are obliged to reveal confidential details about their colleagues and fellow employees. For example, when it is discovered that a paediatric nurse has an unusual bacterial infection that makes it very dangerous for her to work in that unit, particularly with premature babies.

There is clear justification for an occupational safety officer to advise fellow employees to stop working until they are fit to perform their duties. There is also a clear duty for the occupational safety officer to inform his or her employer if the nurse in the example refuses to take leave. The breach of confidentiality is justified by the contract of employment entered into by that nurse. It is always a term of a contract of employment, either express or implied, that an employee will take reasonable care, and practice reasonable skill, in his or her job. Clearly it is unreasonable to continue working if this places patients or fellow employees in danger.

Permitted Disclosure: Summary

1. Confidentiality can only be breached when the recipient of the information learns something that was previously unknown to him or her.
2. It is not a breach of confidentiality to discuss the medical implications of general information that is already known by the recipient.
3. Sharing information with patients about their own health and treatment is an essential part of good practice.
4. The exchange of identifiable information between health professionals caring for a patient, unless the patient has expressly prohibited it, is permitted. This must be done on a strictly 'need-to-know' basis, and must not be shared with health professionals who are not directly involved in the treatment or care of the patient in question at the time that the disclosure is made.
5. Health professionals have a clear duty to reveal confidential information about their fellow employees where the behaviour or condition of those fellow employees poses a threat to patients or fellow employees.
6. It is an implied term in any contract of employment that the employee will not disclose confidential information, learned during or as a result of his or her employment, to unauthorised recipients. This is especially true of the health professional, and a breach of confidentiality is a serious offence that could result in dismissal.

22

THE CONSENT OF THE PATIENT TO DISCLOSURE

> **Learning Outcomes**
> At the completion of this chapter, the reader should know and understand the following:
> - Consent to disclosure must be an informed consent.
> - The principles governing the release of personal health information to partners, family or friends.
> - The principles governing the release of personal health information to third parties for commercial purposes.

Important concepts and phrases that are crucial to an understanding of this chapter

Mandate

A mandate is a commission to act on behalf of another person. In other words, where a person authorises you to act on his or her behalf, you have been given a mandate. A common example of a mandate is a Power of Attorney, where one person authorises another to perform acts on their behalf where those acts will have legal consequences.

Introduction

Disclosure of personal medical information is more often than not performed with the consent of the patient. Again, to be legally valid this consent must be informed consent, which means the consent given by a patient for the release of personal medical or healthcare information must be:

- **Voluntary:** there must be no coercion or duress placed on a patient to disclose.
- **Informed:** the patient must be made aware of the foreseeable consequences of the disclosure.
- **Specific:** the parameters or limits of the disclosure must be clearly set out, and the disclosure must not exceed these limits, which must be set by the patient, and not by the health professional.

In other words, for there to be valid consent to disclosure, it must be a decision freely made in appreciation of its consequences.

Is consent an exception to the principle of confidentiality?

Consent by the patient is often described as an exception to the doctrine of confidentiality. Most textbooks include consent under the heading of exceptions to confidentiality. However, it can be argued that it is not correct to regard the consent of the patient as an exception. An exception implies that the doctrine of confidentiality has no application in certain circumstances. On the other hand, a patient's consent suspends, rather than displaces or overrides, the issue of confidentiality. A patient can withdraw consent at any time. An exception removes the duty of confidentiality as it justifies a breach of confidentiality.

The distinction is essentially academic, but it is important for nurses to clearly understand that consent is exactly that – the patient has voluntarily suspended his or her right to confidentiality. That right has not been taken away from them.

The recognised exceptions to the duty of confidentiality will be discussed in the next chapter.

Express and implied consent

Consent to disclosure can be taken to be implied when a patient, who is aware of the potential for sharing information and that he or she has the right to refuse to disclose or at least limit the disclosure, makes no objection to the disclosure.

Such a situation may arise where a patient has been informed that information may be used for administrative purposes and the patient does not object or refuse. Another common example would be where a team providing care for a patient needs information, and the patient was aware that a team, rather than a sole professional, would carry out the treatment.

Rather than hope that the patient arrives at this conclusion, which might seem obvious to a health professional, it would be better to ensure that patients are informed that information about them is likely to be disclosed to other health professionals or administrative staff in the course of the treatment, and that they have the right to refuse to such disclosure.

If the refusal to disclose means that the patient is effectively refusing the treatment on offer, the patient must be told very clearly what the consequences of that refusal might be.

As a general rule it is unsatisfactory practice to rely on implied consent, and a health professional should take the appropriate steps to inform the patient of his or her rights and thereafter obtain a clear mandate with regard to disclosure.

Consent must be informed

In order for such consent to be valid, patients must have had a realistic opportunity to refuse. Leaflets, posters and letters can all be helpful in letting patients know about the potential uses of their information, although it is arguable that such methods may not be sufficient. There is no real substitute for a face-to-face consultation for the purposes of properly informing a patient.

Health professionals must be aware of their responsibility to disclose information only with appropriate consent, and are advised to consider the needs of their own patients when developing steps to ensure that patients are suitably informed.

When patients refuse to allow their records to be used, this should be clearly noted in the patient's medical file. This refusal to disclose must be respected unless this would expose other people to harm. This scenario is discussed in the next chapter.

The duty of confidentiality is owed to the patient and therefore it is within the patient's power to authorise disclosure. Announcements to the media, notification of family and friends, supplying of information to a solicitor or an insurance company, are all common examples of disclosures made with the consent of the patient. In such instances, the patient must be well aware and fully understand the nature of the health professional's obligations to these third parties. For example, patients often do not realise the potential of massive disclosure when they authorise the release of their personal health information to the insurance industry. Although it might be argued that it cannot be expected that a health professional has the duty to warn the patient of the potential of massive exposure, at the very least the health professional must be certain that the patient knows exactly what he or she is doing when signing the release.

Release of confidential medical information to family or relatives

It is often thought that in circumstances where the adult patient is unable to give consent, for example where the patient is unconscious or has a mental disability that a health professional is entitled to approach relatives or family to consent to disclosures on behalf of the patient. This is not a justification recognised in law, unless the patient has appointed that relative as his agent and given him that authority (to make confidential disclosures). Before a health professional reveals confidential information to relatives or seeks consent from relatives to disclose confidential information, that health professional must be certain that the relative has the legal authority to receive such information or authorise such disclosure.

In the English case of *In the matter of S (Hospital Orders: Court's Jurisdiction)* [1995] 3 All E.R. 290, it was held that blood ties conferred no right to determine the course of treatment or care. It would seem to be a logical step therefore to apply the same principles in respect of confidential information. If family members have no right to determine what treatment the patient is to receive, on what basis would they need to know confidential information or authorise its disclosure?

It follows that an adult patient is entitled to withhold information of his or her condition from partners, relatives and friends. In some cases, even an acknowledgement that a patient is on a particular ward, for example the maternity or psychological ward, will amount to an unauthorised disclosure, as it will inform the third party as to the nature of the patient's condition or illness.

Telephone protocol

Nurses are placed in extremely awkward positions in situations where spouses, partners, relatives or friends request reports or information on a patient, as it is not clear whether the patient has consented to the release of such information. Hospitals should protect nurses and any other health professional in a similar predicament by establishing firm procedures for dealing with telephonic enquiries and front-desk/reception enquires.

When met with a telephonic enquiry, the nurse or other health professional should take the caller's name and number and promise that the caller will be contacted after the hospital records have been checked. Thereafter the nurse should approach the patient and explain the nature of the call. If the patient is agreeable that contact be established with the caller, if possible a telephone should be made available to the patient so that he or she can make the return call, rather than the health professional.

If the patient refuses to allow any information to be disclosed about his or her condition or whereabouts, the matter should be handed over to the hospital authorities or administration. The nurse cannot be expected to shoulder the burden of returning the call and attempting to deceive the caller by stating that the patient is not present in the hospital.

The basic principles of patient confidentiality cannot just be ignored because there are family or friends involved. Clearly the usual requirements for true consent are required. The consent to disclose to partners, family or relatives must be informed consent, it must be freely given, and the patient must have the requisite capacity to understand the implications of the consent.

Constitutional implications

Some questions might be raised about this approach of effectively excluding the family on the instructions of the patient, in the context of the Irish Constitution, with Article 41 expressly stating that it: 'recognises the Family as the natural primary and fundamental unit group of Society'. It is the law of Ireland that the rights guaranteed by Article 41 are recognised as belonging not to individual members of the family, but rather to the family unit as a whole. These rights may be invoked by an individual member on behalf of the family as a whole, but they 'belong to the institution in itself as distinct from the personal rights which each individual member might enjoy by virtue of membership of the family' (*per* Costello J. in *Murray v Ireland* [1985] I.L.R.M. 542 at 547).

Although the courts have upheld the interests of individual members when they appeared to be in conflict with the interests of family unity, this has been in circumstances where the conduct of one member of the family in committing a wrong against another member of the family was seen as an attack on the family itself. So for example, in *DPP v JT* [1988] 3 Frewen 141, a father was charged with the sexual abuse of his daughter, and the mother testified against the father. The father argued that the practice of allowing a wife to testify against her husband was an attack on the constitutional integrity of the family. The Court of Criminal Appeal held that where the offence charged was an attack or an injury on the family itself, then its constitutional duty was to protect the family from such attack, even where the attack was carried out by an individual member of that family.

Could one argue that the interests of the family to know about the condition of one of its members outweighed the interests of the individual member to keep the information from the family? On the other hand, could one argue that the greater good of society (of which the family is the basic unit) is best protected where confidentiality is enforced even against family members?

These are hard questions, but it must be argued that the courts should uphold the interests of individual privacy, even against other family members, on the basis that confidentiality is an essential ingredient of a successful healthcare system.

On the practical side, how can nurses be expected to determine if the caller is a threat to that patient (which would mean that the caller would fit the requirement of being an attacker of the family unit)?

Nurses (or their unions) must therefore insist that their employers establish and implement a protocol in relation to telephonic and reception/front-desk enquiries. This protocol will not only protect the patient, but also the nurse.

Release of confidential medical information to third parties

In its *A Guide to Ethical Conduct and Behaviour and Fitness to Practice* (6th edition, 2004), the Irish Medical Council (IMC) instructs the medical profession that disclosure of clinical details from a patient's medical records, as in the preparation of a medical report for an employer or an insurance company, should only occur in the event that the patient consents to such disclosure while fully understanding the consequences of such disclosure.

Usually a signed consent form should suffice to assure the health professional that it is safe to release details regarding the patient's medical history. The wording of the patient's consent, in the specific case of preparing a medical report for an insurance company, should be along the following lines:

> 'I consent to the company seeking medical information from any doctor who at any time has attended me concerning anything which affects my physical or mental health or seeking information from any insurance office to which a proposal has been made for insurance on my life and I authorise the giving of such information.'

In England, this situation is governed by the Access to Medical Reports Act 1988, which came into force on 1 January 1989. This Act allows the patient to retain some control over the report even after it has been released and also to check the report before it is released. The provisions of this Act are examined in a later chapter. There is clearly a need for similar legislation in Ireland.

Consent to Disclosure: Summary

1. Consent by the patient to disclosure must be informed consent. In other words, the patient must give the consent freely and with full knowledge of the foreseeable consequences of that disclosure.
2. Consent may be express or implied but it is better practice for a health professional to explain to the patient the need for disclosure and thereafter obtain the patient's express consent.
3. Spouses, partners, family or other relatives do not have an automatic right to access confidential information about a patient. The patient must authorise disclosure to these people, and similarly the patient is entitled to prohibit disclosure to some or all of these people.
4. Hospitals should protect nurses and any other health professional by establishing firm procedures for dealing with telephonic enquiries

and front-desk/reception enquiries about patients.
5. The position involving disclosure to other third parties, like employers or insurance companies, is clear. It may only be done with the express consent of the patient, and this consent should be in writing and recorded.
6. Useful websites:
   a. *Medical Council of Ireland* (http://www.medicalcouncil.ie/_fileupload/standards/Ethical_Guide_6th_Edition.pdf).
   b. *Bionet* (http://www.bionetonline.org).

23

EXCEPTIONS TO THE DUTY OF CONFIDENTIALITY

> **Learning Outcomes**
> **At the completion of this chapter, the reader should know and understand the following:**
> - The Guidelines issued by both An Bord Altranais and the Medical Council of Ireland.
> - The four established exceptions to the rule of confidentiality.
> - The public interest exception and the difficulties associated with the interpretation of this criterion.
> - The problems associated with the release of information to law enforcement officials.

Important concepts and phrases that are crucial to an understanding of this chapter

Subpoena
A written order issued by a court ordering a person to be present at a specified time and place in order to give evidence (*subpoena ad testificandum*) or give evidence about certain documents that must be brought along by the witness and produced to the court (*subpoena duces tecum*). If the witness fails to attend court at the time and date specified on the subpoena, that person can be arrested for contempt of court, which could lead to a fine or even imprisonment if he or she has no just excuse for not attending.

Parole
A prisoner can be released on parole before serving a full sentence, usually as a reward for good behaviour whilst in prison, or if there are circumstances, which justify an early release. The release is usually subject to strict conditions, for example daily reporting at the local Garda station, and remaining within a particular district. In Ireland, in terms of section 2 of the Criminal Justice Act 1960 and sections 2 and 4 of the Prisons Act of 1970, the Minister has the power to make rules for the temporary release of prisoners.

Introduction

In *The Code of Professional Conduct for each Nurse and Midwife* (April 2000) issued by An Bord Altranais, it is stated that:

> 'Information regarding a patient's history, treatment and state of health is privileged and confidential. It is accepted nursing practice that nursing care is communicated and recorded as part of the patient's care and treatment. Professional judgement and responsibility should be exercised in the sharing of such information with professional colleagues. The confidentiality of patient's records must be safeguarded. In certain circumstances, the nurse may be required by a court of law to divulge information held. A nurse called to give evidence in court should seek in advance legal and/or professional advice as to the response to be made if required by the court to divulge confidential information.'

The Medical Council's *Guide to Ethical Conduct and Behaviour and to Fitness to Practice* (6th edition, 2004) is more specific, and provides that 'confidentiality is a time honoured principle of medical ethics. It extends after death and is fundamental to the doctor/patient relationship'. Clause 16.3 of the Guide provides that there are four circumstances where exception may be made:

> 'When ordered by a Judge in a Court of Law, or by a Tribunal established by an Act of the Oireachtas.
> When necessary to protect the interest of the patient.
> When necessary to protect the welfare of society.
> When necessary to safeguard the welfare of another individual or patient.'

These are exceptions to the duty, and will arise where the patient has not consented to the disclosure.

When required by a judge in a court of law or by statutory tribunal

The health professional and the patient do not enjoy the same protection from disclosure as that enjoyed by the lawyer and client, known as legal professional privilege. This is because the lawyer-client privilege is what is known as an absolute privilege, which as a general rule will not be tampered with, as it arises from a specifically created legal right.

On the other hand, at the most the health professional-patient relationship enjoys what is known as a relative privilege arising from the nature of the contract between the health professional and patient. Both parties to that contract must always obey the law, which means the court will perform its usual balancing act to decide whether disclosure should be allowed or disallowed after weighing up those two competing demands, the public's right to know versus the patient's right to confidentiality.

A health professional can be subpoenaed by a court to give evidence and must do so. Failure to do so could lead to prosecution for contempt of court.

A well-known decision involving these issues is the English case of *Hunter v Mann* [1974] Q.B. 767.

Facts
A driver in a motor accident ran away from the scene of the accident and was subsequently treated by the defendant doctor. The police requested the doctor to provide the name of the driver but he refused, saying that such information had been given to him in confidence. The doctor was charged with failing to comply with a requirement under section 168(2)b) of the Road Traffic Act 1972 to give information which it was in his power to give and which might have led to the identification of the driver of the vehicle who was alleged to be guilty of dangerous driving, contrary to section 168(3) of the 1972 Act. The doctor was convicted of the charge and appealed his conviction.

Section 168(2) read as follows:

> 'Where the driver of a vehicle is alleged to be guilty of an offence to which this section applies ... any other person shall if required as aforesaid give any information which it is in his power to give and may lead to the identification of the driver ...'.

Issue to be decided by the court
Should the doctor be allowed to rely on patient confidentiality, even if this meant that a criminal would escape prosecution? In other words, whilst it was clearly in the public interest to apprehend and punish dangerous driving, was this more important than the need for the patient to know that he could rely on the confidence of the doctor?

Decision of the court
The court confirmed that the doctor was bound to breach confidentiality when required by law or ordered by a court. The court held that:

> 'I accept that the doctor, in accordance with the first proposition,

has no right to refuse to disclose confidential information in the course of judicial or quasi-judicial proceedings; but I also accept that the judge in certain circumstances, and in the exercise of his, the judge's, judicial discretion, may refuse to compel him to do so. Further than this, in my judgment, the authorities which have been cited to us do not go. Moreover each one of those authorities was concerned with legal proceedings. In the present case it is important to bear in mind the distinction between privilege which is to be claimed in legal proceedings and a contractual duty not to disclose; that distinction is marked by a passage in the judgment of Diplock LJ in *Parry-Jones v The Law Society* ([1968] 1 All ER 171 at 180, [1969] 1 Ch 1 at 9):

"So far as the plaintiff's point as to privilege is concerned, privilege is irrelevant when one is not concerned with judicial or quasi-judicial proceedings because, strictly speaking, privilege refers to a right to withhold from a court, or a tribunal exercising judicial functions, material which would otherwise be admissible in evidence. What we are concerned with here is the contractual duty of confidence, generally implied though sometimes expressed, between a solicitor and client. Such a duty exists not only between solicitor and client, but, for example, between banker and customer, doctor and patient, and accountant and client. Such a duty of confidence is subject to, and overridden by, the duty of any party to that contract to comply with the law of the land. If it is the duty of such a party to a contract, whether at common law or under statute, to disclose in defined circumstances confidential information, then he must do so, and any express contract to the contrary would be illegal and void."

Commentary

The law refuses to grant absolute privilege to the communications between health professional and patient and the resultant confidential medical information, as the right to confidentiality arises as a result of the contract between them and not as a legal right in itself (as is the case with the lawyer and client). The issue before the court is whether the confidential information is relevant as evidence to the issues before the court. If it is, it must be revealed. If the information is not relevant to the issues before the court, or if the court can achieve the same objectives without hearing that evidence, the public interest in secrecy will outweigh the need for it to be before the court.

The court will scrutinise and analyse the confidential medical information as it does all evidence, on the basis of its relevance to the issues at hand. If, as in this case, the health professional's evidence is critical and must be heard to allow the court to uphold the needs of justice, its relevance clearly outweighs the need for that information to remain confidential. If, on the facts of the above case, there was any other way to identify the driver without the doctor having to give evidence, the court would have chosen that other way, thereby allowing the medical information to remain undisclosed.

The patient must be informed of the subpoena
If a health professional is subpoenaed to give evidence in court, it must be made clear to the patient that the professional is disclosing confidential information under legal compulsion and the threat of criminal sanction. It is usual practice for the health professional to wait for the subpoena before giving evidence. This will also allow the patient the opportunity to attempt to block the subpoena by approaching the court.

When questioned in court, the health professional should protest at that stage that the information is confidential, and wait for the judge to order the disclosure of the information as evidence relevant to the issues before the court. This will mean that the fact that the health professional is giving evidence under threat of punishment is noted and recorded. If the health professional is later sued for breach of confidentiality, the evidence is there for all to see that he or she was acting under compulsion.

Until 1995, a court order was necessary to force a health professional to release records. This was time-consuming and very expensive, and therefore in terms of section 45(1) of the Court and Court Officers Act 1995, the Superior Courts Committee may make rules requiring any party to a High Court or Circuit Court action involving personal injury proceedings to disclose medical reports to the opposing party without requiring an application to the court.

There are many statutes that order disclosure of otherwise confidential information. The Road Traffic Act 1961 requires any person to give information to the Garda relating to a road traffic accident involving personal injuries. The National Drugs Advisory Board (Establishment) Order 1966 encourages a doctor to report to the National Drugs Board evidence of adverse reactions to drugs administered to patients, but this information is usually rendered anonymous. If the patient's name is requested, strict guidelines are in place to protect the confidentiality of the patient. There are statutory provisions that require the notification to public health authorities of persons known or suspected to be suffering from certain infectious diseases. These are the Public Health Act 1947, and the Infectious Disease Regulations in terms of the Public Health (Control of Diseases) Act 1984.

The Public Health Act requires a medical practitioner attending a patient who appears to be suffering from an infectious disease to notify the medical officer of the district of the name and whereabouts of the patient and the disease. Examples of notifiable infectious diseases include cholera, plague, smallpox and typhus. HIV is not a notifiable disease for the purposes of the Infectious Disease Regulations. In the United Kingdom, provision is also made under the National Health Service (Venereal Diseases) Regulations 1974 (S.I. No.29 of 1974) for contact tracing.

Disclosure in the interests of the patient

Disclosure between professionals caring for the patient is justified where it can be shown that if information obtained by the doctor and relevant to the care of the patient is not passed on to the appropriate professional, the patient will suffer. An obvious example is the patient's history of allergy to certain medication.

As previously discussed, permission to disclose information to other health professionals should be obtained from the patient in advance of the treatment. There might be occasions, however, where the patient has not consented and it is necessary, to ensure that the patient receives the treatment to which he has consented, that such information is imparted to other health professionals on the treatment team. This scenario is essentially a variation of the defence of necessity.

Disclosure to other (non-medical) health professionals

Traditionally, doctors and nurses have not had difficulty over access to the patient's records. Other professionals have encountered problems, for example occupational therapists, physiotherapists, social workers, social carers and other groups have sometimes been refused access to a patient's records on the grounds that it was unnecessary and a breach of confidentiality. This can pose problems, and is difficult to resolve. On the one hand, for the sake of keeping confidence one wants to limit access to the records to as few professionals as possible, but on the other hand, there is a danger that a professional who is caring for the patient, if acting in ignorance of certain facts known only to the doctor and the nurse, could do the patient considerable harm.

It is clear, however, that the disclosure of confidential information to others is justified if it is necessary in the interests of the health and/or safety of the patient (provided the patient has consented to the treatment in question) or the safety of the health professional.

This justification should only be relied upon where it was not possible to attempt to obtain the patient's consent to disclosure. Of course, where the patient has forbidden disclosure, then this exception cannot be relied upon, unless a person other than the patient is placed in danger. This can be very problematic in practice.

What of the situation where the patient has consented to a particular treatment but refuses consent to disclose to any other health professional involved in the treatment? This often means that the patient cannot receive the treatment in question, and the health professional is therefore receiving mixed messages from the patient consenting to the treatment but refusing to allow that treatment to take place. In the ideal situation, the health professional would need to explain this dilemma, and explain that the treatment is only possible if there is full disclosure to others, and thereafter secure the consent of the patient to disclosure on this basis. The practicalities do not always present this ideal situation however.

The other practical problem is that whilst it is easy to state that the patient's refusal to disclose can be overridden where it places a third party in danger, once again the problem of what constitutes 'danger' arises. For example, can a health professional override an HIV-positive patient's refusal to disclose his or her condition to other health professionals when the chances of cross-infection are negligible, particularly if everybody on the treatment team is adhering to universal precautions? Could it not be argued that if everybody on the medical team follows the required health and safety procedures there is no need to disclose the patient's HIV status? Why should the patient's right to confidentiality be breached because somebody on the medical team has not bothered to follow the procedures that are in place and take the proper precautions? On the other hand, some might argue that a breach of patient confidentiality is a small price to pay if it avoids death or serious injury to any person, even a careless person.

The public interest

Whilst the law of confidentiality has drawn on many areas of law and ethics during its creation, its defining quality is that it is ultimately based on the recognition that it is in the public interest that confidentiality is ensured in the health service. Clearly, health professionals must be guaranteed that the public have confidence in them, and this confidence can only be ensured if a patient or potential patient knows that confidential information imparted to the health professional will not be revealed.

At the same time, it must be understood that this obligation of confidence can be modified or even set aside where competing public interests demand disclosure.

The problematic notion of 'serious harm'

There are circumstances which might justify disclosure, without the individual's consent, where the protection of society is regarded as paramount. The concept that is most often used in these circumstances is that of the risk of 'serious harm' to identifiable individuals or to society at large. Confidentiality is too important a principle to be sacrificed for a vague or minor threat, but it should give way where some 'serious' threat to people looms.

Threats of physical harm to people might be seen as more serious than potential damage to property. The risk of an assault, a traffic accident or an infectious disease might be seen as more compelling grounds for disclosure than the risk relating to fraud or theft. Even in an overtly materialist society, it must be hoped that welfare is more important than wealth.

In reality, however, such neat divisions are not entirely satisfactory and in many cases, the harm is multi-faceted, rather than being one-dimensional in its impact. Serious fraud or theft involving public health resources, for example, would be quite likely to harm individuals awaiting treatment. Even comparatively minor prescription fraud may reveal a serious harm if the forged prescriptions are for controlled drugs.

Health professionals are always encouraged to view the harm from the viewpoint of the victim of that harm. There are examples of serious crime where everybody would agree that there was justification for disclosure of information to the authorities. These would include murder, manslaughter and rape. However, 'serious harm' goes further than physical damage, and must also include the psychological harm that is often suffered alongside the physical damage. For example, child sexual abuse is often more devastating in its psychological impact than the physical harm suffered, and must be included in the category of serious crime.

Again, these are hard questions, and the health professional needs help and guidance in dealing with these complex ethical issues.

An English case which has provided some guidance in situations of potential public harm is *W v Egdell and others* [1990] All E.R. 835 (C.A.).

Facts
The defendant, a consultant psychiatrist, was asked by a firm of solicitors to prepare a report on a prisoner, who was their client. The purpose of the report was to assist a Parole Board to form an estimate of the prisoner's capacity to be paroled. The prisoner had been convicted of a series of murders (five victims) and a number of assaults. The defendant diagnosed the prisoner (the plaintiff) as a 'paranoid schizophrenic' who was capable of killing again, and the defendant advised the solicitors that it was his considered opinion that the plaintiff should be further detained in a secure unit within the prison. Needless to say, the solicitors did not pursue the parole application on behalf of their client, the plaintiff. The defendant sent a copy of his report to the health authority.

The plaintiff brought an action against the psychiatrist (Dr. Egdell), the health authority, the mental health review tribunal and the Secretary of State for breach of confidentiality. The High Court relied on the General Medical Council's *Advice on Standards of Professional Conduct and Medical Ethics* and refused an injunction against the use or disclosure of the report and dismissed the plaintiff's claim for damages. The plaintiff appealed.

Issue before the court
Should patient confidentiality be breached in order to protect the public from potential harm?

Decision of the court
The Court of Appeal dismissed the plaintiff's claim and held that the balance came down in favour of the public interest in the disclosure of the report and against the public interest in the duty of confidentiality owed to the patient. Unlike the High Court, the Court of Appeal considered that the High Court had inappropriately relied on the General Medical Council's rules as the defendant did not have clinical responsibility for the prisoner, as the solicitors commissioned him. The Court of Appeal quoted Article 8(2) of the European Convention on Human Rights which permits intervention by a public authority in the duty of professional secrecy in the interests of public safety and the prevention of crime, and held that the same considerations had justified the actions of the defendant in disclosing his report.

The court quoted with approval from the House of Lords judgment in *Attorney General v Guardian Newspapers Ltd (No 2)* [1988] 3 W.L.R. 776 at page 807:

> 'Although the basis of the law's protection of confidence is that there is a public interest that confidences should be preserved and protected by the law, nevertheless that public interest may be outweighed by some other countervailing public interest which favours disclosure.
>
> ...
>
> It is this limiting principle which may require a court to carry out a balancing operation, weighing the public interest in maintaining confidence against a countervailing public interest favouring disclosure.'

Commentary
The reason why this question of public interest causes so much difficulty is that the public need to know that confidentiality relating to medical

treatment or related healthcare is assured. If the public believes that confidentiality is not guaranteed it will avoid seeking medical treatment, it will avoid revealing necessary information to the person attempting to treat and hopefully cure them, and it will cease to hold the health profession in trust. These can all have disastrous consequences and are the reasons behind the emphasis on the need for confidentiality.

On the other hand, that same public might be harmed if certain facts are not revealed.

The task of the courts is to recognise both of these interests as being in the public good. When these interests compete, however, the court will perform the balancing exercise to decide which interest must have preference over the other. This would be determined by the particular facts at hand, coupled with questions of policy. For this reason, it is difficult to formulate clear guidelines and the law is somewhat confused, and confusing, in this area.

While it is clear that risks of harm to the public might be sufficient to justify disclosure of confidential information, there are no clear guidelines as to what constitutes 'a real risk of consequent danger to the public' (Bingham J. in *Egdell*) sufficient to justify disclosure in the public interest. As was previously discussed, it is dangerous to limit the harm to physical harm, as this would rule out psychological harm in many instances where such harm might be far more serious than the related physical harm, if any. Using phrases like 'real and obvious danger' or 'immediate danger of harm' is similarly dangerous, as these involve a clearly subjective element.

A duty as opposed to a right?

When discussing disclosure in the public interest, the basis of the debate usually rests on the assumption that a health professional is asserting a right to disclose in circumstances where it would be in the public interest to do so. What is clear is that the choice lies with the health professional who must thereafter be able to defend his or her decision to disclose, as an exception to the general duty of confidentiality.

What of the situation where the danger to society would seem so obvious, even certain, that the health professional is no longer burdened with a dilemma whether to disclose or not, but rather (it could be argued) has a duty to disclose? Can there ever be such a compelling circumstance to create this duty?

Situations that spring to mind are where a patient threatens to harm an identifiable third person, or where a patient has the potential to threaten the life of a third party (for example the HIV positive patient who refuses to disclose this fact to his or her sexual partner) or where a patient poses a risk of harm to society at large as opposed to an identifiable third party (for example where a patient has a highly contagious disease and refuses to be quarantined).

An American case which dealt with these complex issues was *Tarasoff v Regents of the University of California* 131 Cal. Rptr. 14(1976) (California Supreme Court).

Facts
The patient of a psychologist threatened to attack and kill a girl who had rejected his romantic advances. The psychologist did not warn the girl or her parents and the patient subsequently killed the girl as he had threatened.

Issue before the court
Should the psychologist have breached the duty of confidentiality to warn the victim or those who could have protected her?

Decision of the court
The court found that the psychologist could be found liable in negligence for failing to warn of his patient's intention to kill a named victim. The court did recognise the competing interests at stake:

> 'We recognise the public interest in supporting effective treatment of mental illness and in protecting the rights of patients to privacy, and the consequent public importance of safeguarding the confidential nature of psychotherapeutic communication. As against this interest, however, we must weigh the public interest in safety from violent assault.
> ...
> The open and confidential character of psychotherapeutic dialogue encourages patients to express threats of violence, few of which are ever executed. Certainly a therapist should not be encouraged routinely to reveal such threats ... (but) his obligations to his patient require that he not disclose a confidence unless such disclosure is necessary to avert danger to others, and even then that he do so discreetly, and in a fashion that would preserve the privacy of his patient to the fullest extent compatible with the prevention of threatened danger.
> ...
> The therapist's obligations to his patient require that he not disclose a confidence unless such disclosure is necessary to avert danger to others".'

The court continued to say that this situation was changed when there was a real risk of physical harm to an identifiable third party.

'If the exercise of reasonable care to protect the threatened victim requires the therapist to warn the endangered party or those who can reasonably be expected to notify him, we see no sufficient societal interest that would protect and justify concealment. The containment of such risks lies in the public interest.'

The conclusion of the court was as follows:

'The revelation of a communication under these circumstances is not a breach of trust or a violation of professional ethics, as stated in the Principles of Medical Ethics of the American Medical Association (1957), section 9: "A physician may not reveal the confidence entrusted to him in the course of medical attendance ... unless he is required to do so by law or unless it becomes necessary in order to protect the welfare of the individual or of the community". We conclude that the public policy favouring protection of the confidential character of patient-psychotherapist communications must yield to the extent to which disclosure is essential to avert danger to others. The protective privilege ends where the public privilege begins ...and we see no sufficient societal interest that would protect and justify concealment. The containment of such risks lies in the public interest.'

Commentary

What the court is saying is that the public would be prepared to sacrifice patient confidentiality in the interests of protecting an identifiable victim against an identifiable threat. Whilst this sounds clear enough, it is very seldom that there is such a clear identification of the victim or the harm to be caused, and it is never definite whether the danger of harm is so compelling as to justify disclosure.

The decision has been applied differently in different jurisdictions within the United States. Some courts have held that the *Tarasoff* decision applies in circumstances where it is foreseeable that there is a threat to the public at large, whilst other courts have held that the *Tarasoff* decision is only applicable where it is possible to identify the particular victim.

The misleading aspect of the *Tarasoff* case is that the facts of that particular case made the decision of the court relatively straightforward, as the threatened party was clearly identifiable. It is highly unusual to have such clear-cut circumstances. When one thinks that the *Tarasoff* case caused huge and prolonged debate, and has been interpreted differently by various American courts, the legal conundrum facing the health professional is apparent.

When faced with a similar decision here, the Irish courts, which have always been slow to impose a duty to act rather than a duty to avoid causing harm, might take a more conservative approach than their Californian colleagues. The courts would be likely to base their approach on the tried and trusted test of foreseeability, with an examination of the likelihood and seriousness of the harm, whether it could be easily avoided or prevented, and the public interest in ensuring that patients who pose a general danger to society would not avoid the rooms of the health professional on the grounds that they had no expectation of confidentiality.

There is an English case dealing with a similar situation that followed the principles of foreseeability in the law of tort. This disturbing case received a lot of media attention at the time, and is *Palmer v Tees Health Authority and another,* The Times Law Reports, 1 June 1998, [1998] Lloyds Rep. 447 Q.B.D.

Facts
A man named Armstrong was born after his mother had an incestuous relationship with her father. His mother sexually abused him during his childhood and teenage years. By the age of seven, Armstrong was deeply disturbed. In 1992 and 1993, during frequent hospital stays after five suicide attempts, Armstrong told nurses that he had sexual feelings towards children and that a child would die if he was released from hospital. The defendants made no attempt to follow up his medical history although he was known to be violent, to abuse drink and drugs and to have been accused of sexually abusing children. He was diagnosed as suffering from personality disorder or psychopathic personality. He was an inpatient until June 1993 and thereafter became an outpatient. He was last seen as an outpatient on 3 February 1994 and failed to attend a further appointment on 5 May 1994.

Armstrong was a neighbour of the Palmer family. On 30 June 1994, Rosie Palmer, aged four, was abducted by Armstrong from outside her home. He sexually abused and murdered her before mutilating her body. He was jailed for life.

As a result of this horrific murder, Mrs Palmer, a 41-year-old nurse, suffered from post-traumatic stress disorder and pathological grief reaction. She lost her job, the care of her other child and attempted suicide.

Mrs Palmer sued for damages in negligence for the death of her daughter and her own psychiatric illness.

Issues before the court
Did the Health Authority owe the murdered victim a duty of care?

Decision of the court
The court held that there was no proximity (i.e. no link) between the actions of the defendant in releasing the patient and the harm caused to the plaintiff as the identity of the victim was unknown to the defendants.

The court quoted from the case of *Caparo Industries plc v Dickman* [1990] 2 A.C. 605:

> 'Thus the postulate of a simple duty to avoid any harm that is with hindsight, reasonably capable of being foreseen becomes untenable without the imposition of some intelligible limits to keep the law of negligence within the bounds of common sense and practicality. Those limits have been found by the requirement of what has been called a "relationship of proximity" between plaintiff and defendant and by the imposition of a further requirement that the attachment of liability for harm which has occurred be "just and reasonable". But although the cases in which the courts have imposed or withheld liability are capable of an approximate categorisation, one looks in vain for some common denominator by which the existence of the essential relationship can be tested. Indeed it is difficult to resist a conclusion that what have been treated as three separate requirements are, at least in most cases, in fact merely facets of the same thing, for in some cases the degree of foreseeability is such that it is from that alone that the requisite proximity can be deduced, whilst in others the absence of that essential relationship can most rationally be attributed simply to the court's view that it would not be fair and reasonable to hold the defendant responsible. "Proximity" is, no doubt, a convenient expression so long as it is realised that it is no more than a label which embraces not a definable concept but merely a description of circumstances from which, pragmatically, the courts conclude that a duty of care exists.'

Commentary
You will remember that when deciding on questions of foreseeability and causation, the courts will introduce questions of policy and equity, even where there is factual causation, in deciding whether on the facts the defendant should be held liable for the harm suffered by the plaintiff. The courts will generally use the tests of foreseeability, fairness and proximity in deciding on questions of policy. In this case, despite the shocking facts before it, the court decided that there was insufficient proximity (closeness of relationship) between the defendant (the Health Authority) and the victim, which made it impossible for the defendant to predict the identity of the victim and when the attack would take place.

As previously mentioned, in regard to the *Tarasoff* decision, what made the facts there somewhat unrealistic is that the health professional concerned knew the identity of the victim before the attack took place. The more likely scenario would be where it was not possible to predict the identity of the victim, and using the usual principles of foreseeability and causation, the courts will have to find that it was not practical to take steps to avoid the harm.

Professional guidelines

Health professionals are able to rely on the guidelines concerning confidentiality as laid down by their respective professional organisations, and the courts have frequently relied on these internal guidelines.

These guidelines for Irish nurses and doctors were quoted at the beginning of this chapter.

As regards confidential patient information, the Medical Council's Guide lists the obligations that the doctor owes his or her patient. These principles apply equally to nurses:

- The doctor must ensure that his or her patient's medical records are protected from improper disclosure while in his or her possession or filed in his or her records.
- If the patient consents to disclosure, the doctor must ensure that the patient fully understands the potential consequences of the disclosure, including what will be disclosed, the reasons for the disclosure, and the consequences of giving consent. The release or disclosure of this confidential information must be in accordance with the terms of the patient's consent, and should not be seen as *carte blanche* to distribute the details freely.
- The patient must be informed when disclosure is to be made to other health professionals and the patient must be made to understand the importance of teamwork in modern medicine. At the same time, the doctor who is disclosing the information to fellow health professionals must ensure that these professionals themselves understand the need for confidentiality and that they adhere to the duty of confidentiality placed upon them.
- Finally, the Guide recognises that there will be situations of emergency where it is not possible to obtain the patient's consent to disclosure, but the Guide makes it clear that disclosure must be limited to only what is absolutely necessary in the circumstances and only on condition that the disclosure is in the best interests of the patient.

Release of confidential medical information to law enforcement officials

There are a number of statutes that state that a citizen, including the health professional, is obliged by law to provide the Garda Síochána with information, and these statutes have been discussed earlier.

What of the situations not covered by any specific statute, where the health professional is either witness to a crime or is in possession of information that could lead to the apprehension of a criminal? The obvious example would be staff in the Accident and Emergency ('A&E') ward who treat a person with injuries consistent with an attack. The Garda arrive asking questions about a suspect involved in a fight ending in fatality, or perhaps where they are seeking a suspected rapist who was injured by his victim in her attempts to defend herself.

Officially, medical records and human tissue or tissue fluid that has been taken for the purposes of diagnosis or medical treatment and which a health professional holds in confidence are subject to special procedures, and application would need to be made to a District Court for a warrant ordering the health professional to produce the documents or body material.

However, on a practical level, staff in the A&E often rely on the assistance of the Gardaí when confronted with violent or aggressive patients, and there is likely to be a good relationship between the hospital staff and Gardaí, which the hospital staff will wish to cultivate.

In such circumstances the health professional would be advised to call the medical officer in charge of the A&E who could determine whether the Gardaí were in possession of a fairly detailed description of the suspect. If this description narrowed down the potential number of patients where it would be possible for discreet screening of these potential suspects, this might be the compromise that would be acceptable to society and achieve the balance that is usually the function of the courts. At the same time, under no circumstances can a health professional allow unrestricted access to all confidential information along the lines of a 'fishing expedition', or allow the removal of documents like the admissions register.

Of course, on an official level, there is no duty on the health professional to be an informer, and he or she could insist that the proper statutory procedures are followed and that a search warrant is obtained.

Even if a search warrant was obtained, it is doubtful that the court issuing such warrant would allow unrestricted access, and the court would stipulate guidelines and limits on the authorised search.

Exceptions to the Duty of Confidentiality: Summary

1. The recognised exceptions to the duty of confidentiality are instances where the law recognises that the public interest in disclosure outweighs the public interest in confidentiality.
2. These recognised exceptions are as follows:
    a. When required by a court of law or by a statute.
    b. When necessary to protect the interests of the patient.
    c. When necessary to protect the welfare of society.
    d. When necessary to safeguard the welfare of another individual or patient.
3. The function of the courts is to attempt to weigh up the competing public demands in the form of confidentiality as a foundation of the healthcare system on the one hand, and the right of the public to have access to information that concerns them on the other. The decision made by the court is a result of this balancing exercise based on the facts before the court.
4. These decisions can be accurately forecast where the facts are relatively straightforward and the danger and/or the potential victim of that danger are capable of identification. Unfortunately, this is not always the case, and it is impossible to formulate hard and fast rules in this regard.
5. Unlike the lawyer and client, a health professional cannot claim absolute privilege from revealing communications with patients. If a health professional is subpoenaed to give evidence in a court of law concerning communications with a patient or concerning the contents of medical records, he or she cannot lawfully refuse to reveal these if ordered by the court to do so.
6. Useful websites:
    a. *Royal College of Nursing* (http://www.rcn.org.uk/publications/pdf/confidentiality.pdf).
    b. *American Medical Association* (http://www.ama-assn.org/).

24

MEDICAL RECORDS AND THE COMMON LAW

> *Learning Outcomes*
> At the completion of this chapter, the reader should know and understand the following:
>
> - The basic principles governing ownership of medical records.
> - The basic principles governing access to medical records.
> - The practical difference between the Canadian and English approaches to the question of access.

Important concepts and phrases that are crucial to an understanding of this chapter

Common law
The common law is like a legal version of stew – it is a well-stirred mixture of all sorts of tasty bits, like unwritten rules, customary practices and judge-made law. It is originally English in character, with the tag 'common' arising from the fact that it was common to the whole of England and Wales after the Norman conquests. Much of the common law of Ireland is identical to that of England, because Ireland was the first country colonised by the Normans after they settled in England, in the eleventh century. Historically the common law accounted for the vast bulk of the law and it remains an important source of law.

Common law is often referred to as case law, but this is not strictly correct. Although most of it does arise from court decisions as opposed to statutes, some very important ingredients of this legal stew came from other sources, custom and equity being the obvious alternate sources.

Countries with common law systems (as opposed to codified systems, where all law is written down in order for it to be law) are usually ex-English colonies, for example South Africa, Zimbabwe, Canada, Australia, New Zealand, Sri Lanka, and India. Although these countries have gone on to create a legal system with features unique to that country, the common law origins of each legal system means that it is possible for courts to seek guidance and be influenced by the law of other countries when their own law is silent on a particular matter. Although Irish law is hugely influenced by English law, our courts can also seek guidance from the judgments of these other countries, Canada and Australia being the obvious choice, when there is no Irish precedent on a specific topic. In this way Ireland can develop its own jurisprudence, rather than simply imitating English law.

Proprietary
A proprietor is a person who has title to property – for all intents and purposes the owner of that property. When speaking about a proprietary right the law is speaking about a person's title to something, in this case the patient's title to his or her medical records.

Introduction

The keeping of up-to-date and accurate medical records is part and parcel of good clinical care. A patient's file must be able to provide a comprehensive history and medical prognosis, a record of the patient's past and present medical treatment, and records of, and references to, any external sources, like second opinions or specialist reports.

Although it is generally accepted practice that a patient should be allowed to access his or her medical records, this practice is largely ethically based, and is seen to be part of the exercise of discretion by the health professional concerned. Problems might arise where a patient claims access to the medical records as a right in itself.

The most obvious basis for a patient's claim to a right of access would be based on the patient's proprietary interest in the medical records.

Ownership of medical records under the common law

Under the common law, the issue of access and disclosure is governed by ownership of the medical record. It would be fair to say that, as a general rule, ownership of medical records is determined by ownership of the material on which the records are stored. In other words, ownership of the paper, or other recording medium, on which the medical record is written or stored, is the same as ownership of the medical record itself.

This is clearly a very clumsy way of dealing with the question of ownership, and the only real advance in this basic principle is that the common law now distinguishes between 'private' and 'public' patients.

In medicine, there are two categories of patient: private and public, and the question of ownership of medical records differs between these two groups.

Private patients

For private patients, ownership of the records is dictated by the contract between the health professional and the clinic/medical institution/hospital. In the absence of any other agreement, ownership must remain with the institution.

On the other hand, if the contract between the health professional and the institution says that the health professional becomes owner of the medical records and is entitled to transfer ownership, the proprietary status of that medical record depends on the relationship between that health professional and the patient.

If the contract is between the patient and the institution, the law is confused, but it is likely that a court would imply a term in the contract vesting ownership in the institution, be it a hospital or clinic.

Where the contract is between the doctor and the patient, ownership will be implied by the court from the term of the contractual agreement.

In both of these scenarios, the ownership of the medical record by the institution or health professional will be limited only to the extent that patient is entitled to access for treatment purposes, whether this is as a result of transferring to another clinic or health professional, or for the purposes of obtaining a second opinion. In this scenario it is really another institution or health professional that is given access to the medical record, as opposed to the patient in a personal capacity.

Public patients

With regard to public patients, the position in Ireland is far from clear. In England, it is established that the medical records are the property of the NHS, as they are usually compiled on forms supplied by the NHS, although the provisions state that the records are the property of the NHS even where the health professional uses his or her own paper.

Accordingly, the NHS provisions have attempted to clarify any confusion that might be caused by the somewhat vague common law.

In Ireland, it is difficult to say with any certainty where the ownership of medical records lies. The question of medical records seems to be dominated by issues relating to access, which are in turn determined by the Data Protection Act 1988 as amended by the Data Protection (Access Modification) (Health) Regulations (S.I. No.82 of 1989) and the recent Data Protection Act 2003 ('the Amendment Act of 2003'). There seems to have been little consideration given to the actual question of ownership.

Under S.I. No.82, access to health data is governed by the health professional acting as data controller (sections 4(1) & 4(2)). If the data controller is not the health professional, then the data controller needs to consult with the health professional, which would appear to suggest that the control of the records is vested in the health professional. Accordingly, the Irish statutory law does not establish ownership, but rather concentrates on the question of control. This is highly unsatisfactory from a legal perspective.

Access to medical records under the common law

The question of ownership of medical records in Irish law is confused. It is therefore necessary to determine if there is clarity in Irish law regarding access to medical records. As previously mentioned, questions of access are regulated by the Data Protection Act and S.I. No.82. The statutory law will be examined in the next chapter. Our understanding of the statutory law will perhaps be improved if we first consider the common law, as hopefully we can identify the gaps in the common law that the statute supposedly sought to clarify.

The common law adopts a more flexible approach to the question of patient access to medical records, and raises two distinct issues on this matter. Firstly, whether a patient's medical records prepared by the health professional were the property of the health professional or the patient and secondly, if the records belonged to the health professional, what rights of access did the patient possess in regard to his medical records?

With regard to the first issue, as previously discussed, the law seems to be reasonably certain that the records belong to the health professional or to the employer of the health professional. They do not belong to the patient.

However, with regard to the second issue, the common law is far from clear.

If one were to describe the nature of the relationship between health professional and patient, it could be convincingly argued that such a relationship is in essence a fiduciary relationship.

By a fiduciary relationship we mean a relationship which is based on trust and confidence, and where one party gains no undue advantage over the other. It would seem to be self-evident that the relationship between a health professional and patient is exactly that.

Medical records contain information about the patient that is revealed by the patient, and that information is acquired and recorded on behalf of the patient. In other words, the patient is the primary source of the record, and records would not be possible if it were not for the disclosure by the patient in the first place.

What is of even more importance is the fact that the records consist of information that is highly private and personal to the patient. It is information that goes to the personal integrity and autonomy of the patient, being secrets about their state of mind or body. Therefore the law recognises that such information remains in a fundamental sense that of the patient, for the patient to communicate or retain as he or she sees fit, as such information is essentially part of the patient's being.

Therefore, as a starting point at least, it might be argued that the patient retains the right to control access to the information and the use and disclosure of such information. While the common law has not given the ownership of the medical records to the patient, it has vested in the patient the right to control those records.

It could therefore be further argued that in the event of the health professional refusing a patient access to the medical records, the onus is on the health professional to justify the decision on the basis of professional medical judgment.

This has been the approach adopted by the Canadian courts, and it is suggested that Irish courts should do the same.

The Supreme Court of Canada in its decision of *McInerney v MacDonald* (1992) 93 D.L.R. (4th) 415 has recognised a common law right of access.

Facts
The patient sought access to her medical records when she discovered that she had been prescribed medicine by previous doctors that was in fact unnecessary. Her current doctor gave her copies of all the notes and reports that she herself had compiled, but refused to give the patient access to the reports in the patient files from her previous doctors, arguing that it would not be ethical for her to release the reports of other doctors.

Issue before the court
Did the patient have a right of access to her entire medical file, or just the records generated by her current personal physician?

Decision of the court
The Supreme Court of Canada confirmed that a patient has no proprietary interest in his or her medical records. However, the court found that the patient had a right of access to all the reports and records contained in her file, including those compiled by health professionals other than her personal doctor. The court held that the relationship between patient and health professional was fiduciary in character. This in turn created a duty upon the health professional to grant access to the information that the health professional relies on in deciding what treatment to choose, and what medicines to administer.

'In characterizing the physician-patient relationship as "fiduciary", I would not wish it to be thought that a fixed set of rules and principles apply in all circumstances or to all obligations arising out of the doctor-patient relationship. ... That being said, certain duties do arise from the special relationship of trust and confidence between doctor and patient. Among these are the duty of the doctor to act with utmost good faith and loyalty, and to hold information received from or about a patient in confidence. (...) When a patient releases personal information in the context of the doctor-patient relationship, he or she does so with the legitimate expectation that these duties will be respected.

The physician-patient relationship also gives rise to the physician's duty to make proper disclosure of information to the patient; ... . The appellant concedes that a patient has a right to be advised about the information concerning his or her health in the physician's medical record. In my view, however, the fiducial qualities of the relationship extend the physician's duty beyond this to include the obligation to grant access to the information the doctor uses in administering treatment.

...

The fiduciary duty to provide access to medical records is ultimately grounded in the nature of the patient's interest in his or her records. As discussed earlier, information about oneself revealed to a doctor acting in a professional capacity remains, in a fundamental sense, one's own. The doctor's position is one of trust and confidence. The information conveyed is held in a fashion somewhat akin to a trust. While the doctor is the owner of the actual record, the information is to be used by the physician for the benefit of the patient. The confiding of the information to the physician for medical purposes gives rise to an expectation that the patient's interest in and control of the information will continue.

...

Rather than undermining the trust inherent in the doctor-patient relationship, access to medical records should enhance it. Indeed, H. E. Emson observes that the practice of giving patients their own records "has been said to improve patient understanding, cooperation and compliance"; see *The Doctor and the Law: A Practical Guide for the Canadian Physician* (2nd ed. 1989), at p. 214. In this sense, reciprocity of information between the patient and physician is *prima facie* in the patient's best interests. It strengthens the bond of trust between physician and patient which, in turn, promotes the well-being of the patient.'

Commentary
The Canadian approach to medical records is that whilst the physical record belongs to the health professional, the information it contains is only there because the patient has confided in that professional, and therefore the content of the file is the patient's.

The English courts have not adopted the same approach. They have held that although the confidential clinical information imparted by the patient did belong to him or her, the medical interpretation of the information received and subsequent diagnosis was the doctor's own professional input to which the patient makes no effective contribution. Consequently the patient does not possess any proprietary claim to the records or to the information stored in the records. The English courts have held that the patient's right to access is based on the health professional's duty to act in the patient's best interests at all times. Therefore access and disclosure would only be justified if made to a fellow health professional who observed a similar duty of confidentiality, or if the patient consents to the preparation of a medical report for his or her solicitor for the purposes of litigation. The patient could be denied access to the records if there was a perceived threat to the patient's physical or mental health in the opinion of the health professional concerned.

The decision which best illustrates this approach is the Court of Appeal decision in *R v Mid Glamorgan Family Health Services Authority, ex parte Martin* [1995] 1 All E.R. 356 (CA).

Facts
The patient sought access to his medical records as he wished to discover details about his previous psychiatric treatment, claiming that this would help him come to terms with his current condition. These requests were refused, primarily on the grounds that this would be detrimental to his best interests.

Issue before the court
The Court of Appeal declined to consider whether a patient has an absolute right of access to his or her medical records. The court held that the question before it was whether a health professional was entitled to deny access where that health professional was of the opinion that disclosure was not in the best interests of the patient.

Decision of the court
The Court of Appeal expressly rejected the approach of the Canadian Supreme Court, and rejected the notion that the relationship between a health professional and patient was fiduciary in nature, as this approach

had been previously rejected by the House of Lords in *Sidaway* (where the court had rejected any comparison between the solicitor-client relationship and the doctor-patient relationship).

The court confirmed that access to medical records could be denied where it was in the best interests of the patient to do so. Although the Health Authority did not have the right to deal with a patient's medical records as it chose, it did have the right to deal with the records in the best interests of the patient.

Commentary
Many would argue that the approach of the English courts will encourage medical paternalism, namely that only the health professional can decide what is good for the patient. The court seemed to be more concerned with the need to clarify the health professional's right to deny access than to decide on the patient's right to access.

It is suggested that the Canadian approach is to be preferred to the English approach, and it is hoped that the Irish courts will follow the lead taken by the Canadian courts. Some would argue that the English approach undermines the special nature of the relationship between a health professional and patient, which should be based on mutual trust and respect, rather than a relationship akin to the old master and servant relationship – 'I speak, you listen'.

The therapeutic nature of the relationship is enhanced when a patient has full confidence in the health professional, and clearly this confidence must be undermined where the health professional refuses the patient access to his or her own medical file. Accordingly it would usually be in the best interests of the patient to be granted access as of right. Where the nature of the record and the circumstances of the patient are such that the health professional is of the reasonable opinion that the harm caused by the disclosure would outweigh the importance of mutual trust, then disclosure must be restricted. These instances should be extremely rare and where the health professional asserts that the circumstances exist, the onus must be on that health professional to justify that stance.

A question of onus – who must prove?

The real difference between the two approaches is really the question of onus. Both approaches recognise that access is determined by the nature of the relationship, be it fiduciary or ethical. However, where the health professional refuses the patient access to his or her file on the basis that disclosure would not be in the best interests of the patient, in terms of the English approach the patient would need to show that the health professional is wrong to make this finding, whereas under the Canadian approach the health professional needs to justify, in objective therapeutic terms, the decision to refuse access.

One can only hope that the House of Lords will follow the Canadian approach, should the question come before them, despite their approach in *Sidaway*. The Irish courts are not bound by *Sidaway*, and it is hoped that they follow the lead of the Canadian Supreme Court.

The confused position in Irish law

The only reported Irish case to consider the issue of patient access to medical records is that of *Toal v Duignan* [1991] I.L.R.M. 135, which concerned a patient born in the Coombe Hospital in June 1961 and who suffered a condition of the right testicle which was not detected and therefore not treated at the time of his birth. The plaintiff sued the hospital for this oversight and demanded discovery of his medical records. The hospital was unable to produce the records as the plaintiff had last attended the out-clinic of the hospital some twenty-six years before, and the hospital had also relocated in that time.

The court stated that a hospital had a duty to keep proper medical records, but did not elaborate on the nature or extent of this duty. The court did not set out the time period that such records should be kept, nor did it specify the legal duty that was breached if the records were stolen or mislaid. Finally, the court did not consider the right of patient access to the records.

The common law in Ireland is therefore in a state of confusion concerning the issue of patient access to medical records. It is therefore necessary to consider the statutory position, which is examined in the next chapter.

Medical Records and the Common Law: Summary

1. Ownership of medical records at common law is determined by ownership of the recording medium, be it a manual file or computer record.
2. In the UK, a distinction is drawn between private patients and public (NHS) patients, with the question of ownership of medical records in the former category determined by the contract between the parties, and in the latter the records are the exclusive property of the NHS. The situation in Ireland is unclear, with the emphasis being on control of the records, as opposed to ownership of the records. It is likely, however, that the Irish common law position would be the same as the UK were the question to come before the Irish courts.
3. The common law regarding patient access to medical records is also

unclear in Ireland. In England the position is that a patient does not have a right to access, and access is at the discretion of the health professional. The position in Canada is different, with the health professional obliged to grant access to the medical records when asked by a patient, and if the health professional were to refuse access, the onus lies on that health professional to justify the refusal.
4. Furthermore, the English courts have refused to categorise the relationship between health professional and patient as fiduciary in nature, whereas the Canadian courts have categorised the relationship as fiduciary in nature.
5. Useful websites:
   a. *Irish Health* (http://www.irishhealth.com/?level=4&con=546).
   b. *Mater Hospital* (http://www.mater.ie/foi/section15/obtain_info.htm).
   c. *Southern Health Board* (http://www.shb.ie).

25

THE STATUTORY POSITION REGARDING MEDICAL RECORDS: DATA PROTECTION AND THE FREEDOM OF INFORMATION

> *Learning Outcomes*
> **At the completion of this chapter, the reader should know and understand the following:**
> - The Data Protection Act 1988 (as amended by the 2003 Act) and its impact on the question of control of, and access to, medical records.
> - The Freedom of Information Act 1997 and its impact on the question of control of, and access to, medical records.

Important concepts and phrases that are crucial to an understanding of this chapter

Before considering the position of the health professional and the Data Protection Act, it is necessary to become familiar with certain definitions and their specific meaning in the Act.

Data means information in a form, which can be processed, and includes both automated data and manual data. This definition originally limited the application of the Act to electronic (computer) data, which meant that a lot of medical files were excluded from the ambit of the Act. The 2003 Act has attempted to improve this situation.

Automated data essentially means any information on computer, or information in a format that would allow it to be recorded on a computer.

Manual data means information that is kept as part of a relevant filing system, or with the intention that it should form part of a relevant filing system.

Relevant filing system means a traditional filing cabinet full of paper files that, while not computerised, is structured by reference to individuals, or by reference to criteria relating to individuals, so that specific information relating to a particular individual is readily accessible. The 2003 Act has brought this type of data into the material now covered by the Act.

Personal data means data relating to a living individual who is or can be identified either from the data or from the data in conjunction with other information that is in, or is likely to come into, the possession of the data controller. This would clearly include a medical file, but would not include aggregated or anonymous medical information.

Processing means performing any operation or set of operations on data, including:
- Obtaining, recording or keeping data,
- collecting, organising, storing, altering or adapting the data,
- retrieving, consulting or using the data,
- disclosing the information or data by transmitting, disseminating or otherwise making it available,
- aligning, combining, blocking, erasing or destroying the data.

Data Subject is an individual who is the subject of personal data.

Data Controller is a person who, either alone or with others, controls the contents and use of personal data.

Data Processor is a person who processes personal data on behalf of a data controller. It is important to note, however, that an employee of a data controller who processes such data in the course of his/her employment is not regarded as a data processor for the purposes of this definition. This qualification regarding employees could be very significant in the healthcare context, as it could be argued that if a Health Board is the data controller, its employees are not. Again we will see that the 2003 Act has attempted to come up with solutions to this problem.

Sensitive personal data relates to specific categories of data that include categories like a person's race, politics, religion, physical or mental health, sexual history, criminal convictions or the alleged commission of an offence, or trade union membership. In other words, information which is regarded as not only confidential, but could be damaging to the individual if it found its way into the wrong hands.

The legal position in Ireland regarding access to mediacl records as governed by the Data Protection Act 1988

Introduction
The Data Protection Act was originally passed after concerns were raised by various bodies and organisations about the vulnerability of computer records, particularly after the 'hacker' became notorious in America. The other main concern that was raised was along the lines of 'Big Brother is watching you', in other words, the ease with which government agencies could access supposedly private information about citizens.

The impact of the Act

Under the Act, the health professional or health board who controls the electronically stored personal data of a patient is a data controller as defined by the Act and that professional must therefore comply with the provisions of the legislation and register with the Data Protection Agency. It is unlawful to disclose data to a person or institution not specified in the registration entry (See section 19(2)). When giving access to a person that is specified in the entry, the health professional must do so always subject to the common law duty of confidentiality. In essence this means that the right of access is subject to the medical judgment of the health professional (which is similar to the paternalistic approach followed in England).

The Act obliges health professionals and other data controllers to comply with certain basic data protection principles and ensure that personal data is accurate. Data must only be used for specified and lawful purposes. Data controllers must take proper security measures to prevent unauthorised access ('hacking') or the alteration, disclosure, or destruction of the data, whether deliberate or accidental.

A weakness of the original Act was that it did not detail what it meant by 'appropriate security measures', but it must be said that it is very difficult to define with any certainty what is meant by that term. The Amendment Act has introduced a new section, section 2C: 'Security measures for personal data', which provides that in determining appropriate security measures for the purposes of the Act, a data controller *may* (not 'must' – in other words, the data controller does not have to do so) have regard to the state of technological development and the cost of implementing the measures, and shall ensure that the measures provide a level of security appropriate to the harm that might result from unauthorised or unlawful processing, accidental or unlawful destruction or accidental loss of, or damage to, the data concerned, and the nature of the data concerned. In addition, the data controller must make sure that his or her employees and agents (a data processor) practice the same security measures when dealing with the personal data in their employment.

The use of the word 'may' rather than 'must' is because not everybody can afford the latest security software and therefore to place a legal duty on people who cannot afford such measures would be to leave them with an impossible choice: buy the software you cannot afford, or close down your business. It must be hoped that the Health Boards and hospitals have installed appropriate security measures like decent firewalls and adequately trained their staff in data security and virus checks and such like. The cost of these security measures is clearly justified when one considers the serious consequences if unauthorised patient information gets into the public domain.

Section 8 sets out the situations where access to information is allowed without the consent of the patient, and this would include the prevention, detection and investigation of criminal offences. Section 8(ii) allows disclosure as a matter of urgency to prevent harm to the patient's health. If the health professional who is the data controller does not obey the principles of personal data protection that are set out in the Act, this would mean that the Act would not protect that person or institution, and there could be liability for an action for breach of confidence.

The Act grants a right to the data subject (the patient) to be informed of the fact that a data controller (the health professional or health board) holds computerised information relating to him or her personally of which he or she is entitled to a copy. If sections of the data are unintelligible, for example the use of medical jargon, the patient is entitled to an explanatory note regarding the use of any technical terms (See section 4(1)(a)(i)-(iii)). One most hope that the test of unintelligibility is determined with reference to the patient, and not to the health professional.

The Act provides that if the data subject (the patient) discovers any inaccuracies and demands that these be remedied, the inaccuracies must be remedied within forty days of the demand, and anybody who has had access to that faulty data in the previous twelve months must be informed of the material modification of the data (See section 6(1)).

The Act contains many examples of medical paternalism. In terms of section 4(8) of the Act, the Minister for Justice is empowered to modify the right of access to personal data concerning physical or mental health should he consider it desirable in the patient's interests. In terms of the Data Protection (Access Modification) (Health) Regulations (S.I. No. 82 of 1989) personal data relating to the physical or mental health may not be supplied to the patient if it is likely to cause 'serious harm'. The health professional is obliged to edit the data in such a way that its release would not cause harm.

As previously mentioned, the original Act only governed computerised records, there was no mention of manual records ('hard copy'), which in practice make up the bulk of medical records in this country, despite the increasing move towards computerised recording. The 2003 Act has attempted to correct this position, as will be seen later.

The Amendment Act of 2003 attempts to extend the existing right of the data subject, which would be the patient in the medical context. In this respect, the new Act provides that more information has to be provided when the data is obtained or in response to an access request. Data controllers who obtain your personal information must inform you of their identity, the reason they are keeping your data, and should also inform you if they intend to pass on the information.

This might have some impact on patients who are asked to provide details by a Health Board, as they will be able to ascertain why the Health Board needs the information and for what purpose the Health Board intends to use the information.

In addition, the new Amendment Act provides that data controllers who have obtained your personal data from someone else must contact you to inform you of the types of data they hold, and the name of the original data controller. This might have a direct impact on patients when health professionals reveal details about patients to other health professionals, as this will at least place an obligation on the receiving health professional to reveal this fact. Again, this might not happen if both health professionals involved in the passing of private medical information are employees of the same health board, as this might make them fall outside the definition of 'data controller' for the purposes of the Act.

Access to manual files – in 2007

The Act is now extended to 'hard copy' files – but only in 2007. Perhaps the most significant improvement is that the definition of 'data' in the Act is now specifically extended to cover manual data in relevant filing systems which are structured by reference to an individual, in other words manual hospital, clinic or practitioner records. As well as providing a copy of personal data held, a data controller must now also describe the types of personal data processed, the purposes for processing, the persons, or categories of persons, to whom the data will be disclosed, the source of the data, unless this is contrary to the public interest, and the logic used in any automated decision-making which is the sole basis for any decision significantly affecting the data subject.

As many medical records are still not on computer, this might have a significant impact on the rights of patients to access their medical records. On the down side, it seems that this part of the Act will only be effective on 27 October 2007 with respect to existing records, but will be immediately effective to newly created manual records. The logic behind this provision is not apparent, and is likely to cause much confusion as a patient will need to show that an entry into a file is 'new' as opposed to 'existing' before the patient can claim access as of right. In addition a patient's file, if they are a long-standing patient, might be partly manual and partly computerised, with the computerised record being 'new', but the manual record closed until 2007. Perhaps a public outcry might speed up the implementation date.

Access to medical opinions

The new Act also provides that where personal data consists of an opinion about an individual, this information may now be provided in response to an access request, without having to seek permission from the person who expressed the opinion, except where the opinion was given in confidence. The Act does not define what is meant by an opinion given in confidence, but it is likely that this will include specialist or second opinions in the field of medicine and health care, and accordingly it would seem that this provision will be of little use to patients seeking disclosure of the entire contents of their medical file.

Sharing of information between health professionals

A final note on the Amendment Act must be to mention the new section 2B, which provides that sensitive personal data shall not be processed by a data controller unless sections 2 and 2A (as amended and inserted, respectively, by the Act of 2003, and which provide that data must be accurate, fair and only kept for as long as necessary) are complied with, and the processing is necessary for medical purposes and is undertaken by a health professional, or a person who in the circumstances owes a duty of confidentiality to the data subject that is equivalent to that which would exist if that person were a health professional. The section continues to define a health professional as including a registered medical practitioner, within the meaning of the Medical Practitioners Act 1978, a registered dentist, within the meaning of the Dentists Act 1985 or a member of any other class of health worker or social worker standing specified by regulations made by the Minister after consultation with the Minister for Health and Children and any other Minister of the Government who, having regard to his or her functions, ought, in the opinion of the Minister, to be consulted; whilst the expression 'medical purposes' includes the purposes of preventive medicine, medical diagnosis, medical research, the provision of care and treatment and the management of healthcare services. This definition is clearly wide enough to include nurses, although why specific mention was not made of nurses is a mystery.

It is difficult to say whether this provision extends the limits of permissible data sharing between health professionals, but the better interpretation is that it does not. That the ultimate test must still be that sharing of information with other health professionals must only be on the basis that it is necessary for the proper treatment of a patient currently in the care of the health professionals concerned.

There is no provision for the destruction of out-of-date records
A provision is needed to make sure that a patient's medical information is destroyed within five years of that patient dying. This is dealt with in the UK in the Access to Health Records Act 1990 (which has been largely repealed except in respect of records of deceased patients). This would protect the deceased patient and his or her estate, and also ease the burden on the medical profession of storing huge quantities of old records.

The Act fails to deal with the question of reports for third parties
Finally, the legislation must deal with the question of preparing reports for third parties. In the UK this is dealt with by the Access to Medical Reports Act 1988, which came into operation on 1 January 1989. It gives a patient a right of access to medical reports prepared by a health professional for an employer or an insurance company. On requesting a medical report concerning a patient, the employer or insurance company is obliged to seek the client's (the patient) consent. The health professional must not supply the report unless the consent of the patient is obtained. The patient is entitled to request access to the medical report before it is supplied to the employer or the insurance company.

The health professional must also allow the patient access to the report in order to check its accuracy and correct mistakes. The health professional has to wait for a period of 21 days after notifying the patient before forwarding the report to the employer or insurance company in the absence of a patient request for access to the report. If the report has already been forwarded to the employer or insurance company, the individual is entitled to access for a subsequent period of up to six months, and the report (or a copy thereof) must be retained by the health professional for at least six months after it has been supplied to the insurance company or employer.

Ireland needs similar legislation as this area is currently regulated by the profession rather than by statute.

The question of onus regarding refusal of access
The Act does contain an exemption from patient access where the health professional is of the opinion that disclosure would be likely to cause serious harm to the physical or mental health of the individual. Unfortunately, the Act does not allocate a burden of proof which would mean that in terms of the English common law, this would be within the discretion of the health professional and the patient would need to show reasons why access should be allowed, which is the English approach, rather than the Australian approach (see Chapter Twenty Four).

Restriction of patient access

Finally, the question of restricted access by the patient needs to be determined to ensure certainty. Particularly, a policy decision needs to be taken, firstly, concerning the question of restricting the patient's right to information on grounds of avoiding serious physical or mental harm to the patient. Secondly, where the doctor does not want to indicate his or her intentions regarding proposed treatment; and thirdly where such access would identify a person who had supplied information about the patient to the health professional, and the informant wishes to remain anonymous.

These are all controversial areas where the accusation of medical paternalism will be made, but these have to be carefully weighed in the light of the health professional's qualifications and insight, and the legal profession must respect the professional competence of doctors and other health professionals. Whilst it is clear that in most instances there is therapeutic value in sharing information with patients, some would argue that there are situations where the health professional must be able to refuse access.

However, it has been previously argued that in these instances the health professional must bear the onus in justifying the decision to bar access, as it is not fair to expect a patient to justify access to his or her own personal information. The Act should spell this out, rather than simply adopting the English approach to access, which is clearly not in line with the new thinking on the therapeutic value of patient autonomy.

Access to information under the Freedom of Information Act 1997 (FOI)

Introduction

The FOI Act was created to allow the citizen access to official information – in other words, information held by state bodies or state-funded bodies. A citizen has the right to ensure the accuracy of information about him- or herself as this could impact on the treatment he or she receives from state departments.

Matters of access and accuracy are relevant to the question of medical records in the possession of a public body, which would usually be the health boards and public hospitals. In the Act, the definition of public bodies includes the Department of Health, the Blood Transfusion Board and the Irish Medicines Board.

The legislation does not deal with medical reports held by private hospitals and clinics.

The crucial position of the CEO

Decisions on access to publicly held records are to be made by the head of the public body and in the case of a patient's medical records it is the Chief Executive Officer ('CEO') of the health board in question. Section 7 makes provision for a legal request for access made by a patient to the CEO. The CEO can refuse this request if it is considered by the CEO that it would be detrimental to the record, infringe copyright, or conflict with a legal duty or obligation of the public body (section 12(2)).

There is also a provision, which would enable a patient to instruct the CEO to correct any personal information, which is incomplete, incorrect or misleading (section 17(1)). The CEO can also refuse this request, but if the CEO does so, a note must be attached to the record stating that an application was made and refused (section 17(4)). Hopefully the note will also provide the reasons for the refusal.

Prohibition of access

Part III of the Act prohibits access to publicly held records used in the deliberation of public bodies, unless it is a factual or scientific report (section 20). Access to publicly held records is also denied on the basis of exemption should it interfere with the proper management of the health board in question (section 21), concerning any records subject to legal privilege (section 22) or refer to any records which are involved in criminal proceedings and which are entrusted to the health board in confidence and from which any individual may be identifiable (section 23). The wide and vague language used in these sections is cause for concern, as it allows the blocking of access to information for very non-specific reasons. It is here that the Office of the Information Commissioner will be valuable, as that office has the power to review decisions by public bodies regarding access to information.

Refusal to allow access to information about yourself

The CEO will deny a third party request for medical records if access would involve the disclosure of personal information (including a deceased patient) (section 28). Where the patient requests information about himself or herself, the CEO may refuse this request if in his opinion he considers that disclosure of such information may be prejudicial to the individual's physical or mental health (section 28(3)). The Act does go on to say, however, that in the event of such a refusal on these grounds, the CEO may allow access to a nominated health care professional who has relevant expertise in regard to the subject matter stored in the medical records (section 28(4)). This section may cause considerable difficulty as it would seem to contradict the provisions in the Data Protection Act and the Regulations, which gives the decision of access to the medical practitioner in question, whereas here the CEO makes the decision. The Act similarly does not define what is meant by a health care professional with relevant expertise in this area – what would happen for example if the patient in question was treated by a team of health professionals, or by both a GP and specialist? Who would decide?

What about independent contractors?
The Act clearly applies to employees, but in the healthcare context there are a number of health professionals who work on a contract for services rather than a contract of service. An obvious example is the GP who contracts with the General Medical Services Scheme, and is therefore an independent contractor rather than an employee. Are the records held by this GP subject to the Act?

A summary of the Act's impact
In summary, it can be said that the Freedom of Information Act will have this affect on the question of patient access to medical records:
- It gives certain patients a statutory right of access to their own medical records.
- Only public patients (whether at GP level or as public patients of a public hospital) can exercise rights under the Act. At present, in the health area, these rights are exercised by way of a request to the relevant health board that provides the service or on whose behalf the service is provided. Voluntary hospitals were directly covered by the Act with effect from 1 September 1999. The Act does not cover the relationship between a health professional and a private patient.
- Medical records can only be made available to a third party with the consent of the patient, except where disclosure of a record is necessary for the protection of a third party or where the release would benefit the patient or where it is decided that the public interest in its release outweighs the privacy rights of the subject. This is essentially a restatement of the common law.
- The Act provides that a record – which is a medical, psychiatric or child-care record – may be refused where, in the opinion of the public body, to release the record might be prejudicial to the subject's well-being. This arrangement mirrors a provision already in the Data Protection Act with the difference being pointed out previously: in that Act the decision-maker is the health professional whereas under the Freedom of Information Act the decision would seem to rest with the CEO.

Access to the records of a child

An area that the Act needs to cover specifically is the question of a parent's right of access to a child's records. Parents do not have an automatic right of access under FOI to the records of their children. In most cases there will be no problem; either the child will have given consent, or is of an age that the consent may be deemed to have been given, or it may be decided that the public interest is best served by the release of the record. What will happen in instances where the child specifically forbids disclosure to parents, or where it is regarded as being contrary to the best interests of the child for disclosure to be made to the parents? It would seem that this scenario will have to be decided along the lines of the English decision of *Gillick*, subject to the constitutional rights of the family and parents.

Conclusion

The Freedom of Information Act has probably created more problems than it solves, particularly with regard to the question of medical records, and there is a crying need for specialised legislation, like the UK's Access to Medical Records Act 1990 and the Access to Medical Reports Act 1988, to govern this area.

On the other hand, it is hoped that patients will not need to rely on the Act to gain access to their medical records. Health professionals must realise that there are many good therapeutic grounds to allowing as much access as possible to their patients.

Data Protection and Freedom of Information Acts: Summary

1. The Data Protection Acts 1988 and 2003 were created to deal with the protection of computer records, although in 2007 this will be extended to include 'hard copy' records, which will be very important with regard to medical records.
2. The Act creates duties that are placed on data controllers to properly manage and protect personal data.
3. The Act fails to deal with the question of destruction of out-of-date records and the supplying of reports to third parties. It is also ambiguous regarding the justification of refusal by a health professional to allow access to a patient of his or her medical records. Specialised legislation is needed to regulate these issues.
4. The 2003 Amendment Act has made a number of improvements to the original Act.
5. The Freedom of Information Act 1997 was created to allow citizens to access information about them held by government or quasi-

government agencies, so as to ensure the accuracy of this information.
6. In the healthcare context, the Act places an enormous amount of power in the hands of the CEO of the Health Board, particularly as regards restriction of access to medical records. The Act seems to contradict the FOI Act in relation to who makes the decision to restrict the access of a patient to his or her own medical records.
7. The Act does not expressly cover the question of a parent's rights to access the medical records of his or her child.
8. Specialised legislation needs to be created that deals specifically with the question of access to medical records.
9. Useful websites:
   a. *Data Protection Commissioner* (www.dataprivacy.ie).
   b. *Office of the Information Commissioner* (http://www.oic.gov.ie).

PART THREE

CRIMINAL LIABILITY

26

THE DISTINCTION BETWEEN THE CIVIL AND CRIMINAL LAW

> **Learning Outcomes**
> At the completion of this chapter, the reader should know and understand the following:
>
> ▸ The important differences between the civil and criminal law with regard to aims, proceedings, proof and sentencing.

Important concepts and phrases that are crucial to an understanding of this chapter

Initiate
To begin or commence something. To initiate proceedings means that a person takes steps to begin the legal process which, if the trial runs its full course, will end in judgment being given for either party to that proceeding.

Pleadings
Printed (or written) documents in a civil action, which are delivered ('served') by the parties to each other, usually alternately and in response to the previous document served by the other side. These pleadings will set out the facts and the law upon which each party will rely on in court.

Summons
A document that is served on the defendant ordering the defendant to attend a particular court on a particular day to answer a specified complaint.

In civil matters heard in the High Court, a summons may be plenary, summary or special. A plenary summons is generally used when there is to be a trial – in other words there will be pleadings and witnesses. A summary summons is used where the proceedings are heard on affidavit (written evidence on oath) without pleadings, usually for a specified (liquidated) sum of money or repossession of land. A special summons is used mainly for probate matters (wills and deceased estates).

In the Circuit Court, civil proceedings are initiated by Civil Bill and Petition, and in the District Court by Civil Process.

Indictment
A written statement which sets out the charges or accusations against the defendant in a criminal trial, and which automatically means that the defendant is entitled to a jury trial.

Arraignment
The procedure that begins the trial of a person charged with a criminal offence (the defendant). The process begins with the name of the defendant being called out in court. The defendant then takes up position at the bar (a box on a raised platform). The indictment is read out to the defendant. The defendant is asked whether he or she understands the charges contained in the indictment. If the defendant confirms that he or she understands, the defendant is asked to enter a plea (in other words, the defendant must say 'guilty' or 'not guilty').

Jury
A group of twelve people who are selected according to certain legal rules, and are asked to make a finding of fact ('a verdict') after hearing the evidence and arguments presented by both sides in a trial. People selected for jury duty must be citizens and must be between eighteen and seventy years of age.

Introduction

Rather than attempt to describe the nature of the criminal process, it is easier to contrast and compare the criminal process with the civil process, in order to understand the essential qualities of the two systems. The nature of the dispute before the court and the mechanisms used in those courts are the obvious differences between the two systems.

Private and public law
Civil procedure involves mainly private law disputes. When speaking of 'private law' one means where the dispute is between two persons acting in their private or personal capacity. The previous part of this book, which dealt with civil proceedings, was always about a dispute between persons (including juristic persons, the concept of which was explained in the previous part). So, examples of private law disputes would be personal injury claims (tort) or claims for breach of contract. Therefore, in private law, the parties themselves drive the proceedings, and the entire process is started by the injured party who initiates the proceedings, which is the legal way of saying 'to get the ball rolling'.

On the other hand, criminal procedure deals with the processing of some activity regarded as a wrong against society or the public in general, and is thus a public law matter. When speaking about the public law, the dispute is between the State (and its powers) on the one hand, and an individual on the other. Apart from the criminal law, other examples of public law would be constitutional law, administrative law, tax law and environmental law. Criminal prosecutions are generally initiated by the Director of Public Prosecutions ('the DPP') or the Garda Síochána, and it is they who 'drive' the proceedings on behalf of the State. It is possible for individuals to initiate private prosecutions in cases where the DPP declines to prosecute, but these are rare.

Compensation and punishment
Generally the purpose of a civil claim is to seek compensation (damages) or some specific relief, like an injunction. Although some aspects of the law of tort are supposed to have a deterrent effect (in other words frighten people off from doing such a thing for fear of the consequences), essentially the aim of civil proceedings is to compensate the victim and place the victim in the position he or she used to be or should be. The money that is awarded will go to the victim as his or her personal property. The victim is the person who drives the civil proceedings as plaintiff, what the law would call a *dominus litis*, which means 'master of litigation'.

The aim of criminal proceedings is to punish wrongdoers. There are many theories about the punishment of crimes, but essentially the four accepted aims of the punishment of criminals is *retribution* (revenge – an eye for an eye), *incapacitation* (imprisonment – removing the criminal from society), *deterrence* (scaring – making people stop committing crime because of a fear of punishment) and *rehabilitation* (repair – making the criminal a better person for the benefit of the wider society). As far as the average person in the street is concerned, punishment is about retribution, but clearly the criminal courts must consider all of these aims when deciding on an appropriate sentence.

When a fine is imposed on a convicted offender, the money goes to the State and not to the DPP in his personal capacity. The victim does not receive the money either, and the victim's involvement in the criminal proceedings is as a witness, and nothing more. It is common to hear about a victim 'laying a charge', but this is incorrect. The victim makes a 'complaint'; but it is the DPP who decides whether to lay a charge after assessing the available evidence. If the DPP is convinced that the charge has no hope of succeeding because the evidence is inadequate, the DPP can decline to press charges, despite the victim of the crime wanting to go on with the prosecution.

The parties
In civil cases we speak of a plaintiff and a defendant, or perhaps applicant and respondent, whereas in criminal cases we speak of the prosecution (cited as 'The People') and the defendant (who used to be known as 'the accused', but that title is no longer favoured). As previously mentioned, in a civil trial the plaintiff and the victim are usually one and the same person, and the plaintiff is the driving force behind the civil action. In a criminal action however, the proceedings are driven by the State, usually in the form of the DPP, with the victim of the crime at the most being a witness, and unable to influence how that criminal case is handled.

The documents used and the initiation of proceedings
In civil proceedings in the High Court, the usual form of initiating document (the document that begins the legal process) is called a Plenary Summons. The Plenary Summons has on it a 'General Indorsement of Claim', which sets out, as briefly as possible, the basis of the plaintiff's complaint against the defendant, and the relief (usually compensation) that the plaintiff is seeking. The defendant enters an Appearance which means he or she informs the plaintiff that the claim will be defended, in other words the defendant intends to oppose the plaintiff. Upon receiving this notice of intention to defend, the plaintiff sends the defendant a far more detailed explanation of his or her case, and this document is called a 'Statement of Claim'.

The defendant will reply to this Statement of Claim by sending a 'Statement of Defence' (often just called a 'Defence'). The plaintiff is entitled to reply to this Defence, by way of a document called a 'Reply'. When the pleadings are closed, the parties can prepare for trial.

As might be obvious by now, there is a lot of paper being exchanged, over quite a long period of time. The collective description for these documents is 'pleadings', and these pleadings make sure that when the parties finally get to court to argue the case in front of the judge, they know exactly what the other side will argue, and so can prepare their opposition in advance.

These are not the only documents in a civil trial, as there is also something called discovery, where the parties exchange lists of the documents they intend to use during the trial; affidavits, witness statements, expert notices (when expert witnesses are used, which is common in medical negligence trials, for example), and so on. A lot of paper changes hands over a considerable time period.

Criminal proceedings, on the other hand, are generally quicker and use a lot less paper. If the crime is not of a very serious nature, a summons is issued which is served on the defendant, calling on him or her to appear at court on such a day to answer the charge that is detailed. When the case comes up for hearing, the judge hears the evidence of the complainant and the defendant and any witnesses there might be, and makes a decision. These are called summary proceedings, as they do not require a jury to hear the matter.

Where the crime is of a serious nature, these are known as prosecutions for indictable offences. These more serious proceedings can still be initiated by a summons, but might also begin with the arrest of the suspect, who is detained and brought to the court. When the defendant first comes to court, he or she will appear in the District Court for what is known as a preliminary examination. At this preliminary examination the defendant is provided with a statement of the charge and of the evidence that the State intends to lead in support of the prosecution. The defendant is also given a list of the witnesses and the exhibits that the prosecution intends to use. At this hearing, both the prosecution and defence can have their witnesses give evidence, which is copied down into the form of a statement (called a transcript) and which is signed by that witness. This sworn transcript of evidence is called a deposition. The defendant may also make a statement that is taken down in writing and can be used as evidence later in trial.

At the preliminary examination, if the judge is of the opinion that the defendant has a case to answer, the case will be sent forward for trial. The defendant will either be returned to jail or released on bail.

If the District Court judge decides to send the case forward for trial, the defendant will receive an indictment from the prosecution, which sets out the offence or offences with which he or she is charged. The defendant is then arraigned before the judge of the Circuit Court or the Central Criminal Court, where the defendant is asked to plead 'guilty' or 'not guilty' to the charges as contained in the indictment.

A jury is selected. The trial begins, with the prosecution calling its witnesses first (and these are cross-examined by the defence lawyer) and presenting its arguments. When the prosecution has completed its presentation, it is the turn of the defendant, who can close the case without presenting evidence, or can do the same as the prosecution – lead the evidence of witnesses (including the defendant if he or she so chooses to give evidence) and these witnesses are cross-examined by the prosecuting lawyer. When all the evidence has been presented, the opposing lawyers deliver a closing argument, the judge instructs the jury (in essence the judge gives the jury a quick law lecture) and the jury is sent off to decide whether the defendant is guilty or not guilty.

As can be seen, there is a lot less paperwork, and the defendant can conduct his or her defence with a minimum of dealings with the prosecution. There is no duty on the defendant to give the prosecution advance warning of what sort of defence he or she will conduct, and the prosecution really have to be ready for any eventuality. The prosecution must compile a Book of Evidence, which contains the statements of the prosecution witnesses and a list of the prosecution exhibits. This must be served on the defendant before the trial, so that the defendant is not caught by surprise, and can conduct a proper defence.

Juries
In criminal cases summary offences are heard by the District Court. A summary offence is an offence which does not entitle the defendant to a trial by jury. This is usually because the offence is regarded as relatively minor (what used to be called 'misdemeanours') or where the defendant has chosen not to have a jury trial (which is permissible in a certain number of crimes). If the defendant is found guilty for a summary offence, the maximum sentence of imprisonment is six months, and the more common sentence is a fine. An example of a summary offence is driving a motor vehicle without insurance.

An indictable offence means that the defendant is entitled to a trial by jury. These are generally heard in the Circuit Court.

The Special Criminal Court is an exception to the rule that serious offences must be heard by a jury. This court was originally set up to hear cases involving paramilitary activity. It was thought that a jury would be exposed to intimidation or worse, and therefore, despite the severity of the offences, there was no jury. The court consists of three judges, with the majority deciding the verdict and sentence. This court has been used in recent years to decide cases which clearly did not involve paramilitary activity, and as a result its continued existence has come under severe criticism, as it is seen as an attack on the constitutional rights of every citizen to be tried by a jury of peers or equal.

There will also be a jury in some civil cases such as defamation and assault cases. However, for the majority of civil cases such as personal injuries actions and family law cases, there is no jury – it is the judge who decides the outcome. This is important in the area of medical malpractice litigation as usually these cases are brought as personal injury cases, which means that there will no jury.

The distinction is based on the consequences of the act
It is not so much the type of wrongful act that distinguishes the civil from the criminal, but the consequences of that wrongful act. If the wrongful act leads to criminal charges, it is governed by criminal law. If it leads to the wrongdoer being sued for damages or having an injunction taken against him or her, or being ordered to perform on a contract, that is governed by the civil law. Therefore it is possible for the same act to lead to both criminal charges and a civil action. An example would be a

negligent driver going through a red traffic light and crashing into another car, causing damage to the car and injuring the passengers. The negligent driver can be charged with the criminal offence of dangerous driving, and can also be sued by the owner of the other car and the passengers of the other car and his own car for damages arising from their injuries.

Intention
In civil law, it is necessary that the person who committed the wrongful act intended to commit the act, but it is not necessary to show that the person intended the consequences of the wrongful act. As a general rule, it is necessary for the plaintiff to show that the defendant committed a voluntary act.

In criminal law, however, it is not only necessary that the prosecution prove that the defendant intended to commit the wrongful act, but also that the defendant intended the unlawful consequences of the act. The physical and mental elements of a criminal offence will be considered in the next chapter.

The evidence and the burden of proof
The final distinction to be made between civil and criminal proceedings relates to the burden of proof, which describes the level of evidence needed to secure a judgement or a conviction. In civil cases, any particular issue as well as the overall question of liability is determined by establishing the issue or the question of liability on a *balance of probabilities*, while in a criminal case all issues and the question of guilt must be proved *beyond reasonable doubt*.

When deciding on a balance of probabilities in a civil case, the crucial question remains whether the version of the party bearing the onus is more probable than not. In a civil case, it is sufficient if the version of the plaintiff is more probable than that of the defendant. This concept has been previously discussed – 'quality is more important than quantity'.

In a criminal case, however, the judge imposes a stricter test in assessing evidence. The judge must be convinced beyond a reasonable doubt that the defendant committed the crime with which he or she is charged. Even where the version of the prosecution is more probable than that of the defendant, this is not sufficient on its own. If the judge has a reasonable doubt about the question of guilt, the benefit of that doubt must be given to the defendant.

Proof beyond reasonable doubt cannot be put on the same level as proof beyond the slightest doubt, because such a high standard of evidence would make the job of the prosecution and the law enforcement agencies impossible. A reasonable doubt is a doubt that exists because of probabilities or possibilities that can be regarded as reasonable on the grounds of generally accepted human knowledge and experience. Where there are no probabilities either way and it cannot be said that the innocent version of the defendant is not reasonably true, then the evidence does not constitute proof beyond a reasonable doubt.

It is not necessary that the judge or the jury should believe the version of the defendant, it is sufficient that it might be substantially true.

In brief, a criminal court or jury cannot convict unless it is satisfied, not only that the defendant's explanation is improbable, but also that beyond any reasonable doubt it is false. If there is a reasonable possibility of the explanation being true, the defendant must be acquitted.

As must be obvious by now, it is difficult to precisely explain what is meant by the phrase 'beyond a reasonable doubt'. Three attempts by three of the greatest judges have been selected, and hopefully they will make things a bit clearer:

Per Denning J. in *Miller v Minister for Pensions* [1974] 2 All E.R. 372 at 373-4:

> '(The evidence) need not reach certainty, but it must carry a high degree of probability. Proof beyond a reasonable doubt does not mean beyond the shadow of a doubt. The law would fail to protect the community if it admitted fanciful possibilities to deflect the course of justice. If the evidence is so strong against a man as to leave only a remote possibility in his favour, which can be dismissed with the sentence "of course it is possible but not in the least probable", the case is proved beyond reasonable doubt.'

Per Kenny J. in *People (A.G.) v Byrne* [1974] I.R. 1 at 9:

> 'The correct charge to a jury is that they must be satisfied beyond reasonable doubt of the guilt of the accused, and it is helpful if that degree of proof is contrasted with that in a civil case. It is also essential, however, that the jury should be told that the accused is entitled to the benefit of the doubt and that when two views on any part of the case are possible on the evidence, they should adopt that which is favourable to the accused unless the State has established the other beyond reasonable doubt.'

Per Walsh J. in *People (AG) v Quinn* [1965] I.R. 366 at 382:

> 'When the evidence in a case, whether it be the evidence offered by the prosecution or by the defence, discloses a possible defence of self-defence the onus remains throughout upon the prosecution to establish that the accused is guilty of the offence charged. The onus

is never upon the accused to raise a doubt in the minds of the jury. In such case the burden rests upon the prosecution to negative the possible defence of self-defence which has arisen and if, having considered the whole of the evidence, the jury is left in doubt whether he was acting in necessary self-defence they must acquit.'

Civil and Criminal Law: Summary

1. The civil and criminal law can be compared according to the consequences of the wrongful act, with the civil law compensating the victim of the wrongful act, while the criminal law punishes the doer of the wrongful act. There is obviously some overlap between these two functions but this is the essential nature of the distinction.
2. Distinctions can also be drawn between the identity of the parties, the nature of the proceedings, the documentation used at the beginning and during the proceedings, the use of a jury, and the type and degree of evidence needed to be successful in court.
3. The function of the victim of the wrongful act is crucial in determining the difference between the two systems. In the civil trial the victim is the initiator and controller of the process, whereas in the criminal trial the victim is no more than a witness, and has no executive or decision-making powers over the process.
4. Useful websites:
   a. *Oasis* (http://www.oasis.gov.ie/) - look under 'Justice'.
   b. *British and Irish Legal Information Institute* (http://www.bailii.org/).

27

ACTUS REUS AND MENS REA

> **Learning Outcomes**
> At the completion of this chapter, the reader should know and understand the following:
>
> ▸ For an act to be regarded as a criminal offence it must have a physical element and a mental element.
> ▸ The physical element is known as the *actus reus*.
> ▸ The mental element is known as the *mens rea*.

Important concepts and phrases that are crucial to an understanding of this chapter

Intention
The purpose or aim of an action. In law the general rule is that a person is presumed to intend the probable and natural and reasonable consequences of his or her actions. As it is a presumption, it is up to that person to prove differently, and if he or she cannot so prove, the intention is taken as fact.

Recklessness
A person is reckless when he or she intentionally creates a risk, where that risk is regarded as being unjustifiable in the circumstances.

Introduction

In simple terms, a criminal act can be described as having a physical element and a mental element.

A crime must always consist of an unlawful (physical) act. Without the unlawful act, there can never be a crime, as you cannot be punished for your thoughts alone. For example, a motorist drives on the right-hand side of the road with the intention of crashing into an oncoming vehicle. The motorist clearly has the mental intention to commit a serious crime. What the driver does not realise is that the road is a double-lane highway and he is entitled to drive in the right-hand lane. The fact that the driver intended to collide with another vehicle does not matter, as his actions are entirely legal. There is no unlawful action, or *actus reus*, which is Latin for 'guilty act'.

An act does not have to be a positive action in order to be an *actus reus*. It can also be a failure to do something. This failure to do something is called an omission – for example, failing to stop when somebody is using the pedestrian crossing.

An act does not make a person legally guilty, unless his or her mind is also legally blameworthy. Lawyers describe this as *mens rea*, which is Latin for 'guilty mind'. What this means is that a person had guilty intent or more precisely, having the intention to commit an act that is wrong in the sense that it is legally forbidden.

As it is often impossible to actually prove the guilty mind of an accused person, the law will often presume or deduce a guilty mind from the actions of the accused person, for example if a person drives at high speed down the wrong side of the road on a dual carriageway, and this caused the death of another, that would be manslaughter, as the driver was so negligent as to be considered to be acting in a way that there was a reckless disregard of danger to the health and welfare of the victim.

We must examine these two concepts in more detail.

Actus reus

One can only speak of a crime once there has been an act that complies with certain requirements.

Firstly, the act must be wrongful, which means it is forbidden or 'proscribed' by law. The definition of the proscription is contained in the definition of the crime in question. The definition of a crime should contain a precise description of the kind of conduct that the law prohibits and seeks to punish. A person cannot be convicted for doing something that was not defined as a crime at the time the act was carried out.

An act can be a commission (a positive action) or an omission (a negative action, or failure to do something). An omission is punishable only if there is a legal duty to act positively, in other words to do something. So for example, there is a legal duty to pay taxes, and a failure to do this is regarded as a wrongful omission, which is punishable by law.

In the criminal law, it is often not only the act that is being punished, but also the result of that act. A person cannot be convicted of murder if there is no proof that somebody died. Therefore the *actus reus* for murder is the beating or stabbing or whatever action was used, and the resulting death. If there was no death, the most a person can be convicted for would be attempted murder.

In exceptional circumstances a mere condition or state of affairs is punishable. For example, it is a statutory crime to be drunk in certain public places, or to be in possession of certain illegal substances. In other words, it is the conduct itself, rather than the result of that conduct, which is being punished.

Secondly, the act must be linked directly ('attributable') to the defendant and not to another person or thing. If the act was committed by a person other than the defendant, the defendant can only be held responsible for that act if he or she incited (persuaded) the other person to do it, or if he or she was acting with a common purpose with that other person (an accomplice). A person can be held liable if he or she acts through the agency of an animal, which is what happens when the animal commits the wrongful act while under the control of the person – for example, instructing your dog to bite somebody might make you liable for a crime, even though you did not lay a finger on the victim.

Finally, the defendant must do the act voluntarily. The act must be one over which the human will exercises control. The defendant must be capable of subjecting his or her bodily movements to his or her control. Therefore the actions of a person carried out whilst asleep or unconscious or during an epileptic attack do not fit into the category of unlawful acts. That person would rely on the defence of automatism, which means acting without conscious control.

Mens rea

Mens rea means a blameworthy state of mind, or a guilty mind. While some people often say that *mens rea* is wrongful intent, this is not accurate, as there are some crimes that do not require specific intent, as will be seen later. Therefore it is better to think of it as a wrongful state of mind.

What the law regards as blameworthy varies from offence to offence.
The purest form of *mens rea* is where the conduct is intentional. Here the defendant intended to perform the wrongful act in order to cause something to happen. The consequence of the intended action was not only foreseen by the defendant, it was desired by the defendant. Crimes requiring intention are the most serious crimes, for example murder. With murder, the defendant must intend to attack the victim, and in so attacking the victim must foresee and desire the death of the victim.

Mens rea may also be in the form of recklessness. This is where the defendant intended to perform the wrongful act, and foresaw the consequences of that act as creating a hazardous risk, but took that risk anyway, although he or she did not desire the results of that act. A well-known crime of recklessness is manslaughter.

A person who kills somebody might be charged with manslaughter where they foresaw that their actions might kill somebody, but nevertheless continued with what they were doing, although they did not mean to kill the victim. For example, a publican burns down the pub of a competitor in order to scare the customers away, and in so doing a number of people are killed. That publican has *mens rea*, as although he intended to frighten people away, he must have foreseen that people could get hurt or killed, but he set the fire anyway and in so doing, consciously took the risk.

Recklessness is a difficult concept to understand as it depends on whether the test is subjective or objective. The subjective test would be that a person is reckless if he or she consciously took an unjustified risk about which the defendant already knew. The objective test says that a person is reckless if he or she consciously took an unjustified risk about which the person did not know but of which he or she ought to have been aware. The Irish courts traditionally favoured the subjective test, but the modern law seems to be drifting towards the stricter objective test.

Finally, *mens rea* may be in the form of negligence. Here the defendant intends to commit the wrongful conduct, but does not foresee the consequences of that conduct in a situation where he or she ought to have foreseen the consequences. This is very similar to the civil concept of negligence, namely behaviour falling below an accepted standard of conduct.

Dangerous driving is an example of a crime by negligence, where the driver might have intended to go quickly but did not necessarily intend to go through the red light, but was going too fast to stop in time. The driver should have realised that his or her excessive speed would make it impossible to stop in a hurry, and therefore can be convicted of dangerous driving even if there was never an intention to go through the red light.

It is sometimes very difficult to distinguish recklessness from negligence, as it would seem to be a matter of degree that distinguishes the two concepts, rather than a fundamental difference of meaning. With recklessness, the law seems to be saying 'you must have seen the risk, but carried on anyway', whereas with negligence the law seems to be saying 'you should have seen the risk before you did what you did'.

Motive

A common mistake is to confuse *mens rea* with motive. This may be a result of too many television shows where the detective always talks about 'means, motive and opportunity' as the unholy triad of crime solving. This might work for the detective, but it is not the law.

A person's motive for committing a crime is legally irrelevant as far as the necessary ingredients for a crime are concerned. A person might rob the rich to give to the poor, and distribute the money to the poor with the purest of motives. That does not mean that the person is not guilty of armed robbery. The necessary *actus reus* and *mens rea* are present, and so the legal definition of a crime is satisfied, and Robin Hood goes to jail for a very serious offence.

Actus Reus and Mens Rea: Summary
1. *Actus reus* means an unlawful act.
   a. The act must be forbidden by law.
   b. The act can be a positive form of conduct (a commission) or a failure to do something where there was a legal duty to do it (an omission).
   c. The act must be done by the defendant personally or by someone that is incited by the defendant or is acting in concert with the defendant, or is under the control of the defendant.
   d. The act must be voluntary.
2. *Mens rea* means blameworthy state of mind, or a guilty mind. What the law regards as blameworthy varies from offence to offence.
   a. It may be intentional wrongdoing as in murder or rape, where the consequences are foreseen and desired.
   b. It may be reckless wrongdoing as in manslaughter, where the consequences are foreseen but not necessarily desired at the time of taking the risk.
   c. It may be negligent wrongdoing as in dangerous driving, where the consequences are not foreseen in circumstances where the law requires foresight.
3. Useful websites:
   a. *Irish Student Law Review* (http://www.islr.ie/).
   b. *Irish Council for Civil Liberties* (http://www.iccl.ie/criminalj/policing/pint93.html).

28
SPECIFIC OFFENCES THAT MAY ARISE IN THE NURSING FIELD

> **Learning Outcomes**
> At the completion of this chapter, the reader should know and understand the following:
> - The Non-Fatal Offences Against the Person Act 1997, and specifically the offence of assault and syringe offences.
> - The offence of manslaughter.

Important concepts and phrases that are crucial to an understanding of this chapter

Provocation
Provocation is a defence to murder and arises where the victim acted in such a way that it caused the defendant to lose control of his thoughts and actions so that he did not know what he was doing (and therefore did not have the necessary intention to murder).

Self-defence
Performing some action (which, in different circumstances, would be unlawful) to protect person or property against an unlawful attack. When used as a defence to a murder charge, the defendant will need to show that he or she used only enough force necessary to protect the person or property under attack. If this necessary force was exceeded, leading to the death of the attacker, the defendant could be guilty of manslaughter, rather than murder, as long as the defender honestly believed that deadly force was necessary in the circumstances. If the defendant knew that deadly force was not necessary to protect the person or property from the attack, but proceeded to kill the attacker anyway, this would be murder, not manslaughter, as intention has replaced recklessness.

Statutory offence
A criminal offence, which is either created as a new offence by the statute, or an existing offence that is modified by statute.

Introduction

It is very seldom that one reads or hears about a nurse being charged with an offence from an incident arising out of his or her duties, but it does happen. It is important for nurses to understand that many of the actions that they perform on patients as a matter of routine are only lawful with the consent of the patient. When the consent is not supplied, the threat of being sued is not the only danger that arises, there is also the danger of the patient laying a criminal complaint.

Criminal law is a huge subject and this chapter will only look at specific offences that are more likely to arise in the nursing context than other types of crime. The subject of drugs will be dealt with separately in the next chapter.

The Non-fatal Offences Against the Person Act 1997

You will remember that in Part Two we considered the tort of trespass to the person, and considered the specific torts of assault, battery and false imprisonment. These three torts have their criminal equivalent, namely the crimes of assault, battery and false imprisonment.

In 1997 the Non-Fatal Offences Against the Person Act was passed, and one of the things that this Act did was abolish the common law offences of assault, battery and false imprisonment, and substitute statutory offences. In addition, the Act created new offences, namely syringe offences; threat, coercion and harassment; and endangerment, all of which were previously unknown to the common law. Finally, the Act codified the existing offences of poisoning, and kidnapping and abduction.

For the purposes of this chapter, offences that are contained in the Act (amongst others) and might be relevant to the area of nursing are considered, namely assault and the syringe offences.

Assault
SECTION 2: Assault

'(1) A person shall be guilty of the offence of assault who, without lawful excuse, intentionally or recklessly—
    (a) Directly or indirectly applies force to or causes an impact on the body of another, or
    (b) causes another to believe on reasonable grounds that he or she is likely immediately to be subjected to any such force or impact,

without the consent of the other.

(2) In subsection (1)(a), "force" includes—

(a) application of heat, light, electric current, noise or any other form of energy, and
(b) application of matter in solid liquid or gaseous form.
(3) No such offence is committed if the force or impact, not being intended or likely to cause injury, is in the circumstances such as is generally acceptable in the ordinary conduct of daily life and the defendant does not know or believe that it is in fact unacceptable to the other person.
(4) A person guilty of an offence under this section shall be liable on summary conviction to a fine not exceeding £1,500 or to imprisonment for a term not exceeding 6 months or to both.'

Commentary
Common law assault was what could be called a 'psychological crime' in that it was committed when the offender made the victim think that he or she was about to be attacked or harmed, whereas battery was the 'physical crime' of touching somebody without consent, for example fondling or punching the victim.

The Act has similarly combined the two in Section 2, and a person would now be guilty of statutory assault if he or she commits either of what used to be common law assault or battery.

The *actus reus* of the crime is the direct or indirect application of force or the causing of an impact upon the victim's body, or causing the victim to reasonably fear (objective test) the immediate infliction of such force or impact.

The first part of the definition of the crime is what used to be the common law offence of battery – the physical crime of uninvited touching. The force or impact can be applied directly or indirectly. An example of direct force would be where the victim is touched or punched on the face by the offender, whereas an example of indirect force would be the pulling away of a chair causing the victim to fall, or the application of acid to a towel causing burns to the victim.

Like the common law before it, the Act does not distinguish between a strong force and a mild force, and therefore any degree of force, no matter how slight, is covered by this offence, ranging from a brutal beating to a caress on the buttock.

The second part of the definition of the crime is what used to be the common law offence of assault – the 'psychological crime' of causing the victim to be afraid that he or she was about to be harmed. It might also be argued that words can now be enough for an assault, although this is a change to the common law position, and it would have been nice if the definition specifically included the concept that words can be used to assault a victim.

The apprehension of harm must be immediate or within a reasonably short period of time. The apprehension must also be objectively reasonable, which means that the threat must be such that a reasonable person would apprehend violence. The apprehension is a mental thought, and therefore a sleeping or unconscious person cannot be assaulted in terms of the common law, but under the statutory definition if a sleeping person was touched without permission, that would fall under the first definition of statutory assault (previously common law battery).

Finally, the Act makes it clear that the assault must be without the consent of the victim. This is a restatement of the common law, with the section going on to define what is known as implied consent – touching or force which is considered quite acceptable in ordinary everyday life, like bumping somebody in a bus queue, or touching the arm of a stranger to attract their attention, or taking somebody's hand at a party.

The *mens rea* of the crime is either intention or recklessness, the first two categories of *mens rea* discussed in chapter twenty-seven.

Therefore, as far as nurses are concerned, where a nurse touches or holds down a patient or administers treatment to a patient without that patient's consent, and whilst the patient was in a position to give or refuse consent, that nurse has committed a crime of statutory assault, and could be charged in terms of section 2 of this Act.

In cases where the patient is unable to consent, the nurse would still be guilty of statutory assault, as there has been unauthorised touching. In these circumstances the nurse would need to rely on the defence of necessity ('emergency medicine').

SECTION 3: Assault causing harm
'(1) A person who assaults another causing him or her harm shall be guilty of an offence.
(2) A person guilty of an offence under this section shall be liable—
   (a) on summary conviction, to imprisonment for a term not exceeding 12 months or to a fine not exceeding £1,500 or to both,
   or
   on conviction on indictment to a fine or to imprisonment for a term not exceeding 5 years or to both.

SECTION 4: Causing serious harm
(1) A person who intentionally or recklessly causes serious harm to another shall be guilty of an offence.
(2) A person guilty of an offence under this section shall be liable on conviction on indictment to a fine or to imprisonment for life or to both.'

Commentary

These sections describe what is usually referred to as 'aggravated assault', as that was the common law offence before the Act. Under the common law there were various types of aggravated assault and the position was very confusing. The Act has simplified matters by having two categories of aggravated assault – assault causing harm and assault causing serious harm.

'Harm' is defined in section 1 as 'harm to body or mind and includes pain and unconsciousness', whereas 'serious harm' is defined in section 1 as 'injury which creates a substantial risk of death or which causes serious disfigurement or substantial loss or impairment of the mobility of the body as a whole or of the function of any particular bodily member or organ'.

Therefore, for the purposes of defining the *actus reus* of these two offences, 'harm' expressly includes psychological harm, whereas 'serious harm' is very specifically defined and is limited to serious physical injury.

Again, the *mens rea* for the crime would be either intention or recklessness.

A nurse might be charged with assault to do harm where he untruthfully told a patient that his penis was to be amputated, causing the poor man to shake with terror. A theatre sister could be charged with assault to do serious harm if she stopped a blood transfusion to a patient immediately after a surgical procedure, in order to save blood, where she knew that the lack of blood could cause cardiac arrest.

Notice also the sentences that can be imposed, including life imprisonment for assault causing serious harm.

Syringe offences

Syringes are extremely useful instruments in the field of medicine, and nurses have ready access to them, and might even be called on to use them occasionally. Unfortunately, syringes also make quite fearsome weapons. The idea of syringes being used as weapons is not a new phenomenon, but with the advent of blood-borne diseases like HIV and Hepatitis, the spectre of the blood-filled syringe has taken on a very sinister connotation, and the Act seeks to cover these situations where that threat is used for criminal purposes. Accordingly, it is important to know what specific offences have been created by the Act that involve the use of syringes.

SECTION 6: *Syringe, etc., attacks*

'(1) A person who—
  (a) injures another by piercing the skin of that other with a syringe, or

(b) threatens to so injure another with a syringe,

with the intention of or where there is a likelihood of causing that other to believe that he or she may become infected with disease as a result of the injury caused or threatened shall be guilty of an offence.

(2) A person who—
   (a) sprays, pours or puts onto another blood or any fluid or substance resembling blood, or
   (b) threatens to spray, pour or put onto another blood or any fluid or substance resembling blood,

with the intention of or where there is a likelihood of causing that other to believe that he or she may become infected with disease as a result of the action caused or threatened shall be guilty of an offence.

(3) A person who in committing or attempting to commit an offence under subsection (1) or (2)—
   (a) injures a third person with a syringe by piercing his or her skin, or
   (b) sprays, pours or puts onto a third person blood or any fluid or substance resembling blood,

resulting in the third person believing that he or she may become infected with disease as a result of the injury or action caused shall be guilty of an offence.

(4) A person guilty of an offence under subsection (1), (2) or (3) shall be liable—
   (a) on summary conviction to a fine not exceeding £1,500 or to imprisonment for a term not exceeding 12 months or to both, or
   (b) on conviction on indictment to a fine or to imprisonment for a term not exceeding 10 years or to both.

(5) (a) A person who intentionally injures another by piercing the skin of that other with a contaminated syringe shall be guilty of an offence.
   (b) A person who intentionally sprays, pours or puts onto another contaminated blood shall be guilty of an offence.
   (c) A person who in committing or attempting to commit an offence under paragraph (a) or (b)—
      (i) injures a third person with a contaminated syringe by piercing his or her skin, or
      (ii) sprays, pours or puts onto a third person contaminated blood,

shall be guilty of an offence.

(d) A person guilty of an offence under this subsection shall be liable on conviction on indictment to imprisonment for life.'

Commentary

Section 6 creates four separate and distinct offences involving syringes, where the definition of a syringe includes the needle that might be attached to the syringe.

Section 6(1) makes it an offence to stab or threaten to stab a person with a syringe. This would include an empty syringe or a syringe filled with another substance which was not blood, where some quality of the syringe itself or of its contents is enough to cause a person to believe they are infected as a result of the stabbing or would be infected if the threat was carried out.

Section 6(2) makes it an offence to spray, pour or put blood or a blood-like substance onto the victim, or threaten to spray, pour or put blood or a blood-like substance onto the victim, using a syringe, with the intention to cause the victim to believe that they are or will be infected.

Section 6(3) refers to what is called transferred intent, where the offender means to hit one person but hits another instead. If a person intended to commit either a crime described in section 6(1) or section 6(2), but did not stab or spray etc. the person that was the intended victim, the offender can still be charged under section 6(3) as if he or she had in fact intended the unlucky bystander to be the victim. This prevents an offender, who admits to intending to commit a crime, from escaping by showing that he or she got the wrong person by mistake. In order to satisfy the section, the prosecution also needs to show that the third party victim actually believed that they were infected. The section does not say that the belief must be reasonable, it must simply exist.

Finally, section 6(5) makes it an offence to stab a person with a contaminated syringe, or spray, pour or put contaminated blood on a victim, or to do any of these things to a third person whilst trying to commit the offence on the intended victim. This offence was clearly created with HIV in mind. Its application is restricted to the use of actual blood rather than a blood-like substance that is mentioned in the other sections. It is also the only sub-section in section 6 that specifically mentions the punishment of life imprisonment, as intentionally infecting a person with HIV is tantamount to murder, although the victim might live for quite a while after the offence. As a person can only be charged with murder if the victim dies 'within a year and a day' of the fatal attack, it was necessary for this statutory offence to be created, as the incubation period for HIV can be a very long time.

For all of these offences the *mens rea* can consist of both intention and recklessness. Therefore the defendant must either know that the syringe or the blood was contaminated, or the evidence must show that the defendant must have known of the contamination of the syringe or the blood contained in that syringe, but proceeded to use it anyway. A nurse could not be charged under this section if he or she caused a needlestick injury, unless the nurse was reckless or intended to stab the victim. Carelessness would not qualify as a crime.

SECTION 7: *Offence of possession of syringe, etc., in certain circumstances and seizure thereof by member of Garda Síochána*

'(1) A person who has with him or her in any place—
  (a) a syringe, or
  (b) any blood in a container,

  intended by him or her unlawfully to cause or threaten to cause injury to or to intimidate another shall be guilty of an offence.

(Sections 2, 3 and 4 describe the powers of search and seizure given to the Garda Síochána and have not been included here).

(5) In a prosecution for an offence under subsection (1), it shall not be necessary for the prosecution to allege or prove that the intent to threaten or cause injury to or intimidate was intent to threaten or cause injury to or intimidate a particular person; and if, having regard to all the circumstances (including the contents of the syringe, if any, the time of the day or night, and the place), the court (or the jury as the case may be) thinks it reasonable to do so, it shall regard possession of the syringe or container as sufficient evidence of intent in the absence of any adequate explanation by the accused.

(6) In this section "blood" includes any fluid or substance resembling blood.

(7) A person guilty of an offence under subsection (1) shall be liable—
  (a) on summary conviction, to a fine not exceeding £1,500 or to imprisonment for a term not exceeding 12 months or to both, or
  (b) on conviction on indictment, to a fine or to imprisonment for a term not exceeding 7 years or to both.'

SECTION 8: *Placing or abandoning syringe*

'(1) Subject to subsection (3), a person who places or abandons a syringe in any place in such a manner that it is likely to injure another and does injure another or is likely to injure, cause a threat to or frighten another shall be guilty of an offence.

(2) A person who intentionally places a contaminated syringe in any place in such a manner that it injures another shall be guilty of an offence.

(3) Subsection (1) does not apply to a person placing a syringe in any place whilst administering or assisting in lawful medical, dental or veterinary procedures.
(4) In a prosecution for an offence under subsection (1) where it is alleged a syringe is placed in a place being a private dwelling at which the accused normally resides, it shall be a defence for the accused to show that he or she did not intentionally place the syringe in such a manner that it injured or was likely to injure or cause a threat to or frighten another, as the case may be.
(5) A person guilty of an offence under subsection (1) shall be liable—
   (a) on summary conviction to a fine not exceeding £1,500 or to imprisonment for a term not exceeding 12 months or to both, or
   (b) on conviction on indictment to a fine or to imprisonment for a term not exceeding 7 years or to both.
(6) A person guilty of an offence under subsection (2) shall be liable on conviction on indictment to imprisonment for life.'

Commentary

Sections 7 and 8 make it an offence to possess or dispose of syringes with intent to cause, or threaten to cause, injury to, or intimidate the victim. Clearly the offender must be aware that he or she possesses the syringe, but the prosecution does not need to prove that the offender had a specific victim in mind. A person who discovers they are HIV positive and places an infected hypodermic syringe or needle in the grass of a playground intending that someone should stand on it and become infected, is guilty of an offence under the Act.

Again, the *mens rea* necessary for these offences is intention or recklessness. Section 8(3) is directly applicable to nurses as it excuses them from liability under section 8(1) if they placed the syringe whilst lawfully performing medical, dental or veterinary procedures. Note that the nurse would have to be engaged in a lawful activity. Note also that in section 8(1) the *mens rea* that is required for this offence is recklessness.

Therefore if a nurse recklessly placed or abandoned an infected syringe whilst performing lawful duties, he or she could escape liability. If the nurse intentionally placed or abandoned the syringe with the intention that somebody be infected, the fact that this was done during a lawful nursing activity shall not be an excuse, as that offence is created by section 8(2), and not section 8(1).

Where a person intentionally infects another person this is regarded as a very serious crime, tantamount to murder, and therefore the punishment can be life imprisonment. Again note that the prosecution will need to show that the syringe was placed with an intention to infect somebody but they do not need to show that the offender had a particular victim in mind. Again, this would cover the situation of leaving or placing an infected needle in a playground with the intent to infect somebody playing there.

Although one would hope that it is highly unlikely that a nurse would fall foul of these provisions whilst carrying out normal nursing duties like disposing of used syringes, the seriousness of these offences and the severity of the punishments are a reminder to nurses that syringes and needles are not playthings, and need to be handled with the utmost care and precaution.

Manslaughter

When a human being in killed, this is a homicide. There are three categories of homicide, namely justifiable homicide (where the law allows you to kill another person – for example, the killing of an armed robber who violently resists arrest); excusable homicide (where the law excuses the fact that you killed another – for example, in self defence) and felonious homicide, where the law will punish you for killing another person.

Felonious homicide is also divided into three categories of crime, namely murder (where you intended to kill a person and knew that it was unlawful to do so), infanticide (the killing of an infant under twelve months by its mother – see the Infanticide Act of 1949) and manslaughter.

Manslaughter is divided into two categories – voluntary manslaughter and involuntary manslaughter.

Voluntary manslaughter occurs either when the offender kills the victim as a result of provocation, or where the offender kills the victim in self-defence but uses more force than was necessary to defend himself, but honestly believed at the time that the degree of force used was necessary in the circumstances.

Involuntary manslaughter is a misleading title as it makes one think that it is a species of automatism, in that it sounds like the person killed whilst not in control of his or her actions. In fact, involuntary manslaughter is no such thing. The offence of involuntary manslaughter is committed when a person is killed but the prosecution cannot show that the defendant possessed the necessary *mens rea* to secure a conviction for murder.

In other words, because murder requires intention (the first and purest form of *mens rea*), if the prosecution can only prove that the killing arose out of the defendant's recklessness or gross negligence, the crime will be manslaughter.

Therefore, the *actus reus* of manslaughter is the unlawful killing of another human being. The *mens rea* is either recklessness or gross negligence leading to the death of that person.

If a nurse was grossly negligent and this resulted in the death of a patient, the nurse would be charged with manslaughter, not murder, as there was no direct intention to kill the patient.

Specific Offences: Summary

1. The Non-Fatal Offences Against the Person Act has replaced the common law offences of assault and battery with a new offence of assault that is a combination of the two common law offences.
2. The Act has also created a number of syringe offences, which penalises the use of a syringe to infect somebody or threaten to infect somebody, either by stabbing that person with the syringe, or leaving or placing the syringe somewhere so that a person is infected with the contents of the syringe (in other words the needle on the syringe does the damage) or where a syringe itself is used to spray or pour its contents over the victim, so that the person is infected or thinks that he or she is infected.
3. As a general rule the Act requires *mens rea* to be in the form of intention or recklessness.
4. Manslaughter can be either voluntary or involuntary.
5. Voluntary manslaughter occurs where the killing is a result of provocation, or where the limits of self-defence are exceeded.
6. Involuntary manslaughter occurs where the defendant is held not to have intended the death of the person, but rather acted recklessly or was grossly negligent.
7. Useful websites:
    a. *Law Reform Commission Report on the Act* (http://www.lawreform.ie/publications/data/lrc77/lrc_77.html).
    b. *Homebirth Association of Ireland* (http://ireland.iol.ie/~hba/childbirth_medical_legal_minefield.htm).
    c. *RTE News* (poisoning story) (http://www.rte.ie/news/2004/0526/mulhollandn).

29

DRUGS

> **Learning Outcomes**
> At the completion of this chapter, the reader should know and understand the following:
> - The Misuse of Drugs Acts 1977 and 1984.
> - The Misuse of Drugs Regulations 1988 (updated in 1993).
> - The status of drug protocols.

Important concepts and phrases that are crucial to an understanding of this chapter

Possession

The ordinary meaning of possession is the physical detention or keeping of something. In the legal sense a person must not only physically possess something, but must also have the intention to keep that thing as his or her own. Neither the Drugs Act nor the Regulations specifically define possession, and therefore the ordinary meaning must be given to the concept when it is used in the Act or Regulations. As a general rule in the Misuse of Drugs Act, it is an offence to unlawfully possess scheduled drugs, but it is not an offence to use them, with the exception of opium. This distinction might be academic, as generally you must possess before you can use, but the distinction is also practical: it is much easier to prove possession than it is to prove use.

Although section 1 (Interpretation) of the Misuse of Drugs Act does not contain a specific definition of possession, it does make it clear that possession includes what is known as constructive possession – if you are controlling or instructing somebody to possess the drug on your behalf, the Act regards you as the possessor, even though you do not have physical possession.

Section 1(2) provides that:

> 'For the purposes of this Act any controlled drug, pipe, utensil or document of which a person has control and which is in the custody of another who is either under the person's control or, though not under the person's control, acts on his behalf, whether as an agent or otherwise, shall be regarded as being in the possession of the person,

and the provisions of section 16 and section 18 together with the provisions of this Act relating to the possession of controlled drugs shall be construed and have effect in accordance with the foregoing.'

Therefore the *actus reus* of illegal possession is actual (physical) or constructive possession. The *mens rea* of the offence is knowledge of the drug in question. The prosecution must prove that the defendant knew of the existence of the drugs in his or her possession. It is not a defence for the defendant to show that he or she did not know or made a mistake as to the type of drug (heroin as opposed to morphine, for example) as section 29(1) of the Act says that such a mistake is not a defence:

> 'In any proceedings for an offence under this Act in which it is proved that the defendant had in his possession or supplied a controlled drug, the defendant shall not be acquitted of the offence charged by reason only of proving that he neither knew nor suspected nor had reason to suspect that the substance, product or preparation in question was the particular controlled drug alleged.'

In other words, the prosecution need only show that the defendant is in illegal possession of a controlled drug, and that the defendant knew he or she was in possession of a controlled drug – irrespective of the type of drug.

Use
The ordinary meaning of use is to employ or handle something for a purpose. In the legal sense, particularly with regard to drugs, the concept of use is equated with personal use. To illegally possess a controlled drug for personal use is less serious than possessing it for supply. Neither the word 'use' nor the concept 'personal use' is defined in the Act or the Regulations, and therefore the ordinary meanings must be applied.

Supply
The ordinary meaning of supply is to provide something that is needed. Once again, the concept is not defined in the Misuse of Drugs Act, with the interpretation section merely stating 'supply' includes 'giving without payment'. Therefore, once again, the ordinary meaning of supply must be used in the Act, and this meaning becomes very important, as the distinction between 'use' and 'supply' is crucial. If a person is convicted of illegal possession with intent to supply controlled drugs, as opposed to possession for personal use, the sentences that can be handed down to the convicted offender are a lot harsher.

Again, it is difficult to prove that a person had an intention to supply, and therefore the Act has created a presumption.

A rebuttable presumption of law allows the court to assume that something is a fact unless and until it is proven that it is not a fact. It is often referred to as a 'persuasive presumption'. Where a person illegally possesses controlled drugs, and the amount of drugs so possessed is more than seems necessary or adequate for personal use, that person is presumed a supplier, rather than a user. The evidential burden is then placed on the defendant to show that despite the large quantity of drugs, they were for personal use only, and evidence and argument will need to be led by the defendant to show that.

SECTION 15: Possession of controlled drugs for unlawful sale or supply

'(1) Any person who has in his possession, whether lawfully or not, a controlled drug for the purpose of selling or otherwise supplying it to another in contravention of Regulations under section 5 of this Act, shall be guilty of an offence.

(2) Subject to section 29 (3) of this Act, in any proceedings for an offence under subsection (1) of this section, where it is proved that a person was in possession of a controlled drug and the court, having regard to the quantity of the controlled drug which the person possessed or to such other matter as the court considers relevant, is satisfied that it is reasonable to assume that the controlled drug was not intended for the immediate personal use of the person, he shall be presumed, until the court is satisfied to the contrary, to have been in possession of the controlled drug for the purpose of selling or otherwise supplying it to another in contravention of regulations under section 5 of this Act.'

Section 15(2) of the Misuse of Drugs Act creates a rebuttable presumption as it provides that where a person is found to be in possession of controlled drugs in a quantity that the court considers reasonable to assume exceeds the amount required for immediate personal use, there will be a presumption that he intended to supply others. In addition to the quantity of the drugs, the court may also take into account any other factors that it considers to be relevant. The prosecution will therefore introduce evidence that the quantity and purity of the drugs found in the defendant's possession are sufficient to raise the presumption. See *The People (DPP) v Lawless* (1985) 3 Frewen 30.

Therefore rather than charging a person with supply in the ordinary sense, the Gardaí will usually charge a person with an offence under section 15 – 'possession with intent to supply', on the basis that the quantity of drugs found raise the presumption created by that section.

Article 4 of the 1988 Regulations prohibits the supply of controlled drugs, except by authorised persons in specific circumstances. Contravention of these Regulations can lead to severe penalties, including up to fourteen years' imprisonment.

Dispense
The ordinary meaning of dispense is to distribute or hand out. Once again, the term is not defined either in the Act or in the Regulations and therefore the ordinary meaning must be used.

Administer
The ordinary meaning is to give or furnish or apply. The word is not defined in the Act or in the Regulations. In the nursing context, to administer drugs usually means to dose the patient with the specific drug. In a legal sense, to administer a drug is in effect to supply a drug to another. Common methods of administering drugs would be orally, by suppository or pessary, and intravenously.

Section 10 of the 2000 *Guidance to Nurses and Midwives on the Administration of Medical Preparations* (issued by An Bord Altranais) says the following about intravenous administration:

10.0 Administration of Intravenous Medical Preparations

'(a) (*not relevant for our purposes*).
(b) Nurses/midwives shall have theoretical instruction and supervised clinical practice in the administration of intravenous medical preparations. The nurse/midwife shall be satisfied with her/his competence and be aware of her/his personal and professional accountability.
(c) Nurses/midwives may administer such medical preparations by the following methods:
   (i) addition to an intravenous infusion (bag, buretrol or infusion pump), or
   (ii) through the appropriate section of an intravenous giving set, or
   (iii) via an in-situ intravenous cannula.
(d) Midwives, in accordance with currently accepted midwifery practice, may administer specified medical preparations directly into a vein by venepuncture.'

Introduction

Every nurse in every sector will at some stage in his or her career be asked to handle, control and administer drugs, and these skills are an important part of any nurse's training. Drugs are clearly a huge asset to the health sector, but at the same time are potentially lethal if misused or abused.

The Misuse of Drugs Act of 1977, as amended by the 1984 Act, is the most important statute governing the regulation and administration of drugs. It is a very large and complex Act, and this Chapter can only provide a brief outline of the main features of the Act.

From a practical point of view, the Regulations passed by the Minister in terms of the Act are more useful than the Act itself, as they give the sort of information needed by somebody who has to deal with controlled drugs as part of their job. The latest full Regulation is the 1988 Regulation, and its full title is: Misuse of Drugs Regulations 1988 (S.I. No. 328 of 1988). The 1988 Regulations replaced the 1979 Regulations (S.I. No. 32 of 1979) and the 1987 Amendment Regulations (S.I. No. 263 of 1987).

The 1988 Regulations have been updated by the Misuse of Drugs (Amendment) Regulations 1993, but the changes were minimal and required exports of controlled drugs to be properly documented and to ensure that the relating shipping documentation properly identifies the drug. This was to conform with Article 16 of the United Nations Convention against Illicit Traffic in Narcotic Drugs and Psychotropic Substances. The remainder of the amendments added a substance each to Schedules One, Two and Three, transferred a substance from Schedule Two to Schedule Four, and deleted a substance altogether from the Schedules.

The 1988 Regulations are in four Parts, followed by the Schedules. Part 1 is the Introduction, which includes the important interpretation section. Part 2 deals with the production, supply, importation and exportation of controlled drugs, which includes Article 8 dealing with the supply of drugs in hospitals. Part 3 deals with documentation and record keeping, and includes Article 13 that sets out the format and content of a valid prescription, and Article 14 that deals with the question of the supply of drugs in response to a prescription. Part 4 contains miscellaneous provisions, including details of the destruction and disposal of drugs, and Article 24 that deals with the question of forged prescriptions.

Finally, there are the Schedules of controlled drugs, which is the topic covered next.

The schedules of controlled drugs

The drugs that are mentioned in the Act are what are known as controlled drugs, and these controlled drugs are sorted into five main categories, or schedules.

Schedule One is a list of drugs in their raw form, in other words before they are processed into pharmaceuticals. Well-known examples are cannabis and opium. Schedule One drugs can only be possessed under licence for research purposes by registered drug manufacturers and other State bodies conducting research. This licence will allow possession but does not allow the use of these substances for any other purpose except research. In other words, a researcher can possess cannabis under licence but cannot legally smoke a cannabis joint unless the smoking process is part of an authorised clinical trial.

A nurse need have nothing to do with Schedule One drugs unless he or she is an authorised participant in licensed research.

Schedule Two drugs are drugs that are used for medicinal purposes, but are dangerous in that they are either highly addictive or potentially toxic. Morphine and Pethidine are two well-known examples of Schedule Two drugs.

Schedule Three drugs are drugs that are used for medicinal purposes but are slightly 'softer' than Schedule Two drugs in that they are usually in a more diluted form and often do not possess such toxic or highly addictive properties as Schedule Two drugs. Well-known examples are Valium and a number of Antibiotics.

Schedule Four drugs are 'over the counter' (as opposed to 'on the shelf') drugs that can be purchased in a pharmacy but are kept behind the counter and must be requested from the pharmacist. Examples are Paracetemol and Aspirin.

Schedule Two and Three drugs are only available to patients on prescription issued by a registered medical practitioner or a registered dentist or a registered veterinary surgeon (the vet may only issue prescriptions for drugs for the purposes of treating an animal, not a human).

Schedule Five drugs are drugs that may be imported or exported, examples of which are substances with Codeine, Ethylmorphine, Nicocodine, and Nicodicodine as their base. As these contain opium bases, the schedule provides that these substances must be diluted, or in a form that prevents extraction into their pure form, so as to prevent these being used in a drug smuggling operation.

The lawful use of drugs

Only certain people can possess and supply drugs. Article 8 of the 1988 Regulations lists these people as:

'(a) The matron or acting matron of a hospital or nursing home which is wholly or mainly maintained by a public authority out of public funds or by a charity or by voluntary subscriptions, and the drug is a medical preparation,

(b) the sister or acting sister for the time being in charge of a ward, theatre or other department in such a hospital or nursing home where the drug is a medical preparation supplied to her by a person responsible for the dispensing and supply of medicines at such hospital or nursing home,

(c) a person in charge of a laboratory the recognised activities of which consist in, or include, the conduct of scientific education or research and which is attached to a university or a hospital referred to in paragraph (a) of this sub-article, or a person in charge of any other laboratory engaged in the conduct of scientific education or research and which is attached to any other institution approved for the purpose by the Minister,

(d) the State Chemist,

(e) the Director of the Forensic Science Laboratory of the Department of Justice,

(f) a public analyst appointed under section 10 of the Sale of Food and Drugs Act, 1875,

(g) the Medical Director of the National Drugs Advisory Board,

(h) a person employed or engaged in connection with any arrangements made for testing the quality or amount of the drugs, medicines and appliances supplied for the purpose of section 59 of the Health Act, 1970,

(i) a person employed or engaged as an inspector in connection with a scheme for the licensing of manufacturers or wholesalers of medical preparations under the Health Acts 1947 to 1985,

(j) a person authorised under and in accordance with Regulations made under section 65 of the Health Act, 1947 (as amended by section 39 of the Health Act, 1953 and by section 36 of the Act) for the purpose of enforcement and execution of the said Regulations,

(k) a person appointed as an inspector by the Pharmaceutical Society of Ireland, acting under the directions in writing of the Registrar of the said Society; provided that nothing in this sub-article shall be construed as authorising—

(i) the matron or acting matron of a hospital or nursing home, having a pharmacist responsible for the dispensing and supply of medicines, to supply or offer to supply any drug, or
(ii) a sister or acting sister for the time being in charge of a ward, theatre or other department to supply any drug otherwise than for administration to a patient in that ward, theatre or department in accordance with the directions of a registered medical practitioner or a registered dentist.'

Commentary
Note that although a matron and sister or acting sister are included in this list, they are only entitled to possess and supply any drug where, in the case of the matron, there is no pharmacist in the hospital, and in the case of the sister, only to a patient on the instructions of a doctor or a dentist.

Midwives are in a special category of lawful possessor and supplier

Article 10 of the 1988 Regulations permits a midwife to possess and administer to patients the drugs Pentazocine and Pethidine, but only after the midwife has obtained a written order signed by herself and an 'appropriate medical practitioner' (a practitioner specialising in gynaecology and obstetrics). The order must contain the name and address of the midwife, the purpose for which the drug is required and the quantity to be obtained.

As Pethidine is a Schedule Two drug, Article 17(3) provides that the midwife must record in a book on each occasion she is supplied with Pethidine. She must also record in the book the date, the name and address of the person from whom the drug was obtained, the amount obtained and the form in which it was obtained. On administering Pethidine to a patient, she must enter in the book the name and address of the patient, the amount administered and the form in which it was administered.

Pentaxocine is a Schedule Three drug. Article 20 deals with Schedule Three drugs and it provides that any person (and this would include a midwife) who is entitled to possess and supply a Schedule Three drug must keep every invoice or other like record issued in respect of each quantity of such drug obtained by her and in respect of each quantity of such drug supplied by her. As the 'supply' in this case would be administration, these details would need to be recorded – the name and address of the patient, the amount administered and the form in which it was administered.

The supply of drugs

Where a supplier supplies drugs (as opposed to prescribing or administering them) Article 12 provides that this shall only be on receipt of a written requisition, signed by the recipient of the drugs, and which sets out the address and contact details of the recipient, and sets out the purpose for which the drug is to be used, and the quantities required. If the drug is urgently needed, and the requisition has not yet been obtained, the supplier is entitled to supply the drugs on an urgent basis, with the stipulation that the requisition is supplied within 24 hours of the supplying of the drugs.

The recipient of these drugs can be a practitioner, the matron or acting matron of a hospital or nursing home, a person in charge of a laboratory, the owner of a ship, or the master of a ship which does not carry a registered medical practitioner on board as part of her complement, the master of a foreign ship in a port in the State, or the installation manager of an offshore installation.

Where a requisition is furnished by the matron or acting matron of a hospital or nursing home, it must be signed by a registered medical practitioner or a registered dentist employed or engaged in that hospital or nursing home.

Where the person responsible for the dispensing and supply of medicines at any hospital or nursing home supplies a controlled drug to a sister or acting sister in charge of a ward, theatre or other department in a hospital or nursing home, that supplier must obtain a requisition in writing, signed by the sister or acting sister, which specifies the total quantity of the drug to be supplied; and mark the requisition in such manner as to show that it has been complied with. In these circumstances the requisition must be retained at the dispensary at which the drug was supplied and a copy of the requisition must be retained by the sister or acting sister.

A person who supplies a controlled drug to a matron or acting matron of a hospital or nursing home must provide a receipt with the consignment. The matron must check the receipt against the drugs supplied, note on that receipt any discrepancies between the contents of the receipt and the drugs received, enter the date on which the drugs were received, sign the receipt, and return that receipt to the supplier not later than three working days after receiving the drugs.

The Regulation does not specify that the matron must keep a copy of the receipt that is returned to the supplier, but for obvious reasons this should be done.

Prescriptions

Article 13 of the Misuse of Drugs Regulations of 1979 sets out the requirements for a valid prescription. In order to be valid and enforceable, a prescription must have the following qualities:

- The full name, qualifications and contact details of the prescribing practitioner (where practitioner is defined in Section 1 of the 1977 Act as 'a registered medical practitioner, a registered dentist and a registered veterinary surgeon').
- It must be completed (in other words the blank spaces must be completed) in the handwriting of the practitioner concerned. The handwriting must be in ink and must be 'indelible', which means that the writing must be not be capable of being blotted out (at least not so it will not be noticed).
- It must be signed by the practitioner, and the signature is not allowed to be a pre-printed signature, but must be an original signature in ink.
- It must contain the name and address of the patient for whom the drugs are prescribed. If it is a prescription by a vet for the medication of an animal, the prescription must specify the name and address of the person to whom the medicine is to be delivered.
- It must exactly specify the name and quantity of drugs prescribed (the quantity must be described in both words and figures).
- It must exactly specify the dose to be taken. Where the prescription is for a preparation of a controlled drug, it must specify the form and the strength of the preparation, and either the total quantity (in both words and figures) of the preparation or the number (in both words and figures) of dosage units to be supplied.
- If the prescription is for a total quantity of drugs that are to be dispensed in instalments, it must contain a direction specifying the amount of the instalments and the intervals at which the instalments may be dispensed.

Article 14 of the 1988 Regulations specifies that the pharmacist (or chemist or druggist) who dispenses on the strength of a prescription must be satisfied that the prescription is a valid prescription in that it must satisfy the above specifications. In addition, the dispensing pharmacist must be satisfied that the prescription is issued by a practitioner legally practising as such in Ireland. If the pharmacist is not familiar with the signature on the prescription, he or she must take 'reasonably sufficient steps' to make sure that the prescription is genuine, which would usually mean that the practitioner's rooms should be consulted by telephone, hence the need for the contact details on the prescription.

The pharmacist must mark on the prescription the date on which the drug is supplied, and must thereafter retain the prescription.

Article 14(3) governs a prescription by instalments:

'(3) In the case of a prescription for a controlled drug other than a drug specified in Schedule 4 or 5, which contains a direction that specified instalments of the total amount may be dispensed at stated intervals, the person dispensing it shall not supply the drug otherwise than in accordance with that direction and—
(a) sub-article (1) shall have effect as if for the requirement contained in paragraph (e) thereof there were substituted a requirement that the occasion on which the first instalment is dispensed shall not be later than fourteen days after the date specified in the prescription;
(b) sub-article (2) shall have effect as if for the words "at the time of supply" there were substituted the words "on each occasion on which an instalment is supplied";
provided that no instalment shall be supplied later than two months after the date specified in the prescription.'

Commentary

If there is a date of commencement of medication on the prescription, the pharmacist must not dispense the drugs to the patient before that date, and not later than two weeks after the prescription date. For an instalment prescription, the first instalment of that prescription must be dispensed less than two weeks after the date specified in the prescription, and no instalment may be supplied later than two months after the date specified in the prescription.

The question that must be raised is whether this description of an instalment prescription is wide enough to cover what is usually known as a 'repeat prescription'. If it is wide enough, the requirement at the end of the sub-article is somewhat ambiguous as it might mean that any subsequent instalment cannot be dispensed later than two months after the date on which the prescription was issued, in which event any repeat prescription can only last for two months. As this could cause many problems, the other interpretation would be that any subsequent instalment cannot be later than two months after the date specified in the prescription itself as the next instalment date (in other words, if each instalment was dated). This is also problematic as it does not make sense to place a two-week limit on the first instalment, but a two-month limit on subsequent instalments. The first interpretation effectively means that a patient will need to return to the practitioner every two months in order to obtain a fresh prescription, and it is perhaps this result that the Article attempts to achieve. However, this might be impractical.

The dispensing pharmacist must also be satisfied as to the identity of the person tendering the prescription, which should match the details of the patient's name and address appearing on the prescription. This would mean that the pharmacist who does not know or recognise the patient would be entitled to ask for some form of positive identification before handing over the prescribed drugs.

Clearly a prescription can only be in written form, which means that a prescription cannot be made over the telephone or in conversation. It must be in the form specified by Article 13.

Article 13 ends with an exception to these general rules, and the exception is an important one for nurses to know. The exception is that when dealing with a patient in a hospital or nursing home, it is sufficient if the prescription is written on the patient's bed card or case sheet.

Section 18 of the 1977 Act makes it a criminal offence to either forge a prescription or alter a valid prescription with the intent to deceive. Section 27 of the 1977 Act (as amended by the 1984 Act, which made the penalties tougher) provides that if a person is summarily convicted (a judge-only trial, without a jury) under section 18, he or she can be fined (the euro equivalent of) £400, or sentenced up to six months imprisonment or both. If a person is convicted on indictment (a jury trial) for an offence under section 18, the court can fine an offender an 'appropriate' amount (in other words, the court has a discretion) or sentence the offender to imprisonment for up to three years, or both a fine and imprisonment.

Pharmacists need to have faith in prescriptions and must be able to take them at face value. If there was widespread prescription forgery the whole basis of trust would break down leading to chaos in the drug regulation system. Accordingly, prescription forgery is regarded as a serious offence, and this is made quite clear by the Act, which has prescribed tough penalties for anybody convicted of the offence.

Recording of drugs

Article 16 of the 1988 Regulations deals with the keeping of a register for Schedule One drugs, which are the drugs in their crude form and very often are the most dangerous and addictive drugs. It is highly unlikely that a nurse will be involved in any dealings with Schedule One drugs. However, the Article also governs the recording of Schedule Two drugs, and here there is a high probability that nurses will be asked, at some stage, to assist in the administration of Schedule Two drugs.

Whenever a drug is administered, a record must be kept of that administration in a register, recording who withdrew the drug and to whom it was administered, and the quantity that was administered, and when it was administered. The register must be in the prescribed form (set out in Schedule Six and Seven of the Regulations), and must be divided up into sections, with each section dedicated to a specific drug. The entries in the sections must be in chronological order, and there must be a corresponding column next to the chronological entry which shows a running stock balance – in other words, it must be possible to know from a reading of the register just how much of a particular drug is in stock at the time.

A register must be stored for a period of at least two years after the last entry in that register is made. The creation and maintenance of such a register would usually have nothing to do with the nursing staff, but it is the duty of the nurse to ensure that when a patient is administered a prescribed drug, that the drug is consumed in his or her presence, and that fact is thereafter recorded, usually on the patient's drug chart.

Guidelines issued by An Bord Altranais

The Nursing Board has issued guidelines concerning the possession, control and administration of drugs, and these provide an excellent practical guide to nurses in an area that is flooded with regulations, orders and protocols.

The *Guidance to Nurses and Midwives on the Administration of Medical Preparations 2000* contains guidelines on a wide area of subjects involving drugs, including an explanation of some of the more important sections in the Misuse of Drugs Act, the contents of a valid prescription, dispensing requirements, labelling of containers, and the supply and possession of controlled drugs in both public and private hospitals and nursing homes. It replaced the document of the same title issued in 1990.

The 2000 Guidelines has been supplemented and updated by the 2003 *Guidance to Nurses and Midwives on Medication Management*. The 2003 Guidelines specifically provide that it 'supercedes' the 2000 Guidelines. This probably means that it replaces the 2000 Guidelines, but it would have been better if this was clearly stated, as it might mean that it is an updated supplement, rather than a replacement. The better way to approach this problem is to follow the 2003 Guidelines, unless there is an area that is not covered in the 2003 Guidelines, but which is covered in the 2000 Guidelines, in which event the 2000 Guidelines should be followed.

The 'Introduction' in the 2003 document contains this very important advice:

'The nurse/midwife should have knowledge of the relevant statutes and legislation regarding the practices of prescribing, dispensing, storing and supplying scheduled medicinal products (this includes controlled, prescription-only and over-the-counter medications). There is an obligation to practice according to the legislation governing nursing and midwifery practice, and the current standards and policies of regulatory bodies and health service providers.

The nurse/midwife should be aware of the legal and professional accountability with regard to medication management. It is acknowledged that local need may dictate specific policies and protocols authorising the practices of individuals involved with medicines. The health service provider and health care regulatory and professional organisations have a responsibility to the patient/client to assure safe and effective medication management practices.'

Part 2 of the 2003 Guidelines sets out the principles of medical management, and makes the important point that whilst only doctors and dentists (and vets) can prescribe medicine, the Act does allow the nurse to possess and supply drugs to the patient. The Guide emphasises the importance of knowing and keeping up to date with the policies and protocols practiced in your particular institution.

Paragraph 2.1 contains very useful principles regarding medication management. It makes the important point that verbal or telephone prescriptions are only to be used in emergencies. What the guideline does not say in so many words is that verbal prescriptions are against the law, as the Regulations specifically provide for written prescriptions. The emergency situation means that a nurse can rely on the defence of necessity if charged with contravening the Regulations by administering controlled drugs on a verbal or telephonic prescription. It must therefore be stressed that this practice can only happen in a true emergency, and must not become a habit of convenience.

Paragraph 2.3 recognises the use of fax prescriptions but stresses that the practitioner involved must provide the original prescription thereafter (although no time-limit is specified) for insertion into the patient's chart or file. In this regard, the 2000 Guidelines provided (although not in so many words) that if the practitioner did not subsequently supply the original, the nurse should thereafter refuse to accept a prescription by fax from that specific practitioner. This is not repeated in the 2003 Guidelines, perhaps because nurses were too scared to oppose a doctor, even a lazy or careless one.

Paragraph 2.6 is perhaps the most important in the context of this chapter as it deals with the criminal law implications of drug management and administration. The paragraph concerns scheduled controlled drugs and summarises the various sections in the Act that were discussed earlier in this chapter. The Guidelines make the important point that private institutions are not covered by the Act and therefore do not have a statutory right to possess or administer drugs like a public hospital. Drugs in a private institution are treated exactly the same as drugs in a person's home – there must be a valid prescription authorising their possession and use. However, private institutions may now hold licences issued in the terms of the Act, which allow the supply, distribution, and control of scheduled drugs similar to the arrangements in public hospitals.

The Guidelines provide the following critical advice regarding the management of Schedule Two drugs:

'i) Local health service provider policy may require two persons to conduct the administration of MDA Schedule 2 drugs one of whom is a nurse/midwife. This is not a legal requirement. Local policy may dictate that the checking, preparation, administration or destruction of these drugs should be witnessed.

ii) The nurse/midwife manager or her/his nurse/midwife designee should keep the keys of the controlled drugs cupboard on their person.

iii) Policies and procedures should be in place for checking a stock balance at each transaction of MDA Schedule 2 drugs. At changeover of shifts a nurse/midwife from each shift should complete the count of these scheduled drugs.

iv) Appropriate documentation of the administration of the MDA Schedule 2 drug should be entered in the patient's/client's chart/notes and in the ward-controlled drugs register.

v) Requisition copies (or a note) detailing the requested MDA Schedule 2 drugs submitted to the pharmacist, or nursing/midwifery director who supplies the drugs, are required to be kept by the nurse/midwife manager.'

Community nurses are the exception to the general rule that nurses are not allowed to possess or carry drugs on behalf of patients. The community nurse can receive written authorisation allowing the transport of drugs to patients in the community. Possession is only for the purpose of transporting the drug to the patient, and the nurse is not entitled to store the drug on behalf of the patient. The patient can store the drug at home if there is a valid prescription allowing this.

Paragraph 2.7 details the regulations surrounding the supply of drugs by a nurse under the direction of a doctor, which is governed by the Medicinal Products (Prescription and Control of Supply) Regulations

1996. The paragraph emphasises the importance of local written policies and protocols in this regard. There are restrictions to this practice where the community hospital or clinic is providing mental health services, in which event that hospital or clinic is limited to holding no more than three days' supply.

Paragraph 2.8 recognises the increasing use of complementary therapies, and paragraph 2.9 similarly recognises the increasing use of unauthorised or unlicensed medicinal products. In both cases, the most important underlying principle is the need for a full and frank consultation with the patient, including full disclosure and discussion about the interaction and impact of these therapies and medicinal products on more conventional treatments and drugs that the patient may be taking.

Paragraph 2.10 deals with medication errors, and what is emphasised here is that upon the discovery of a medication error, the patient's health must be carefully and constantly monitored. Again, the importance of a local policy or protocol dealing with medication error is emphasised.

The final paragraph, paragraph 2.11, deals with the storage of drugs, and emphasises the need for secure storage, and the importance of storing medicinal products separately from antiseptics, disinfectants and cleaning products. The paragraph emphasises the need for a policy or procedure governing the ordering of products from the pharmacy, the checking and recording of deliveries, the immediate reporting of any discrepancies either in goods delivered or in existing stocks, and the storage of products for self-administration by patients.

The status of protocols

Section 5 of the 2000 Guidelines contains important principles regarding the administration of medical preparations, and in particular stressed the need for institutions to develop their own protocols and practices:

> 'Employers shall have written policies and procedures for nurses/midwives on the administration of medical preparations. These policies and procedures should have regard to the different competences of nurses/midwives and the various settings in which they practise. Nurse management must be involved in the formulation of such policies and procedures for the administration of medical preparations by nurses/midwives. These policies and procedures should cover the issues outlined at Point 9.0, together with any other issues relevant to the institution.'

This very useful advice was not repeated in the 2003 document, which is a shame, as it is something that should be stressed to both employers and employees alike. Protocols are an extremely valuable part of any day-to-day administration of a health facility. At the same time, it must be stressed that protocols have no independent legal status, and should always conform to the provisions of the Act and to the Guidelines issued by An Bord Altranais. Accordingly, employers should ensure that the protocols that are practiced in their institution conform to the Act and the Guidelines.

It is recognised that protocols are often a product of local conditions, but if the Act or guidelines prohibit a practice contained in a protocol, that protocol will not protect the employer (and perhaps not the employee either) if charged with a contravention of the Act or if sued for any drug mishap involving a patient. The onus is upon the employer to change the protocol or seek a change in the Act or the Guidelines to accommodate the protocol based on local needs.

As a change in the Act or even in the Guidelines is very difficult to accomplish, it usually means that the protocol must conform to the law and to the guidelines, until those are changed. A protocol that contravenes the law or a guideline must not be left unchanged in the hope that the law will change in the future.

If a nurse becomes aware that a protocol contravenes the Act or the Regulations, this fact must be reported to his or her employer immediately, preferably in writing, and a personal record kept of that report. A protocol that does not comply with the law has serious implications for all involved.

Conclusion

It is critically important for a nurse to be familiar with the Misuse of Drugs Act, and more particularly, the Regulations to the Act. Contravention of the Act is regarded as a serious offence, with large fines and the possibility of imprisonment. Dismissal for drug-related offences or contraventions is virtually guaranteed. The necessary information on drug management is readily available, and therefore ignorance of these provisions will never be a valid defence, particularly as a nurse is expected to be familiar with these provisions as part and parcel of the job.

The Guidelines issued by An Bord Altranais are extremely useful documents containing a lot of vital information. They can be accessed from the website of An Bord Altranais and nurses are encouraged to download and print a copy for reference purposes.

Nurses are urged to become familiar with these Guidelines, as it will be a good defence to any charge involving the storage or administration of drugs for a nurse to show that he or she was following these Guidelines.

Drugs: Summary

1. The Misuse of Drugs Act 1977 (as amended by the 1984 Act) is the primary statute concerning the regulation and administration of controlled (scheduled) drugs.
2. The Misuse of Drugs Regulations of 1988 (updated in 1993) is equally important from a more practical point of view.
3. Contravention of the Act or the Regulations can lead to a criminal record, harsh punishments, and almost certainly to dismissal.
4. An Bord Altranais have issued guidelines on the regulation and administration of drugs, the latest being issued in 2003. Courts are often guided by the principles contained in guidelines issued by professional bodies, and therefore it is important that a nurse is familiar with these.
5. The use of practices and protocols with regard to drugs is an established institution in the health service. These protocols have no legal status as such, and therefore it is important that they comply with the Act and the Regulations.
6. Useful websites:
   a. *Irish Health.com* (http://www.irishhealth.com/?level=4&id=5784).
   b. *Oasis* (http://www.oasis.gov.ie/health/alcohol_and_drug_treatment_services/drug_offences.html).
   c. *An Garda Síochána* (http://www.garda.ie/angarda/gndu.html).
   d. *Clubscene Ireland* (www.clubscene.ie/drugsandthelaw.htm).
   e. *Drug Awareness Group* (www.athlone.ie/drugawareness/drug_laws.htm).

30

GENERAL DEFENCES IN THE CRIMINAL LAW

> *Learning Outcomes*
> **At the completion of this chapter, the reader should know and understand the following:**
>
> ▸ The general defences to a criminal charge, namely:
>   ▸ Infancy.
>   ▸ Insanity.
>   ▸ Intoxication.
>   ▸ Duress.
>   ▸ Self-defence.
>   ▸ Necessity.

Important concepts and phrases that are crucial to an understanding of this chapter

Culpability
To be culpable is to be blameworthy, or held legally responsible or accountable for a breach of the law.

Acquittal
The defendant in a criminal trial is discharged after being found not guilty or if a plea from the bar is successful (in other words an argument that the criminal trial is inherently faulty in some way). The court will no longer have the power to deal further with the acquitted defendant – he or she may leave the courtroom as a free person. What happens outside the courtroom after the acquittal is beyond the power of the court at that stage.

Presumption
In law, a presumption is a conclusion or inference that is reached on the basis of facts that have already been proved. There are two kinds of presumptions – irrebuttable and rebuttable. An irrebuttable presumption is really a rule of law as it is taken as fact, and nobody is allowed to even attempt to disprove it. A rebuttable presumption is taken as fact until it is disproved.

Incontrovertible
Something that is beyond discussion and cannot be disputed. An irrebuttable presumption in law is incontrovertible as it is really a rule of law and cannot be disputed, but is taken as fact. Incontrovertible evidence is evidence that cannot be challenged in a court of law, but is accepted as fact.

Introduction

Readers will remember that when studying the law of torts, there were what are known as common defences to any tort, for example, consent. The criminal law has a very similar idea, in that there are defences that can be raised against virtually any criminal charge. However, as the types of crimes differ quite markedly, it is dangerous to talk of these as 'common' defences, as certain defences clearly cannot be used in regard to certain crimes. For example, it would be quite difficult to argue self-defence in response to a charge of theft, but it might be possible to argue necessity in response to a charge of theft.

In addition, the criminal courts have held that certain defences are not allowed to be used in respect of certain crimes – for example, duress can never be used as a defence to a charge of murder. These exceptions are based on public policy, where the good of society as a whole is seen as being more important than the individual rights of the defendant.

As these defences cannot be raised against each and every criminal charge, it is perhaps better to refer to these defences as 'general' rather than 'common'.

These general defences are infancy, insanity, intoxication, duress, self-defence and necessity. Each defence will be dealt with separately.

Infancy

The law has always recognised that a child should be treated differently to an adult concerning the question of criminal culpability. What has changed over the centuries is the level of understanding concerning the difference between children and adults in relation to criminal culpability.

The common law divided children into three categories for the purposes of criminal responsibility. Children under the age of seven years, children aged between seven and fourteen years, and children aged fourteen years and older.

In terms of the common law, a child under the age of seven years was said to be *doli incapax* (incapable of committing a legal wrong). It was, and is, believed that an infant child could not tell the difference between right and wrong. This rule was known as an irrebuttable or conclusive presumption, which meant that the child's incapacity was accepted as an absolute fact, and was admitted as incontrovertible evidence. The prosecution was not entitled to lead evidence to show that the child was capable of committing a crime. Accordingly, the DPP would not bother to charge a child under the age of seven.

The common law presumed children between the ages of seven and fourteen to be *doli incapax*. However, with regard to this age category, the presumption was a rebuttable presumption. In other words, the prosecution could lead evidence to show that a young defendant knew full well that what he or she was doing was wrong. Clearly, as the child grows older and approaches his or her fourteenth birthday, it will be easier for the prosecution to rebut the presumption. The evidence must show that the child knew that his or her actions were seriously wrong, as opposed to just being naughty.

Once a child reached the age of fourteen, the common law treated the child as an adult for the purposes of criminal responsibility.

These common law rules have been modified by statute. The Children Act 2001 raised the age of the irrebuttable presumption of *doli incapax* of an infant from seven to twelve years. Therefore, a child under the age of twelve cannot be charged with a crime in Ireland.

The Act further provides that a child between the ages of twelve and fourteen shall be rebuttably presumed to be *doli incapax*. Therefore the upper limit of the common law's rebuttable presumption has been left unchanged. To rebut this presumption the prosecution must still show that the child knew that his or her actions were seriously wrong, as opposed to just being naughty.

Insanity

With certain exceptions, adults are held to be liable and responsible for their acts and adjudged to be capable of exercising control over them. This is known as the presumption of sanity, and this principle is a rebuttable presumption. If the defendant pleads insanity as a defence to a criminal charge, it is the defendant who must prove the insanity, on a balance of probabilities, and in so doing discharge the presumption of sanity.

Broadly speaking, insanity is relevant to the criminal law in two ways.

Firstly, the defendant must be fit to plead to the criminal charge. If it is shown that the defendant, because of insanity, is unable to understand the charge, or is unable to understand the difference between guilty and not guilty, or is unable to instruct lawyers in his or her defence, or is unable to challenge jurors, or follow the evidence; the trial cannot proceed, as the fairness of the trial cannot be guaranteed due to the defendant's condition.

This test is not limited to any particular medical definition of insanity, but is rather a measurement of criminal capacity. If the defendant does not have the ability to understand what is going on in the trial, then he or she is found 'unfit to plead'. Section 2 of the very unpleasant sounding Criminal Lunatics Act 1800 provides that he or she should be detained in strict custody 'until the pleasure of the government be known'.

The second use of insanity in the criminal law is where the defendant is found fit to plead, which means that the trial proceeds, but the defendant raises the defence of insanity during the trial. As previously mentioned, the law presumes every person (in criminal law over the age of fourteen) to be sane and fully accountable for his or her actions. However, if the defendant can show, on a balance of probabilities, that at the time the offence was committed he or she was legally insane, this is a valid defence, as the defendant will be incapable of having a guilty mind, or *mens rea*.

The McNaghten Rules have been used for a long time in criminal law to assess the insanity defence. They have been criticised and added to, but they still exist and are still used:

1. A partial delusion (i.e. insane as regards one issue only) will be no defence if the defendant still knew, despite the delusion that his or her actions were against the law.
2. Every person is presumed to be sane, and therefore accountable for his or her actions, until the contrary is proven.
3. To establish insanity, the defendant must show that at the time the act was committed, he or she was suffering from a defect of reason arising from a disease of the mind such that he or she did not know the nature and quality of his or her actions, or if the nature and quality of the actions were known, he or she did not know that they were wrong. Wrong in this respect means unlawful.
4. A person suffering from a partial delusion only should be treated as if the facts of the delusion were real.

Accordingly, if a defendant knew, despite being (medically) insane, that what he or she was doing was wrong, there can still be a conviction according to these Rules. The real test of criminal insanity is therefore knowledge, as set out in rule 3. It must be shown that the defendant's knowledge was so affected by a disease that he or she did not know what they were doing or that he or she knew what they were doing but did not know that the act was unlawful. If the defendant can prove this on a balance of probabilities, the presumption in rule 2 will be rebutted and the defendant will be acquitted. If the defendant cannot prove this, the presumption of sanity will stand and the defendant will be culpable.

The Irish courts have found that the McNaghten Rules are not the only basis on which a defendant can be found guilty but insane. The Rules are narrow in that they tend to concentrate on whether a person knows right from wrong, but do not consider the situation where a person knows right from wrong but, because of his or her mental illness, is unable to stop doing wrong. This is often called the defence of 'irresistible impulse' and the Irish courts have recognised that this could be used as a component of the defence of insanity.

Where the defendant is found 'guilty but insane' this is in fact an acquittal. Despite the acquittal, the defendant is not free to go anywhere that he or she chooses to go. The defendant will be detained in a psychiatric hospital. As the defendant was acquitted, he or she is no longer under the jurisdiction of the courts, and the decision whether to release him or her from the psychiatric hospital is an executive decision, in other words a decision of the government of the day.

There are a number of popular misconceptions about mental health and criminal law. The first is that people often claim that most crime is committed by those who are psychiatrically ill. This is simply not true, and in fact a relatively minor proportion of crime is committed by the psychiatrically ill. Your average criminal knows exactly what he or she is doing.

The second popular misconception is that where a defendant charged with murder is allowed to use the insanity defence, this is a 'soft-option'. Again, this is not necessarily true. A finding of guilty but insane carries with it a mandatory committal to the Central Mental Hospital 'at the government's pleasure'. The offender is no longer dealt with by the courts, but rather relies on the Minister for Justice for a discharge, which means that the issue of a discharge becomes a matter of politics and the uncertainty that brings, as opposed to clearly delineated laws and access to the courts.

The law and psychiatry do not happily co-exist. As an English judge, Devlin J. pointed out in *R v Kemp* [1957] 1 Q.B. 399 at 407:

> '…the law…is not concerned with the origin of the disease of the cause of it but simply with the mental condition which has brought about the act. It does not matter, for the purposes of the law, whether the defect of reason is due to degeneration of the brain or to some other form of mental derangement. That may be a matter of importance medically, but it is of no importance to the law, which merely has to consider the state of mind in which the accused is, not how he got there.'

In other words, the law is directed at the issue of criminal responsibility for the actions of the accused person, not at a clinical definition of psychiatric disability. The law speaks of a 'disease of the mind', not a defective or injured brain. The law is concerned with the mental faculties of reason, memory and understanding. The condition of the brain is irrelevant in legal terms. One of the main reasons why the McNaghten Rules have caused so much controversy and confusion is that they are essentially psychiatric rules being used to decide criminal responsibility.

Intoxication

This defence is often referred to as 'drunkenness', but it is recognised that the defence could be used by a defendant acting under the influence of drugs, as well as alcohol. Therefore, it is better to speak of the defence of intoxication.

The common law did not distinguish between intoxicated and sober defendants. It was argued that the act of becoming intoxicated was a voluntary act and therefore the offender should not be allowed to hide behind this fact. It would be simple for a person to get really drunk before committing a crime and thereafter use it as a defence.

There is, however, a problem with this approach, as it must be recognised that a person might not have *mens rea* if they are so intoxicated that they do not know what they are doing.

There is a clear conflict between the theory of criminal law and public policy.

The English law deals with this problem by categorising crimes that require 'basic intent' and crimes that require 'specific intent'. With regard to the first category, intoxication is not a defence, but it is a defence with regard to the second category, as intoxication would prevent a person from forming a 'specific intent'. This is seen as a compromise between the strict theory of the law, and public policy, as the law must protect the public from offenders who commit crimes whilst under the influence of drugs or alcohol. So for example, if an intoxicated person unlawfully killed somebody, he or she might use intoxication to beat the charge of murder (specific intent) but would still be convicted of manslaughter (basic intent).

There has been much discussion about the exact meaning of the phrases 'specific intent' and 'basic intent', but it can be said that they roughly correspond to the first two categories of *mens rea* that were discussed in an earlier chapter. Specific intent is the first category of 'pure' intention, whereas basic intent is the second category of recklessness or gross negligence, and obviously the third category of negligence.

Irish law is in a somewhat confused state regarding the defence of intoxication. Current principles of Irish law suggest that it would agree with the basic principle that if intoxication removes *mens rea*, this should be a defence. What is not clear is whether the Irish courts will follow the 'specific versus basic intent' test used in English law. There have been no definitive decisions by the Irish courts on the topic.

The Law Reform Commission of Ireland ('the LRC') released a report in 1995, titled *Report on Intoxication*. In that Report, the LRC recommended that a statute be passed which ruled out the defence of intoxication for any charge. This harsh approach was probably a reaction to a belief that alcohol and drug abuse was a serious problem in Irish society and should not be seen to be encouraged in any way. As far as involuntary intoxication is concerned (for example, where a person's drink is 'spiked' without their knowledge), the LRC recommended that this could be used as a defence to any charge where the level of intoxication was such that the offender did not have *mens rea*.

Duress

The common law recognised two defences based on duress, namely duress by threats and duress by circumstances. Duress by circumstances is essentially the defence of necessity, which will be dealt with later.

Where a person commits a crime because he or she has been forced to do so by threats either to their person or to their family, this can be used as a defence to the charge.

The leading Irish case in this regard is *The People (Attorney General) v Whelan* [1934] I.R. 518.

Facts
The defendant received stolen money. His defence was that he was forced to keep the stolen money under threats of violence.

Issue to be decided
Was the threat sufficient to take away the freedom of choice of the defendant?

Decision of the court
The court recognised that the defence of duress had to be restricted, as its potential was huge. Therefore the court set out limitations on the use of the defence:
- The will of the defendant must have been overcome by the threats.
- The defence does not apply to murder.
- The duress must be operating on the defendant at the time of committing the crime.

If the defendant could escape the duress and reassert his or her own will, and that opportunity was not taken, the defence cannot be used.

The Court of Criminal Appeal described the defence and its limitations as follows:

'...threats of immediate death or serious personal violence so great as to overbear the ordinary power of human resistance should be accepted as a justification for acts which would otherwise be criminal.

Where the excuse of duress is applicable it must ...be clearly shown that the overpowering of the will was operative at the time the crime was actually committed and, if there was a reasonable opportunity for the will to reassert itself, no justification can be found in antecedent threats.'

Necessity

The defence of necessity in criminal law is virtually identical, at least in principle, to the one in tort. Where a defendant commits a lesser evil in order to avoid a greater evil, the defendant can plead the defence of necessity, where that lesser evil is a criminal offence.

The example that was used earlier in the tort section can also be used here. A person pulls another out of the river, but in so doing breaks the victim's collarbone. In response to a charge of (statutory) assault, the defendant can lead evidence that the person was drowning and would have died if he had not been pulled out of the river.

In criminal law, the defence is limited:

It cannot be used as a defence to murder

For policy reasons, and for the same reasons that duress is not a defence to murder, a person cannot argue that he killed one (faultless) person in order to save the life of another (faultless) person. This would leave the court with an impossible task of deciding whether one person's life is more valuable than the life of another person.

The defendant needs to show that there was no alternative action available to take at the time

The defendant must show that the only reasonable way he or she could avoid the greater evil was to commit the crime, which is the basis of the criminal charge. A healthcare example would be where a nurse responds to a patient's call and discovers that the patient is having difficulty breathing. The nurse administers aggressive CPR, causing severe bruising to the chest and much pain to the patient.

The patient lays a charge of (statutory) assault. The nurse pleads necessity, but it is shown that an oxygen canister and mask were next to the bed, and would have been more than adequate to help the patient to breathe. The court might decide on those facts that the defence of necessity should fail, as the use of CPR was not the only alternative available to the nurse.

The defendant must show that in committing the lesser evil he or she did no more than was necessary at the time

Again, the defendant must do enough to prevent the greater evil, but no more than that. If we used the previous example of the nurse using CPR on a patient having difficulty breathing, but on this occasion there was no oxygen available. If it is shown that the use of aggressive CPR was not justified, and the problem could easily have been solved by mouth-to-mouth resuscitation, again the nurse might fail on the defence of necessity, as he or she went further than was necessary when assaulting the patient.

The defendant must show that he or she did not create the situation that necessitated breaking the law

Clearly the defendant cannot justify committing the lesser evil if he or she was the cause of the greater evil in the first place. For example, a nurse places a pillow over the face of a terminally-ill patient, in an effort to stop the suffering of the patient, who is facing a long and painful death. The patient stops breathing. The nurse has a change of heart and successfully administers CPR by punching the patient's chest, but fractures a rib in the process. The nurse is charged with attempted murder and (statutory) assault, and pleads guilty to the attempted murder but not guilty to the assault as he argues that he had to punch the patient to start his heart beating.

It is true that the patient's death (the greater evil) was avoided by the assault (the lesser evil). However, the nurse caused the greater evil, and so the defence of necessity as a defence to the assault charge is not available to the nurse. The nurse is likely to be convicted of both attempted murder and assault, but the fact that the nurse thereafter saved the patient's life will be taken into consideration by the court when passing sentence.

The statutory defence of necessity

Section 21 of the Non-Fatal Offences Against the Person Act 1997 creates a statutory defence of necessity against a charge of criminal damage:

'Amendment of section 6 of the Criminal Damage Act, 1991

Section 6(2) of the Criminal Damage Act, 1991, is hereby amended by the substitution for paragraph (c) of the following paragraph:

"(c) if he damaged or threatened to damage the property in question or, in the case of an offence under section 4, intended to use or cause or permit the use of something to damage it, in order to protect himself or another or property belonging to himself or another or a right or interest in property which was or which he believed to be vested in himself or another and the act or acts alleged to constitute the offence were reasonable in the circumstances as he believed them to be."'

Self-defence

The use of objectively reasonable force in defence of person or property will allow the defendant to escape from being convicted of assault or damage to property and even to escape from a murder charge.

If the defendant used force that was not reasonable, he or she will face conviction. Where the charge is murder, and it is shown that the defendant used unreasonable force but truly believed that the force used was necessary in the circumstances, he or she will be convicted of manslaughter, as the *mens rea* will be in the form of recklessness, rather than intention. If the charge is not murder, but assault or criminal damage, the fact that the person truly believed that the force used was necessary will not allow the person to escape the conviction, but can be used to mitigate (lessen) the sentence.

Statutory self-defence

Again, the Non-Fatal Offences Against the Person Act 1997 has created a statutory defence of self-defence, by providing the defence of justifiable use of reasonable force in sections 18, 19 and 20. Section 18(1) lays the framework for the defence:

'*Section 18: Justifiable use of force; protection of person or property, prevention of crime, etc*
  (1) The use of force by a person for any of the following purposes, if only such as is reasonable in the circumstances as he or she believes them to be, does not constitute an offence—
   (a) to protect himself or herself or a member of the family of that person or another from injury, assault or detention caused by a criminal act; or
   (b) to protect himself or herself or (with the authority of that other) another from trespass to the person; or
   (c) to protect his or her property from appropriation, destruction or damage caused by a criminal act or from trespass or infringement; or

(d) to protect property belonging to another from appropriation, destruction or damage caused by a criminal act or (with the authority of that other) from trespass or infringement; or
(e) to prevent crime or a breach of the peace.'

Section 19 deals with the justifiable use of reasonable force in carrying out a lawful arrest, or the assisting in the carrying out of a lawful arrest. Section 20 deals with the meaning of the phrase 'use of force' as it is used in sections 18 and 19. Section 20(1) sets the scene:

'Meaning of "use of force" and related provisions
(1) For the purposes of sections 18 and 19—
(a) a person uses force in relation to another person or property not only when he or she applies force to, but also where he or she causes an impact on, the body of that person or that property;
(b) a person shall be treated as using force in relation to another person if—
(i) he or she threatens that person with its use, or
(ii) he or she detains that person without actually using it; and
(c) a person shall be treated as using force in relation to property if he or she threatens a person with its use in relation to property.'

Conclusion

As has been previously stated, it is important to remember that these are general defences, which can be used to defend oneself against a variety of charges, although not necessarily all charges.

The defences of necessity and self-defence have been encoded in the Non-Fatal Offences Against the Person Act, and have effectively replaced the common law, although the earlier decisions of the courts can still be used to interpret these statutory provisions.

It is hoped that a nurse will never have the need for these defences. Clearly infancy cannot be used by a nurse as a defence, as it is unlikely that somebody will qualify as a nurse whilst younger than fourteen years of age. The defence of intoxication might be used, if a nurse became involuntarily intoxicated by a gas leak, for example.

A defence of duress might be used where a nurse is forced to commit a criminal act by superiors, for example, an employer forcing a nurse to obey a protocol that was clearly illegal. A nurse might snap under the pressure and commit crimes whilst in a state of insanity or automatism.

Clearly, if a nurse is attacked by a deranged patient or visitor, the defence of self-defence is available.

In practice, however, the defence that is most likely to be used by a nurse who faces a criminal charge is that of necessity. Emergency medicine is based on the principle of necessity, and clearly this would be a valid defence if the nurse was forced to break the law, subject of course to the limits of the defence that have been developed by the criminal courts.

In the unlikely event that a nurse is charged with assaulting an unconscious patient by treating that patient, the defence of necessity is available. The previously used example of a nurse supplying drugs to a patient on the basis of a verbal or telephonic prescription, where the patient needed those drugs on an emergency basis (to save life or prevent serious or irreparable damage) again would justify the defence of necessity.

For most nurses these situations will never occur, but it is useful to know that there are defences available where the nurse has acted in good faith.

There are also other defences that would fit under the description of general defences, for example entrapment and diplomatic immunity, but these have not been considered here.

General Defences: Summary

1. General defences to a criminal charge include
   a. Infancy.
   b. Insanity.
   c. Intoxication.
   d. Duress.
   e. Self-defence.
   f. Necessity.
2. The use of the phrase 'general defences' as opposed to 'common defences' is preferable as these defences will not be available as a defence to every criminal charge.
3. Most of these defences still exist as common law defences but some have been codified in the Non-Fatal Offences Against the Person Act.
4. Some of these defences are absolute defences, which means that a person will be acquitted if they are successful. The defences of infancy and insanity are 'capacity defences' as the defendant claims not to have the capacity for criminal intent. With self-defence the defendant will be acquitted where reasonable and justified force was used to protect person or property.

5. Other defences might be relative defences where they will be a defence against certain crimes but might still lead to a conviction for a lesser or different crime (for example self-defence where the force used was unreasonable but the defendant believed it was necessary) or where they cannot be used at all against certain crimes (for example, duress and necessity can never be a defence to a charge of murder).
6. Useful websites:
   a. *The Law Reform Commission* (http://www.lawreform.ie/publications/data/lrc87/lrc_87.html).
   b. *Memorandum on the Criminal Law Insanity Bill* (http://www.feargalquinn.ie/m/mcrimins.htm).
   c. *Kent Law School* (https://www.kent.ac.uk/law/undergraduate/modules/criminal/self_defence.htm).
   d. *DPP* (http://www.dppireland.ie).

PART FOUR

ACCCOUNTABILITY TO THE EMPLOYER

31

THE CONTRACT OF EMPLOYMENT

> **Learning Outcomes**
> **At the completion of this chapter, the reader should know and understand the following:**
> - Who or what is an employee.
> - The common law duties of the employer and the employee.
> - The law relating to contracts of employment.

Important concepts and phrases that are crucial to an understanding of this chapter

Liquidation
In the ordinary sense, to liquidate something is to make it disappear, or if the word is used in an action film, it means to kill ('with extreme prejudice'). In the legal sense, to liquidate means the same as 'winding up', which is an expression used to describe the process whereby a juristic person (for example, a company) is closed down (in other words, the juristic person is 'killed').

The winding up process consists of collecting the assets of the company and selling them, and using the money from that sale to pay off the debts of the company, including the salaries of its former employees. If there is any money left over after all the debts of the company are paid, this is given to the members of the company.

Creditor
A person to whom money is owed.

Debtor
A person who owes money.

Express terms and implied terms of a contract
A term in a contract is a provision in that contract which creates legal obligations between the parties to that contract. If the parties specifically agree on things that must be contained in that contract, these are said to be express terms. On the other hand, the contract might contain terms

that were not specifically agreed between the parties, but which are in the contract either because the type of contract needs those provisions to function properly, or because the express terms cannot make sense or cannot function without these additional provisions being present. These additional terms are called implied terms.

Introduction

Although many might not realise the implications of being one, most nurses are employees, usually of a health board. Employees in Ireland are protected by a whole host of laws. It is important for a nurse to know firstly his or her status, and secondly, what laws are out there to protect employees.

Who or what is an employee?

Those who work for others fall into two main categories: Employees who work under a contract of service, and the self-employed (sometimes called an independent contractor) who work under a contract for services.

There is another category of worker, who is known as an office holder. This person has their position created for them by statute, rather than by a contract. What this means is that the person's appointment, suspension, dismissal and remuneration are all determined by the statute, rather than by a contract. This category is relevant to the nurse as certain nurses might be held to be officers of a health board, in which event they are office holders in terms of the Health Act 1970. This would mean that they are not employees and are therefore excluded from the protection of a number of statutes. This complex question will be dealt with in the chapter on dismissal.

An example can explain the difference between the two types of contract. Let us imagine that a lady named Susan telephones Jack, a fencing contractor, and asks Jack to come out to her house and give her a quotation for a fence around the perimeter of her property. Jack does so and Susan accepts the quoted price. Susan and Jack have entered into a contract for services. Jack is not an employee of Susan; he has contracted with her to provide a service, namely the erection of a perimeter fence in return for the payment of the agreed sum of money. She is his client, and he is providing her with a specified service.

The agreed day arrives and Jack arrives with two workers, Liam and Alan, and the three of them erect the fence. Liam and Alan are employees of Jack, and he pays them a salary in return for their labour. Susan has no control over Liam and Alan, who follow the orders of Jack. If Susan wanted the fence to be erected in a certain way, she would need to talk to Jack, and he would then tell Liam and Alan what to do. Susan has no right to give orders to Liam and Alan directly.

When the fence is complete, and Susan is satisfied with the result, she will pay the agreed sum to Jack. Out of that money, Jack will pay the salary of Liam and Alan, with the rest of the money going into his back pocket.

Therefore there are two contracts in existence in our example. There is a contract for services between Susan and Jack, with Jack being an independent contractor. There is a contract of service between Jack as employer, and Liam and Alan as employees, who each have their own contract with Jack.

The importance of the distinction

It is important to determine whether a contract of service or a contract for services governs the relationship between parties, for the following reasons:

- The contract of service has certain implied terms, for example the employer's extensive duties to ensure the safety of employees, and in turn, the employee's duty of fidelity towards the employer. This is not necessarily so in the contract for services.
- As a general rule, an employer owes a special duty of care to employees arising from the contract itself, but not to independent contractors.
- Most of the employment protection legislation applies only to employees. For example, the Unfair Dismissals Acts 1977-93 and the Redundancy Payment Acts 1967-2001 apply only to employees.
- Employers in certain industries are required to pay a levy to FÁS in the terms of the Industrial Training Act 1967. The value of the levy is calculated according to the number of employees at the employer's firm, but would not include the number of independent contractors.
- An employer is vicariously liable for the wrongs of an employee, but it is very seldom that an employer is liable for the wrongs of an independent contractor.
- As a general rule, trade unions represent employees rather than independent contractors.
- When a company goes into liquidation the employees of that company are protected, as their outstanding wages are treated as preferred debts of that company. In other words, the employees will be placed near the beginning of the queue when it comes to the company paying out the people to whom it owes money.
- Employees have their tax deducted from their salary by their employer, who must then pay that tax to the State. Independent contractors are personally responsible for paying their tax.

Perhaps the most important consequence of the type of contract is the question of dismissal, as an independent contractor cannot be dismissed, which is why the Unfair Dismissal Acts only apply to employees. If a person is dismissed and goes to the Employment Appeals Tribunal (EAT) claiming unfair dismissal, an employer might raise the defence that the person was not an employee and therefore cannot be dismissed.

The courts have applied a number of tests to determine whether a person working for another is an employee working in terms of a contract of service or a self-employed person working in terms of a contract for services.

The control test

This test recognises that there must be some element of control exercised over the employee by the employer. The control test soon became inadequate with the increase in the number of highly-skilled employees, who possessed more knowledge and expertise than their employer. It was difficult to talk of the employer controlling the employee when the employer did not really understand what it was that the employee was doing. An extreme example would be the nuclear scientist, who is generally involved in work that could never be understood by mere mortals, but technically he or she is an employee.

A more common example would be highly skilled computer programmers, who are employed by software companies, where the owner/employer might not know half as much about computers and programming as the employees, and yet asserts the right to 'control' those employees. In the healthcare context, a nurse might be highly specialised in a certain area, for example a theatre sister, whilst her employer, the health board, might consist of people employed more for their management skills than their knowledge of nursing.

The case of *Dr Seamus O'Friel v The Trustees, Saint Michael's Hospital Dun Laoghaire, Co. Dublin* [1982] I.L.R.M. 260 is a good example of the difficulty of distinguishing employees and independent contractors through the use of the control test alone.

Facts
Dr O'Friel acted as a consultant surgeon at St Michael's for almost three years before the contract between them was terminated by the hospital. During that time Dr O'Friel had treated both public and private patients, had taken an outpatient clinic once a week, and had been 'on call' every Wednesday. His income came from private patients, from the hospital, and from the Department of Health. Dr O'Friel claimed that he was an employee and that the termination of the contract by the hospital was an unfair dismissal.

Issue to be decided
In order to be dismissed, Dr O'Friel had to be an employee. Was he an employee or an independent contractor?

Decision of the court
The Employment Appeals Tribunal (EAT) found that Dr O'Friel was not an employee, and it emphasised the importance of the control test.

> 'In the case of Brian & Brendan Scanlon v Browne & Carolan Ltd (M60, M74/1977) the tribunal considered a number of tests which may be applied in finding the distinction. These were:
> 1. The element of control;
> 2. The right to 'hire and fire';
> 3. The requirement that service must be personal or may be delegated;
> 4. Liability in the event of a worker on the premises being injured by the negligence of a fellow worker;
> 5. Responsibility for custody and stamping of Social Welfare cards.
>
> ...
>
> Of these five tests the most important is the element of control. The degree of control by the respondent was very limited in this case, but we appreciate the argument of the claimant's counsel that this limitation is due to the nature of the work since the administrators of the hospital are not qualified doctors or surgeons. But there would undoubtedly be a greater degree of control over a full-time salaried surgeon as employed by the Regional Health Board. That control is administrative only — it does not effect or override the surgeon's exercise of his professional judgment. But his regular salary, his pension, his hours of work (subject to a certain amount of flexibility) are controlled, and his is a contract of service. On the other hand the claimant did not receive a salary. He provided his services to the respondent for reward, which would be better described as fees, the control of which was in the hands of himself and his colleagues. And it was he and his colleagues separately or together who controlled the hours of work.
>
> Claimant's occupation is described accurately or otherwise, as "consultant surgeon". In answer to the tribunal the claimant said that the word "consultant" in that context meant a surgeon who had reached a certain level in his profession. We were told that the description is applied to full-time salaried surgeons in the employment of the Regional Health Boards. Perhaps the word has developed a derived or secondary meaning in a medical context.

Nonetheless its primary meaning implies the opposite of a contract of service. A consultant is primarily an independent person whose opinion is sought and who may possibly also perform certain services as such independent person.'

Commentary
This case illustrates the difficulty of formulating any hard and fast rules when it comes to distinguishing between the employed and the self-employed. As soon as one test seems to have the answer, the market place creates a new form of relationship, and the test is suddenly inadequate. Although control remains a critical factor, it can never be seen as the only, or even the ultimate, factor. In the case of skilled employees, there might be very little control but the court might still find that there was a contract of service. On the other hand, where the individual is totally unskilled, there might be a high level of control but the court could still find that there was a contract for services.

A useful way in which to use the control test, and attempt to avoid these problems as previously mentioned, is to recognise that the right of the employer to control an employee must simply exist in theory, although not necessarily in practice. As long as the employer has the right to control somebody (for example, to tell the employee to get to work, to finish work, and to take leave at a particular time) the chances are good that there is an employer/employee relationship, rather than a contract for services.

A highly specialised nurse, or a midwife, might operate almost independently within a hospital and thereby give the appearance of being an independent contractor. If the nature of the relationship between nurse or midwife and hospital is such that the hospital has the right to tell the nurse or midwife what to do (rather than how to do it) or where to go, that relationship is more likely to be categorised as a contract of service.

The control test has proved inadequate in another important aspect, and that is the situation where the worker under consideration seems to have 'two masters'. This is a common scenario in the modern commercial world where a person who seems to be working for one person, spends all his time working at the premises and under the control of another person. For example, a bookkeeper is originally hired by an auditing firm, but continuously and permanently works on the premises of a construction firm, doing their books. Who is responsible for the employee, if for example he was injured on site at the construction firm, or if he 'cooked the books' and broke the taxation laws?

This situation of 'two masters' has become very common, with many so-called labour bureaux being specifically created to hire out workers to other employers. The Unfair Dismissals (Amendment) Act 1993, supplemented by the Terms of Employment (Information) Act 1984, provides that where an employee works for an employer through the services of an employment agency, that employee is deemed to be employed by the person for whom the work is being done. In other words, the employer who is a client of the employment agency is deemed to be the employer of the employee, despite the fact that the original contract is between the employee and the employment agency.

This could also be important in the healthcare context where many nurses become private nurses known as 'agency nurses' and are given work through employment agencies at hospitals or clinics, along the same lines as the 'locum' system. The hospital or clinic will be deemed to employ that nurse, rather than the agency.

The integration test

This test looks at the facts surrounding a person's work to determine whether his or her work is an integral part of the business, rather than simply being an accessory to the business. This inquiry can raise very difficult questions when the nature of the business means that even self-employed persons are highly integrated in the business – for example, the freelance journalist working at but not for the newspaper. In other words, it might be the nature of the business, as opposed to the contractual relationship that determines a person's degree of integration.

In the case of *In the matter of The Sunday Tribune Ltd* [1984] I.R. 505, the weakness of this test was clearly illustrated.

Facts
The Sunday Tribune had been placed into liquidation and was in the process of being 'wound up'. Employees are regarded as preferred creditors of an insolvent employer, which means that they get paid their salaries before most of the other creditors get paid. This can be very important if there is not enough money to pay all the debts, as those at the end of the queue will lose out. The court had to decide whether a number of journalists were employees or independent contractors, as employees would be preferred creditors, whereas contractors would be ordinary creditors. These journalists were loosely referred to as 'freelance'.

Issue before the court
Was it possible to classify the journalists as employees or independent contractors?

Decision of the court
One of the journalists wrote a weekly column for the entire year, apart

from her two weeks' annual leave, and she took part in editorial conferences and received holiday pay. The court found that she was an integral part of the enterprise and therefore she was an employee. On the other hand, another journalist regularly contributed pieces to the paper but they were not always published. The topic of her pieces was usually decided in consultation with the editor and she would not work on a piece until the editor had commissioned it. She was not paid per word but rather at a rate agreed between the newspaper and the trade union. The court concluded that she was not an integral part of the newspaper and therefore found that she was an independent contractor.

Commentary
It is difficult to distinguish clearly between employees and independent contractors using the integration test, where the nature of the business, rather than the nature of the relationship, makes it necessary for anybody in that business to be integrated in the enterprise. Freelance journalists often work very closely with a particular newspaper and might regularly contribute to that newspaper so that they become identified with a that newspaper, even though they have a contract for services rather than a contract of service.

Again, this might impact on private nurses as the nature of many hospitals and clinics means that even the private nurse will become highly integrated into the workings of the hospital or clinic, particularly if the contract is a lengthy one, despite the fact that the nurse might have been originally hired to perform a specific task with autonomy.

As a general rule, if a person assumes some commercial risk in doing the job, he or she will most likely be classified as self-employed, even though he or she might be highly integrated in the business.

The integration test has not enjoyed a lot of support as its success is heavily dependent on the type of industry under scrutiny, and it seems to raise more questions than answers.

The enterprise test

The enterprise test asks whether the person who is performing the service is performing it as a person in business on his or her own account. For example, if the performance of the task requires significant capital investment on the part of the person, as opposed to being supplied by the business he or she serves, it is likely that he or she will be classified as self-employed.

This is a useful test, and operates on the simple principle that employees receive salaries and generally their employment does not place them in a position of commercial risk, whereas the self-employed work for themselves and therefore pay their own salaries, but also must stand the risk of making a loss. The case of *Tierney v An Post* (unreported, Supreme Court, 6 October 1999), shows the value of this test.

Facts
The applicant ran a rural post office. He provided the premises, and he was entitled to employ others to assist him in the running of the business. He was subject to the control of the head postmaster of the area. The post office was carried on in the same premises as the applicant's grocery business.

Issue before the court
Was the applicant an employee?

Decision of the court
The Supreme Court held that the although the applicant was subject to the immediate direction of the head postmaster for the area, the question of control was a factor to be taken into account but could not be the only factor that needed to be considered. A crucial factor was that the profit of the business went to the applicant and therefore the court found that the applicant was not an employee.

Commentary
Whilst this is a very valuable test, the changing nature of the job market has revealed gaps in the enterprise test. It is quite common to find employees working on a commission-only basis in the modern commercial world, but at the same time they might have a high degree of control exercised over them. The fact that the profit or loss is borne by the employee is no longer as critical as it used to be.

The mixed test

The courts have realised that each of these previously described tests have important contributions to make to a difficult question, and therefore the accepted test that is currently used is really a mixture of all the good bits of these tests, which is called the 'mixed' test, for obvious reasons. In this mixed test, the courts still give dominance to the control test, but are prepared to be influenced by other factors, rather than just looking at control. The mixed test was used in the English case of *Readymix Concrete Ltd v Minister for Pensions* [1968] 2 Q.B. 497 and was applied by the EAT in *Kirwan v Dart Industries Ltd and Leahy* (UD 1/80).

Facts
Dart Industries is the manufacturer of Tupperware. Leahy was the local

distributor, and Kirwan sold Tupperware for Leahy. Leahy supplied Kirwan with a car, but Kirwan paid for petrol and upkeep. Kirwan earned commission on the Tupperware that she sold, and also earned commission on the sales of the dealers that she had trained.

The contract was terminated and Kirwan claimed that Dart Industries and Leahy were her employers and that she had been unfairly dismissed.

Issue before the court
Despite a lot of freedom and relatively little control, could it be said that Kirwan was an employee?

Decision of the court
The EAT declined to consider the question of control as the sole determining feature of the relationship. Instead it looked at a variety of factors. It recognised that although Kirwan had a lot of freedom, Leahy was in ultimate control. It recognised that Kirwan was an integral player in the successful distribution of the product. It recognised that the provision of the car was an inducement towards greater sales through mobility.

McKenna J. argued that no one test could be regarded as conclusive. He suggested that an obligation to work under the control of the 'employer' was a necessary condition of a contract of service. He went on to say, however, that control alone was not sufficient. Once the control test had been satisfied the court must ask whether there is anything in the contract which is inconsistent with it being a contract of service.

Commentary
In using the mixed test the court is mindful of the fundamental importance of control (or the right to control) in any contract of service. At the same time the court recognises that in certain circumstances the control test on its own is inadequate, and it assesses the type of contract by looking at other factors as well. Therefore the court starts by looking at the question of control, but is prepared to continue assessing the facts if the control test appears inadequate.

The reality test

The 'reality' test is so-called because the court takes a step back and looks at the reality of the situation. Some commentators argue that it is distinguishable from the mixed test in that the reality test gives equal weight to all factors, and the element of control is just one of many things that the court will consider. In some countries this reality test is called the 'dominant impression' test, as the court determines the overall impression created by the elements of the relationship between the parties. It is difficult to see any real difference between the mixed test and the reality test.

In trying to work out this dominant impression, the courts will ask questions like the following:

Who actually provides the services?
If the engaged person is permitted to get somebody else to do all or any of the work contracted for, it is likely that the person is self-employed or an independent contractor. Generally a contract of employment contemplates that an employee will provide his or her own work and skills, and not those of somebody else.

The power to engage and dismiss
If the alleged employer does not have the power or authority to 'hire or fire', this is a good indication that the alleged employer is not, in law, the employer. This scenario would apply where there is a sub-contractor hiring out labourers to a construction firm. However, if the construction firm exercises such close control over the work being done and pays the workers their wages and is entitled to dismiss those workers, the court might hold that the workers have become the employees of the construction firm. This scenario of 'two masters' is now controlled by statute, as discussed before.

Remuneration
An employee cannot contract to work for nothing. A contract of employment must contain an agreement that one party will work for the other in consideration of a wage or other remuneration. Very often an employee will be paid according to the time spent at work (of service), whereas an independent contractor will be paid for a specific task (for services). Again, this test is not absolute, as certain employees do get paid for specific tasks, for example a piece worker.

Times of work
As a general rule, an employee does not determine his or her own hours of work, but again, this test is not infallible, particularly with the introduction of flexi-time.

Workplace
An employee generally works at premises supplied by the employer. Again, this test is not conclusive, for example the computer operator who works from home, or conversely, the sub-contractor who works on the client's site.

Tools of the trade

If the worker pays for his or her own tools, this is often a strong indication that he or she is self-employed or an independent contractor. There are clear exceptions to this rule, with many artisans preferring to buy their own tools, despite being employees.

As there are so many variables, the courts will look for clues and decide what dominant impression is created by the relationship between the parties. Things that the courts will look for are:

- An employee is usually controlled and supervised, whereas an independent contractor is not obliged to obey instructions concerning how to do the job;
- an employee works on orders from the employer, whereas the independent contractor usually exercises a wide discretion in how the job is to be done, as long as the final product is that which was contemplated by the parties when the deal was struck;
- an employee usually works in or on premises owned or controlled by the employer, whereas the independent contractor usually has his or her own premises but often completes the job on the site of the client;
- an employee usually can only work for one employer; an independent contractor can do jobs for a number of different clients;
- an employee is usually a member of the employer's organisation (for example, he or she will have an employee number), whereas the independent contractor must obviously be independent;
- an employee usually has deductions taken off his or her salary by the employer, for example PAYE (tax) and other deductions like insurance and trade union subscriptions. In addition, an employer will often contribute to pension and medical aid schemes, whereas an independent contractor must personally take care of these things;
- an employee usually gets paid annual leave and sick leave, whereas an independent contractor decides when to work or not to work (and usually only takes some leave when the annual income target has been reached);
- an employee usually receives a fixed salary, which is not dependent on his or her production. However, this is one area where things are changing rapidly as many employees now receive a basic salary and thereafter commission, whilst other employees often receive commission only (for example telesales). Analysts have predicted that this form of employment (i.e. short-term and results-based employment) will become more and more common and therefore it is necessary to be flexible when deciding whether a person is an employee. An independent contractor usually quotes for a job and a price is agreed for a specific product.

This list can never be a closed list, because the marketplace is such that new varieties of the employment relationship are being created every day. If one were to go through the above list, it becomes obvious that a lot of the 'clues' can be interpreted either way. However, if the answers to these questions create a dominant impression that the relationship is that of an employer and employee, then the law will recognise the contract between the parties as such.

The leading modern Irish case on the distinction between employee and independent contractor is *Henry Denny & Sons (Ireland) Ltd v The Minister for Social Welfare* [1998] 1 I.R. 34, where the Supreme Court considered the question.

Facts
Sandra Mahon worked for Denny as a demonstrator of its products in supermarkets. She signed a contract on an annual basis, and the contract described her as an independent contractor. Some of the more important provisions in the written contract were that Denny was not obliged to provide work to Mahon, she should be punctual and dress properly, that the contract could be terminated for 'serious misconduct' or on one month's notice by either party, and that she would be paid on presentation of an appropriate invoice (which had to be signed by the store manager). The contract expressly stated that Mahon was not an agent of Denny and had no authority to bind Denny, and that she was an independent contractor. Attached to the contract were 'Notes'. These stated that Mahon would be responsible for her own tax affairs and again repeated that she was an independent contractor.

Mahon received no formal training. She was briefed on the products that she was to demonstrate. She wore a company coat and demonstrated from a Denny stand, using Denny products only. She did not work at Denny's premises but rather used Denny products from the store in which she was demonstrating that day. She was paid a fixed sum per demonstration, and received a petrol allowance. She worked for the entire year (50 weeks). She was not entitled to sick pay or paid annual leave. She was not a member of the company pension scheme, and was not a member of the trade union.

Of importance was that both parties regarded Mahon as an independent contractor, although both parties recognised that Denny had the right to direct and control the demonstrations, including the manner, time and place of the demonstration.

Issue to be decided
The Supreme Court had to decide whether Sandra Mahon was an insurable person under the Social Welfare (Consolidation) Act 1981. In

order to be an insurable person under this Act, one had to be an employee. The Act did not apply to independent contractors.

Decision of the court
Despite the parties to the contract regarding Mahon as an independent contractor, and the written contract between them describing her as an independent contractor, the Supreme Court decided that she was an employee. The court made it clear that the contract was the starting point of the investigation into the status of the person performing the work, rather than the only consideration. In addition, the court made it clear that a variety of factors needed to be considered when deciding on the status of the person performing work, and control was only one of these factors.

Keane J. reviewed the Irish and English decisions on the subject and concluded:

> 'It is, accordingly, clear that, while each case must be determined in the light of its particular facts and circumstances, in general a person will be regarded as providing his or her services under a contract of service and not as an independent contractor where he or she is performing those services for another person and not for himself or herself. The degree of control exercised over how the work is to be performed, although a factor to be taken into account, is not decisive. The inference that the person is engaged in business on his or her own account can be more readily drawn where he or she provides the necessary premises or equipment or some other form of investment, where he or she employs others to assist in the business and where the profit which he or she derives from the business is dependent on the efficiency with which it is conducted by him or her.'

Murphy J. dealt with the issue of the contract expressly stating that Mahon was an independent contractor:

> 'The document known as the "Demonstrators' General Terms and Conditions", which was applicable to Ms Mahon and all other demonstrators whose names were from time to time included on the panel maintained by Kerry Foods as persons available to provide the services of a demonstrator, is reasonably lengthy but not very informative. It is clear that the panellists might have been called upon "to demonstrate, promote, market and sell Kerry Foods" products at different locations but little guidance is forthcoming as to the manner in which those operations would be carried out or the

skills which the panellists might possess or would be required to exercise in carrying out their functions. The document is silent as to the contract between the parties. Whether Ms Mahon was retained under a contract of service depends essentially on the totality of the contractual relationship express or implied between her and the appellants and not upon any statement as to the consequence of the bargain. Certainly the imposition of income tax and the manner of its collection falls to be determined in accordance with the appropriate legislation and the regulations made thereunder as they impinge upon the actual relationship between parties and not their statement as to how liability should arise or be discharged.

The terms and conditions governing the engagement of Ms Mahon were not 'the unique source' of the relationship between her and the appellants. I am satisfied that the appeals officer was correct in his conclusion that he was required to consider "the facts or realities of the situation on the ground" to enable him to reach a decision on the vexed question whether the respondent was an employee or an independent contractor. In seeking to ascertain the true bargain between the parties rather than rely on the labels ascribed by them to their relationship the appeals officer was expressly and correctly following the judgment of Carroll J in *Re Sunday Tribune Ltd* [1984] IR 505 . Of course the appeals officer was not entitled to ignore the terms and conditions under which the respondent was engaged nor did he do so. His report analyses fully and fairly the relevant written conditions in the context of the oral evidence heard by him and the arguments addressed to him. I have no doubt that the officer was entitled to reach the conclusion that he did and that the learned trial judge was correct in upholding that decision.'

Commentary

The Supreme Court has endorsed what can be called the reality test. The court will look at the totality of factors in deciding the nature of the contract between the parties. Even where the written contract between the parties gives labels to that relationship, the court will not follow those labels where the facts indicate that the contract is different to what it is titled. This is necessary as parties could attempt to mislead third parties by describing their contract as one thing whilst knowing that actually it is another thing.

The common law duties between employer and employee

In terms of the common law, every contract of employment, whether written or verbal, is deemed to have the following terms contained in it, where the parties owe certain duties towards each other. These do not have to be expressly agreed by the parties, the common law says that every contract of employment must contain these duties, whether agreed or not. In terms of the common law, the parties could agree to expressly exclude some of these implied duties, but as we shall see later, most of these duties (specifically those duties imposed on the employer) are now imposed by statute and cannot be excluded by contract.

The common law duties of the employee

To give personal service
The employee must do the work in person, and as a general rule cannot delegate this work to another.

To obey lawful orders
An employee must obey all lawful orders, provided that such orders were contemplated by the terms of the contract, do not place the employee in personal danger, and do not ask the employee to break the law.

To exercise reasonable care and skill
In addition to exercising reasonable care and skill in all work done under the contract, where an employee claims specialised skills, these skills must be rendered according to that special level of expertise.

To act in good faith
Employee must never work against the interests of their employer. They must not accept bribes or make secret profits. They must disclose all inventions made using the employer's facilities or made during work hours.

To maintain secrecy
Employee must never disclose confidential information received during or as a result of the work done for the employer. They must not exploit the employer's trade secrets. They may, however, disclose information if it is in the public interest to do so, or to someone who is legally entitled to receive that information.

The common law duties of an employer

To provide work
As a general rule, employers are not obliged to provide work, as long as they continue to pay the wage of the employee. However, where the provision of work is essential for future employment (e.g. to establish a reputation in the trade), or where the amount of remuneration is

determined by the work performed (e.g. commission work or piece work), or where the employee is undergoing training or is an apprentice, or if the employee is employed to fill a certain post or do a particular task, the employer cannot summarily abolish that post or task.

To pay wages or remuneration
As previously mentioned, an employee does not work for nothing, and an employer is obliged to pay the employee a salary. However, in the modern world of commerce, this salary might take a number of different forms, like commission, or goods for resale, or shares, and so on.

To provide for the safety of the employee
An employer has a special duty of care towards its employees, and must:
- Employ competent employees who are not a danger to other employees,
- provide and maintain a safe place of work,
- provide and maintain proper equipment,
- devise a safe system of working, and
- indemnify employees in respect of all losses and expenses incurred whilst acting on the employer's behalf, unless the employee acts unlawfully whilst knowing that such act was unlawful, or where the employee obeys an unlawful order, knowing the order to be unlawful.

The contract of employment

The common law recognised that a contract of employment could be either written or verbal, or even created by the behaviour of people, without any words. This is still the case today, and many contracts are struck by a simple handshake and very few words, and often no writing.

Anyone who works for an employer for a regular wage or salary has automatically a contract of employment whether written or not. Section 23 of the Industrial Relations Act 1990, states that a contract of employment, for the purposes of the Industrial Relations Acts of 1946 – 1990, may be 'expressed or implied, oral or in writing'.

Many of the terms of a contract of employment may emerge from the common law, statutes or collective agreements made through trade unions or may be derived from the custom or practice in a particular industry.

This lack of a written record clearly creates problems, both for the parties themselves and for any agency that is seeking to monitor the area of employment. Accordingly, the law has stepped in to ensure that a record is kept of any employment contracts.

The terms of Employment (Information) Acts

The Terms of Employment (Information) Acts of 1994 and 2001 provide that an employer must provide an employee with a written statement of certain particulars of the terms of employment. The Act defines a contract of employment as:

'(a) a contract of service or apprenticeship, and
(b) any other contract whereby an individual agrees with another person, who is carrying on the business of an employment agency within the meaning of the Employment Agency Act, 1971, and is acting in the course of that business, to do or perform personally any work or service for a third person (whether or not the third person is a party to the contract),

whether the contract is express or implied and if express, whether it is oral or in writing.'

Section 3(1) of the Act sets out the details of the contract of employment that must be provided to the employee in writing:

'(1) An employer shall, not later than 2 months after the commencement of an employee's employment with the employer, give or cause to be given to the employee a statement in writing containing the following particulars of the terms of the employee's employment, that is to say—
   (a) the full names of the employer and the employee,
   (b) the address of the employer in the State or, where appropriate, the address of the principal place of the relevant business of the employer in the State or the registered office (within the meaning of the Companies Act, 1963),
   (c) the place of work or, where there is no fixed or main place of work, a statement specifying that the employee is required or permitted to work at various places,
   (d) the title of the job or nature of the work for which the employee is employed,
   (e) the date of commencement of the employee's contract of employment,
   (f) in the case of a temporary contract of employment, the expected duration thereof or, if the contract of employment is for a fixed term, the date on which the contract expires,
   (g) the rate or method of calculation of the employee's

remuneration,
(h) the length of the intervals between the times at which remuneration is paid, whether a week, a month or any other interval,
(i) any terms or conditions relating to hours of work (including overtime),
(j) any terms or conditions relating to paid leave (other than paid sick leave),
(k) any terms or conditions relating to—
  (i) incapacity for work due to sickness or injury and paid sick leave, and
  (ii) pensions and pension schemes,
(l) the period of notice which the employee is required to give and entitled to receive (whether by or under statute or under the terms of the employee's contract of employment) to determine the employee's contract of employment or, where this cannot be indicated when the information is given, the method for determining such periods of notice,
(m) a reference to any collective agreements which directly affect the terms and conditions of the employee's employment including, where the employer is not a party to such agreements, particulars of the bodies or institutions by whom they were made.'

Commentary
The important principle to understand about this statute is that it does not say that an employment contract is only a contract when it is in writing. That is not the law. The employment contract comes into existence when the parties agree on the terms of that contract, whether that is in writing, in words, or simply by their behaviour. That principle is made clear by the definition of a contract of employment at the beginning of the Act.

What this law provides is that certain aspects and details of that existing contract must be recorded in writing so that they are available not only to the parties themselves but to third parties, like labour inspectors.

It is also quite clear that the provisions of this Act apply to virtually any contract of employment, including employees working under a contract of apprenticeship, or employed through an employment agency, or employed by the State (and this would include people employed by health boards).

The Act does not apply to employees who have only been employed (continuously) for less than a month (although, strangely, the Act says that the employer must provide this written statement of particulars to the employee within two months of the employee starting work). Before December 2001, the Act did not apply to employees who worked for less than eight hours per week, but this exclusion was removed by the Protection of Employment (Part-Time Work) Act 2001.

The Act makes further provisions about the written statement:
- The statement must be signed by or on behalf of the employer;
- the statement must be retained by the employer during the employment of the employee and for one year after the contract is terminated;
- even where the employee leaves his or her employment during the first two months of the contract, the employer must still provide the ex-employee with the written statement;
- after 1 March 1998, the statement must include details of rest periods and breaks allowed to the employee;
- the statement must indicate the pay reference period for the purposes of the National Minimum Wage Act 2000;
- the statement must state that the employee may request from the employer a written statement of the employee's average hourly rate of pay for any pay reference period falling within the previous twelve months, as set out in Section 23 of the National Minimum Wage Act 2000.

Other statutory provisions providing for written records

There are also other statutory provisions that order employers to provide their employees with certain details of the employment contract in writing. Again, it is important to note that these articles of writing do not themselves make the contract valid. The contract of employment is already in existence, and all these statutes provide is that certain details of that contract must be recorded in writing.

Employers are required by section 14(1) of the Unfair Dismissals Act of 1977 – 2001 to give a notice in writing to each employee setting out the procedure which the employer will observe before, and for the purpose of, dismissing the employee. This must be given not later than twenty-eight days after entering into a contract of employment.

The Payment of Wages Act 1991, gives every employee the right to a written statement, every pay day, of wages and with every deduction itemised.

Contract of Employment: Summary

1. The law distinguishes between two types of contract when looking at the law of employment. The contract of service between an employer and employee, and the contract for services between a client and an independent contractor.
2. The distinction is important for a number of reasons, but most important are that an independent contractor cannot be dismissed, and that a number of protective statutes do not apply to independent contractors, only employees.
3. The courts have formulated a number of tests to determine whether a contract is one for services or of service, but the modern approach is to look at the entire relationship and dealings between the parties, and thereby gain a dominant impression of the nature of the relationship between the parties.
4. A contract of service between an employer and an employee can be agreed with a handshake, or in words, or in writing. The existence and validity of this contract does not depend on it being reduced to writing.
5. There are statutes, which direct that the parties to a contract of service must record certain details of that contract in writing. These details do not create the contract, which is already in existence. The details are rather a written record of an existing contract, so that the parties and others can refer to those written details when they are needed.
6. Useful websites:
    a. *Department of Trade and Enterprise* (http://www.entemp.ie).
    b. *Oasis* (http://www.oasis.gov.ie/employment/starting_work/contract_of_employment.html).

Annexure 1

Fixed Term/Specified Purpose Contract with a Health Board

1. You are employed as a _____ .
2. Your employment commences on_____.
3. Your employment with the South Eastern Health Board (the Board) shall be for the purpose of filling a vacancy.
4.. The Unfair Dismissals Acts, 1977–1993 shall not apply to your dismissal, consisting only of the cesser of the said purpose (or expiry of the period stated).
5. The position for which you have been recruited is in _____.
6. You will report directly to _____.
7. The main duties of your position are set out in the attached job description.
8. In addition to your normal duties, you may be required to undertake other duties appropriate to your position as may be assigned to you by your supervisor.
9. You will be paid at __ point of the Department of Health and Children salary scale: €_____. Statutory deductions will be made in respect of PAYE and PRSI (Class A). You will be paid _____ in arrears by paypath.
10. The normal attendance hours for your position are € _____ (times to be worked, days, shifts, etc.). You may be required to work overtime, depending on service requirements. Overtime will be paid at the rates approved by the Department of Health and Children.
11. Annual leave and public holidays are granted in accordance with the provisions of the Organisation of Working Time Act, 1997. Your annual leave entitlement will be _____ days per completed year of service.
12. The granting of sick pay is entirely at the discretion of the Chief Executive Officer and is subject to compliance with the Board's sick leave procedure.
13. Your work performance and conduct will be regularly appraised during the period of your employment.
14. Details of the Board's grievance and disciplinary procedures are contained in the Staff Handbook, which shall be issued to you on commencement of your employment.
15. The Board is committed to ensuring the safety, health and welfare of its staff and to this end, a safety statement has been prepared setting out all the safety arrangements, which are in force. You will be familiarised with these arrangements on commencement of your

employment and will be obliged to adhere to them at all times.
16. Confidential information must not be divulged or discussed except in the performance of normal duty.
17. Notwithstanding the fact that this is a specified purpose contract (or fixed term), the Board reserves the right to terminate this contract prior to the cesser of the purpose (or duration) on the giving of the appropriate period of notice set down by the Minimum Notice and Terms of Employment Act, 1973–1991.
18. Your employment with the Board shall cease on _____. The Unfair Dismissals Act, 1977–1993 shall not apply to your dismissal consisting only of the expiry of your contract on this date.
19. You will be required to give the Board at least one week's notice in writing of your intention to terminate your employment.
20. On the cesser of the purpose of this contract (or duration), you shall cease to be an employee of the Board. Any further employment offered to you shall be at the sole discretion of the Board.
21. A copy of the Board's employee handbook is enclosed and forms an integral part of your contract.
22. I am aware that I will be liable for the payment of Superannuation contributions. The rate of deduction of Superannuation will be in accordance with the relevant legislation.
23. Your terms and conditions may be revised in accordance with agreements reached between the union representing your grade and the Board.

I accept and agree to be bound by the above terms and conditions.

SIGNED: _____ (Employee). DATE: _____

SIGNED: _____ (for the Board)
POSITION: _____ DATE: _____

Annexure 2

Portion of Contract of Appointment of a Staff Nurse Employed by a Health Board

Post of staff nurse.
Responsible to: CNMI / CNM2
Accountable to: Director of Nursing

Professional qualifications: Experience
Candidates must, on the latest date for receiving completed application forms for the office:
  (a) Be registered in the General Division of the Register of Nurses kept by An Bord Altranais or be entitled to be so registered.
  (b) 6 months Post registration experience is desirable.
  (c) A specialist qualification or at least one years experience in a specialist post is desirable.

Essential qualifications
Each candidate must:
  (a) Be of good character.
  (b) Each candidate must be under 65 years of age on the first day of the month in
  (c) which the latest date for receipt of completed application forms for the office occurs.
  (d) Be free from any defect or disease which would render him/her unsuitable to hold the office and be in a state of health such as would indicate a reasonable prospect of ability to render regular and efficient service.
  (e) Produce satisfactory documentary evidence of Hepatitis B vaccination including dates of vaccination and Hepatitis B surface antibody level.

OR

Satisfactory documentary evidence of the result of a test for Hepatitis B surface antigen performed within the last six months.

If you are not in a position immediately to provide either of the above you should arrange to have a blood test for Hepatitis B carried out by a recognised Hospital and have the results forwarded to the Nominated Medical Officer. Alternatively you may arrange with the Nominated Medical Officer to carry out this blood test.

Arising from your blood test if you are shown to be susceptible to Hepatitis B infection, you are then required to be vaccinated and must provide satisfactory documentary evidence of Hepatitis B vaccination including dates of vaccination and Hepatitis B surface antibody level.

Please note that an offer of employment may not be made to you unless the requirements described above which will identify you as not being a carrier of Hepatitis B are compiled with to the satisfaction of the Nominated Medical Officer.

(f) be prepared in the event of appointment to an Institution devoted wholly or part to the treatment of Tuberculosis to furnish a written agreement that he/she shall after taking up duty undergo the following medical examination periodically;
 (i) Tuberculin and B.S.R. tests;
 (ii) General medical examination;
 (iii) Chest x-ray examination.

(g) Must be prepared to accompany, when deemed necessary by the Medical Staff, patients who are being conveyed by ambulance to any of the Health Board's institutions or to extern hospitals.

Desirable:
Certification in Intravenous Drug Administration is desirable or to give a commitment to pursue training in the event of appointment.

Have completed a training programme in Manual Handling & Lifting Techniques and if not give a commitment to undergo training if appointed.

Overall objectives:
1. Manage the Ward/Department in CNM1/CNM2 absence.
2. Provide and maintain a caring, efficient and highly professional nursing service to all patients in his/her care.
3. Actively participate in the teaching and assessment of student nurses undergoing diploma training and encourage and assist the development of support staff.
4. Monitor the work of support staff in the Ward/Department and provide necessary training and guidance to ensure that high standards of care are maintained in accordance with hospital policy and protocol.

Professsional:
1. To receive patients and their relatives in a calm, courteous and reassuring manner and ensure they are kept informed of progress and treatments and participate in providing support and help.
2. Maintain absolute confidentiality and respect of all medical and nursing records.
3. Prepare reports for and receive reports from CNMI/CNM2 and night staff. Maintain an awareness of the need for information and support through 24 hour nursing services.
4. Assist medical staff with procedures and treatments ensuring that all instructions are faithfully executed and that observations are documented and reported.
5. Provide and maintain a high standard of clinical practice at all times.
6. Ensure that nursing procedures are carried out in accordance with the nursing procedure manual.
7. Ensure the proper control, storage and administration of drugs and medicines.
8. Adhere at all times to An Bord Altranais code for nurses.
9. Anticipate and respond to the needs of patients and their relatives.
10. Attend In Service training sessions where possible and keep abreast of developments and trends within the clinical speciality and the profession as a whole.
11. Maintain a quiet calm atmosphere in the ward environment and by encouragement and example, foster a happy team spirit to ensure the safety and well being of patients and staff.
12. Actively promote the concept of total patient care within the Ward or Department.
13. To have a knowledge of Cardiac Pulmonary Resuscitation.
14. Provide returns and statistics required by Hospital policy.
15. Participate in:
    (a) Arranging meals and serving meals and refreshments to patients.
    (b) Co-ordinating all requirements for the discharge of patients.
16. Ensure that all staff are conversant with the Fire Regulations of the hospital and within the Ward/Department including the sitting of appliances and exits.
17. Participate in the control of infection.
18. Attend meetings as required.
19. Be aware of health and safety hazards associated with working procedures. Ensure own safety and that of others with particular reference to:
    (a) Lifting,
    (b) Disposal of sharps,

(c) Disposal of infected equipment/material.
20. Supervise and support other grades of staff in the course of their duties in the interest of patient care.

Administration
1. Observe all nursing and administrative policies and procedures as laid down by the South Eastern Health Board.
2. Ensure that the Ward/Department is maintained in good order, that supplies are adequate, and that all equipment is in good working order and ready for immediate use.
3. Ensure that the appropriate and efficient use of supplies is made and exercise economy in the use of consumables.
4. Share the responsibility for the day-to-day running of the ward with other trained staff.
5. Liaise continuously with the CNMI/CNM2 and ensure that effective communications systems are maintained within the Ward/Department.
6. In the absence of CNMI/CNM2, report all absenteeism, lateness and sickness to the Senior Nurse Manager.
7. Ensure that the admission, transfer and discharge of patients is conducted in accordance with hospital policy.
8. Arrange for the care of patient's property, safe custody of valuables or cash and distribution of mail.
9. Co-operate and liaise with all Wards and Departments within the hospital e.g. Pharmacy, Chaplains, Catering and Physiotherapy.
10. Report and record accurately any accidents to patients or staff to Director of Nursing Office and initiate any action necessary.
11. Co-operate with the Director of Nursing in estimating the need for household staff in terms of the maintenance of desirable standards of cleanliness and methods to be used.

Personnel:
1. Assist with induction programmes for newly appointed staff.
2. Wear uniform in accordance with Hospital Policy and ensure that professional standards are adhered to with regard to uniform changing per hospital and infection control protocols.

General:
1. Assist in other Ward/Departments as requested by Director of Nursing.
2. Undertake any other duties as requested by Director of Nursing.
3. Initiate and undertake approved clinical nursing research within the Ward/Department.

General conditions
The appointment will be made under Section 14 of the Health Act, 1970 and Circular 10/71 from the Department of Health.

The above Job Description is not intended to be a comprehensive list of all duties involved and consequently, the post holder may be required to perform other duties as appropriate to the post which may be assigned to him/her from time to time and to contribute to the development of the post while in office.

Particulars of officce

1. The officer appointed will hold office under Part II of the Health Act, 1970 on such terms and conditions and shall perform such duties as the Chief Executive Officer from time to time determines, subject to any directions from the Minister for Health.
2. The office is whole time, permanent and pensionable
3. *Salary*
   € _____ X 9 annual increments to € _____. LSI € _____.
   Payment will be made by the Pay Path System. Incremental Credit may be granted in respect of previous approved service.
   Superannuation
   (a) With effect from the 6th April 1995:
      (i) Persons who become pensionable officers of a health board, who are liable to pay the Class A rate of PRSI contribution will be required in respect of their superannuation to contribute to the health board at the rate of 1.5% of their pensionable remuneration plus 3.5.% of net pensionable remuneration (i.e. pensionable remuneration less twice the annual rate of social insurance old age contributory pension payable at the maximum rate of a person with no adult dependant of qualified children).
      (ii) Persons who become pensionable officers of a health board who are liable to pay Class D rate of PRSI contribution will be required, in respect of their superannuation, to contribute to the health board at the rate of 5% of their pensionable remuneration.
   (b) All persons who become pensionable officers of a health board, are required, in respect of the Local Government (Spouses and Children's Contributory Pension) Scheme 1986, to contribute to the health board at the rate of 1.5% of their pensionable remuneration in accordance with the terms of the Scheme.

Repayment of Gratuity or Contributions
Please note that under the Superannuation Code, a person who has been granted a gratuity (or a refund of superannuation contributions) shall be entitled to repay such gratuity or superannuation refund and if these monies are repaid, the entire period of previous permanent service will reckon for superannuation purposes. Repayment of contributions/gratuity will be subject to compound interest.

4. The person appointed will reside within a convenient distance.

   Previous Temporary Service
   Where previous temporary service is involved the person appointed will be required to reckon such service for superannuation purposes. Officers appointed who pay modified P.R.S.I. contributions i.e. "D" class; the charge will be 5% of salary earned in respect of periods of temporary Health Board service after 1/1/1986. For service prior to 1/1/1986 the charge is 2Y2% of salary earned.

   Officers appointed paying full rate of P.R.S.I. contributions i.e. "A" class will have their temporary health board service charged at uprated salary and emoluments at the time of paying contributions.

5. *Probation:*
   Where a person who is not already a permanent officer of a Health Board is appointed the appointment shall be subject to the conditions that:
   (a) The person appointed shall hold office for a probationary period of 12 months which the Chief Executive Officer may at his discretion extend, and
   (b) The person appointed shall cease to hold office at the end of his/her probationary period unless during such period the Chief Executive Officer has certified that the service of such a person is satisfactory.

6. *Travelling Expenses:*
   The person appointed will be paid travelling expenses at the approved rate of travelling necessarily performed in the discharge of his/her official duties.

7. A person appointed to an office shall pay to the health board any fees or other monies (other than his/her inclusive salary) payable to or received by him/her by virtue of his/her appointment or in respect of service which he/she is required by or under any enactment to perform.

8. For the purpose of satisfying the requirements as to health, it will be necessary for each successful candidate, before he/she is appointed to undergo a medical examination by a qualified medical

practitioner to be nominated by the Health Board. Defects reported as a result of this examination in respect of teeth, vision, tonsils or other such matters must be remedied before appointment.
9. The person appointed to the office is transferable to similar office under the control of the Health Board.
10. When resigning, an officer is required to give one month's notice in writing previous to resigning the office, or in default, to forfeit one month's amount of salary, to be deducted as liquidation damages from any remuneration due at the time of such resignation.
11. The person appointed will be required to retire on reaching 65 years of age.

Annual leave

24-27 days annual leave applies to this post.

General conditions

I. Fire Orders must be observed and staff must attend fire lectures periodically.
II. All accidents within the Department must be reported immediately.
III. In accordance with the Safety, Health and Welfare at Work Act 1989, all staff must comply with all safety regulations.

Appointment and asssignment

The appointment to this post shall be to the _____ Health Board with initial assignment to _____ General Hospital. This assignment may be changed at the discretion of the _____ Health Board having regard to the service needs in the Board's area.

Confidentiality

In the course of your employment you may have access to, or hear information concerning the medical or personal affairs of patients and/or staff or other health services' business. Such records and information are strictly confidential, unless acting on the instructions of an authorised officer, on no account must information concerning staff, patients or other health service business be divulged or discussed except in the performance of normal duty. In addition records must never be left in such a manner that unauthorised persons can obtain access to them and must be kept in safe custody when no longer required.

32
TERMINATION OF THE EMPLOYMENT CONTRACT

> *Learning Outcomes*
> **At the completion of this chapter, the reader should know and understand the following:**
> - The difference between termination by expiration and termination by dismissal.
> - The types of dismissal.
> - The Unfair Dismissal Acts.
> - The position and status of officers appointed in terms of the Health Act 1970.

Important concepts and phrases that are crucial to an understanding of this chapter

Adjudication
The process of analysing, comparing and judging competing claims that is carried out by a tribunal or a court.

Redress
The relief or remedy granted to a litigant (e.g. reinstatement, re-engagement or compensation).

Introduction

The most common dispute between employees and employers concerns dismissal. Disputes are usually about whether a dismissal has taken place, or if the dismissal is admitted or proved, whether that dismissal was fair and lawful.

The difference between termination by expiration and termination by dismissal

A contract expires or ceases to exist either because the parties to that contract agree it should end, or the contract itself has a limited life and a term in that contract specifies that it shall end at a stipulated date or at the completion of a stipulated task. The contract will also expire if one of the parties dies, as the contract of service is a personal contract, where the specified identity of the parties to the contract is an essential part of the contract.

On the other hand, a dismissal will occur when the one party unilaterally ends the contract, without agreement by the other party. The party that unilaterally ends the contract in a dismissal is usually the employer, except in the case of constructive dismissal, where the employee ends the contract.

The types of dismissal

The common law of dismissal has for all intents and purposes been overtaken by statutory law. Of course the interpretations by the courts of these statutory provisions form part of our common law. The different classifications of dismissal are still used and these were originally formulated by the courts and are part of the common law.

Types of dismissal that are recognised by the modern law are wrongful dismissal, unfair dismissal, lawful dismissal, summary dismissal and constructive dismissal.

Wrongful dismissal

An employee will allege wrongful dismissal when the termination has breached (broken) a term of the contract. For example, if a contract provides that an employee must be given three months' notice, and the employer terminates the contract after one month's notice, the employee can claim wrongful dismissal.

This is an alternative cause of action to unfair dismissal and is the most popular cause of action after an action for unfair dismissal.

The primary reason for the popularity of wrongful dismissal as an alternative cause of action is because the action is based on the terms of the employment contract, and therefore the usual contractual remedies apply, namely specific performance or damages.

The remedy of specific performance orders the wrongful party, in this case the employer, to fulfil its duties arising from the contract, which means that the employer must allow the employee to continue working as before.

At one stage the courts were reluctant to grant specific performance on a contract of employment. This attitude has relaxed somewhat.

A good example of this changing attitude is illustrated in the case of *McCann v Irish Medical Organisation* (unreported, High Court, 2 October 1989).

Facts
McCann was the Secretary-General of the Irish Medical Organisation (IMO). The executive of the IMO passed a resolution removing McCann from his office of Secretary-General. McCann applied to the High Court for an injunction ordering the IMO to allow him to continue as Secretary-General. In effect, he sought specific performance on his employment contract.

Issue before the court
Should specific performance be granted on the contract between McCann and the IMO given that the Secretary-General needed to be able to work with the executive?

Decision of the court
Egan J. granted interim injunctive relief to McCann. Injunctions were ordered firstly preventing the dismissal of McCann and secondly, preventing the IMO from replacing McCann with another employee and thirdly, preventing the IMO from removing McCann from the office of Secretary-General until the legal proceedings were completed. At the court hearing, the parties agreed that McCann was, and continued to be, the holder of the office of Secretary-General of the IMO and the resolution terminating McCann's employment was withdrawn.

Commentary
Traditionally, there were three grounds for the court refusing to grant specific performance on an employment contract. Firstly, it was argued that the contract of employment was based on mutual confidence and trust and once these were no longer in existence, the parties should not be forced to work with each other. Secondly, the courts argued that the contract of employment was based on the concept of mutuality or reciprocity — the courts will not force an employee to perform the work against his or her wishes, and likewise employers should not be forced to keep them in service. Thirdly, the courts did not want to order specific performance because that order could require constant supervision, something the courts could not provide.

These justifications for refusing specific performance have diminished as the modern employment contract has been characterised by lessened contact between employer and employee. As organisations have grown and become diverse, the nature of employment in the modern age means infrequent personal contact. If the employee wants to return to work this should be allowed, and the fact that the primary relief for unfair dismissal is reinstatement or re-employment is testimony to this fact. The courts have begun to realise that specific performance can be granted on an employment contract, as *McCann*'s case illustrates.

Similar arguments could be used in the healthcare context where a nurse might never come into direct contact with his or her employer, particularly if the employer is a health board. If a nurse has a dispute with an immediate superior and is wrongfully dismissed as a result, specific performance is possible if the nurse (or the superior) was transferred to another hospital or even to another wing of the same hospital, thereby avoiding contact and further conflict.

The second important reason for wrongful dismissal being a popular alternative to unfair dismissal as a cause of action is that the other available remedy is damages. The Unfair Dismissal Act places a limit or ceiling on the amount of damages an employee is entitled to receive when unfairly dismissed. However, if one brings an action based on wrongful dismissal in the High Court, the amount of damages that one can be awarded could substantially exceed the limit of two years' salary imposed by the Unfair Dismissal Act. An award of damages by a court is not limited to lost salary but can include damages for loss of reputation, costs of retraining, or even some starting capital to set up your own business. This difference in compensation could be worth a lot of money, particularly where the employee can show that his or her future earnings would have been considerable but for the wrongful dismissal.

Lawful dismissal

A lawful dismissal is one that complies with the express and implied provisions of the contract between the parties, including terms imported into the contract by statute. For example, a dismissal with proper notice would be a lawful dismissal.

The definition of unfair dismissal means that although a dismissal is lawful, it might still be unfair if, for example, it was for an arbitrary reason or due to an ulterior motive.

Summary dismissal

In this scenario the employer brings the contract to an immediate end, without giving notice. This usually happens in cases of serious misconduct like the assault of a fellow employee, or theft from the employer. The employee's actions must be such that the employer cannot be expected to continue the contract at all, not even for the purposes of giving notice.

Constructive dismissal

This type of dismissal differs from the others as the employee, and not the employer, brings the contract to an end. In other words, the employee resigns.

Under normal circumstances, a resignation is the employee's way of unilaterally ending an employment contract, and would be the opposite of a dismissal. However, if the employee resigns because the employer acted in such a way that it was intolerable for the employee to continue working, that forced resignation is regarded as a dismissal, as the employer's conduct is effectively the cause of the termination.

The test is an objective test. For example, an overly sensitive employee could not claim constructive dismissal after resigning as a result of the employer raising his voice at the employee. The employer's conduct that forced the employee to resign must be objectively improper or unlawful, and must be in a manner calculated to destroy or seriously damage the relationship of confidence and trust with the employee. Examples would be a dramatic cut in pay without warning or explanation, a significant change in a job description (usually in a worse job), or a relocation to some remote branch of the employer's organisation, forcing the employee to travel considerable distances to get to and from work.

A leading Irish case dealing with constructive dismissal is *Byrne v RHM Foods (Ireland) Ltd* (UD 69/1979).

Facts
Byrne was employed as the personal assistant to the marketing manager. The marketing manager was suspended from his job, but Byrne was assured by the managing director that her job was safe, that she had nothing to worry about, and should continue with her work as before. However, Byrne soon discovered that it was not possible to continue as before. The keys to the filing cabinet were removed, she was given no work, and she was effectively cut off from her colleagues. The last straw was when her telephone was disconnected. Byrne resigned.

Issue before the court
Had the employee been unfairly dismissed?

Decision of the court
The EAT held that Byrne had no option but to resign, and therefore this was not a genuine resignation, but rather a dismissal.

The EAT stated in its finding that the employee's position of 'continuous isolation without knowledge of what was going on or contact by any person made it reasonable and understandable that her confidence and trust in her employer should be undermined to the extent that she could tolerate it no longer'.

Unfair dismissal

Even in cases where the employer sticks to the letter of the contract by giving proper notice and any payments that are due, the employee can still allege unfair dismissal if the reason for that contract being terminated is an arbitrary or unfair reason (for example, the employer did not like the employee's dress sense or religious beliefs – something that is not connected with the employee's ability to perform the job). This type of dismissal was not recognised by the common law, where an employer could dismiss an employee for virtually any reason, as long as the terms of the contract relating to notice or severance pay were fulfilled. As this left most employees extremely vulnerable to the whim of the employer, the question of unfair dismissals was extensively regulated by the Unfair Dismissal Acts 1977-2001, and it is these Acts that will be studied next.

The Unfair Dismissal Acts

The Unfair Dismissal Acts 1977-2001 protect employees from being unfairly dismissed. The Acts set out the rules by which dismissals are judged. Where an employee is unfairly dismissed, the Acts have created an adjudication system, which allows the employee to seek justice and redress. The principal Act is the 1997 Act, with the 1993 and 2001 Acts making some important amendments to the original Act.

Section 1 of the 1977 Act contains an extended definition of dismissal:
'"Dismissal", in relation to an employee, means—

(a) the termination by his employer of the employee's contract of employment with the employer, whether prior notice of the termination was or was not given to the employee.

(b) the termination by the employee of his contract of employment with his employer, whether prior notice of the termination was or was not given to the employer, in circumstances in which, because of the conduct of the employer, the employee was or would have been entitled, or it was or would have been reasonable for the employee, to terminate the contract of employment without giving prior notice of the termination to the employer, or

(c) the expiration of a contract of employment for a fixed term without its being renewed under the same contract or, in the case of a contract for a specified purpose (being a purpose of such a kind that the duration of the contract was limited but was, at the time of its making, incapable of precise ascertainment), the cesser of the purpose.'

Commentary

Paragraph (a) of the definition covers the situation where the employer unilaterally ends the contract, either with notice or summarily. This is obviously the most common form of dismissal. Paragraph (b) describes constructive dismissal.

Paragraph (c) describes the dismissal of an employee on a fixed-term or specific-purpose contract. At first, this definition looks like it has substantially modified the common law, as in terms of the common law, such contracts expire rather than being a dismissal. However, it is important to notice that the expiration of the fixed-term or specific-purpose contract is not the moment of dismissal. The dismissal happens when the employer fails to replace the expired contract with another fixed-term or specific-purpose contract of the same or similar nature.

The definition says that it must be replaced by 'the same contract' and therefore it is possible to have a situation where an improved replacement contract would technically amount to a dismissal. For example, a fixed-term contract of six months is replaced by a fixed-term contract of three years. Technically, in terms of this definition, that person has been dismissed, as the replacement contract is not the same as the original contract. For obvious reasons however, it is highly unlikely that the employee will challenge the replacement contract or the 'dismissal' as being unfair.

This leads on to a very important point about this extended definition of dismissal that is found in section 1. The definition only tells us what a dismissal is. It does not define whether that dismissal is fair or lawful or not. The fairness, or otherwise, can only be determined once the existence of the dismissal is established. It could be argued, however, that the definition of constructive dismissal, by its very nature, can only be fulfilled where the conduct of the employer is unfair or unlawful.

At first, the definition of dismissal in section 1 of the Unfair Dismissal Act 1977 does not seem wide enough to include the situation where an employee takes statutory leave (for example, maternity leave in terms of the Maternity Protection Act 1994) but then is not permitted to return to work by her employer. As the courts will attempt to bring all dismissals within the definition, it is likely that the employer's action in refusing to allow the employee to return to her job will be interpreted as being a dismissal in terms of paragraph (a).

Therefore the statutory definition of dismissal covers four scenarios or types of dismissal: the unilateral termination by the employer, the constructive dismissal, the failure to repeat a fixed-term or specific-purpose contract of employment, and the refusal to allow an employee to return to his or her job after taking statutory leave.

Certain employees are not protected by the Unfair Dismissal Acts

Section 2 of the 1977 Act excludes certain employees from the protection of the Act. These include an employee who has not worked continuously for the same employer for a year; an employee reaching the normal retirement age; a person employed by a family member or relative to work in a domestic setting or farm where both employer and employee reside; a person in employment as a member of the Defence Forces, the Judge Advocate-General, the chairman of the Army Pensions Board or the ordinary member thereof who is not an officer of the Medical Corps of the Defence Forces; a member of the Garda Síochána; an apprentice or trainee on a training allowance; a civil servant; officers of a local authority; officers of a health board or officers of a vocational education committee or officers of a committee of agriculture.

The various categories that are excluded are self-explanatory, except perhaps section 2(1)(a), which says that employees with less than one year's service are not protected by the Act, except where that dismissal is in contravention of another statute.

It would seem to be easy for an employer to avoid the Act by making sure that an employee never has more than a year's service. For example, an employer might employ the same employee for a considerable length of time, but always on six-month contracts, with perhaps a couple of weeks' break between each contract. If the employee is dismissed, and claims unfair dismissal, the employer can argue that the employee has only been employed for six months, and therefore is not protected by the Act.

The 1993 Amendment Act amended this exclusion section by saying that a Rights Commissioner, the EAT, or the Circuit Court may decide whether the employment of a person on a series of two or more contracts of employment, between which there was a break of no more than twenty six weeks, was for the purpose of avoiding the provisions of the Unfair Dismissal Acts. If it is decided that the motive behind this series of fixed-term or specific purpose contracts was to avoid liability under the Act, the length of these various contracts may be added together to calculate the length of service of the employee and so decide whether that employee is protected by the Acts.

The Acts apply to all employees who have had at least a year's continuous service with the same employer. Before 20 December 2001, the Acts did not apply to a person who worked for less than eight hours a week, but on that date the Protection of Employment (Part-Time Work) Act 2001 removed this exclusion.

An employer and an employee are allowed to enter into a written fixed-term or specific-purpose contract, and to put an express provision in that written contract saying that the Unfair Dismissal Acts do not apply to that contract. This is the only time that the Act allows its provisions to be excluded. In any other type of contract, a clause that excludes the provisions of the Unfair Dismissal Acts will be treated as null and void, and ignored by the tribunal or the court.

As was discussed earlier, in relation to the 'two masters' scenario, persons engaged through employment agencies are covered by the Acts. For the purposes of the Acts, the person for whom the hired employee works is deemed to be the employer of that employee.

The Acts do not apply to the dismissal of an employee who is standing in for an employee who is on statutory leave, provided that the employer informs the replacement employee, in writing, at the beginning of the job, that his or her employment will terminate when the employee on leave returns.

The other exclusion that must be mentioned given the nature of this book, are people employed by health boards as officers. These officers of health boards are part of another category of worker that falls outside the employee-independent contractor distinction, namely that of an office holder. Officers of health boards are expressly excluded from the protection of the Unfair Dismissal Acts as their appointment, remuneration and termination are governed by another statute, the Health Act 1970. However, a temporary officer is still protected by the Unfair Dismissal Acts. This aspect is dealt with at the end of this chapter, as it affects most nurses employed by the health boards.

It must also be mentioned that an agency nurse used to be categorised as an independent contractor and therefore was not protected by the Unfair Dismissal Acts. However, the Unfair Dismissal (Amendment) Act 1993 has included agency nurses under the protection of the Unfair Dismissal Acts, as the nurse is employed by an employment agency to work in a hospital and therefore the hospital is deemed to be the employer of the nurse.

Proving the fairness of the dismissal

Section 6 of the 1977 Act provides that every dismissal of an employee will be deemed (presumed) to have been unfair unless the employer can show substantial grounds justifying the dismissal. In order to justify a dismissal, an employer must show that it resulted from one or more of the following causes, which are listed in section 4 of the 1977 Act. These are:
- The capability, competence or qualifications of the employee.
- The employee's conduct.
- The redundancy of the employee.
- The fact that continuation of the employment would contravene another statutory requirement.

It is necessary to look at these grounds a little more closely.

The capability, competence or qualifications of the employee

These are often called 'incapacity dismissals', and arise when an employee is unable to do the job he or she was originally employed to do. An example would be the dismissal of an ambulance driver after the driver had his or her driver's licence suspended or revoked.

These dismissals can be quite tricky as it is sometimes difficult to distinguish incapacity from misconduct. For example, an employee is constantly late in the morning and this leads to the employee's job not being done properly. Is the employee dismissed for the offence of always being late (despite repeated warnings) or is the dismissal because the employee was not doing the job properly as a result of being late?

The other difficulty often raised in this type of dismissal is just how much should the employer do to ensure that the employee can do his or her job? For example, is it incapacity if the employer does not train its employees in the latest techniques or equipment, with the result that the employee can no longer do the job properly?

The employee's conduct

This is usually a dismissal as a result of the employee's misconduct. Questions that will be asked of an employer are whether the act of misconduct complained of was sufficiently serious to deserve summary dismissal (serious misconduct), or dismissal with notice (misconduct that makes it impossible to continue the employment relationship in the long term), or whether the misconduct in question was serious enough to justify dismissal at all, and a lesser punishment might have been more appropriate. These are all substantive grounds, and look to the inherent fairness of the dismissal.

The tribunal will also look at the procedural fairness of the dismissal, and make sure that the employer followed a proper disciplinary procedure and that the employee was given a full and fair hearing before the dismissal was decided upon.

In the case of *Hennessy v Read & Write Shop Ltd.* (UD 192/1978), the EAT stated that its function was not to determine the guilt or innocence of a claimant, but at the same time the employer must be able to show that it reasonably arrived at the decision to dismiss, backed up by evidence that was led at the dismissal hearing. The EAT described the test that it used to decide whether the employer's decision was reasonable:

'1. The nature and extent of the enquiry carried out by the employer prior to the decision to dismiss the claimant, and
2. the employer's conclusion following such enquiry that the claimant should be dismissed.'

Enquiry 1 can be labelled the 'procedural justice' of the dismissal, whilst Enquiry 2 can be labelled the 'substantive justice' of the dismissal. The EAT must be satisfied that the employer reasonably fulfilled both requirements before taking the decision to dismiss.

The redundancy of the employee

Redundancy is defined fully in the Redundancy Payments Act 1967 as amended by the Redundancy Payments Act 1971, and occurs where a dismissal is as a result of the employer ceasing to trade or carry on business, or where the employee's function is no longer required by the business of the employer, or where the employer must reduce the workforce, or where the work that the employee used to do must now be performed by somebody with superior qualifications.

Redundancy is a substantial ground justifying dismissal. In other words, the act of making a person redundant can be fair. It is included in the Unfair Dismissal Acts because a redundancy dismissal can be unfair if the selection of the employee for redundancy was based on unfair criteria. Although the act of making an employee redundant is in terms of the Redundancy Payments Act, the employer must justify the selection of employees for redundancy in terms of the Unfair Dismissal Acts.

What this means in practice is that the employer needs to show that there was a redundancy situation, that the only way to solve the problems of the business was through redundancy, that the employee was a reasonable choice for redundancy, and finally, that redundancy was the whole or main reason for the employee's dismissal.

In the case of *Daly v Hanson Industries Ltd* (UD 719/1986), the EAT said that a redundancy defence raised by an employer would be tested in two ways:

'(a) was the redundancy genuine, or did the dismissal take place under the cloak of redundancy?
(b) was there a cause and effect relationship between the redundancy and the dismissal?'

It is necessary to be sure that there are circumstances justifying redundancy. An employer could disguise its ulterior motives for dismissal by simply labelling the dismissal as a redundancy. Therefore, the employer must not only show that the reason for the dismissal was a redundancy, but that there was a genuine need to make the employee redundant. Once the employer has proven that, it must thereafter show that there was a fair selection process.

The fact that continuation of the employment would contravene another statutory requirement

This is really another form of incapacity dismissal. The employee is incapable of performing under the employment contract as the existence of the employment contract contravenes a law. A common example in modern Irish employment law is of the employee who is an illegal alien, having failed to secure or renew a residence permit.

This scenario might arise in the healthcare sector, as there are a lot of much-needed foreign-born doctors and nurses in Irish hospitals. Such was the case in *Ponnampalam v Mid-Western Health Board* (UD 300/1979), where the claimant was a consultant surgeon appointed in a temporary capacity to carry out clinical surgery duties. The Mid-Western Health Board did not obtain the required statutory authority for him to fill this post (the sanction of Bord na n'Ospideal was required in terms of the Health Act 1970) and the contract between the claimant and the health board was terminated as a result. When this matter went on appeal to the Circuit Court it was held that the claimant was in fact an officer of a health board and therefore was not protected by the Unfair Dismissal Acts in any event.

There were other substantial grounds for dismissal

Although the previous four categories of justified dismissal in section 4 of the Act seem to cover any conceivable situation and type of dismissal, this final category in section 6 is a 'catch-all' category where a dismissal does not fit any of the other categories. An example would be where the employee's continued employment poses a threat to the employer's business.

For example, in *Kavanagh v Cooney Jennings Ltd* (UD 175/1983) the employee was convicted on charges of indecent assault, and his employer dismissed him as it was felt that he would scare away customers. The EAT upheld the dismissal as justified.

On the other hand, the threat must not be trivial or remote as in *Merrigan v Home Counties Cleaning Ireland Ltd* (UD 904/1984) where the employee was a widow with seven children, three of whom were heroin addicts. Her story was featured in the local newspaper. The employee cleaned at the local hospital, as her employer was a contract cleaning company. The secretary of the hospital telephoned the employer and said that it would look bad if the employee was allowed to continue cleaning at the hospital after the publicity of the newspaper article. The employer offered the employee cleaning positions at two other places but she refused. She was dismissed. The letter of termination that she received made it clear that her dismissal was as a result of the complaint by the secretary of the hospital. The EAT held that the threat to the employer was 'remote' and found that the dismissal was unfair.

An employer who has dismissed an employee must, if asked, furnish in writing within fourteen days the reason for the dismissal.

Certain types of dismissals are deemed unfair

Section 6(2) states that dismissals are unfair under the Acts where it is shown that they are as a result of one or more of the following grounds:

'(a) The employee's trade union membership or activities, either outside working hours or at those times during working hours when permitted by the employer,
(b) the religious or political opinions of the employee,
(c) the race or colour or sexual orientation of the employee,
(d) legal proceedings against the employer where the employee is a party or a witness,
(e) the unfair selection of the employee for redundancy, where the reason for the selection was based on a prohibited ground,
(f) the employee's pregnancy, the employee having recently given birth or is breastfeeding or any matters connected with pregnancy, birth or breastfeeding,
(g) the exercise or proposed exercise by an employee of the right to leave in terms of the Maternity Protection Act of 1994,
(h) the exercise or proposed exercise of the right to leave in terms of the Adoptive Leave Act of 1995,
(i) the exercise or proposed exercise by the employee of the right to leave in terms of the Parental Leave Act of 1998,
(j) the age of the employee,
(k) the employee's membership of the travelling community.
(l) the employee's rights or proposed exercise of rights under the National Minimum Wage Act 2000,
(m) the exercise or proposed exercise by the employee of the right to leave in terms of the Carer's Leave Act of 2001.'

As section 6 of the Unfair Dismissals Act already states that dismissals are deemed unfair until the employer can show otherwise, it must be asked why is this special category only deemed unfair, rather than making them illegal? In other countries, for example South Africa, these dismissals are called 'automatically unfair dismissals' and the employer is not allowed to argue that these dismissals could ever be justified.

The Unfair Dismissal Acts does not have a concept of 'automatically unfair dismissal'. Section 6(1) applies to all dismissals, and this means that the employer has the right, no matter what the reason for the dismissal might be, to argue that there are substantive grounds justifying the dismissal. In other words, an employer would be entitled to argue that under the circumstances, dismissal on the grounds of racism or religious discrimination was justified. Of course, because society generally frowns on discriminatory practices, the employer will have quite a job convincing a tribunal or court that its actions were justified.

This seems to be the real difference between dismissals under this section and the 'ordinary' dismissals under section 4. With dismissals under this section the employer will need to lead more compelling evidence to justify the dismissal.

Employees claiming dismissal due to paragraphs(a), (f), (g), (h), (i), (l) or (m), may bring an unfair dismissal claim even though they do not have a year's continuous service with their employer. This is the other important distinction between dismissals under section 6(2) and dismissals under section 4.

Remedies for unfair dismissal

The redress for unfair dismissal is one of three options:

- **Re-instatement** in the original position. In other words, the employee is returned to his or her original job as if the dismissal never took place;

or

- **re-engagement** in a suitable alternative job on conditions, which the tribunal considers reasonable (as close as possible to the original position, at least as concerns salary and benefits and length of service). This might be the case where the employee's original position no longer exists, and the only relief available is a similar job with the same employer on similar terms. This will often happen when a redundancy was unfair only because the procedure for selecting the employee was unfair. In other words, the redundancy was real, and the employee's position has disappeared. In such a situation, the employer will be ordered to provide another job that is similar and suitable to the employee's qualifications and training, or, if such a position does not exist in the employer's entire enterprise, the employer might be ordered to train the employee to fill another position on the same salary and benefits as his or her previous position;

or

- **financial compensation** up to a maximum of two years' pay. The amount of compensation will depend on factors like the reasons for the dismissal, and whether the employee was in any way at fault, whether the employee tried to minimise his or her loss by looking for another job, and whether there was procedural fairness leading up to the dismissal.

An employee found to have been unfairly dismissed but who has suffered no financial loss may be awarded up to four weeks' pay. For example, an employee is unfairly dismissed but immediately finds another job, either with the same or better salary and benefits as the previous job. Despite not suffering any financial loss, the employee can still receive token compensation, more for the purpose of slapping the employer's wrist than significantly compensating the employee.

An employee who claims to be unfairly dismissed and wishes to challenge the dismissal under the Acts, must lodge a written claim within six months of the dismissal with a Rights Commissioner. If either the employer or employee objects to the matter being heard by a Rights Commissioner, they can apply directly to the EAT. In exceptional circumstances, the time limit for lodging an application can be extended for up to a year.

Officers of a Health Board appointed in terms of the Health Act 1970

As previously mentioned, a category of worker that falls outside the distinction of employee versus independent contractor is the office holder. The officer of a health board could be regarded as an office holder as he or she takes up a position created, and regulated, by the Health Act.

Permanent officers of health boards may be removed from their positions because of 'misconduct or unfitness' (section 23(2) of the Health Act 1970). The permanent officer can also be removed by order of the Minister if he or she is absent from his or her duties 'without leave or reasonable cause' (section 23(3) of the Health Act 1970). Prior to this removal, the officer can be suspended from duty without pay by the CEO of the health board, whilst the allegations of misconduct are investigated by a committee headed by a chairperson chosen by the Minister.

These measures have the potential to be very harsh in practice. Permanent (as opposed to temporary) officers of a health board are not protected by the Unfair Dismissals Acts.

The vast majority of nurses in Ireland work for health boards, and it is the policy of health boards to appoint their nurses as officers (or temporary officers).

The reasoning behind this policy was confirmed in the judgment of *Western Health Board v Mrs Bridget Teresa Quigley* [1982] I.L.R.M. 390.

Facts

Mrs Quigley was a registered psychiatric nurse. In 1974, she was appointed to St Mary's Hospital by the Western Health Board as a temporary staff nurse. In October 1974, she was notified that her temporary employment was being extended up to 31 December 1974. However, she continued to work beyond this date but received no other notification clarifying her position. In November 1977, she received a letter, which stated that her temporary employment was to be terminated on 31 December 1977. Mrs Quigley regarded this as a letter of dismissal, as she had assumed that her position was permanent. She brought proceedings under the Unfair Dismissals Act 1977. The Employment Appeals Tribunal decided that she had been unfairly dismissed. This decision was affirmed on appeal to the Circuit Court. The Western Health Board appealed this decision to the High Court.

Issue before the Court
Was Mrs Quigley an officer of the health board, or an employee of the health board? If she was an officer, the Unfair Dismissals Act did not apply to her termination which meant that the EAT did not have jurisdiction over her dispute.

Decision of the Court
The High Court held that Mrs Quigley was an officer and not 'a servant', and therefore the EAT was not entitled to hear her application. Accordingly, the ruling of the EAT and the judgment of the Circuit Court were null and void. The court held that:

> 'There is no doubt that Mrs Quigley is a trained professional person and that she was carrying out the highly responsible duties of a psychiatric nurse. I do not think that she can properly be described as a *"servant"* as that term is used in s. 14 of the Health Act, 1970. Psychiatric nurses and their predecessors, *"mental nurses"* have traditionally been regarded as officers and not servants. For instance the Mental Hospitals (Officers and Servants) Order 1946 (No. 203 of 1946) provides at paragraph 3 sub-s. 3 that a Mental Hospital Authority shall appoint persons to be *"male and female mental nurses and attendants to assist in the administration of Mental Hospitals and to perform the duties specified in any declaration of the Minister for the time being in force defining the duties of such officers."*
>
> It then goes on to provide in sub-article 4 that a Mental Hospital Authority shall for each of their institutions appoint such number of suitable persons to be servants as the Minister may from time to time direct or approve *"for the discharge of minor and subordinate duties in or about the institution."*
>
> I do not think that one could describe a psychiatric nurse exercising her profession in a Mental Hospital as carrying out *"minor and subordinate duties in or about the institution."* The phrase must in my opinion be interpreted as referring to much less responsible duties such as those of maid, caretaker, porter or groundsman.

Moreover it appears to me that a psychiatric nurse who is employed by the Health Board must be employed either as a *"temporary"* or as a *"permanent"* officer. There is no alternative position carrying the emoluments of a temporary officer but giving the permanency of a permanent officer. A Health Board has no power to employ permanent staff to carry out the duties of officers without going through the procedures laid down under the Local Authorities (Officers and Employees) Acts for the appointment of such staff. If it were to attempt to do so expressly it would be violating the provisions of those Acts and acting *ultra vires*. But if it cannot validly appoint them expressly, neither, it appears to me, can it appoint them by implication.'

Commentary

This judgment confirms the existing practice of health boards to appoint nurses as officers of the health board, which means they can be dismissed for 'misconduct' or 'unfitness' in terms of the Health Act 1970.

It also means that nurses who are appointed as permanent officers will not be protected by the Unfair Dismissal Acts.

If a nurse is charged with misconduct or unfitness, he or she will face an internal disciplinary committee, with leave to appeal to the High Court.

Sections 23 and 24 of the Health Act 1970 deal with the procedure to be adopted when an officer is faced with removal.

Section 23 is fairly brief in its explanation of the procedure to be followed, and limits itself to saying that a 'permanent officer' shall not be removed under this section for a reason other than misconduct or unfitness except with the approval of the board.

The section continues to say that removals of officers must be carried out in accordance with regulations made by the Minister.

The Health (Removal of Officers and Servants) Regulations 1971 (S.I. No. 110 of 1971) provide that whenever it is proposed to remove an officer of a health board, the officer shall be given notice in writing by the chief executive officer or an officer authorised to act on his behalf—

'(a) of the intention to remove;
 (b) of the reasons for such removal;
 (c) that the chief executive officer will consider any representations made by the officer or on his or her behalf before the expiration of seven days after the giving of such notice;
 (d) of details of any proposal to appoint that officer to another office or employment (for example, a transfer or a demotion).'

This can be interpreted to mean that a nurse will receive a 'charge sheet' detailing the allegations that are made against him or her.

The Regulations go on to say that the removal may not happen unless and until this notice has been given, and any representations made by or on behalf of the officer have been considered.

In other words, the officer will have the right of reply to the charges. The Regulations state that this right of reply must be 'before the expiration of seven days after the giving of such notice'. A week to reply to charges is not a long time and the officer (for example, a nurse) must get in touch with his or her union or representative immediately upon receiving such a notice.

Section 24 provides for the appointment by the Minister of a committee that will hear the case against a permanent officer charged with misconduct. The Minister appoints the chairperson of the committee, and thereafter half of the committee members are chosen from a panel nominated by the various unions in the health sector, and half are chosen from a panel nominated by the CEO of the health board.

The Health (Removal of Officers and Servants) Regulations 1971 provide that during the proceedings of the committee, the chairperson shall have discretion in the running of things, and in particular shall—

'(a) decide the order of appearance of persons appearing before the committee,
(b) permit the officer to appear in person or to be represented or assisted by another person, and
(c) hear, if he or she thinks fit, any person who is not a party to the proceedings.'

After hearing the evidence the committee shall vote and the majority decision goes forward as a recommendation to the CEO.

Where the committee recommends the removal of the permanent officer, this shall not be done by the CEO until twenty-one days has passed. The officer facing removal has a chance to appeal his or her removal to the Minister, who can confirm, reverse or substitute the decision to remove.

The rules of natural justice must apply to these hearings and an officer will be entitled to an impartial hearing, to challenge accusers, and to present his or her own version and evidence.

A right of appeal or review shall lie to the High Court, where an officer is a permanent officer. A temporary officer of a health board is protected by the Unfair Dismissals Act, and can therefore appeal to the EAT.

The status of nurses in the 'private sector'

We have discussed the status of nurses in the 'public sector', in other words nurses employed by a health board. What about nurses working in the private sector?

As a general rule, these nurses are employees and are therefore protected by the Unfair Dismissals Act, with a right of appeal to the EAT.

The fact that a private or agency nurse is described as an employee is not necessarily conclusive of the matter, as the employment contract may go on to describe a disciplinary procedure as set out in the Health Act 1970, rather than one contemplated by the Unfair Dismissals Acts. This is what occurred in the case of *Celine Traynor v John Ryan* [2002] 13 E.L.R. 245, where the plaintiff was a consultant anaesthetist employed under a 'consultant's common contract', with the contract specifying that the disciplinary procedure was that as set out in the Health Act, despite the plaintiff being employed by a private hospital.

It would therefore be advisable that the status of a nurse working in the private sector is clearly stated in his or her contract of employment, including the fact that the nurse is an employee and is protected by the Unfair Dismissals Acts.

'Unfitness' versus 'Unfitness to Practise'

A question that is related to status concerns the distinction between unfitness that could lead to dismissal, and unfitness to practise, that could lead to a nurse being removed from the Nurses' Register.

A finding of unfitness to practise can result in the removal of a nurse's name from the Nurses' Register, in other words it has a direct affect on his or her professional status, and prevents that nurse from practicing as a nurse, for the duration of the removal. A dismissal for unfitness impacts on the nurse's employment status, but does not prevent him or her from finding work as a nurse in another institution, or becoming an agency nurse. It is therefore important to distinguish the two types of unfitness.

The scenario is further confused as the Health Act provides for the possible removal of a nurse for both misconduct and 'unfitness', whereas the Nurses Act deals with 'unfitness to practise'. In other words, there are a possible three categories of offence with which a nurse can be charged, with the categories under the Health Act leading to dismissal, and the category under the Nurse's Act leading to removal from the Register.

Whilst a nurse is always subject to the Fitness to Practise Inquiry in terms of the Nurses Act 1985, these investigations should be limited to instances where there has been a complaint about the nurse's professional misconduct.

Accordingly it is recommended that a nurse's standard contract of employment with a health board should specify what is meant by 'unfitness' in the Health Act as opposed to 'unfitness to practise' in the Nurses Act, and stipulate a mechanism whereby the two are distinguished in cases of doubt or disagreement.

As a starting point, it can be argued that misconduct (including unfitness) can lead to dismissal, whereas professional misconduct can lead to removal from the Nurses' Register. The Medical Council's *Guide to Ethical Conduct and Behaviour* defines 'professional misconduct' as 'conduct which doctors of experience, competence and good repute, upholding the aims of the profession, consider disgraceful and dishonourable'. The *Code of Conduct for each Nurse and Midwife (April 2000)*, which is issued by An Bord Altranais, does not contain such a precise definition, but the meaning would be as clear if the Medical Council's definition was used and the word 'nurses' was substituted for 'doctors'. Professional misconduct deals with offences that are 'disgraceful and dishonourable'.

Can 'disgraceful and dishonourable' conduct ever amount to conduct that is not professional misconduct? For example, if a nurse assaulted another nurse, that conduct is clearly disgraceful and dishonourable but it has nothing to do with the nurse's medical or caring capabilities in relation to patients, and therefore one could argue does not amount to professional misconduct, but rather 'ordinary' misconduct.

Perhaps the easiest and most practical method to distinguish between disciplinary offences which constitute 'professional misconduct' leading to a finding of 'unfitness to practise' as opposed to 'ordinary' misconduct leading to dismissal, would be to list the most common examples of both as an annexure to the contract of employment.

Professional misconduct can be dealt with in terms of the Nurses Act whilst other forms of misconduct can be dealt with in terms of the Health Act. For incidents of misconduct that seem to fall between the two categories, the previously mentioned mechanism to distinguish the two can be used, with the test being whether the conduct complained of had a direct impact on the safety and sanctity of the patient. For example, in the previous example of one nurse assaulting another nurse – whilst there might be an indirect impact on the patients as the offender would be suspended from duty and the victim might be released from duty, meaning that the hospital or clinic would have fewer nurses to call upon, this at best is an indirect impact on the patients' welfare, and should not qualify as professional misconduct. On the other hand, if a nurse intentionally or negligently hooks up a saline drip instead of a blood plasma drip, for example, causing harm to a patient, this would be professional misconduct.

However, even this 'direct impact on the patient' test does not answer all questions. What of an incident where a nurse negligently spills hot food over a patient? The patient's welfare is clearly impacted, as the patient is burned. Is this professional misconduct, however, as the serving of food is hardly something that the nurse studied to do? It is a function that can also be carried out by others without nursing qualifications.

This is clearly an area that An Bord Altranais and the Department of Health and Children need to consider carefully. Questions that need to be answered and made clear in contracts of employment are:

- That the nurse is an officer for the purposes of the Health Act.
- That in cases of professional misconduct the nurse will be subject to the disciplinary procedures set out in the Nurses Act (The Fitness to Practise Enquiry), which could ultimately lead to the removal of that nurse from the Register, with a right of appeal to the High Court.
- That in cases of other misconduct the nurse will be subject to the disciplinary procedures in terms of the Health Act, with the ultimate sanction being dismissal from employment, with a right of appeal to the High Court.
- That a list of professional misconduct ('unfitness to practise') offences and 'ordinary' misconduct (dismissal) offences be established, as well as a dispute mechanism and guidelines for distinguishing between the two.

Termination: Summary

1. An employment contract can be terminated by one party, or it may expire when its purpose is concluded or if the parties agree that it shall end.
2. In terms of the common law, a party could unilaterally terminate an employment contract for any reason as long as the procedure of termination was in accordance with the provisions of the contract (usually notice periods and severance payments).
3. As this meant that employees were extremely vulnerable, the Unfair Dismissal Acts were created which provided that a dismissal must be both substantively and procedurally fair.
4. An employee alleging unfair dismissal can have his or her case heard by a specialised tribunal called the Employment Appeals Tribunal (the EAT).
5. If a dismissal is found to be unfair, the employee can be reinstated into his or her previous position, or re-engaged in a similar position, or financially compensated.

6. The above provisions will apply to nurses who are employed by private employers, or by health boards as temporary officers.
7. An employee can still approach the civil courts on the basis of wrongful dismissal, as an alternative cause of action to the unfair dismissal, where the termination of the contract is in violation of one of the provisions of that contract (for example, insufficient notice or premature termination of a fixed-term contract).
8. A nurse who works for a health board and is appointed as a permanent officer of a health board in terms of the Health Act 1970 is not protected by the Unfair Dismissals Acts. The procedure for removal of a nurse, who is a permanent officer, is governed by the Health Act in terms of misconduct and unfitness (which can lead to dismissal).
9. All nurses on the Register of Nurses, whether private or public, employees or officers, permanent or temporary, can be charged as being unfit to practise in terms of the Nurses Act, which can lead to removal from the Register of Nurses.
10. It is sometimes difficult to distinguish between misconduct leading to dismissal and professional misconduct leading to removal from the Register of Nurses.
11. Useful websites:
    a. **The EAT:** (*http://www.entemp.ie/employment/appeals/*).
    b. **College of Chiropractors of Ontario:** (*http://www.cco.on.ca/professional_misconduct.htm*).

33
STATUTORY REGULATION OF EMPLOYMENT

> **Learning Outcomes**
> **At the completion of this chapter, the reader should know and understand the following:**
>
> ▸ Minimum Notice and Terms of Employment Acts 1973–1994.
> ▸ Payment of Wages Act 1991.
> ▸ Organisation of Working Time Act 1997.
> ▸ National Minimum Wage Act 2000.
> ▸ Redundancy Payments Acts 1967–2003.
> ▸ Protection of Employees (Part-Time Work) Act 2001.
> ▸ Protection of Employees (Fixed-Term Work) Act 2003.

Important concepts and phrases that are crucial to an understanding of this chapter

Collective agreement
An agreement, usually in writing, that is entered into by an employer, or an association of employers or an employer organisation, on the one hand, and a group of employees, or an employee body or a trade union, on the other hand. These collective agreements are usually specific to a particular industry and will deal with issues like wages, hours of work, over-time pay and such like, where these are usually in excess of the statutory minimum. The law provides that a provision in a collective agreement that contravenes the principle of equal treatment is null and void. Very often a collective agreement is incorporated into the contracts of employment of those employees subject to its provisions.

Gross and net salary
A gross salary is the entire salary that a person is paid before any deductions are made.

A net salary is the money that the employee actually receives, after all deductions have been made.

Most deductions are made with the written consent of the employee, for example, VHI or BUPA deductions, but statutory deductions, like tax and pension, are automatically made by the employer as a statutory duty – the employee cannot object to these deductions being made and the employer cannot refuse to make these deductions from an employee's salary.

Introduction

Employment law is largely governed by statute, although the interpretation of these statutes by the courts forms part of our common law and is an important component of our employment law.

As nurses are generally employed as officers of a health board in terms of the Health Act 1970, a reader must be careful when looking at any of these Acts, to carefully check the exclusion section to determine whether nurses are protected by the statute in question.

Minimum Notice and Terms of Employment Acts 1973-1994

These Acts apply to an employee who has been in continuous service with the same employer for at least thirteen weeks.

The minimum notice period to which an employee is entitled is calculated according to that employee's length of (continuous) service. Where the employee has:
- Thirteen weeks to less than two years of continuous service: One week's notice.
- Two years to less than five years of continuous service: Two weeks' notice.
- Five years to less than ten years of continuous service: Four weeks' notice.
- Ten years to less than fifteen years of continuous service: Six weeks' notice.
- More than fifteen years of continuous service: Eight weeks' notice.

On the other hand, employees only have to give an employer one week's notice of intention to resign.

Remember that these are minimum notice periods. What this means is that the parties to an employment contract can agree to longer notice periods but can never agree to shorter notice periods. Either party can waive their right to notice or accept payment in lieu of notice. This is a regular occurrence, for example, where an employee gets a job offer but needs to start with his or her new employer immediately, or where an employer wants to get in the employee's replacement immediately.

Payment of Wages Act 1991

An employee's rate of pay is normally agreed between the parties at the beginning of the contract. If there is no agreement, the employee must be paid at least the statutory minimum wage, as specified in the National

Minimum Wage Act 2000. Legal minimum rates of pay for particular categories of employees are also laid down through Joint Labour Committees and the Registered Employment Agreement system. If an Employment Regulation Order or a Registered Employment Agreement governs an employee's pay, employers will be guilty of an offence under the Industrial Relations Acts if they fail to pay wages at less than the statutorily prescribed rate.

Section 2 of the Act describes the mode of payment of wages and says that every employee has the right to a readily negotiable mode of wage payment, including cheques, postal orders, bills of exchange or negotiable instruments. What this means is that the wage must be in cash or easy to convert into cash. Most employees in this age of electronic banking have their wages paid directly into their bank accounts. The definition of wages says that payments in kind are not regarded as part of a wage – for example, when your employer gives you goods from the store, this shall not form part of your wage. Therefore, for example, if a nurse was allowed to take home medicine for her family (which is highly unlikely, one hopes) the cost of those medicines do not form part of his or her wage and he or she would need to give consent in writing for the cost of those medicines to be deducted from his or her salary.

Section 4 of the Act orders employers to give to each employee a wage packet accompanied by a payslip which sets out the gross wage, and thereafter each deduction must be itemised and the final balance clearly shown. It is an offence not to do so. If the wage is paid in cash or by bill of exchange or negotiable instrument the payslip must accompany the payment, and if the payment is made by electronic means directly into the employee's account, the payslip must be delivered to the employee as soon as possible after payment is made.

Employers may not make deductions from wages or receive payment from their workers unless these deductions are required by law, like tax or pension, or if the written contract expressly allows certain deductions (and only after the employer has given the employee advance warning that the deduction is to be made), or with the written consent of the employee (like medical insurance payments).

This Act applies to all employees. Employees can complain about unlawful deductions or non-payment of wages to a Rights Commissioner.

Organisation of Working Time Act 1997

This Act regulates hours of works, rest and lunch breaks, and holidays. Again, the Act sets the minimum, and parties are always free to agree to longer breaks or more holidays, but never less.

There are many collective agreements in a large number of industries, which set out employees' entitlements to rest and meal breaks, overtime and annual holidays. These collective agreements will, for example, vary the times at which rest is taken or vary the averaging period over which weekly working time is calculated.

The Organisation of Working Time Act does not protect all employees. Section 3 of the 1997 Act provides that the Garda Síochána, the Defence Forces, junior hospital doctors, transport employees and workers at sea are not covered by the limits imposed in respect of rest and maximum working time. In addition, those who control their own working hours or persons employed by a close relative in a private dwelling house or farm in or on which both reside, are not covered by the rest and maximum working time rules. The Minister also has the power to exclude employees in the transport industry and those who are working in the civil protection services, and also various enterprises working on shift systems. Nurses are not excluded, and are therefore protected by the Act.

Section 15 of the 1997 Act provides that the maximum average working week is forty-eight hours. The reason it is called an average working week is that in certain industries there are peak periods, where employees need to work a lot of hours, followed by quiet periods, where there are not a lot of hours for employees to work.

What happens in these industries is a practice called averaging, where the forty-eight hours per week is averaged out over a period which is longer than a week. For example, if the averaged period was a month, in the first and second week the hours might be fifty-four hours per week and in the third and fourth week the hours might be forty-two hours per week, but the weekly average over that month is forty-eight hours per week, as the monthly total is the same, namely one hundred and ninety-two hours per month.

Averaging may be balanced out over a four, six or twelve month period depending on the nature of, and practices within, the industry concerned. The usual averaging period in most industries is the four-month period, but in industries which have busy seasons followed by quiet seasons (for example the tourist industry, which is busiest in Spring and Summer or certain manufacturing plants where the product manufactured is needed for a specific period) this can be extended to six months. In industries that want to average the maximum working week over the entire year, the employees and employers must enter into a collective agreement and this collective agreement must be approved by the Labour Court.

Section 11 of the 1997 Act provides that every employee must have a daily rest period of eleven consecutive hours during every twenty-four hour period, and section 13 provides that once a week every employee must have a rest period of at least thirty-five consecutive hours.

Section 12 of the Act provides that during the working day every employee must have a rest break of fifteen minutes where more than four and a half hours have been worked; or a rest break of half an hour where more than six hours have been worked, which may include the first break. Shop employees who work more than six hours and whose hours of work include the period 11.30 a.m. - 2.30 p.m. must be allowed a break of one hour during that period of 11.30 a.m. - 2.30 p.m. Most industries have varied and lengthened these time periods through collective agreements and in other industries these rest periods have been varied by Regulations made by the Minister.

Section 16 of the 1997 Act regulates employees that are known as 'night workers', who are employees that work at least three hours during the period between midnight and 7.00 a.m., and the number of hours they work during the night in a year equals or is more than half of their total working time in that year. As a general rule, night workers are allowed to work forty-eight hours per week averaged over two months or a longer period if permitted by a collective agreement that has been approved by the Labour Court. Where these night workers perform work that is characterised by 'special hazards or heavy physical or mental strain', they are not allowed to work more than eight consecutive hours in any twenty-four hour period.

Certain industries have collective agreements which exempt those industries from the rest break requirements, but in these industries the employees must receive equivalent compensatory rest. The Organisation of Working Time (General Exemptions) Regulations 1998 (S.I. No. 21 of 1998) has exempted certain sectors from the rest break requirements, but stipulate that these employees must also receive 'equivalent compensatory rest'. Similar provisions exist in other Regulations, for example S.I. No. 20 of 1998 Exemption of Transport Activities, and S.I. No. 52 of 1998 Exemption of Civil Protection Services provide exemptions from the rest and maximum working week provisions of the Act, but these Regulations do not require equivalent compensatory rest.

Section 19 of the 1997 Act deals with annual leave. Employees who work for a full working year are entitled to four weeks' annual paid holiday. Where the employee has worked less than a year, this holiday entitlement is calculated on a pro-rata basis against time worked. This applies to all employees, whether they are full-time, part-time, temporary or casual. Therefore, where an employee works for the same employer at least 1365 hours in any year, he or she is entitled to four weeks' annual paid leave.

Where the employee works at least 117 hours in any month, the employee is entitled to a paid holiday equivalent to one-third of the working week, for each of those completed months. In any other situation, the employee is entitled to eight per cent of the hours worked in any year, up to a maximum of four weeks' holiday.

Section 20 states that holidays must be taken in consultation with the employer, and this involves balancing the employer's operational needs with the employee's personal and family needs. If the employer wants employees to take their annual leave at a particular time, this must be communicated to the employee or the trade union at least a month in advance of that chosen period. Holidays must be taken in the year that the holiday is earned, unless the employee consents to taking the holiday during the following year, as long as this is within the first six months of that following year. The employee must receive his or her holiday pay before going on holiday.

There are nine public holidays, and these fall on New Year's Day, St. Patrick's Day, Easter Monday, the first Monday in May, June, August and October, Christmas Day and St Stephen's Day. An employer has the choice to give the employee a day's paid leave on the actual public holiday, or if the employee needs to work on a public holiday, the employer must give him or her a day's paid leave on another day, or another day of holiday leave, or an extra day's pay.

If the employee does not work on the public holiday, and that holiday falls on a day that the employee usually works (for example a Bank Holiday Monday) the employee must be paid for that day. Section 21 of the 1997 Act deals with employees that work on public holidays, and their treatment is essentially the same as that of Sunday workers.

Section 14 of the 1997 Act deals with Sunday workers. Sunday workers are generally paid a special rate, which is calculated according to the industry or sector in which that business operates. The premium can be in the form of an allowance, or an increased rate of pay, or paid time off, or a combination of these.

Section 18 of the 1997 Act provides that if employees are on standby ('on call'), but are not called to work, under normal circumstances they must still be paid at least a quarter of their salary for working what are known as 'zero hours'. Again, these percentages have usually been increased by collective agreement.

National Minimum Wage Act 2000

The National Minimum Wage Act 2000 applies to all employees, including full-time, part-time, temporary and casual employees. However, employees who are close relatives of the employer, and apprentices, are not protected by the Act.

The Act applies to those employees who are adults (over the age of eighteen years) and who are experienced, in other words they are not on training or an apprentice.

Section 14 of the Act provides that an experienced adult worker must be paid an average hourly rate of pay that is not less than the national minimum wage in a pay reference period. A pay reference period may be a week, or a fortnight, but no longer than a month.

Section 14 applies to employees who are not only older than eighteen years, but who have completed at least two years of employment since turning eighteen, and are not a trainee. Where the employee is under eighteen or still within the first two years of employment, the Act provides for lesser rates of pay, either eighty or ninety per cent of the minimum wage.

As previously mentioned, a trainee is not entitled to receive the minimum statutory pay, and section 16 sets out the percentage of the minimum wage that a trainee can be paid (ranging from 75 to 90 per cent). However, to prevent an employer from abusing this exemption and simply calling all employees 'trainees', an employee must be on a genuine training course to qualify as a trainee. The criteria that a course of training or study must satisfy for the purposes of the Act, in order for an employer to pay an employee the trainee rates, are set out in the *Detailed Guide to the National Minimum Wage Act 2000* which is available from the Employment Rights Information Unit. In addition, section 16(4) provides that where an employee changes his or her job but remains with the same employer, the employer is not allowed to pay that employee trainee rates a second time unless the employee undergoes a course of training or study that is different in purpose or content from the previous training or study undertaken by the employee.

An employee may make a complaint about payment that is less than the statutory minimum wage to a Rights Commissioner or the Labour Inspectorate at the Department of Enterprise, Trade and Employment. Before an employee refers the dispute, section 24(2) says that he or she must request, in writing, from the employer, a written statement of his or her average hourly rate of pay, and must stipulate the pay reference period or periods that are the subject of the dispute. The details and format of this statement are set out in section 23. If the employer does not comply within four weeks of the written request, the employee can proceed without the written statement.

An employee must refer the dispute to a Rights Commissioner within a period of six months from the date the employee obtained the written statement or, in the case where an employer fails to supply the written statement, within six months from the latest date the employer was obliged to supply the statement. This time limit may be extended to twelve months, at the discretion of the Rights Commissioner.

Redundancy Payments Acts 1967-2003

The Redundancy Payments Acts 1967-2003 oblige employers to pay compensation to employees dismissed for reasons of redundancy. As previously explained, an employee becomes redundant where his or her position ceases to exist and he or she is not replaced by another employee because the employer is in financial difficulties, or where there is not enough work to justify the further employment of that employee, or where the employer reorganises its operation or closes down altogether. Clearly, in circumstances where an employee is dismissed for reasons other than redundancy, this Act does not apply.

To qualify for payment of a redundancy lump-sum, the redundant employee must have had at least a hundred and four weeks' continuous service with the same employer, and must be between sixteen and '66' years of age. Part-Time workers are included in this scheme because of the changes introduced by the Protection of Employment (Part-Time Work) Act 2001 and the Redundancy Payments Act 2003.

This lump-sum entitlement is calculated as follows:

> Two weeks pay for every year of service under the Redundancy Payments Act 2003, subject to a ceiling, which at last count was €507.90 a week (since April, 2001). Added on to that figure is a bonus week's gross pay (i.e. no deductions) as long as the ceiling has not been reached.

Protection of Employees (Part-Time Work) Act 2001

This Act applies to all part-time employees as defined in the Act, but the definition process set out in the Act is very complicated. A part-time employee means an employee whose normal hours of work are less than the normal hours of work of a comparable employee in relation to that part-time employee. This definition is therefore dependent on the definition of a comparable employee. Section 7(2)(a) of the Act provides that a comparable employee is a full-time employee (who is defined as somebody who is not a part-time employee) to whom a part-time employee (defined in the Act as a 'relevant part-time employee') can compare himself or herself where the following conditions are met:

Where the comparable employee and the part-time employee are employed by the same or associated employer and one of the following conditions is met:
- where both employees perform the same work under the same or similar conditions or each is interchangeable with the other in relation to the work,
- where the work performed by one of the employees concerned is of the same or a similar nature to that performed by the other and any differences between the work performed or the conditions under which it is performed by each, either are of small importance in relation to the work as a whole or occur with such irregularity as not to be significant, or

- the work performed by the part-time employee is equal or greater in value to the work performed by the other employee concerned, having regard to such matters as skill, physical or mental requirements, responsibility and working conditions.

Section 7(2)(b) of the Act provides that where the comparable employee and the part-time employee are not employed by the same employer, the Act can still apply where the full-time employee is specified in a collective agreement to be a comparable employee in relation to the part-time employee, or section 7(2)(c) states that where the full-time employee is employed in the same industry or sector of employment as the part-time employee and one of the abovementioned (three) conditions is met.

According to section 9(1) of the Act, where the part-time employee is protected by the Act, this means that the part-time employee cannot be treated in a less favourable manner than a comparable full-time employee in relation to conditions of employment.

However, section 9(2) of the Act does allow a part-time employee to be treated less favourably than a comparable employee where such treatment can be justified on objective grounds. By 'objective grounds' is meant a ground that is based on considerations other than the status of the employee as a part-time worker and the less favourable treatment is for the purpose of achieving a legitimate objective of the employer and such treatment is necessary for that purpose. An example would be a shop selling tourist goods, which would employ one salesperson on full salary as a permanent post, but during the tourist season (Spring and Summer) another part-time salesperson, with a lesser salary due to his or her inexperience, might be employed.

Section 9(4) of the Act also allows a part-time employee to be treated less favourably than a comparable full-time employee in relation to any pension scheme, as long as the part-time employee works for less than one-fifth of the hours of the comparable full-time employee. This is a very specific and limited exclusion – it only applies to pension benefits, and can only be justified if the part-time employee in question works less than one-fifth of the hours worked by the comparable full-time employee, which is a very small portion indeed.

Protection of Employees (Fixed-Term Work) Act 2003

This Act is very similar in structure and content to the previous statute considered, namely the Protection of Employees (Part-Time Work) Act 2001. This Act applies to all fixed-term employees, who are defined as a person who has entered into a contract of employment with an employer where the end of the contract is determined by an objective condition such as arriving at a specific date, completing a specific task or the occurrence of a specific event.

Section 2 of the Act provides that the term 'fixed-term employee' does not include employees in initial vocational training or in apprenticeship schemes or employees with a contract of employment concluded within the framework of a publicly-supported training, integration or vocational retraining programme.

More importantly for the purposes of this book, the Act does not protect a trainee nurse within the meaning of Parts III and IV of the Nurses Act 1985. Neither does it protect a member of the Defence Forces, nor a trainee in the Garda Síochána. Section 17 expressly excludes these employees from the protection of the Act.

Section 6 of the Act declares that a fixed-term employee cannot be treated in a less favourable manner than a comparable permanent employee in relation to conditions of employment. All the statutes that protect the comparable permanent employee will also protect the fixed-term employee.

Section 5 of the Act defines the comparable permanent employee as follows: if the permanent employee and the fixed-term employee are employed by the same or associated employer, or where both are employed in the same industry or sector of employment as the fixed-term employee, and both employees perform the same work under the same or similar conditions or each is interchangeable with the other in relation to the work, or the work that they perform is the same or similar in nature with the difference in work conditions being insignificant to the bigger picture, or the work performed by the fixed-term employee is equal or greater in value to the work performed by the permanent employee, after considering matters such as skill, physical or mental requirements, responsibility and working conditions.

Where the fixed-term employee and the permanent employee do not have the same employer and are not employed in the same sector or industry, the permanent employee can still be a comparable employee in relation to the fixed-term employee where the permanent employee is specified in a collective agreement as being a comparable employee for the purposes of this Act.

Section 6(2) of the Act does allow a fixed-term employee to be treated in a less favourable manner than a comparable permanent employee where such treatment can be justified on objective grounds. A ground will be defined as an objective ground for the purposes of this Act if it is based on considerations other than the status of the employee and is for the purpose of achieving a legitimate objective of the employer and such treatment is necessary for that purpose.

Section 6(5) of the Act provides that a fixed-term employee may be treated less favourably than a comparable permanent employee in relation to any pension scheme when his or her normal hours of work are less than one fifth of the working hours of the comparable permanent employee. Again, this is a very limited and specific exclusion. It only applies to pension benefits under a scheme, but nothing else, and in addition, only applies to the fixed-term employee who works for less than one-fifth of the hours worked by the comparable permanent employee.

Section 8(1) of the Act provides that a fixed-term employee shall be informed in writing by his or her employer as soon as practicable of the objective condition determining the contract. In other words, whether the contract ends on a specific date, or ends on the completion of a specific task, or ends on the happening of a specific event.

Section 8(2) of the Act also provides that where an employer proposes to renew a fixed-term contract, the employee shall be informed in writing, not later than the date of renewal, of the objective grounds justifying the renewal of the fixed-term contract and the failure to offer a permanent contract of indefinite duration.

The Act prevents an employer from 'rolling-over' fixed term contracts, and simply employing the employee indefinitely with successive fixed-term contracts. Section 9(1) of the Act says that when employees on fixed-term contracts, including those which commenced prior to the passing of the Act, have worked for three years for that same employer, the employer can renew the contract for a fixed term on one further occasion only and that renewal may be for a period of no longer than one year. Since the passing of this Act an employee may not be employed for more than four years on fixed-term contracts. If the employer exceeds this time limit, the contract is viewed in law as a permanent contract of indefinite duration, unless the employer can show that there are objective grounds justifying the continuation of a fixed-term contract in relation to that employee.

According to section 11, a fixed-term employee must have the same chances as any other employee to secure a permanent position, and the employer must inform all employees, including fixed-term employees, of vacancies that occur in that employer's business. Surprisingly, an employer only has to provide training to a fixed-term employee where this is practicable.

Disputes under this Act can be referred to a Rights Commissioner for adjudication within six months of the complaint arising or the end of the contract, whichever is the earlier. The Rights Commissioner can declare whether the complaint was or was not well founded; and/or require the employer to comply with the relevant provision; and/or require the employer to re-instate or re-engage the employee (including on a contract of indefinite duration); and/or require the employer to pay to the employee compensation up to the equivalent of two years' salary.

Statutory Regulation: Summary

1. The Acts that have been dealt with in this chapter are:
   - Minimum Notice and Terms of Employment Acts 1973-1994.
   - Payment of Wages Act 1991.
   - Organisation of Working Time Act 1997.
   - National Minimum Wage Act 2000.
   - Redundancy Payments Acts 1967-2003.
   - Protection of Employees (Part-Time Work) Act 2001.
   - Protection of Employees (Fixed-Term Work) Act 2003.
2. There are of course a number of other acts that affect your rights as an employee, particularly the Acts dealing with different types of leave, for example parental leave and carer leave.
3. These have not been dealt with in this chapter, for lack of time and space.
4. Information can be obtained about any of these Acts from the Department of Trade and Enterprise or any of the websites maintained by the various trade unions or organisations like Oasis or Comhairle.

34
DISCRIMINATION IN EMPLOYMENT AND THE EMPLOYMENT EQUALITY ACT 1998

> **Learning Outcomes**
> At the completion of this chapter, the reader should know and understand the following:
> - The concept of direct discrimination.
> - The concept of indirect discrimination.
> - The concept of positive discrimination.
> - Justifications of discrimination available to an employer.
> - The concept of sexual harassment.
> - The provisions of the Employment Equality Act 1998 that deal with the above concepts.

Important concepts and phrases that are crucial to an understanding of this chapter

Arbitrary
Something that happens by chance, often random and without any logic or pattern to it. When a person makes an arbitrary choice, it is a choice made without any logical reason or objective justification, and is usually a matter of opinion or personal prejudice.

Introduction

The original Employment Equality Act 1977 was repealed by the 1998 Act, in order to comply with various EU directives on sexual harassment, equal pay and equal treatment in the workplace. The 1998 Act has been recently modified by the equality Act of 2004, in order to comply with recent EU Directives on discrimination. These changes are largely technical, as the Act already covered the various forms of discrimination mentioned in the Directives. In addition, the definition of sexual harassment was broadened and the concept of positive action was extended to all nine grounds of discrimination.

The scope of the Employment Equality Act

The Act covers employees in the public and private sectors as well as applicants for employment and training. It outlaws discrimination on any of the prohibited grounds, and seeks to cover all areas relevant to employment. After Part One, which is primarily dedicated to definitions and repeals, Part Two of the Act establishes the scope of the Act.

Section 8 deals with discrimination by employers with regard to access to employment, conditions of employment, training and promotion. Section 9 deals with discrimination in collective agreements with regard to access to and conditions of employment and equal pay for like work. Section 10 deals with discriminatory advertising or advertising that might reasonably be understood as indicating an intention to discriminate.

Section 11 deals with discrimination by employment agencies against any person seeking employment or other services of the agency, for example training. Section 12 deals with discrimination in the provision of vocational training or any instruction needed to carry on an occupational activity. Finally, section 13 deals with discrimination by trade unions, professional and trade associations as regards membership and other benefits.

The Act is clearly intended to be as comprehensive as possible, covering all sectors and all aspects of employment. The 2004 Equality Act has extended the scope of the Act even further, for example, to self-employed peersons working in people's homes. These changes are unlikely to have any significant imapct on the nursing sector.

The concept of discrimination

Discrimination is not defined in the Interpretation section, but Section 6 of the Act explains what is meant by the concept, at least for the purposes of the Act.

> '(1) For the purposes of this Act, discrimination shall be taken to occur where, on any of the grounds in subsection (2) (in this Act referred to as "the discriminatory grounds"), one person is treated less favourably than another is, has been or would be treated.
>
> (2) As between any 2 persons, the discriminatory grounds (and the descriptions of those grounds for the purposes of this Act) are—
>
>   (a) that one is a woman and the other is a man (in this Act referred to as "the gender ground"),
>
>   (b) that they are of different marital status (in this Act referred to as "the marital status ground"),
>
>   (c) that one has family status and the other does not (in this Act referred to as "the family status ground"),

(d) that they are of different sexual orientation (in this Act referred to as "the sexual orientation ground"),
(e) that one has a different religious belief from the other, or that one has a religious belief and the other has not (in this Act referred to as "the religion ground"),
(f) that they are of different ages, but subject to subsection (3) (in this Act referred to as "the age ground"),
(g) that one is a person with a disability and the other either is not or is a person with a different disability (in this Act referred to as "the disability ground"),
(h) that they are of different race, colour, nationality or ethnic or national origins (in this Act referred to as "the ground of race"),
(i) that one is a member of the traveller community and the other is not (in this Act referred to as "the traveller community ground").

(3) Where—
(a) a person has attained the age of 65 years, or
(b) a person has not attained the age of 18 years,
then, subject to section 12(3), treating that person more favourably or less favourably than another (whatever that other person's age) shall not be regarded as discrimination on the age ground.

(4) The Minister shall review the operation of this Act, within two years of the date of the coming into operation of this section, with a view to assessing whether there is a need to add to the discriminatory grounds set out in this section.'

Commentary

It is important to establish the meaning of discrimination. Discrimination as a concept means that one thing is distinguished or treated differently from another thing. For the purposes of the Act, it is the impact of the discrimination, and whether that discrimination is unfair, that is important.

The Act simply says 'when one is treated less favourably than another', which is a good starting point in relation to the remainder of the Act. However, one would understand the Act a lot better, if one first understood the concept of discrimination before reading the Act.

Direct discrimination

When we speak of 'direct discrimination' in employment law, what is meant is a labour practice or policy that treats employees, trainees or job applicants differently. This different treatment is based on arbitrary characteristics, which have nothing to do with that person's value as an applicant, trainee or employee. These arbitrary characteristics are often called 'prohibited grounds'.

An employer discriminates when it treats one employee in a less favourable way than another. That discrimination becomes unfair and unlawful when the reason for the differential treatment is only because those employees have different but arbitrary characteristics. Section 6 of the 1998 Act expressly states the prohibited grounds, namely gender, marital status, family status, sexual orientation, religious belief, age, disability, race and membership of the traveller community.

A test to determine whether there is unfair direct discrimination is as follows:
1. Is there a distinction made between employees or groups of employees?
2. Is the distinction based on one or more of the prohibited grounds?
3. Is the distinction justified?

For an employee to prove direct discrimination, it is unnecessary to show that the employer intended to discriminate. Proof of the discriminator's state of mind, intention or motive is not required. It is enough to show that the effect of the action is less favourable treatment on the prohibited ground. In the English case of *James v Eastleigh Borough Council* [1990] I.R.L.R. 288, the House of Lords approved of the following test in cases of alleged direct gender discrimination: 'Would the complainant (the employee) have received the same treatment from the defendant (the employer) but for his or her sex?'

Indirect discrimination

Indirect discrimination in employment law can be defined as policies and practices that do not explicitly distinguish between employees or job applicants on the basis of any prohibited ground but that nonetheless have a discriminatory effect on particular groups of employees or individual employees. For example, during an economic downturn an employer dismisses the 'casual' employees before the 'permanents'. Although this might appear neutral on the face of it, if it was shown that casual workers were usually women and that most of the permanent employees were men, then such a redundancy policy will indirectly discriminate against women.

A test for indirect discrimination would be:
1. Has a requirement or condition been applied equally to both sexes or all racial groups or communities?

2. Is the requirement or condition one which a considerably smaller number of women or persons of a racial group or community in question can comply with than those who are not protected?
3. Is the requirement or condition justifiable irrespective of the protected grounds (For example, business necessity)?
4. Does the requirement or condition operate to the detriment of the complainant?

An employee has been indirectly discriminated against when the treatment in question is neutral on the face of it, but has a discriminatory impact on that employee. This is termed 'disparate impact' in the USA. In *Griggs v Duke Power Company* 401 US 424 (1971), the American Supreme Court held that it was unnecessary to prove intention to discriminate. The employee must simply show the disparate impact of the employer's practice on minorities or women. The burden then falls on the employer to show that such a practice was justified in the circumstances, usually by showing that the practice was established through business necessity or by showing that these relate to the successful performance of the job in question.

It has often been argued that in order to prove indirect discrimination, it must be shown that there is a causal connection between the prohibited ground and the manner in which the employee is being treated. However, the Irish Supreme Court rejected this test in *Nathan v Baily Gibson Ltd.* [1998] 2 I.R. 162.

Gender discrimination

In addition to gender being a prohibited ground specified in section 6, the Act expressly provides for indirect discrimination on the gender ground in section 22(1):

'Indirect discrimination on the gender ground.

(1) Where a provision (whether in the nature of a requirement, practice or otherwise) which relates to any of the matters specified in paragraphs (a) to (e) of section 8(1) or to membership of a regulatory body—
   (a) applies to both A and B,
   (b) is such that the proportion of persons who are disadvantaged by the provision is substantially higher in the case of those of the same sex as A than in the case of those of the same sex as B,

   and

(c) cannot be justified by objective factors unrelated to A's sex,

then, for the purposes of this Act, A's employer or, as the case may be, the regulatory body shall be regarded as discriminating against A on the gender ground contrary to section 8 or, as the case may require, section 13.'

Commentary

The section begins on the premise that the condition or practice in question applies to both genders. This is the difference between direct and indirect discrimination. Whereas direct discrimination expressly targets a certain group, a provision might appear neutral on the outside, but still indirectly discriminate against a certain gender, race, group or community.

It is the secondary impact of that condition or practice that is important when it comes to deciding on indirect discrimination.

A recent judgment of the High Court in *Mid Western Health Board v Maura Fitzgerald* (unreported, High Court, 28 November 2003) is a good example of discrimination on the gender ground.

Facts

Ms Fitzgerald was appointed Acting Deputy Matron of Limerick Regional Hospital in 1996. In 1998, the Matron of the hospital was due to go on maternity leave. The Mid-Western Health Board (MWHB) advertised the post of 'Acting Matron/Locum Director of Nursing'. Ms Fitzgerald was one of three applicants interviewed for the advertised post. The other applicants were a female and a male. In September 1998, the MWHB appointed the male applicant to the post, after giving him more points for the interview than Ms Fitzgerald, who was placed second. The third applicant, another woman, was not even graded by the interview committee.

Ms Fitzgerald applied to the Labour Court in terms of section 2(a) of the Employment Equality Act, claiming that she had been discriminated against by the MWHB on the grounds of her gender in filling the post of Acting Matron/Locum Director of Nursing.

The Equality Officer appointed by the Labour Court found that Ms Fitzgerald had been discriminated against as alleged and recommended that:

- The MWHB should pay Ms Fitzgerald the difference in pay, which she would have received had she been appointed to the disputed post;
- The MWHB should pay the plaintiff compensation in the amount of IR£3,000 (€3,809.21); and

- In all future cases when the matron was absent from duties Ms Fitzgerald, while holding the post of Deputy Matron, should deputise for her, the Matron.

The Labour Court upheld the recommendation of the Equality Officer, and found that the advertised position consisted of duties that were already being carried out by Ms Fitzgerald, and the failure to appoint her to that position raised a presumption of discrimination which the MWHB had failed to rebut. The MWHB appealed to the High Court.

Issue before the court
Was Ms Fitzgerald a victim of unfair gender discrimination?

Decision of the court
The High Court upheld the Labour Court's finding of fact, namely that Ms Fitzgerald was already performing the tasks required of the advertised position. The High Court further upheld the Labour Court's finding in law that the MWHB had failed to rebut the presumption of discrimination, and accordingly had contravened the Employment Equality Act. The appeal by the MWHB was dismissed.

Commentary
This case is difficult to define as being either direct or indirect discrimination, because whereas the interview would seem to appear neutral on the face of it, it was clearly the premise of the interview that caused a problem, as the employer did not take into account the fact that Ms Fitzgerald already occupied the post and was doing her job successfully. In addition, the fact that the interview committee did not even bother to grade the other applicant, who was also a woman, would suggest a hidden agenda. It would seem to be a case involving both direct and indirect discrimination.

This case is useful as it illustrates that the burden of proof is originally on the employee who must put forward evidence to show that there has been discrimination. This is called a *prima facie* case, which means 'on the face of it'. In other words, would a reasonable person, after considering the evidence of the employee, think that the employer had a case to answer?

This does not mean that the employee has won the case. What the *prima facie* case does is raise a presumption; the employee's version is considered the truth unless and until the employer manages to disprove it.

Once the employee has produced sufficient evidence to raise this presumption of discrimination, the burden of proof falls on the employer to produce evidence to show that despite the appearance of things, there was no discrimination. If the employer fails to disprove the discrimination (or 'rebut the presumption'), the employee's version is conclusively regarded as the truth, and the employee will win the case.

In this case the employer needed to show that the male applicant's qualifications and experience were sufficiently superior to Ms Fitzgerald's, to the extent that he would be able to a better job than she was, in essence, currently performing. Clearly the MWHB failed to show this.

Sexual harassment

The issue of sexual or intimate contact between employees, and the potential for the misuse of power in the employment relationship, is a constant problem for most employers, who are expected to act quickly and decisively when learning of this behaviour. The problems of definition when distinguishing between the appropriate and inappropriate, the welcome and unwelcome, and the physical and psychological, make this area of employment law a legal (and political) minefield. This does not mean that an employer must ignore the problem – it must deal with it as best as is reasonably possible in the circumstances.

Section 14A of the amended Act has an extended definition of sexual harassment. By deleting the 'reasonable' requirement it would seem that the Act is contemplating a more subjective test.

Section 15 holds an employer vicariously liable for the discriminatory acts of an employee done in the course of his or her employment. Section 15(3), and thereafter section 26, also provides that the employer of the employee who is being sexually harassed will have a defence to a discrimination claim, if that employer can show that it took reasonable steps to prevent the employee from being treated differently in the workplace because of that employee's rejection or acceptance of the sexual harassment, or, if the employee has already been treated differently, to take reasonable steps to reverse that different treatment. In addition, the employer can have a defence if it can show that it took reasonable steps to stop and prevent further harassment. These issues were explored in the case of *A Female Employee v A Hospital* [2001] E.L.R. 79.

Facts

The employee was a female nurse employed by the respondent hospital. In 1990 a male colleague had sexually harassed her. A meeting between the nurse and the harasser (Mr A) was held in 1990. At the meeting the hospital informed Mr A that his behaviour would not be condoned. The meeting was closed on the basis that the dispute was 'amicably resolved'. In 1993, Mr A was promoted to a position where he supervised the nurse's work. The nurse claimed that since then Mr A had victimised, intimidated and bullied her, making her position within the hospital intolerable. Without success, she had requested that Mr A be transferred to another area. On several occasions she requested a transfer for herself, but this had not happened.

The nurse was satisfied that she had exhausted all avenues to resolve the complaint and that management had failed to deal with it adequately or sufficiently. The nurse applied to the Labour Court in terms of the Employment Equality Act, and the Labour Court in turn referred the matter to an Equality Officer for investigation and a recommendation.

Issue before the tribunal
Was the nurse a victim of unlawful discrimination?

Decision of the tribunal
The Equality Officer found that the nurse had been unfairly penalised for reporting the harassment. Accordingly, the hospital had unfairly discriminated against the nurse. The nurse was awarded £3,000 as compensation for her suffering, and the hospital was ordered to transfer Mr A to another area.

Commentary
If an employee's actions against another employee fall within the definition of harassment, and this harassment is brought to the attention of the employer, the employer is under a statutory duty to do all that is reasonable in the circumstances to resolve the matter. If the employer does not do all that is reasonable in the circumstances, it will be held to have discriminated against the complainant employee in terms of the Act.

Therefore it is not the harassing employee that falls foul of the Act, it is the employer which fails to do anything about the harassment that is penalised by the Act. The harassing employee is guilty of misconduct, and must be punished in accordance with the employer's disciplinary procedures. The Employment Equality Act is more concerned with the impact of the sexual harassment upon the victim, and the employer's efforts (or lack thereof) to prevent or remedy that impact.

Equal pay for like work

The Act confirms the concept of equal pay for work of equal value, which was introduced into Irish law by the Anti-Discrimination (Pay) Act 1974, and has been championed by the European Court of Justice.

Like work may be shown by making a comparison between the work of the claimant (the dissatisfied employee who is getting less pay) and another employee (who has more pay) of the same or an associated employer. The 'comparator' (the title used in the Act to describe the employee with whom a comparison is being made) must be employed at the same time as the claimant or during the previous or following three years. There is no longer the requirement of the 1974 Act that the claimant be employed in the same place as the comparator. Sections 7 and 19 allow an employer to show that there are objective grounds for the different rates of pay, as long as the ground is not the gender ground.

Section 30 of the Act makes the principle of 'equal pay for like work' a term of every employment contract, as it says that if a contract does not contain an express equality clause, it shall be taken to have one. In other words an equality clause is either expressly placed into a contract of employment by the parties themselves, or it is implied by law. The end result is that every contract of employment contains an equality clause.

The 'occupational requirement' defence

The emphasis is on unfair discrimination, which means that discrimination on valid grounds is not unfair. For example, if it is shown that certain jobs can only be performed by somebody with specific but arbitrary characteristics (like a height requirement). This claim by the employer will be closely tested. Very often certain jobs are given to certain people as a result of a mentality that says 'this is the way things are and always have been, and there is no reason to change'. A better approach would be: 'This is how it should be or could be'. Employers need to examine their own beliefs in deciding why they think certain jobs can only be done by certain people.

The so-called 'inherent requirement criteria' used by the employer must be shown to be necessary, rather than just convenient. The requirements must relate to the core function of the job. In other words, if the requirement was excluded, the nature of the job would be fundamentally changed or it could not be performed. The burden of proof lies with the employer to prove that the discrimination is justified by the inherent requirements of the job.

The 'inherent requirement of the job' defence is recognised in section 25 of the 1998 Act. Instead of using the 'inherent requirement', the Act uses the phrase 'occupational requirement'.

An interesting case that examined an issue that was similar to the occupational requirement was *Martin Smyth v Eastern Health Board* [1996] E.L.R. 72, a case that dealt with the practice of 'specialing'.

Facts
Mr Smyth was a nurse working in a psychiatric hospital. He made a written request to his employer that he be given time off in lieu of accumulated time. The agreement in place allowed for this, as long as staffing levels at the time of the request permitted the employee to be

absent. The request could be denied if there was a staff shortage or if other staff had requested time off at the same time.

Mr Smyth's request was refused and he claimed that he had been directly discriminated against, and he argued that if he had been a female his request would have been granted. Mr Smyth also claimed that he had been indirectly discriminated against as the proportion of female nurses was substantially higher than male nurses, and therefore there should have been more female nurses on duty at any one time then there were male nurses on duty, but this was not the case. The Psychiatric Nurses Association represented Mr Smyth, and it referred the case to the Labour Court, which in turn referred the dispute to an Equality Officer for investigation and recommendation.

The Health Board argued that Mr Smyth was required to work in a male ward where some of the patients were aggressive and volatile. The employer had told him that if he could find another male nurse to replace him, he could take leave. Evidence was led that the ward in question was staffed by both male and female nurses, but that 'specialing' was a practice whereby aggressive patients were escorted by two nurses.

The union argued on behalf of Mr. Smyth that this practice was based on the supposed strength and stamina of male nurses and this was specifically excluded from the grounds of occupational qualification and therefore the Health Board could not rely on these to justify the need for male nurses over female nurses.

The union pointed out that this practice of 'specialing' was increasing whilst at the same time the Health Board was employing fewer male nurses and more female nurses (in order to remedy the gender imbalance) which meant that the male nurses employed by the Health Board were increasingly being called upon to do this dangerous job of 'specialing'.

In response, the Health Board admitted that the gender of Mr Smyth was a factor in refusing him leave, but argued that the same could have happened to a female nurse in another situation that demanded that a female fill the role. This was just a question of operational needs at the time of the request, and was not discrimination.

The Health Board gave evidence that both male and female nurses were involved in 'specialing', but the consultant psychiatrist had specifically instructed that a certain patient be 'specialed' by two male nurses as the patient was particularly aggressive. It was therefore an operational requirement that two male nurses were always on duty in respect of this particular patient.

Issue before the tribunal
Was Mr Smyth a victim of gender discrimination?

Finding of the tribunal
The Equality Officer found that the Health Board was not guilty of discrimination against Mr Smyth. The Officer held that 'none of the female psychiatric nurses could have provided the nursing services required in this instance. A consultant psychiatrist specifically requested two male nurses to undertake this "specialing" duty and both the PNA and the Health Board accept that this request was made'.

Commentary
Whilst the decision reached was probably the correct one, it was difficult to reconcile it with the then section 25, as the need for two male nurses was based on strength and stamina, and the specific request for two male nurses by the consultant psychiatrist does not change this fact. This illustrates the extreme difficulty in implementing this section. It is perhaps for this reason that the amended section 25 has deleted all referencees to 'physiology' or 'strength and stamina', and relies solely on the occupational requirement defence.

There are other sections, which recognise the occupational requirement defence.

Section 26(1) allows 'an employer to arrange for or provide treatment which confers benefits on women in connection with pregnancy and maternity (including breastfeeding) or adoption'. Whilst the first two attributes are clearly dependent on being a woman, it is not clear why benefits in relation to adoption should be confined to women.

Positive or 'fair' discrimination
There is such a thing as fair discrimination, and it is usually allowed where an employer practices 'positive discrimination' in favour of a clearly disadvantaged group. For example, in section 11(5), the Act recognises that an employment agency may provide services exclusively for employees with disabilities. In addition, section 28 allows measures to be taken in favour of women where these measures are in connection with pregnancy and maternity. Section 24(1) allows employers to introduce measures in order to 'promote equal opportunity', and mentions 'specific advantages so as to make it easier for an under-represented sex to pursue a vocational activity.'

Therefore in areas where women are traditionally under-represented, employers could justify the employment of a female candidate instead of a male candidate where those candidates had equivalent qualifications. The employer would need to prove that in the past, where candidates of equal gender had the same qualifications, the male candidate tended to get the job because of historical prejudice associated with that occupation. At the same time the employer must be careful not to introduce a quota system, where women are employed purely because they are women, irrespective of their qualifications and the qualifications of the male candidates.

The 2004 Equality Act extends the provision of positive action to all the grounds of discrimination recognised by the Employment Equality Act (section 33 of the Employment Equality Act).

Retirement age

Section 34 of the Act contains a recognised defence to a claim of discrimination on the grounds of age. This arises in situations where the employee's contract of employment is terminated because he or she reaches a certain age, and that age is the agreed or traditional retirement age in that particular industry. The accepted approach to retirement terminations is that the contract of employment has lapsed or expired, as opposed to the employee being dismissed.

It is possible to have different retirement ages for different jobs provided there is no direct or indirect discrimination based on arbitrary grounds, more especially gender. Section 34 goes on to say that it shall not be discrimination on the grounds of age for an employer to specify that applicants for a position must be under a certain age where it can be shown that the period required to train a person for that position requires that the trainee be under a certain age to make the training cost- or time-effective.

Clearly it does not make financial sense to train a person for an extended period at great expense, in the knowledge that the person will only be working for you for a limited period of time before retiring. The difficulty of course is to determine 'cut-off points' – at what age or what length of prospective service when compared to the cost of training can it be said to be uneconomical to train that person?

The complaint process

Claims of discrimination are investigated by the Director of Equality Investigations (the Equality Officer), who may order in equal pay cases a maximum compensation of three years' pay. In non-pay cases, the Director may order equal treatment and maximum compensation of two years' pay. The Director can also order further action to stop any further discrimination. This usually takes the form of a Recommendation, which is sent to the Labour Court for confirmation where the matter was contested.

If the case involves dismissal based on discrimination, it can go directly to the Labour Court, but the Labour Court can refer this to the Director if it wishes. In addition to financial compensation, the Labour Court can order reinstatement or re-engagement.

Discrimination: Summary

1. Discrimination occurs when two or more employees or two or more groups of employees are treated differently. Unfair discrimination occurs when this different treatment is because of an arbitrary reason (a prohibited ground), which cannot be justified.
2. Discrimination can be either direct or indirect.
3. Not all discrimination is unlawful or unfair, and positive discrimination is encouraged where it promotes disadvantaged groups who have been the victims of discrimination in the past.
4. In the employment context, employers can raise defences to practices, which are discriminatory. The most popular defence is 'occupational requirement' (sometimes called 'inherent requirement' in other countries).
5. The Employment Equality Act inserts into every contract of employment an equality clause, which guarantees equal pay for like work.
6. The Act prohibits discrimination on nine grounds, these being gender, marital status, family status, sexual orientation, religious belief, age, disability, race and membership of the traveller community.
7. Useful websites:
    a. *The Equality Authority* (http://www.equality.ie/).
    b. *The Equality Tribunal* (http://www.equalitytribunal.ie/).
    c. *Department of Justice, Equality and Law Reform* (http://www.justice.ie/).
    d. *Centre for Equality Studies* (http://www.ucd.ie/esc/)
    e. *Monster* (http://equality.monster.ie/)

HEALTH AND SAFETY IN THE WORKPLACE

> *Learning Outcomes*
> **At the completion of this chapter, the reader should know and understand the following:**
> ▸ Safety, Health and Welfare at Work Act 1989.
> ▸ Safety, Health and Welfare at Work Regulations 1993.

Introduction

It is important that hospitals and clinics practice the most stringent health and safety practices. These places are often crowded, with a lot of people and equipment concentrated in a relatively small place. The danger of accidents is aggravated by the fact that many of the people walking the corridors of hospitals are not well, and will not be as aware or alert as they would usually be concerning potential sources of danger.

The current health and safety laws are drawn from different sources such as the common law and statute law. European Union (EU) Directives have impacted significantly on domestic law, particularly in relation to general work safety, as well as specific sectors, for example the construction industry, which is governed by industry-specific regulations. Curiously, there are no industry-specific regulations for the health sector, which is governed by the general regulations.

The origins of health and safety law in the common law

The common law recognises two bases for the duty of care that an employer owes to its employees.

Firstly, the tort of negligence says that an employer owes a personal duty of care to its employees. The test would be that of the prudent or reasonable employer. This duty of care is described under four headings, namely the duty to provide safe and proper equipment, a safe place of work, a safe system of work, and competent fellow staff.

The duty to provide safe and proper equipment
The employer is expected to provide and maintain proper equipment so that employees using that equipment will not be exposed to unnecessary risk.

The duty to provide a safe place of work
The employer is expected to provide and properly maintain the place of work to ensure the safety of its inhabitants.

The duty to provide a safe system of work
By system of work is meant the process by which that particular business operates, and usually entails a beginning, a process and a final product. Clearly a hospital is not a manufacturing process, but it is clear that within the hospital there are a number of systems that operate, for example an outpatient system, an emergency and casualty system, a surgery system, and so on, and these must be safe for the health professionals and patients within that hospital.

The duty to provide competent fellow staff
Clearly it is of little use for some employees to observe safety procedures if others ignore the same procedures, as this would endanger all employees, regardless of their personal habits. The employer is under a duty to ensure that it recruits employees who are already familiar with safety procedures, and if they are not, the employer must take the necessary steps to ensure that new employees receive adequate training in this area.

The second basis for the duty of care is that it is a common law duty and an implied term in any employment contract that an employer will provide safe and secure working conditions for its employees.

The employer's duties in relation to the health and safety of employees, particularly in the tort of negligence, existed independently of statutory provisions and were developed over time by the courts. Although the current health and safety law comes mostly from statute, these statutes are based on principles developed by the courts.

The common law made it difficult for an employee to prove a claim against his or her employer, as the employee needed to prove the usual elements of negligence. The employee had to rely on the courts to develop the common law of health and safety, and this did not happen in a hurry.

Judicial formulation of health and safety principles

The first principle that has been developed by the courts is that when establishing the standard of care expected of a reasonable employer, the courts will take evidence of the existing practices of other employers, either from the same industry, or within the same geographical area. This was of little help to the employee if the industry as a whole was dangerous and the average employer failed to implement adequate safety measures.

The second principle developed by the courts is that the law will seek to strike a balance between the employee's right to a safe working environment, and the costs to the employer of providing those safeguards. At the time of the Industrial Revolution, the emphasis on progress seemed to overshadow the sanctity of human life, and the common law was very slow to produce a law that properly protected the worker.

There was clearly a need for statutory intervention, as the common law was moving too slowly in its efforts to protect the worker.

Safety, Health and Welfare at Work Act 1989

The nature of the 1989 Act is preventative rather than punitive. What this means is that the Act seeks to encourage people to be safe by providing guidelines, rather than just punishing unsafe practices.

Section 28 says that the Minister for Enterprise, Trade and Employment can make regulations on occupational health and safety matters after consultation with the Health and Safety Authority (HSA). The formulation of these regulations has allowed the introduction of various EU Directives regulating the safety, health and welfare of employees into Irish Law.

In terms of the legislation enacted before it, the 1989 Act was substantial, both in size and impact. It was the first legislation to protect all employees, regardless of their place of work. It was designed to reduce accidents by forcing employers to reduce risks. This was supported by mainly criminal sanctions, although section 28 of the Act does allow for the making of regulations that attract civil liability.

Sections 6 to 11 establish the general duties of employers under the Act.

SECTION 6. General duties of employers to their employees

'(1) It shall be the duty of every employer to ensure, so far as is reasonably practicable, the safety, health and welfare at work of all his employees.
(2) Without prejudice to the generality of an employer's duty under subsection (1), the matters to which that duty extends include in particular-
  (a) as regards any place of work under the employer's control, the design, the provision and the maintenance of it in a condition that is, so far as is reasonably practicable, safe and without risk to health;
  (b) so far as is reasonably practicable, as regards any place of work under the employer's control, the design, the provision and the maintenance of safe means of access to and egress from it;
  (c) the design, the provision and the maintenance of plant and

machinery that are, so far as is reasonably practicable, safe and without risk to health;
(d) the provision of systems of work that are planned, organised, performed and maintained so as to be, so far as is reasonably practicable, safe and without risk to health;
(e) the provision of such information, instruction, training and supervision as is necessary to ensure, so far as is reasonably practicable, the safety and health at work of his employees;
(f) in circumstances in which it is not reasonably practicable for an employer to control or eliminate hazards in a place of work under his control, or in such circumstances as may be prescribed, the provision and maintenance of such suitable protective clothing or equipment, as appropriate, that are necessary to ensure the safety and health at work of his employees;
(g) the preparation and revision as necessary of adequate plans to be followed in emergencies;
(h) to ensure, so far as is reasonably practicable, safety and the prevention of risk to health at work in connection with the use of any article or substance;
(i) the provision and the maintenance of facilities and arrangements for the welfare of his employees at work; and
(j) the obtaining, where necessary, of the services of a competent person (whether under a contract of employment or otherwise) for the purpose of ensuring, so far as is reasonably practicable, the safety and health at work of his employees.'

Commentary

Section 6(1) of the Act provides that it is the duty of employers to ensure the safety, health and welfare at work of all employees, in so far as is reasonably practicable. This first section sets the standard and the context in which the remainder of the section must be read, and the preface to section 6(2) is clear that the remainder of the section must not be seen to take anything away from the comprehensiveness of this first sub-section.

Section 6(2) specifies ten matters which an employer must consider when fulfilling the duty imposed by section 6(1) of the Act, such as provision and maintenance of place of work including design, access, systems, information, instruction, training and supervision, control and elimination of hazards and provision of protective clothing/equipment.

However, what is clear is that section 6(2) must never be interpreted to contain a closed or exhaustive list. None of the other sections is allowed to restrict its scope or reduce the comprehensive duty placed on employers by section 6(1), and therefore section 6(2) is setting the scene, rather than limiting the options. There will always be variations of duties placed on employers, which will be dependent on the type of industry and sector. The specific dangers associated with the health care sector, for example contaminated blood and contagious disease, means that the health and safety practices of a hospital will be different from, for example, a school or sports stadium, although all of these cater to the public.

Section 7 of the Act addresses the general duties of employers and the self-employed to persons other than their employees. In effect, this section covers the general public, as it provides that the duty of care extends to an open-ended category of persons, namely those other than employees. This section is particularly relevant to the health care institutions, as members of the public are continually in and around a hospital, or visiting the community care centres and clinics run by the health boards.

Section 8 of the Act imposes duties on people who provide a place of work for employees of other employers. Again, and for similar reasons, section 8 is as important to the health care sector as section 7. Section 8 is slightly more restricted in its application than section 7, but clearly applies to those people working on the site, either as self-employed workers (for example, consultants), or the employees of other persons (for example, agency nurses), and to whom the person who is in overall control of the site (the administrator of the hospital) owes a duty of care, provided that the place of work is 'made available to them'.

SECTION 9. General duties of employees

'(1) It shall be the duty of every employee while at work-
- (a) to take reasonable care for his own safety, health and welfare and that of any other person who may be affected by his acts or omissions while at work;
- (b) to co-operate with his employer and any other person to such extent as will enable his employer or the other person to comply with any of the relevant statutory provisions;
- (c) to use in such manner so as to provide the protection intended, any suitable appliance, protective clothing, convenience, equipment or other means or thing provided (whether for his use alone or for use by him in common with others) for securing his safety, health or welfare while at work; and
- (d) to report to his employer or his immediate supervisor, without unreasonable delay, any defects in plant, equipment, place of work or system of work, which might endanger safety, health or welfare, of which he becomes aware.

(2) No person shall intentionally or recklessly interfere with or misuse any appliance, protective clothing, convenience, equipment or other

means or thing provided in pursuance of any of the relevant statutory provisions or otherwise, for securing the safety, health or welfare of persons rising out of work activities.'

Commentary
Section 9 sets out the duties owed by all employees while at work. The employee's main duty is to take reasonable care for his or her own safety, health and welfare as well as that of others. The employee must co-operate with the employer, use protective equipment and clothing provided and report dangerous risks of which he or she becomes aware.

An employer could possibly use this provision to try and escape liability by claiming that the employee failed to comply with his or her responsibilities and was thus contributorily negligent, which will not allow the employer to escape liability, but could certainly be used by the employer to reduce its liability. The employer might also claim ignorance of hazards on site if these are not formally reported. The duties of nurses in this regard are particularly important, as being the people 'on the ground', they are more likely to notice hazards and potentially dangerous situations.

As it is the employer who is liable for any damage caused by the nurse during his or her employment, an employer would be justified in dismissing a nurse for a serious infringement of safety regulations.

Section 10 of the Act deals with the duty owed by persons who design, manufacture, import or supply articles for use in the workplace. It attempts to make sure that all articles and substances used in the workplace are properly designed, constructed and tested prior to supply and use. The section also says that there must be enough information supplied with the articles to make it possible to safely dismantle and dispose of the articles if necessary. This could apply to hospital equipment that is outdated or beyond repair but cannot simply be thrown away on the dump.

Section 11 places a duty on any persons who design places of work to design them so that they are, so far as is reasonably practicable, safe and without risk to health. A similar duty is imposed upon people who construct places of work. Again, hospitals should be designed to make sure that there are handy entrances and exits, easy access to patients in the wards, and so on.

Sections 10 and 11 could be critically important in the health care sector when one considers the amount of extremely sophisticated and potentially lethal equipment found in any hospital. In support of these provisions, the regulations have imposed an onerous duty on manufacturers to comply with safety standards in the manufacture of equipment, and this is particularly true in the health care sector. Unfortunately, the courts have not yet been called upon to interpret sections 10 and 11.

'Reasonably practicable'

A reader of the Act could not fail to notice the number of times the phrase 'reasonably practicable' appears in the text, particularly in section 6 with regard to the duties of employers in securing and making safe the worksite of their employees, and indeed third parties on that worksite. The phrase has been included in the Irish and UK safety legislation for a long time, but has been given central status in the 1989 Act.

It is therefore important that the meaning and implications of the phrase 'reasonably practicable' are fully understood.

The most widely quoted explanation of what is meant by the phrase is that of Lord Justice Asquith in the English Court of Appeal, in the judgement of *Edwards v National Coal Board* [1949] 1 All E.R. 743 (CA):

> '"Reasonably practicable" is a narrower term than "physically possible" and seems to me to imply that a computation must be made by the owner in which the quantum of risk is placed on one scale and the sacrifice involved in the measures necessary for averting the risk (whether in money, time or trouble) is placed in the other, and that, if it be shown that there is a gross disproportion between them – the risk being insignificant in relation to the sacrifice – the defendants discharge the onus on them. Moreover, this computation falls to be made by the owner at the point of time anterior to the incident.'

Commentary

The test used by the courts involves balancing the risk of an accident happening on the one hand, against the expense needed to avoid that risk on the other. If the risk is minimal, but precautions expensive, then it is not 'reasonably practicable' to spend the money on putting the precautions in place. If, on the other hand, the risk of somebody being injured is great, and the cost or expense of avoiding that injury can be afforded by the employer, then it is 'reasonably practicable' to have the precaution put in place.

In a later English case, *Marshall v Gotham Company Limited* [1954] 1 All E.R. 937 (HL) the phrase was once again considered.

Facts

The roof of a gypsum mine had collapsed, largely as a result of a rare geological fault known as 'slicken-slide'. The owner of the mine had not provided any artificial support for the roof, and it argued that it was not financially feasible to spend the large amount of money to provide the support, particularly as the support would not necessarily prevent this type of accident, which was caused by earth movement and therefore could not be controlled.

Issue before the court
Was it reasonably practicable for the mine owners to support the roof?

Decision of the court
The decision was finally made in the House of Lords, the highest court in the UK, where the judges accepted that the cost of providing systematic support throughout the mine would have been very high and in any event, it was doubtful whether such support could have prevented the accident in question. The court decided that it was not 'reasonably practicable' to install the necessary support and the employers were found to be not in breach of the statutory duty to make the mine safe. The House of Lords quoted the *Edwards* case with approval, and Lord Reid added the following:

> '... if a precaution is practicable it must be taken unless in the whole circumstances that would be unreasonable. And as men's lives may be at stake it should not be lightly held that to take a practicable precaution is unreasonable.'

Lord Reid continued to say that in the present case, however:

> 'The danger was a very rare one. The trouble and expense involved in the use of precautions, while not prohibitive, would have been considerable. The precautions would not have afforded anything like complete protection against the danger, and their adoption would have had the disadvantage of giving a false sense of security.'

A more recent Irish authority is the case of *Boyle v Marathon Petroleum (Ireland) Limited* (unreported, High Court, 12 January 1999).

Facts
Boyle was an operative working on an offshore rig drilling for gas. The defendant company owned the rig and Boyle was an employee of the defendant. The platform on the rig was originally constructed as two floors with a space of twenty-two feet between them.

It was necessary to check the readings on various gauges, some of which were five feet above the bottom floor, whilst others were eight feet above the bottom floor. A ladder was used to reach the top valves and gauges, and as the bottom floor was very wet and slippery and cluttered with fire-fighting and electrical equipment, it was very difficult, and dangerous, to move the ladder to read these gauges and adjust the valves.

The employees complained about this, and the defendant company responded by building a middle floor so that all the valves and gauges could be reached from a standing position. Due to the position of the lowest valves, the height of the area between the mid-floor and the bottom floor was less than five feet. The middle floor was supported by girders every two feet, and these protruded which reduced headroom to just over four feet. This meant that anybody working and moving on the bottom floor had to do so in a crouching position.

Boyle was cleaning the bottom floor of the platform when he struck his head on one of the girders and jerked his neck backwards ('whiplash'). He sued the employer under the common law and also in terms of the Safety, Health and Welfare (Offshore Installations) Act 1987, which required the installation manager to ensure that every workplace on the installation was 'so far as is reasonably practicable' made and kept safe.

Issue before the court
Were the measures introduced by the employer, namely the erection of the middle floor, 'reasonably practicable'?

Decision of the court
The High Court accepted that it was difficult and even hazardous to work on the lower floor. However, the plaintiff worked on this floor perhaps six times a year, whereas the new middle floor was used continuously. The middle floor was inserted after the employees had complained. Boyle's was the first complaint in ten years since the middle floor was inserted. On balance therefore, the High Court concluded that the insertion of the middle floor was the provision of a workplace that was safe 'so far as is reasonably practicable'.

The High Court (McCracken J.) held that:

> 'The use of the words "reasonably practicable" seems to me to recognise that offshore installations do have practical problems which differ from onshore factories or other workplaces. I have to consider whether the conditions under which the plaintiff was required to work were as safe as was reasonably practicable, and this must be a test based on the actual circumstances of each individual offshore installation. When considering the necessity of the insertion of the middle floor, I must balance the benefits and additional safety to people working on the blocks from the middle floor against the possible dangers to the people working on the bottom floor.'

Accordingly, as the bottom floor was not used nearly as often as the middle floor, it was 'reasonably practicable' for the employer to have inserted that middle floor. McCracken J. held that the dangers complained of by Boyle, namely low ceilings and obstructions, were dangers that it was not reasonably practicable to avoid in this type of work. He did not, however, specifically define the phrase. This judgment, and the approach adopted by the High Court, was upheld by the Supreme Court. O'Flaherty J., in the Supreme Court, stated:

> 'This duty is more extensive than the common law duty which devolves on employers to exercise reasonable care in various aspects as regards their employees. It is an obligation to take all practical steps. That seems to me to involve more than they should respond that they, as employers, did all that was reasonably to be expected of them in a particular situation'.

Commentary
When using the balancing of interests test, the court will consider the risk and the probability and extent of that risk on the one hand, and on the other hand the cost of taking measures to avoid that risk, and whether the cost is justified in avoiding the harm complained of.

The courts will look at each situation against the background of the particular conditions and risks that are encountered in that industry, as an overall general test would be impractical, and not much use. In the hospital context, there are many examples that one could use to illustrate this principle. For example, the use of Universal Precautions to avoid infection and possible death from contaminated blood is clearly 'reasonably practicable' and something that every employer must implement. The cost of providing these precautions is not expensive, and when compared with the risk, which is death, the expense is far outweighed by the risk. On the other hand, it might not be 'reasonably practicable' to have washing and toilet facilities in every hospital ward, particularly day wards, where patients can safely walk down the corridor to go to the toilet.

Safety statements

The safety statement is a useful device in that it is well known amongst most employees with the result that in most workplaces its absence would be noticed and hopefully remedied. It is for this reason that section 12 is arguably one of the most successful sections in the Act. Of course, the question of whether the contents of the statement are read and obeyed is another matter. As always, the success or failure of any safety law depends on the attitude of the people who control the causes of danger, be they employers or employees.

Under section 12 of the Act, every employer must, as soon as possible, prepare or cause to be prepared a statement in writing known as a safety statement. The statement must describe the manner in which the safety, health and welfare of the workers and third parties shall be protected in the workplace. Failure to comply with section 12 is a criminal offence and there may also be civil liability.

A safety statement is a written commitment by the employer to safeguard the health and safety of his or her employees and others whilst on or in the workplace. It forces the employer to properly bring its mind to the problem and it helps employees monitor the employer's efforts in this regard. For that reason alone, it is an extremely useful document, and nurses amongst others must insist that these are prominently displayed in hospitals, clinics and any other institutions within the health care sector, where safety measures do not always receive the prominence that they should.

A safety statement must also identify the cooperation required from employees and include the names of persons responsible for the safety tasks assigned to them under the Act. The employer must bring the terms of the safety statement to the attention of all employees and others who may be affected by the safety statement. In a hospital situation one could argue that this should include patients, who need to be made aware of hazards in the hospital that should be avoided. Whether a court would ever be prepared to go this far is debateable.

In summary the safety statement should:

- Clearly explain how the health and safety of employees will be protected. In describing the duty on the employer, general sweeping terms should be used, making the duty on employers comprehensive rather than exclusive.
- Provide details of how the employer is going to manage its employees' health and safety, and this must include a commitment to comply with all statutory and other legal duties, and to provide the necessary equipment and funding to make sure that all is done to protect the safety of all health professionals and patients or clients.
- Identify the hazards and assess the risks in the workplace. An assessment of risk is the examination undertaken by a reasonable employer, which identifies work activities that could foreseeably result in harm to employees, and the provision and practice of reasonable safeguards to guard against the occurrence of that harm. This is similar to the duty of care in tort, where a person must guard against all foreseeable risks where it is reasonable and possible to do so. In hospitals, for example, certain safeguards

would seem obvious, like keeping corridors open and free from obstacles, easily accessible toilet facilities, non-slip floors, fire escapes, regular servicing of lifts, and so on.

- Clearly explain the cooperation required from employees on health and safety matters. A safety statement should make it clear that the employer, managers, supervisors and the employees themselves should make sure that their workplace practices conform to the safety statement. Supervisory checks and audits should be carried out to determine how well the aims of the safety statement are being achieved, for example a regular fire drill. Corrective action should be taken when required. All health professionals, but nurses in particular, should be extremely vigilant when carrying out their duties and make notes and report on dangerous hazards in their workplace. They must not stop at just reporting the hazard, but must make sure that the health statement is amended where necessary to record the hazard. Too many reports are dropped into dusty drawers and forgotten, and it is up to the vigilant employee to make sure that this is not allowed to happen. Nurses should become involved with their safety representatives and union officials to force employers to act on reports from employees.

- Include the names and job titles of the people who have been appointed to be responsible for the health and safety within the workplace. A good safety statement is a particular and detailed safety statement. Rather than simply contain general duties, a clear and easy-to-understand record should be made of the more significant hazards, and the practical steps needed to be taken in order to safeguard against that particular danger. For example, 'Electrical installations like bedside lamps and call buttons: earthing and insulation to be checked every three months and/or after any modification – by Ward Sister'. Employees must be informed of these findings and referred to any specific procedures contained in other manuals and where these manuals are kept. As a rule therefore, the duty on an employer must be comprehensive, whilst duties of employees should be specific.

- Clearly set out a timetable and procedures for consultation with employees on the health and safety issues. Employees are required to report to their employer, manager or supervisor about any defects in plant, equipment, place or system of work that might endanger health and safety. Therefore the safety statement should indicate the system for doing so. In addition, employers are required to put in place a safety consultation programme that allows and encourages participation by all employees in health and safety matters. This is an important aspect of safety management as

it empowers employees to exercise significant control over their workplace. It will also provide an understanding of the benefits of workplace safety, and as such plays an important educative function. The names and functions of the safety representatives should also be clearly displayed.
- Contain details of information available to employees on health and safety. For example, the nature and location of any manuals dealing with safety procedures in relation to specific machinery (for example, a kidney dialysis machine) or specific substances (for example, ether or oxygen).

Consultation with employees

Section 13 of the Act orders every employer to consult with employees on safety, health and welfare matters at work. In so far as is reasonably practicable, the employer must implement the recommendations made by employees. If employees point out a hazard and suggest a practical and affordable way of preventing or controlling the hazard, and the employer does not put this into practice, the employer would have a difficult time explaining its failure to do so if an accident were to happen.

Employees can make representations to the employer on matters of safety, health and welfare and can appoint a safety representative from among their number to act on their behalf. This representative has a right to information and to investigate accidents, potential hazards and complaints.

The Health and Safety Authority

The National Authority for Occupational Safety and Health (the Health and Safety Authority) was established under Part III of the 1989 Act. Parts V, VI, VII, and VIII set out the powers of the Authority. Under section 16 of the Act, the Authority has several functions including enforcement of the statutory provisions. The Authority must also review on a regular basis the relevant legislation and it can issue Codes of Practice with the consent of the Minister. These Codes are merely aids to safe practice and are not legally binding, although they will hopefully be used by the courts as guidelines in an effort to achieve consistent judicial interpretation of the statute.

Section 33 of the Act authorises the Authority to appoint inspectors to enforce the legislation. Section 34 gives these inspectors the powers of entry, inspection, examination, search, seizure and analysis. In terms of sections 35, 36 and 37, an inspector has the authority to issue improvement directions and plans, improvement notices and prohibition notices.

The Authority or its agent can investigate the circumstances surrounding any accident, disease, occurrence, situation or any other matters. Failing to comply with the Authority in the performance of its functions is a criminal offence and penalties such as fines or imprisonment may be imposed.

Both natural and juristic persons may be prosecuted, and this would include the officers or management of a hospital or health board, for example. Prosecutions must be brought under section 51(3) within one year from the date of the offence. Subsection (4) provides, however, that where a report about an investigation is required by a statute or a regulation, or where an inquest is held, summary proceedings must be brought within six months of the making of the report or the conclusion of the inquest.

It would appear that the Authority can prosecute both summary and indictable proceedings, in its own name, without it being necessary to obtain the authorisation of the DPP. The Authority is empowered to apply to the District Court for the issue of summons alleging offences contrary to the provisions of the 1989 Act.

In addition to the provisions of the main body of the Act itself, there have been numerous regulations made by the Minister in terms of section 28 the Act, both of general application and industry-specific regulations.

Safety, Health and Welfare at Work (General Application) Regulations 1993

Perhaps the most noticeable aspect of these Regulations, which are heavily influenced by the various EU directives on health and safety, is that, unlike the Act, they do not contain the limiting phrase 'so far as is reasonable practicable'. It can therefore be argued that when enforcing these Regulations, the Health and Safety Authority are not bound by the previously discussed decisions, which interpreted this phrase. Most of the duties contained in these Regulations are strict duties (the employer must comply absolutely) and many are described in absolute language.

The 1993 Regulations are divided into ten sections and impose duties on employers and employees for the benefit of employees. Although the terms of 'employer' and 'employee' are not defined in the regulations, their meaning can be ascertained from the definitions in the Act itself, which are found in section 2, the Interpretation Section:

> ' "Employee" means a person who has entered into or works (or in the case of a contract which has been terminated, worked) under a contract of employment with an employer;

"Employer" in relation to an employee, means the person by whom the employee is employed under a contract of employment; for the purpose of this definition a person holding office under or in the service of the State or of the Government shall be deemed to be employed by the State or the Government (as the case may be) and an officer or servant of a local authority or of a harbour authority, health board or vocational education committee shall be deemed to be employed by the local Authority, harbour authority, health board or vocational education committee (as the case may be).'

Part I of the Regulations provides that they shall 'also apply in respect of the use by [the employer] of the services of a fixed term employee or temporary employee'.

Part II of the Regulations imposes specific duties in respect of matters such as training, health surveillance, protective and preventative services, etc. Some of the main duties of the employer under the Regulations are as follows:

- To ensure that safety measures are reviewed on a regular basis and kept up to date, in terms of new technology and new law;
- To ensure that known risks caused by equipment, substances and the fitting out of a place of work, are periodically evaluated by the employer;
- To coordinate measures in relation to the protection from and prevention of occupational risks;
- To inform employees or safety representatives of any risks involved in their work activities;
- To ensure that any measures taken do not involve financial cost to the employees;
- To provide personal protective equipment free of charge, where the use of such equipment is exclusive to the place of work.

These duties are particularly relevant in the health care sector, where sophisticated equipment is used continuously, making maintenance and upgrading essential, although sometimes difficult when waiting lists are long and patient demand is extreme. In addition, effective protective clothing is a necessity, and can and should be regularly renewed and improved.

Regulation 7 details the steps and measures that need to be taken in the event of an emergency occurring in a place of work. The employer is obliged to provide facilities for the emergency evacuation of employees, to arrange contacts with the appropriate emergency services and to ensure that there are sufficient employees trained in emergency procedure, and that they have adequate training and equipment to properly carry out that function.

Regulation 10 obliges an employer to inform employees who are or may be exposed to 'serious and imminent danger' of any risk involved and of the steps taken, or to be taken, for their protection. Should such 'serious, imminent and unavoidable danger' arise the employer must ensure that work is stopped immediately and employees evacuated to safety.

Hospitals pose huge challenges as regards emergencies, particularly when it comes to evacuating patients, and it is necessary that all staff are thoroughly prepared for emergency procedures. However, it is difficult to have regular practice drills, for the obvious reason that one cannot expect patients to be taken out of bed or transported outside on a too-regular basis. Regulation 10 would also include measures taken by the employer to avoid infection of employees by body fluids, blood or other dangerous substances like radioactive material or poisons.

Regulation 16 defines a place of work as:

'A place of work intended to house workstations on the premises of the undertaking and any other place within the area of the undertaking to which an employee has access in the course of his employment but does not include –
(a) means of transport used outside the undertaking or a place of work inside a means of transport;
(b) construction sites;
(c) extractive industries;
(d) fishing boats;
(e) fields, woods and land forming part of an agricultural or forestry undertaking but situated away from the undertaking's buildings'.

Regulation 17 further limits the scope of the duties of an employer to any place of work within its control.

These Regulations are clearly wide enough to include hospitals and clinics, even where these premises are spread over a wide area, consisting of many separated buildings.

Part IV of the Regulations deals with the issue and use of work equipment. All work equipment acquired before 31 December 1992, for use by employees at a place of work must comply with certain minimum standards set out in the Fifth Schedule of the Regulations. Equipment provided after that date must comply with both the minimum requirements and any relevant applicable EU directive. Furthermore, the equipment must be maintained to the requisite standard throughout its life.

Under the regulations standards are set in relation to stability and solidity, ventilation of enclosed places, room temperature, lighting, floors, walls, ceilings, roofs, doors, gates, vehicle danger areas, loading bays, ramps, etc. Other areas include windows, skylights, escalators and such like.

Regulations 18 to 20 deal with work equipment. Work equipment should be fit for its intended purpose. The employer must also ensure that competent employees use and service the equipment.

Control devices should be clearly visible and identifiable, and must be located outside 'danger zones', which are zones within or around work equipment in which an employee is subject to a risk to health or safety. Alarms must be put in place and controls must be provided to allow equipment to be switched off and override start controls. Emergency stop devices should be used as should clamps, safety guards and the like.

Part IV is clearly applicable to all hospitals and clinics, where the risk of fire and electrical accidents is relatively high, particularly in some of the older hospitals.

Part V of the Regulations deals with personal protective equipment. Where risk to health and safety cannot be avoided by technical measures and procedures an employer is obliged to provide personal protective equipment for use by employees. Before issuing personal protective equipment, the employer must make sure that the equipment is effective and compatible with other equipment. Furthermore, every employer must ensure that the equipment is kept in good working order. The employee must be provided with training and instruction in the use of the equipment. Instruction and training regarding Universal Precautions and the supply and use of the accompanying protective clothing is the most obvious example of this duty placed on employers in the health sector.

Part VI of the Regulations deals with manual handling of loads. The Regulations regard the manual handling of loads as a last resort. Where it is necessary, an employer is obliged to minimise the risk involved and provide, where possible, information concerning the weight and centre of gravity of a load to the employee. The Eighth Schedule details the factors that must be taken into account by an employer for the manual handling of loads. The Ninth Schedule identifies individual risk factors in the manual handling of loads. It could be argued, for example, that the risk of repetitive strain injury should be assessed. These Regulations are applicable to employees in the health care sector who are involved in lifting patients, and health boards must make sure that proper lifting training is given to any nurse who might be required to lift patients.

Part VII and the Tenth and Eleventh Schedules of the Regulations impose duties on an employer to protect an employee who habitually uses display screen equipment as a significant part of his or her normal work. An example would be the computer at the reception desk of a hospital or clinic, or the display screen of an ultra-scan machine.

Part VIII of the Regulations apply to the generation, storage, transmission and provision of electrical energy. Part IX refers to first aid, Part X and the Twelfth Schedule to notification of Accidents and Dangerous Occurrences.

Health and Safety: Summary

1. The Safety, Health and Welfare Act 1989 is a very comprehensive statute which deals with all aspects of health and safety in the workplace.
2. Sections 6 to 11 impose a very broad duty of care on employers to their employees and others, to ensure the health and safety of those people whilst at work in the workplace.
3. The use of the phrase 'so far as is reasonably practicable' dominates these sections, and has been interpreted by the courts to mean that in deciding whether the provision of any safety feature or equipment or measure is 'reasonably practicable', the courts will balance the risk that the hazard poses on the one hand, against the cost and effort of removing or controlling that risk on the other.
4. From a practical point of view, the duty on the employer to produce and maintain a safety statement for any workplace is perhaps the most important aspect of the Act, as it forces an employer to properly consider all potential hazards in a workplace and suitable measures to prevent or control these.
5. The 1993 Regulations to the Act have been heavily influenced by the EU Directives on health and safety, and are capable of a stricter interpretation than the Act, as they do not contain the 'reasonably practicable' phrase that is used so extensively in the Act.
6. Useful web site:
The Health and Safety Authority (http://www.hsa.ie).

VICARIOUS LIABILITY AND THE NURSE

> **Learning Outcomes**
> At the completion of this chapter, the reader should know and understand the following:
> - The principle of vicarious liability.
> - The current law relating to vicarious liability.
> - The position of the nurse as employee as regards vicarious liability.

Important concepts and phrases that are crucial to an understanding of this chapter

Authority – express and implied

An employer can authorise an employee to do something in words or writing, and this is called express authority. On the other hand, an employee might have implied authority to do something when, although the employer has not said so in as many words, the employee cannot do his or her job properly without being able to do certain things.

The employee can argue that there was implied authority from the employer to do the things that are necessary to perform his or her job properly. For example, an employer instructs an employee to take the company vehicle and deliver a parcel to a neighbouring city. The employee takes the parcel, jumps into the car, and heads off. During the journey the employee notices that the petrol tank is almost empty. The employee stops and buys petrol without asking the employer whether he can do so. The employee can argue that he was acting under the employer's implied authority, as he needed to buy petrol in order to deliver the parcel. The act of buying the petrol was incidental to the delivery of the parcel.

Therefore if a nurse was instructed to make a patient comfortable after a particularly painful procedure, the nurse can claim implied authority to do all the things necessary to make the patient comfortable, without needing to be given permission to do each and every thing. Clearly, when we say that something is incidental to the job in hand, it can only be things that the nurse knows or reasonably ought to know he or she is allowed to do. For example, the instruction 'make the patient as comfortable as possible' cannot be taken to confer implied authority to give the patient a dose of morphine, as the nurse is prohibited from doing such a thing. On the other hand, it would probably allow the nurse to administer paracetemol and arrange for some extra blankets and pillows out of the stores.

Indemnity insurance
The essential principles of indemnity in insurance are:
- The insurer gives an undertaking to make good any damage or loss.
- The insured person is not allowed to make a profit from the policy.
- Indemnity insurance is different from life insurance. For obvious reasons, you cannot take out indemnity insurance on somebody's life.

What amount is recoverable? As a general rule, the contract will state that the insurer will pay the sum insured, or the amount of the actual loss suffered, depending on which is the lesser amount.

Example 1
John insures his car for €10,000. He crashes it, causing damage, which will cost €1,000. John may only claim €1,000.

Example 2
Joan insures her painting for €10,000. The painting falls off the wall and is torn. It will cost €15,000 to restore the painting. Joan will only receive €10,000.

Therefore a nurse can take out an indemnity insurance policy which will cover that nurse for damages and expenses up to a certain amount, for example €100,000. If the damages and expenses of a medical malpractice claim cost the nurse €80,000, the insurance company will pay the entire bill. If the claim and expenses cost the nurse €120,000, the insurance company will pay €100,000, and the nurse will have to find the other €20,000. Obviously, the more cover the nurse takes (in other words the ceiling is lifted) the higher the premium (the money you pay to the insurance company every month) will be.

Introduction – the concept of vicarious liability

Vicarious liability simply means that one person is held liable for the wrongdoing of another. This concept is not limited to employment law. A driver might be vicariously liable for the actions of a passenger. A host might be liable for the actions of a guest. In very rare circumstances, a parent might even be held vicariously liable for the actions of a child. However, in this chapter, the specific question of employer liability for the torts of an employee will be examined. This is known as the doctrine of *respondeat superior*.

One of the most important advantages of being an employee is that as a general rule the employer is liable for any damages caused by an employee in the course of employment, rather than the employee being personally liable for the consequences of his or her actions.

The law of vicarious liability is complicated. It is often a difficult question as to whether an employee's actions are within the course of employment.

In order to hold an employer liable for the actions of an employee, the plaintiff needs to prove three things:
- That the wrongdoer is an employee of the employer being sued.
- That the employee was negligent.
- That the negligent action causing the damage was within the employee's scope of employment.

The first two aspects have been covered elsewhere in this book. The third requirement needs to be examined further.

In deciding whether an employee acted in the course of his or her employment, the English courts adopt a slightly wider test than the Irish courts. The English courts ask two questions:
(1) What was that employee employed to do?
(2) When the employee carried out the wrongful act in question, was he or she acting for the benefit of the employer?

As far as the first question is concerned, the English courts have held that where the wrongful actions of the employee are closely connected with the duties of the employee, the test is satisfied.

It is the second question that causes considerable problems, as the English courts have said that even where the employee is clearly in the wrong, perhaps even contravening a code of the employer, this does not automatically mean that the wrongful action is outside the scope of employment, and all facts must be considered.

The English courts have similarly held that the term 'in the course of employment' will cover all acts authorised by the employer, but will also cover acts not authorised by the employer if those acts are performed for the purpose of the employer's business, or where the acts are incidental to the employer's business, or where the acts protect the property or assets of the employer, and even acts that are prohibited by the employer but that prohibition does not take those acts outside the sphere of employment.

The Irish courts have adopted a stricter test and have held that an employer is only vicariously liable for an act of the employee where:
- It is a wrongful act authorised by the employer.

or
- It is a wrongful and unauthorised mode of doing some authorised act.

The leading Irish case in this regard is *Reilly v Ryan* [1991] I.L.R.M. 449.

Facts
A robber burst into a pub waving a knife and demanded money from the till. The bartender grabbed a customer and shoved the customer between himself and the robber. The customer was stabbed in the arm, and sued the employer of the bartender for compensation for his injuries.

Issue before the court
Was the bartender acting in the course of his employment when he grabbed the customer and used him as a shield? The employer argued that the bartender was not acting to protect the bar, but only himself. The customer argued that the bartender was doing what he thought was necessary to protect the interests of the employer and therefore the employer should be vicariously liable for the actions of the bartender.

Decision of the court
The court held that although the bartender had a clear duty to defend the employer's property and to defend himself, he had gone too far when he defended the property by assaulting the customer (by grabbing him) and thereafter allowing the customer to be stabbed. These actions were outside the course of employment.

> 'On these facts, can it be said that Mr Heffernan was acting in the course of his employment by reacting as he did, that is, by assaulting the plaintiff and using him as a shield, thus causing him to be stabbed? Clearly what he did was not expressly authorised by the defendant, but was it a wrongful and unauthorised mode of doing something that he was if not expressly, at least impliedly authorised to do?
> ...
> He chose to interpose a human barrier between himself and the intruder. This involved a physical assault on the plaintiff and putting him in a position of great danger. It was a wholly unreasonable and excessive means of dealing with the emergency.
>
> Was it so excessive as to take it out of the class of acts, which are impliedly authorised? In my opinion it was. What he did has to be looked at in the context of his duties as the defendant's manager. His principal duty was to serve the defendant's customers. This involved also, as the defendant said in evidence, looking after their comfort and safety. But instead of looking after the plaintiff's safety, as was his duty, Mr Heffernan was the cause of his being injured. His reaction was accordingly excessive in the sense that what he did

went wholly outside what he was employed to do, being in fact the precise opposite of what his duty was at the time. Instead of trying to protect the plaintiff, he assaulted him and was the cause of his being injured. In my opinion it could not be said that such behaviour was impliedly authorised by the defendant.'

Commentary
This case clearly displays the difficulties faced when deciding on questions of vicarious liability. It was clearly within the employee's duty to protect the bar takings, and it was clearly in the interest of the employer that the bartender do all in his power to stop the money being stolen. Therefore, if this was an English decision it could be argued that the two tests are satisfied. However, the employee went just a little too far, and it could also be argued that it was not in the employer's interests to have the customer stabbed, as not only would the employer need to compensate the customer, but that customer and perhaps other customers would not go back to that pub for a drink after hearing about what happened, and in the long run the employer would lose a lot more money than just what was in the cash register (the thief demanded forty pounds). Therefore, even on the wider test the English courts would probably have found the employer not liable.

If we were to apply the stricter Irish test, the problem is still not easily solved. The employee was clearly authorised to defend the pub, but could it not be argued that his actions were an unauthorised mode of defending the pub? The court said that his actions went beyond an unauthorised mode of defending the pub. The court had to make a policy decision and decide at what point an unauthorised mode went too far.

'A frolic of his own'

An employer will also not be vicariously liable for the actions of an employee if that employee goes off on 'a frolic of his (or her) own'. For example, if a delivery driver stops on the route and gets drunk, and thereafter causes an accident, the employer can argue that this had nothing to do with the delivery, and the employee was pursuing his own interests when he got drunk. A similar scenario would be where the driver went off the agreed route to visit a friend and had an accident whilst on the detour. Clearly in both of these situations the drinking and the visit were for the employee's own benefit, and could not be said to be in the interests of the employer.

The logic behind the *Reilly v Ryan* decision can be based along the same lines – the bartender was not trying to protect the pub or the takings when he pulled the customer in front of him, he was trying to save his own skin, and therefore could be said to be on a frolic of his own.

Accordingly, he was not carrying out an unauthorised mode of defending the pub, but rather he was carrying out an unauthorised mode of saving himself.

In deciding whether a health board was liable for the actions of a nurse, the same questions would need to be asked. Was the nurse carrying out a wrongful act (impliedly) authorised by the employer, or was it a wrongful and unauthorised mode of doing some authorised act?

Again, this can pose problems. Take the following example: a patient complains that he did not receive his lunch, and it seems that somebody forgot to serve him. The duty nurse takes the patient down to the kitchen so he can make himself a sandwich, despite knowing that only kitchen staff are allowed in the kitchen. While they are in the kitchen, some hot oil is spilled, and the patient suffers serious burns to the leg.

Is the nurse doing what she was employed to do? It could be argued that she is looking after the patient, as is her duty. If we were to apply the English test: Is the nurse acting in the employer's interests? Again, if all had gone well and the patient had received his sandwich, he would have been very pleased with the service provided by the nurse, and might have sung her praises. However, the employer can argue that it could never be in its interests, as it would prefer a patient to miss a meal, even if this meant grumbles about being hungry, as opposed to the patient being exposed to danger.

On the other hand, if the nurse had responded to the patient's requests for some lunch by saying that it was not her problem as it was outside her job description, would this have been in the employer's interests, as the patient would have been angry with the lack of concern on the part of the nurse? The other factor in the nurse's favour is that she is hardly acting in her own interest, as it would have been easier for her to tell the patient that she could do nothing about it, and he would have to go hungry. It is therefore difficult to talk about the nurse being on a 'frolic of her own'.

If we were to apply the Irish test, the nurse clearly has an implied authority to look after the interests of a patient, as that is what she is there for. It might even be argued that she has implied authority to commit an unauthorised act, namely go into the kitchen, as the patient was hungry and her job was to look after the patient. Was her action an unauthorised mode of looking after a patient? Most probably. Did she go beyond the limits by taking the patient to the kitchen with her? Probably, and it is here that the employer might succeed. If the nurse had gone into the kitchen herself and caused an accident, the employer would probably be found vicariously liable, but the action of the nurse in taking the patient down to the kitchen, might place her outside that zone of unauthorised but acceptable actions.

It is clear that the issue of vicarious liability raises many difficult questions, none of which can be answered very easily. In addition, the answers are often influenced by policy. Again, certainty must sometimes step aside to make way for equity.

Indemnity insurance for the vicarious liability of an employer for the actions of a nurse

The Clinical Indemnity Scheme (CIS) is the State-funded scheme that provides an indemnity to health service agencies funded in whole, or in part, by the taxpayer, against the cost of claims brought against those agencies for personal injury arising from clinical negligence.

The CIS has been established on the principle of 'enterprise liability'. What this means is that a health service agency (a hospital, or health board, or other similar agency) covered by the CIS assumes vicarious liability for the acts and omissions of its employees providing clinical services. The distinguishing feature of enterprise liability is that the plaintiff does not sue the individual health professional, as the agency agrees to take vicarious responsibility for its clinical staff. In other words, vicarious liability is admitted by the employer and does not have to be proven by the plaintiff-patient, provided of course that the employee is providing professional medical services, and is therefore covered by the CIS policy.

The stated benefit of this is that it will not be necessary to have a number of co-defendants in a medical malpractice action – for example, Minister, health board, and health professional – but only one defendant, the CIS, will be sued. This will save on the trauma and expense of separate defendants with separate legal representation, and will hopefully mean fewer and/or shorter trials.

This is good news for employees where the actions of the employee are clearly covered by the scheme, but not good news when they are not. Whereas the common law was a confusing series of tests to decide vicarious liability, that confusion might be replaced by a new confusion in deciding whether the employee's actions are covered by the scheme.

The CIS covers all claims alleging medical malpractice or clinical negligence against an agency and/or its staff arising from the delivery of 'professional medical services'. It will therefore cover services provided at hospitals, clinics and other facilities owned or operated by the health boards as well as services delivered in patients' homes and other community facilities, under the auspices of the health boards or other similar agencies.

In terms of the National Treasury Management Agency (Delegation of Functions) Order, 2003, 'professional medical services' means:

(a) 'services provided by registered medical practitioners or registered dentists of a diagnostic or palliative nature, or consisting of the provision of treatment in respect of any illness, disease, injury or other medical condition,

(b) services provided by other health professionals in the performance of their duties, including pharmacists, nurses, midwives, paramedics, ambulance personnel, laboratory technicians, or

(c) services connected with the provision of health or medical care provided by persons acting under the direction of a person to whom paragraph (a) or (b) applies;'

Employees of health boards and hospitals cannot rely on the employer for protection on the basis of vicarious liability if their actions do not fall within the above definition. It could be argued that the definition is more restrictive than the previous (already strict) tests used by the Irish courts, and which were discussed with the *Reilly v Ryan* judgment.

Whilst the CIS cover is quite extensive, the question still remains whether it will give the employee as much protection from being sued in a personal capacity as did the common law of vicarious liability. If the answer to that question is no, it will not, the next question to be asked is whether the patient can still elect to sue in terms of the common law vicarious liability rather than sue the CIS? If the answer to that is no, it means that the employee, for example a nurse employed by a health board, is more likely than before to be found personally liable.

Another problem with the CIS cover, which has caused a lot of controversy concerns so-called 'Good Samaritan' acts, for example, stopping to help an injured motorist. The CIS only covers claims arising from Good Samaritan acts which occur in an agency's premises. It does not cover Good Samaritan acts which take place elsewhere. What this means is that a health professional who undertakes Good Samaritan work outside the premises of the hospital or health board will need to find additional private insurance, or alternatively, give up the Good Samaritan work.

In addition, the CIS does not cover the costs of representation before a disciplinary body, for example a Fitness to Practice Inquiry. Similarly, the CIS will not cover legal fees where a health professional is charged in a criminal court from actions arising from the practice of medicine. The CIS will provide cover for personal injury claims arising from the alleged criminal behaviour, where the allegations of criminal behaviour arise from the delivery of clinical care. The scheme will not cover claims arising from criminal activity which does not fall within the accepted definition of professional medical services, for example the assault of a fellow employee.

For example, if a health professional performed a procedure on a patient against the wishes of the patient and was charged with criminal assault, the employee would have to pay for the lawyer at the criminal trial. However, if the unauthorised procedure fell within the definition of professional medical services, the CIS would cover the costs of the civil trial if the patient sued for damages for the alleged assault.

In summary therefore, the problem that this scheme can cause for employees is that in instances where the CIS does not cover the employee's actions, it is not clear whether the common law of vicarious liability still operates, or whether the employee will be personally liable for these actions. The better approach would seem to be that the common law cannot be excluded where the statutory scheme does not go as far as the common law, unless the common law is expressly excluded by the statute in question. In addition, it could be argued that a patient has a constitutional right to sue the health professional in a personal capacity, and the employer on the basis of vicarious liability, and that a statute cannot take away this cause of action. However, this is a worrying aspect of the scheme, and something that needs to be clarified by the courts.

If the common law action based on vicarious liability is excluded, it will mean that employees, including nurses, will need to have indemnity insurance to cover those situations that are not covered by the CIS policy. This will be expensive.

It also means that if a nurse wanted to ensure proper legal representation at a disciplinary hearing or a criminal court hearing, he or she would need to pay those fees, or would need to take out an expensive insurance policy, as the CIS does not cover the legal fees in these instances.

Vicarious Liability: Summary

1. The principle of vicarious liability is that one person is held liable for the actions of another.
2. As a general rule, an employer will be held liable for the actions of an employee 'in the course of employment'.
3. In deciding what actions are in the course of employment, the Irish courts have a two-legged test:
    a. Is the act a wrongful act authorised by the employer?
    or
    b. Is the act a wrongful and unauthorised mode of doing some authorised act?
4. When speaking of authorised acts, acts that are both expressly and

impliedly authorised by the employer are included.
5. The CIS scheme, which is based on 'enterprise liability', rests on the premise that the employer will admit vicarious liability if the actions of the employee that lead to the injury are 'professional medical services' as defined.
6. What is not clear is whether this system replaces the common law system of vicarious liability or whether the patient will have an election of either suing the CIS under the new scheme or suing the employee in a personal capacity and the employer in a vicarious capacity, as co-defendants in terms of the common law.
7. The CIS does not cover the cost of legal fees for disciplinary proceedings, nor for criminal trials. The cover will however include civil damages arising from criminal action where the action leading to the criminal charge is regarded as falling within the definition of 'professional medical services'.
8. The CIS does not cover an employee who performs a Good Samaritan act outside the premises of the employer.
9. Useful websites:
    a. **C.I.S.** (http://www.imt.ie/faqs.doc).
    b. **Department of Health and Children** (http://www.doh.ie/enterprise_liability/faq.html).

PART FIVE

DEMONSTRATING YOUR KNOWLEDGE

37
WRITING ESSAYS AND ANSWERING EXAM QUESTIONS

Introduction

It is perhaps unfortunate that the most popular manner of testing a student's knowledge is the written 'sit-down' examination. Unfortunate, as there are other more creative and pleasant ways of testing knowledge; but unfortunately necessary, as the numbers of students make any other assessment method practically impossible.

The biggest problem about sit-down written examinations is that they teach students to memorise huge chunks of information, as opposed to understanding the underlying principles. Written examinations also teach students to accept what they are being told, as the emphasis is on getting the information down, rather than questioning the information itself. Many lecturers also find it easier simply dictating information for students to write down, rather than challenging students, and themselves, by analysing the issues behind the information, or asking the students to find the information for themselves.

In order to take some of the pressure off the final examinations, students are often asked to hand in written work during the year (usually called 'continuous assessment'), and generally these take the form of written essays or assignments.

Therefore, if a student perfects the techniques necessary to write a good essay, and learns how to answer examination questions as quickly and efficiently as time allows, that is most of the battle won, as these two forms are the dominant methods of assessment.

Writing essays

Essay topics can generally be lumped into two main categories. The first is the descriptive essay, usually found in the early years of study, which asks the student to research a particular topic and summarise the information in his or her own words. The second type of essay topic, which is often used with senior students, is the question or debate-style essay, which is similar to the style used in academic journal writing, where a thesis is proposed and defended.

Answering exam questions

As far as examination questions are concerned, there is the descriptive question, which asks the student to list the information, and is essentially a memory test with minimal or no analysis. Again, these types of questions are reserved for students in their first or second years of study. The second type of question is the problem or scenario question, and students are likely to face more and more of these as they progress in their studies. It is certainly favoured in law examinations, as lawyers are essentially legal problem solvers.

The need for problem solvers

Knowledge is useless if it cannot be applied, used and tested. It is simply impossible to memorise everything that has been written about a particular topic. In practice, a professional often has to research a particular topic when advising a client or patient, particularly if the problem is not something that he or she deals with on a regular basis. What distinguishes a good professional from a so-so professional is the ability to apply book knowledge to the facts, in a way that ensures the problem is solved, rather than compounded or altered. Whilst a good memory is always an asset, the fact is that most information is at our fingertips, thanks to the latest communications technology. However, merely being able to recite reams of information does not make a good professional; it is what he or she can do with that information that matters.

A good nurse will be distinguished from the average nurse by his or her enquiring mind and problem solving capabilities. It is therefore a good idea during your studies to start developing these skills by thinking creatively and trying to solve problems, rather than simply writing them out, or memorising the information without properly understanding it or challenging it.

The techniques used in answering problem questions and essay questions differ quite substantially, and the fifth part of this book is dedicated to teaching you about these techniques, and thereafter provides examples of problem and essay questions, which can be answered with reference to the main text. Remember that these techniques are not limited to legal questions; they can be used in any discipline or subject where you are tested by written examinations or essays. This section does not deal with descriptive exam or essay questions, as they are essentially a matter of memory or summarising.

Problem questions

Problem questions in a law examination can be answered by a simple formula, which is:

Facts – Problem – Law – Application – Conclusion.

Facts

Read the whole scenario/question very carefully, at least twice, in order to fully understand and comprehend the question and the events described. Make a note, in particular, of the following:

Parties: who are the people mentioned and what is their relationship?

Places and objects: where did the scenario take place and what objects does it involve?

This formula provides a useful starting point to analysing and answering any problem.

The problem

Analyse what the legal issue or question of law is.

What is the basis of the case?
What is the **legal issue** arising from the facts?
Is there **any defence** to the legal action?
What **relief** is being asked for? For example, damages.

A useful formula to identify what a legal issue in a question is:

Classification

Look beneath the facts and decide what branch (or branches) of law are involved. It is important to remember here that the fact that one area of law is involved does not automatically exclude other areas of law. For example, you already know that one incident might have both civil and criminal law implications. Read the question carefully, as the examiner might limit the area of law in the question, if there is not enough time to cover everything in your answer. If the examiner does not limit the question, be sure to consider all the possibilities, but keep an eye on the time allocation.

Question

Decide what the specific question is that needs to be answered in order to provide a solution to the factual problem.

This step is perhaps the most important step in answering any problem question, as your decision at this stage will irrevocably influence the remainder of your answer.

The law

Consider the applicability of each source of law with which you are familiar. Consider whether the legal issue is dealt with in:

- The Constitution.
- Legislation (including EU legislation where applicable).
- Case law or common law.
- Other sources (for example, an article that you might have read).

You might find this hard to believe, but the process up to this point should have taken you no more than ten minutes where you have forty-five minutes per answer. Most of this process is done very quickly in your mind, and is written down in a very brief opening paragraph. For example:

> *'This problem involves Sean, the wrongful driver, who drives through a red traffic light and crashes into Michael, the innocent driver. Michael sues Sean for negligence. Sean is also charged with dangerous driving. The negligence action will be heard in the civil court, whereas the case of dangerous driving will be heard in the criminal court. I must advise Sean about the implications of both.'*

In this very short paragraph, the writer has identified the parties and their relationship, summarised the facts, identified the areas of law and set out the task asked of the writer. The bulk of the answer hereafter will involve the application of the law to the facts. This opening paragraph not only informs the examiner that the writer knows what is going on, but it also focuses the writer as to the task at hand.

Application of the law to the facts

Each one of the facts you have isolated as key must now be considered, step by step, in the light of the rule of law.

This is the longest and most significant part of your answer, as it is here that every detail of the problem is carefully weighed up against the law. Each key fact must be tested against the stated law, to see whether it fits within or is resolved by the governing rule of law.

Where the facts presented are identical to a known case/judicial decision then it is easy. If you do not know a case with the same facts, you would argue by analogy. What this means is that you compare the facts before you to the facts of cases or decisions that you have studied, noting the similarities and differences, perhaps arguing that the similarities are important, whereas the differences are of no importance.

Conclusion and comments

The conclusion is based directly on what has been argued in the application section.

After stating the conclusion, you may comment on it, for example whether you think the solution is just or fair and whether the law needs to be changed or challenged.

Example problem questions

Problem one
A patient consents to an operation for the removal of a hernia, and signs a consent form to this effect. Whilst operating on the hernia, the surgeon notices two additional problems: the patient has an ingrown toenail (which was pointed out to the surgeon by the theatre nurse), and the patient has a malignant tumour in his stomach wall.

The surgeon removes both the ingrown toenail and the tumour. The patient sues the surgeon in tort for battery, on the basis that his consent to a hernia operation did not extend to the removal of the ingrown toenail, or the removal of a tumour.

Advise the surgeon

Problem two
Sheila Molony has signed a form to consent to an operation for the investigation of a lump in her breast. She is very distressed to be undergoing surgery and ever since she has come into hospital she has been taking in very little of what is said to her.

The surgeon explains that 'a biopsy will be carried out and if that is positive then further surgery will be performed'.

It is apparent to Nurse Mary Murphy that Sheila has not realised that a radical mastectomy could be performed.

What should Nurse Murphy do?

Problem three
A pregnant woman is due to give birth by caesarean section. The normal procedure is for the patient to have an epidural before the commencement of the operation.

The patient suffers from needle phobia and refuses to have the anaesthetic.

The surgeon declares that it is impossible to perform a caesarean section without the use of an epidural and orders the anaesthetist to administer the epidural. When the patient hears this, she becomes highly agitated, making it impossible to administer an epidural. The anaesthetist orders two nurses to restrain the patient, and administers a general anaesthetic by gassing the patient. The patient finally loses consciousness, and the caesarean is performed. The operation is a success, with the birth of a healthy child.

The patient subsequently sues the surgeon, the anaesthetist and the nurses for battery.

Advise the surgeon, the anaesthetist and the nurses.

Problem four
A patient enters the clinic and informs the duty nurse that he has a very sore throat.

The patient sits down in the chair and opens his mouth and the nurse determines that the patient's throat is badly infected. She informs the patient of her diagnosis and suggests an antibiotic spray.

The patient nods and opens his mouth again. The nurse sprays penicillin spray onto the back of the patient's throat.

The patient complains that he thought the nurse wanted to take another look to confirm her diagnosis. When the nurse tells him that she has only sprayed some penicillin spray, the patient becomes agitated and informs the nurse that he is allergic to penicillin. The nurse complains to the patient that he should have informed her of his allergy when she mentioned the need for an antibiotic.

The patient has to receive emergency treatment for penicillin shock.

Advise the patient.

Problem five
A diagnosed paranoid schizophrenic is brought to the casualty ward with a dog bite. The dog's owner transports him to the casualty ward.

The patient makes it clear that he understands exactly what has happened to him. The staff at the hospital know the patient well as he is an outpatient.

When it is explained to the patient that he will need a tetanus injection, the patient refuses to have the injection, and asks only that the bite is cleaned and dressed. It is explained to the patient that tetanus can be fatal but the patient persists in his refusal.

Advise the staff at the casualty ward.

Problem six
A young woman is injured in a car crash. Her condition is stable but she has lost a lot of blood and there is a possibility that she might require a blood transfusion in the future.

The attending nurse explains this to the patient. The patient informs the nurse that she is a member of the Jehovah's Witness Church and she refuses to have a blood transfusion, as it is against her beliefs to allow another person's blood into her body. When it is explained that this might be life-threatening, the patient is adamant and states again, very clearly, that under no circumstances does she want a blood transfusion.

The patient subsequently loses consciousness through lack of blood. A doctor is called and orders that the patient receive a pint of blood. The nurse explains about the patient's belief and her explicit instruction that she must not be given a blood transfusion under any circumstances.

The doctor informs the nurse: 'This is an emergency, we are acting to save this young woman's life. Proceed with the transfusion immediately, nurse.'

What should the nurse do?

Problem seven
A sixteen-year old girl attends clinic and asks the doctor that he prescribes her an oral contraceptive as she is sexually active and wishes to avoid becoming pregnant.

The girl further orders the doctor that he is not to tell her parents as 'my father would kill me if he knows that I am sleeping with my boyfriend'.

Advise the doctor.

Problem eight
Padraig O'Connell is an elderly patient who is operated on for ulcers. During the operation it is discovered that he is riddled with cancer and the surgeon closes him up without operating and recommends that Padraig begins a course of morphine.

In consultation with his wife, it is agreed that Padraig will not be informed of the cancer, as he has a few months to live, and the news would cause unnecessary trauma and further shorten his life. Nurse Egan is present during the operation and is also present during the consultation with Padraig's wife.

That night Nurse Egan visits Padraig as it is the end of her shift and she wants to ensure that he is comfortable. Padraig asks Nurse Egan:

> 'Nurse, I notice that they are giving me some powerful drugs, which make me feel quite dizzy. What is happening, have I got cancer or something?'

How should Nurse Egan respond?

Problem nine

A nurse is on his way home after working a particularly exhausting twelve-hour shift in the casualty department. He stops when he sees a crowd at the side of the road. There is an overturned car and the driver has been thrown clear, and is lying on her back. She is conscious and complains that her lower back is very sore and she cannot move her legs.

The nurse decides that the woman might be bleeding and instructs the onlookers to lift the woman up and turn her over.

It is subsequently discovered that the woman had a damaged spine, and in turning her over the spinal column had completely severed, causing permanent paralysis of the legs.

Was the nurse responsible in law for this?

Problem ten

A nurse administers an injection of Bicillin into the deltoid muscle of the upper arm of a patient who is injured in the buttock.

The patient develops gangrene in his hand, which is subsequently amputated.

Evidence is led that it is dangerous to inject into the deltoid muscle having regard to the pressure of the circumflex artery.

The nurse leads the evidence of other staff at the hospital that there was nothing in the standing procedures or Codes of Conduct prohibiting an injection into the deltoid muscle.

Was the nurse responsible in law for this?

Problem eleven

As a result of the defendant's negligence, there is a motor vehicle accident, and the plaintiff suffers brain damage, which means that he will walk with difficulty and his memory will be severely impaired. The plaintiff is a nurse.

Evidence is further led that the plaintiff suffers from a rare bone disease, which at the time of the accident was in remission but has been aggravated by the accident. The expert witness testified that the plaintiff will suffer a withering of all his limbs, making it impossible for the plaintiff to hold down a health care job of any description.

What damages would you award the plaintiff and why?

Problem twelve

In breach of her duty of care, a nurse failed to properly dispose of contaminated dressings and a syringe, which were left on a stainless steel trolley in the treatment area. By chance, two youths broke into the hospital in search of syringes and needles. Whilst the youths were ransacking the trolley, they heard somebody approaching. Grabbing as much as they could from the trolley, the youths ran. In their haste, they picked up some of the contaminated dressings and the used syringe. Subsequently an outbreak of disease occurred in the neighbourhood. Investigation established the cause as being the contaminated dressings or the syringe.

Was the nurse responsible in law for this?

Problem thirteen
In breach of her duty of care, a nurse puts some drops in the wrong eye of a patient. The drops were meant to dilate the pupil of the other eye. The drops would not normally have caused any harm, but because of an existing defect, the patient loses sight in that eye.

Was the nurse responsible in law for this?

Problem fourteen
Eileen was involved in a serious road accident and admitted to hospital. A telephone request came in asking for information on her progress. The nurse taking the call asked who the caller was, to which came the reply: 'Her husband'. The nurse then gave the caller full details of Eileen's progress, and details of visiting times.

The nurse thereafter went through and told Eileen about the telephone conversation and that her husband was coming to the hospital. The nurse is shocked when Eileen becomes hysterical and starts shouting: 'What have you done? What have you done?'

The nurse discovers that Eileen has been in hiding from her husband pending the criminal trial where he is charged with serious assault and marital rape.

Advise the nurse.

Problem fifteen
Bill accepts a job to drive a school bus, after he retires from his full-time job as a driver of long-distance haulage vehicles.

April is a nurse in the neurology ward, and is Bill's neighbour. She is horrified when Bill's wife tells her about his new job, as April knows that Bill is a diagnosed epileptic (the reason for his early retirement) and he is not yet responding to medication.

Advise April.

436 NURSING LAW FOR IRISH STUDENTS

Problem sixteen
Brenda works as a nurse in the occupational health department and is horrified to discover that a paediatric nurse, Karen, has an unusual bacterial infection which makes it very dangerous for her to work in that unit, particularly with premature babies.

However, Brenda knows that Karen has used up all her paid sick leave, and she is a single mother with three young children, which means she cannot afford to lose any pay.

Brenda notices that Karen does not appear ill in any way, and it is probable that she is a carrier of the disease rather than a sufferer of this particular germ.

Karen is anxious to work and begs Brenda not to notify the hospital authorities about her infection.

Advise Brenda.

Problem seventeen
Eoin is Duty Nurse in the Casualty Department when the Gardaí arrive to enquire about the possibility of a young man in his late twenties having been admitted and/or treated with severe lacerations to his face and neck.

The Gardaí tell Eoin that about two hours earlier, a fourteen-year-old girl had been found in a serious condition after having been raped. The girl had told them that she tried to prevent the attack by picking up a broken bottle lying in the grass and stabbing her attacker in the face, and she believed that she had cut him severely.

Eoin is asked by the Gardaí if they can go through the admissions book to check admissions during the last two hours.

What should Eoin do?

Problem eighteen
Michael is a nurse on night duty. He receives a call from Dr Murphy who informs Michael that he is running very late. The doctor asks Michael if he would give one of the patients his morphine as he will arrive too late to do it himself by which stage the patient could be in considerable pain. When Michael checks the patient in question, he is fast asleep and seems to be quite comfortable, but Michael administers the morphine in any event. A short while later the patient goes into cardiac arrest and is only saved by the intervention of a 'crash team'. It turns out that the patient had already been given a morphine injection by the matron and Michael had in fact overdosed the patient.

Michael is charged under the Misuse of Drugs Act for unlawfully supplying a Schedule One drug, and in addition is charged with attempted murder alternatively serious assault.

Advise Michael whether he has a defence to these charges.

Problem nineteen
An elderly patient goes berserk in the ward and threatens a nurse with a hypodermic needle. The patient is about to stab the nurse and the nurse grabs a metal crutch and hits the patient on the head. The patient is killed instantly. The nurse is charged with murder as the prosecution argues that the nurse could have simply run away from the elderly patient, and in addition, the needle was new and unused and did not present any serious danger.

Advise the nurse.

Problem twenty
Jennifer is a nurse in a very small country hospital. There is a serious accident on the highway near the hospital and ten patients are rushed into the hospital. There are only seven beds available and Jennifer decides that three of the victims are going to die anyway and so she leaves them outside in the passage, whilst the others are placed in bed and tended. One of the patients in the passage subsequently dies, amongst other things from exposure, as the passage was very cold and draughty.

Jennifer is charged with manslaughter but pleads necessity, as she argues that she had to save the lives of the patients that had a chance of survival.

Advise Jennifer.

Problem twenty-one
Tom is a senior nurse who has worked in the same hospital for a number of years. A new matron is appointed to Tom's section and from the word go she and Tom do not get on. The matron undermines Tom's position by insisting that the junior nurses report directly to her, whereas previously they reported to Tom. In addition Tom's responsibilities are gradually but deliberately taken from him until in the end he finds himself doing the dirty and menial tasks, like emptying bed pans and disposing of soiled bandages.

Tom feels he has no option but to resign. However, he is not sure that he will get another job immediately, and cannot afford to lose any wages.

Advise Tom.

Problem twenty-two
Siobhan is the receptionist at the main desk of a hospital. She begins work at 8.30 a.m. A junior doctor by the name of Lucy begins work at 9.00

a.m., and each morning as she walks past the main desk she says to Siobhan:

'Hiya sexy, what colour are your knickers today?'

Siobhan is not sure whether she can complain about this behaviour, and what steps she should take.

Advise Siobhan.

Problem twenty-three
A patient is admitted into hospital to have a small mole removed from his calf under local anaesthetic. The patient arrives at 9.00 a.m., has the procedure at 11.00 a.m., and is due to be discharged at 4.00 p.m. on the same day. The patient is resting in the day ward, and is 'hooked-up' to a glucose drip, as his blood-sugar levels plummeted after the procedure. The patient needs to go to the toilet and the nurse explains that there is no toilet in the day ward, and points out the toilet at the end of the passage. The patient starts to move down the passage, with the glucose drip on a mobile platform. The patient slips and falls on his elbow, resulting in a very painful fracture.

The patient files a complaint with the Health and Safety Authority, complaining that the hospital did not fulfil its duty of care by failing to have a toilet in the ward itself. The hospital claims that it cannot afford to have toilet facilities in the day wards.

What statute is relevant to this situation and what test must be used in assessing this complaint?

Problem twenty-four
Gary is a nurse in the general wards of a small hospital. He notices that the electrical sockets in the general ward are loose and one is hanging out of the wall with the wires exposed. Gary reports this to the Administrator. Nothing is done about it. Gary makes another report. Nothing is done about it. Gary makes a third report in writing. Still nothing is done.

Gary sends a copy of his report to the Health and Safety Authority, with another copy to the local newspaper, which prints the report after the Administrator had refused to comment.

Gary is dismissed by the hospital for breaching confidentiality.

Advise Gary.

Writing essays

Some of you, and particularly those of you who enter the teaching or academic professions, will be asked to do a piece of academic writing at some stage in your careers. It is a good idea to get into the discipline required for academic writing as soon as possible in your student career, so that as time goes on, your way of thinking becomes structured in such a way that you will automatically take an idea and subject it to analysis and criticism, both positive and negative. If you learn to think this way, you will automatically question and challenge ideas, rather than simply accepting them by writing them down and memorising them.

Some general pointers about formal academic writing before starting:

Things to avoid
Never Use the First Person 'I'
Some people will regard this as an old-fashioned rule, and this might be so. It is, however, true to say that a piece of writing seems to have more authority and is more impressive when it is written in the third person. The difference between 'I think the world is round' and 'It can be argued that the world is round' is obvious, even though they might mean the same thing. Therefore, try and remember that formal writing is always done in the third person. You are not writing a novel or an autobiography.

Nver Use Slang or Colloquial Language or Swear Words
Academic writing is formal writing. You are not speaking to your mates in a pie shop. At the same time, target your audience and use language that they will understand. If you are writing a piece with a particular reader in mind, use language (good language) that the person will understand and appreciate. For example, this book is written in an informal style, which is not found in a lot of legal textbooks. That is because it is not aimed at lawyers, but at people who do not necessarily know anything about the law.

Planning an essay
Many students place a piece of paper in front of them or sit at the computer and scribble or hammer away until the essay is finished. This might work well for popular fiction, but academic writing is all about preparation and structure. The planning beforehand is as important as the writing itself.

What is the point?
Every piece of writing is a communication to the reader. A descriptive essay is to communicate to the reader that you have read certain material

and have now summarised that material and got the main points down on paper. However, an essay can also be used to get a point across. Therefore, the first thing that needs to be done is to decide what that point is.

Getting an idea
The usual method of formal writing is to think up an idea (a 'thesis') and thereafter assemble material and sources and authority in support of that idea. When it comes to essays your range of ideas is clearly limited by the topic posed by the lecturer, unless of course you are allowed to choose your own topic to write about a particular subject. Usually, however, the idea is provided for you, and you must decide whether you agree or disagree with that idea, after presenting both sides of the argument.

Relevance
Whatever the limitations imposed upon you in your subject matter, it is important to have that idea or thesis fixed firmly in your mind throughout the essay process. The reason for this fixation is that whatever you write must be written in order to prove or disprove your original thesis. If you write something that has nothing to do with the original idea or thesis, the chances are good that you have written something irrelevant. Irrelevant writing annoys your reader, particularly when your essay is one of many that the lecturer needs to read. 'Waffling' or 'padding' must be avoided at all costs. Apart from being annoying, it is saying to the reader that you have nothing of value to contribute in your essay and this will also alienate your reader.

Structure

Plan your assignment in full before you start to write
Get a blank piece of paper and jot down very briefly what you intend to do in each section of your essay.

Never let 'the muse take you' and make it up as you go along
Only start writing the essay itself once you know exactly what you are going to write, from beginning to end.

Always stick to your structure and always write in order to prove your original thesis
Stick to your original structure. This does not mean that you cannot think up new ideas during the writing of your essay. This will often happen, and you will also notice gaps in your thinking, or that your content does not flow in a logical progression. That is the creative process and is fine, as long as it happens within a general structure, so

that there is at least some sort of control to your wandering. In other words, don't just scribble madly. A common structure for an essay is as follows:

> Introduction.
> Definition of terms.
> Arguments in support of thesis.
> Arguments against your thesis.
> Your response to the arguments against your thesis.
> Conclusion.

The introduction
Your introduction is your guide map, both for the reader and yourself. The introduction introduces the idea that you wish to support and expand upon in your writing. The introduction tells the reader how it is that you propose to introduce and defend your idea.

Some argue that the introduction is the most important section in an academic essay as it affects the reader and influences him or her for the remainder of the essay. If you think about it, this makes a lot of sense. If your introduction is rubbish, the reader is going to regard the rest of your essay in a negative light, and might not be so keen to notice that the writing has improved later in the essay. On the other hand, if you write a brilliant introduction, the reader is in a very positive frame of mind and might be more willing to forgive a few weak moments later on in your essay. This is also a good tip when writing essay-style answers in an examination – examiners are generally tired and irritable as they have been reading piles of examination scripts for days, even weeks. It takes very little to irritate a person in that condition, and a bad introduction is more than likely to put the reader in a negative frame of mind and mark the student down, even where the answer might improve later on.

Definition of terms
This is essentially part of your introduction. Although you will generally be writing your essay for your lecturer, who is supposedly an expert, this is still a good habit to get into, as if you go on to write for a journal or even a newspaper, you cannot assume specialist knowledge on the part of every reader. Always write for the layperson. For example, if you write an article for a nursing journal, and it is read by a lawyer who does not know medical terminology, that lawyer is essentially a layperson when it comes to nursing. If you use a whole lot of medical terms in your article, the lawyer will not know what you are talking about. Therefore, if any of the terms that you are going to use in your essay have a specialist or particular meaning in the context of the piece, you must define them.

So for example, if you were writing an essay about children consenting to medical treatment, you would write the following in your 'Definition of Terms' section (although some writers simply put their terms at the end of the 'Introduction' section – that is a matter of choice):

'In this piece, when speaking of a "child", the writer means an unmarried person who is younger than the chronological age of eighteen years'.

Arguments in support of your thesis
Again, relevance is the key. Before presenting any argument (i.e. before you start writing) always be certain in your own mind that the argument you are putting forward is relevant to your original idea or thesis. If your thesis is composed of a number of arguments, always make sure that the arguments complement each other (rather than contradict each other) and try and get these arguments in a progressive order (in other words, you draw the reader along with you as you expand your idea to its conclusion).

Arguments against your thesis
It would not be honest if you did not consider the ideas of others who do not agree with your ideas. If you are aware of any writings where people have taken another line on the same topic, you should refer to these. This will give your writing credibility, as it will not be one-sided propaganda. It will also impress the reader that you have done this, and should improve your result. Most importantly, it will force you to think about things that you might previously have taken for granted.

Your response to the arguments against your thesis
Once you have referred to these opposing or different ideas, you must try and deal with them, by either disproving or negating them, or distinguishing them from your present thesis. Again, your counter-arguments must be relevant to your original thesis, don't go off at a tangent just for the sake of a good argument.

Conclusion
Once you have considered the arguments both for and against your original thesis, you must come to a conclusion as to whether your original idea was a good one or not.

The use of the word 'conclusion' is somewhat of a controversial area, as it means different things to different people. Ask your lecturer what he or she understands by the term before writing the essay.

For some people a conclusion is used to set out the main points of the essay. In essence therefore, these people regard a conclusion as being the same as a summary. A summary is a repeat. It is an exercise in setting out the main points again so as to remind the reader. The chapters in this book contain summaries at their end. The ideas in those summaries are to be found in the main body of the chapter – they are not new ideas.

In this chapter, it is argued that a conclusion is not the same as a summary or a *précis*. A conclusion is a part of the argument, as a conclusion brings together all the strands of your arguments contained in your essay and allows you to reach some form of closure.

What this means is that a conclusion in this sense is a new piece of writing and is still part of the creative process. It is not a repeat, it is an ending. It can and should contain new ideas, which have been created through the process of arguing around the original thesis and considering opposing or different ideas. It might happen of course that you wish to change or modify your original thesis, if the counter arguments seem better than your arguments. The conclusion is the place to do it. This is also the place where you might suggest future directions in the area under discussion. This often happens in the social sciences. For example, if you have successfully argued that the current mental health policy is rubbish, rather than leaving it at that, you might suggest what needs to be done about it. Again, this would not happen in a summary, but can happen in a conclusion.

As previously mentioned, this is not everybody's idea of what a conclusion should be, and it would be wise to question your lecturer on this topic, and determine what it is that he or she wants before writing your essay.

Referencing

There is not enough time or space to fully discuss the techniques of referencing. Just remember that if you write down an idea that you did not think up, you must give credit to the person that did think up the idea. To do otherwise is plagiarism, which is a serious academic crime.

Similarly, if you use somebody else's words, these must appear in the form of a quotation, and again the creator of those words must be acknowledged in a reference. Again, a failure to use quotation marks around somebody else's words is plagiarism.

The most popular system of referencing in Ireland is what is known as the Harvard System. There is an excellent, and very comprehensive, booklet on the Harvard System in Ireland that can be found on the Internet as a PDF document. The title of this document is as follows:

National College of Ireland, Library and Information Services, *'How to Reference Harvard Style'* **edited by Alison Nolan.**

If you open up the Google search engine (*www.google.ie*), limit the search to Ireland, and type in the words 'Harvard' 'Style' 'Alison' 'Nolan' you should find it without a bother.

Some examples of essay questions
Question one
Describe the stages in the Fitness to Practice Inquiry, with reference to the relevant legislation and case law.
(Note: This is a descriptive essay).

Question Two
The Fitness to Practise Inquiry is a complicated and drawn-out process, with the odds stacked heavily against the nurse.

Comment on this statement.

Question Three
There has taken place a systematic exclusion of the midwife's independence, and a downgrading of her status, to the extent that midwifery is currently a marginalised profession in Ireland.

Comment on this statement.

Question four
The *Gillick* test has no place in Irish law, as it promotes sexual promiscuity amongst our children, undermines parental authority, and poses a real threat to the family.

Comment on this statement.

Question five
The so-called therapeutic privilege is a fancy name for bald-faced lying to patients and has no place in Irish law.

Comment on this statement.

Question six
By introducing the Clinical Indemnity Scheme the Minister for Health and Children has sold the health care profession down the river and it is now a case of 'everybody for yourself'.

Comment on this statement.

INDEX

absolute privilege, 221, 223
academic writing, 439–444
access
    medical records, to, 225, 238–246
    nursing profession, to, 25–28
accident and emergency staff
    disclosure of information to Gardai, 235
accidents
    inevitable, 61
    prevention. *see* health and safety
accomplice, 272
acquittal, 304, 308
actionable conduct, 58, 60
acts of God, 61
actual cause. *see* factual causation
actuary, 172
actus reus, 271–272, 274
    assault, 277
    manslaughter, 284
    possession of drugs, 287
adjudication, 349
admonishment, 49–50
adoptive leave, 361
adversarial court system, 172, 174
advice
    complaints, in relation to, 49–50
age
    capacity, and, 82
    criminal responsibility, of, 304–305
    retirement, of, 395
aggravated assault, 279
aggregated medical data, 204, 206, 208
alcohol abuse, 31
alternative practitioners
    duty of care, 148–150
Alzheimer's disease, 90
American law
    disclosure of risks, 110–111, 113, 118, 119
    DNR orders, 85–86
    informed consent, 74, 75
An Bord Altranais. *see* Nursing Board
annual leave, 375–376
anonymous data
    permissible use of, 206–208
antiobiotics, 291
appeals
    conditions to retention on register, 48
    erasure/suspension decision, from, 45–46, 47
arraignment, 262
Aspirin, 291
assault
    actus reus, 277
    aggravated, 279
    causing harm, 278–279
    causing serious harm, 278–279
    consent of victim, 278
    criminal offence, 276–278
    degree of force, 277
    direct force, 277
    harm, apprehension of, 278
    mens rea, 278
    psychological crime, 277
    tort of, 68–69, 73–74
audi alteram partem, 37, 38–39
authority, express and implied, 415–416
automated data, 247. *see also* data protection
automatism, 272
autonomy. *see* patient autonomy

Bachelor of Science in Nursing, 35
balance of probabilities, 136–137, 139, 267
battery, 69–70, 72, 73–74, 277
    consent, and, 75–76, 78, 91, 131, 136
    disclosure, and, 120
    necessity, defence of, 131–132
    physical crime, 277
Bentham, Jeremy, 204
best interests test, 93–94, 96, 102, 122
bias, 39
binding judgments, 108–109
binding precedent, 109
Blood Transfusion Board, 254
Bolam test, 112, 155–157, 160, 161, 183
Book of Evidence, 266

Bord Altranais, An. *see* Nursing Board
breach of confidence, action for, 194. *see also* confidentiality
British Medical Association, 83
burden of proof, 267–269
    balance of probabilities, 136–137, 139, 267
    civil standard, 136–137
    negligence, 136–137
    reasonable doubt, 267–268
    res ipsa loquitur, 137–138, 139
'but for' test, 180–187, 191

Canadian law
    medical records, access to, 241–243, 244, 245, 246
    necessity, defence of, 132–133
cannabis, 291
capacity
    age, and, 82
    child, 100–102
    consent to treatment, to, 73, 77–78, 80–86. *see also* informed consent
    criminal, 304–305
    legal, 87
    mentally incapacitated adults, 88–91
    refuse treatment, to, 83–86, 88–91
    relative capacity, 82–83, 88
carer's leave, 361
carer's rights, 93–94
case law, 237
causation, 58, 136, 179–191
    Bolam case, 183
    'but for' test, 180–182, 187, 191
    alternatives, 182–187
    Civil Liability Act 1961, 182–186
    concurrent liability, 182–183
    conspiracy or concerted action, 182, 183
    factual causation test (actual cause), 179–187, 191
    foreseeability rule, 189, 190, 191
    joint duty of care, breach of, 182, 183
    legal causation (proximate cause), 179–180, 187–190, 191
    material and substantial factor test, 185–186, 191
    public policy considerations, 189, 191
    thin skull ('eggshell skull') rule, 189–190
    vicarious liability, 182, 183, 185
censure, 49–50
Central Criminal Court, 265
Central Mental Hospital, 308
Central Midwives Board, 4–5, 6
    dissolution, 8
    elections, 7
    new Board (1944), 6–7
    powers, 7
    regulatory measures, 7
    rule-making powers, 7
chain of causation, 58
child
    capacity, 82, 100–102
    consent to medical treatment, 82, 100–102
    parents, by, 98–107. *see also* parental consent
    constitutional rights, 102–103, 104–105
    contraceptive advice, 100–102, 106
    criminal responsibility, 304–305
    definition, 80, 99
    guardian *ad litem*, 99, 105
    medical records, access to, 257, 258
    welfare principle, 104–105
Circuit Court, 261
    criminal proceedings, 265
civil law. *see* civil proceedings
civil liability
    criminal liability, and, 59–60
    civil proceedings
    aim of, 263
    appearance, 264
    balance of probabilities, 136–137, 139, 267
    burden of proof, 267
    civil and criminal law, distinction between, 262–269
    compensation, 263
    defence, 264
    discovery, 264
    evidence, 267
    general indorsement of claim, 264
    initiation, 261, 264
    intention, 267
    juries, 266
    parties, 264
    plaintiff, 263
    pleadings, 264
    private and public law, 262–263

standard of proof, 136–137
statement of claim, 264
Clinical Indemnity Scheme (CIS), 174, 421–423
Code of Professional Conduct (Nursing Board), 24, 29–31, 368
    confidentiality, 194, 221
Codeine, 291
coercion, 125
collaborative decision–making, 66
collective agreements, 371, 373–374
commercial promotions, 31
common law, 237–238
    duties of employee/employer, 334–335
    medical records, access to, 238–246
    offences, 276, 277
community nurses
    drugs, transport of, 300
company liquidation, 319, 321
compensation, 263
    unfair dismissal, 362–363
competence, 30, 31
complaints
    injunction applications, 50–52
    procedure, 40–44. *see also* Fitness to Practise inquiry
complementary therapies, 301
computation of damages, 175–178
computerised data. *see* data protection
concurrent liability, 182–183. *see also* vicarious liability
    breach of joint duty, 182, 183
    conspiracy or concerted action, 182, 183
conditions to retention on register, 47–49
    appeals, 48
conduct. *see* misconduct
confidentiality, 95, 122, 192–203
    action for breach of confidence, 194
    anonymous data, permissible use of, 206–208
    Codes of Conduct, 194, 200, 221
    consent to disclosure, 213–219
    constitutional rights, 195, 200–201
    courts, function of, 200–202
    deceased person, duty owed to, 210
    definition, 192
    disclosure to other health professionals, 209–210, 212
    doctrine, 193–196, 202–203
    duty of, 193–203, 215
    duty of care, 193
    enforcement, 200–202
    ethical duty, 194–195, 196
    European Convention, 195–196
    exceptions to duty, 214, 220–235, 236
        judicial proceedings, 220, 221–225
        law enforcement, for, 235
        patient's interests, 225–226
        public interest, 226–234
    family or relatives, disclosure to, 215–216, 217
    Hippocratic Oath, 194–195
    identifiable information, sharing of, 209–210
    implied contractual duty, 193–194, 211, 212
    information subject to, 196–197
    medical records, 29–30, 31
    moral duty, 194–195
    objective test, 197–198
    permitted disclosure, 209–212, 213–219
    personal health information, 205–208
    principles, 198, 201, 202
    privacy, right of, 195, 200–201
    privileged communications, 199–200
    professional guidelines, 234
    professional requirement, 194
    public domain, information in, 209
    purpose, 193
    reasonable person test, 196–197
    sharing information with patients, 209, 212
    statutory duties, 195
    subjective test, 198
    telephone/inquiries protocol, 216, 217
    third parties, disclosure to, 218, 219
    unauthorised disclosure, 209, 211, 212
    voluntary suspension of right to, 214
    workplace, in, 211
conscientious objection, 30
consent, 59, 276. *see also* informed consent; refusal of consent; voluntary consent
    battery, and, 75–76, 78

consent, *continued*
   capacity, 77–78
   constitutional right, 66
   defence to action in tort, 62–63, 70–71
   disclosure of confidential information, 213–219
   DNR orders and, 84–86
   emergency treatment, 72, 78, 84, 95
   implied, 278
   law of, 74
   necessity, and, 72, 95, 131–133
   parents, by, 98–107
conspiracy or concerted action, 182, 183
Constitution of Ireland 1937, 3, 4, 66
   child, rights of, 104–105
   confidentiality, rights of, 195
   dignity, rights of, 195
   education provisions, 102–103
   family, rights of, 102, 103, 217
   parents, rights of, 102–103
   privacy, rights of, 195
   refusal of medical treatment, right to, 96
   unenumerated rights, 195
constructive dismissal, 352–353, 355
contempt of court, 41–42
contraceptive advice
   minors, to, 100–102, 106
contract, 98
   employment, of. *see* employment contract
   express terms, 99, 319–320
   implied terms, 99, 319–320
   medical treatment, for, 100
   minor, by, 98–99, 99–100
   void and voidable contracts, 98–99
control test, 322
controlled drugs. *see also* drugs
   schedules of, 290, 291
courts. *see also* High Court
   adversarial system, 172, 174
   common law, 237–238
   confidentiality, enforcement of, 200–202
   hierarchy, 108–109
   precedent, 108–109
   subpoena, disclosure under, 220, 222, 236
CPR
   DNR orders, 84–86
creditor, 319

criminal act. *see also* criminal offence
   accomplice, 272
   actus reus, 271–272, 274
   animal, agency of, 272
   automatism, defence of, 272
   common purpose, 272
   incitement, 272
   intention, 270–271
   manslaughter, 272–273
   mens rea, 271, 272–273, 274
   motive, 273–274
   omissions, 271
   requirements, 271
criminal culpability, 304, 305
criminal law
   arraignment, 262
   civil law and, distinction between, 262–269
   general defences. *see* defences in criminal law
   indictment, 262
   intent, 309
criminal liability
   civil liability, and, 59–60
criminal offence, 50, 70, 275–284. *see also* criminal act
   assault, 276–278
   drugs, 286–289
   manslaughter, 284–285
   murder, 284
   Non–Fatal Offences Against the Person Act 1997, 276–284
   statutory offences, 276–284
   syringe offences, 279–284, 285
criminal proceedings, 262–263, 264–266
   aim of, 263
   arrest and detention, 265
   'beyond reasonable doubt', 267–269
   book of evidence, 266
   burden of proof, 267–268
   courts, 265, 266
   defence, 265–266
   defences to. *see* defences in criminal law
   deposition, 265
   evidence, 267
   fines, 263
   indictable offences, 265, 266
   indictment, 265
   initiation, 264–265

intention, 267
jury trial, 266
parties, 264
preliminary examination, 265
prosecution, 263, 265
punishment, aims of, 263
summary offences, 266
summary proceedings, 264–265
summons, 264
trial, 265–266
victim's involvement, 263
witnesses, 265
criminal responsibility
  children, 304–305
  insanity, defence of, 306–309

Dáil Éireann, 3
damage, 136
damages, 59, 60, 172–178
  computation, 175–178
  contractual, 178
  general, 175–177, 178
  liquidated and unliquidated, 175
  loss of wages, 175, 178
  medical expenses, 175, 178
  negative *interesse*, 177–178
  no-fault compensation, 173–175
  pain and suffering, 175, 178
  Personal Injuries Assessment Board, 174
  purpose, 178
  special, 175–177, 178
  types of, 178
  danger to society
    disclosure of information, justification for, 226–229
danger zones, 413
data. *see also* data protection
  aggregated, 204, 206, 208
  anonymous data, permissible use of, 206–208
  confidentiality, duty of. *see* confidentiality
data controller, 248, 249
data processor, 248
data protection, 195
  appropriate security measures, meaning of, 249
  confidentiality, 249
  definitions, 247–248
  inaccuracies, correcting of, 250

manual files, access to, 247, 250, 251
medical opinion, 252
  medical paternalism, 250
  medical records, access to, 239–240, 248–254, 257–258
  out-of-date records, 253, 257
  processing of data, 248
  rights of patient, 250–251
  serious harm, risk of, 250
  sharing of information, 252
  third parties, reports for, 253
  unintelligible data, 250
death with dignity, 31
debtor, 319
deceased person
  confidentiality owed to, 210
deemed, 80
defamation, 109–110
defence
  criminal prosecution, to, 264, 265–266
defences in criminal law
  duress, 310–311, 314
  general defences, 304–315, 315–316
  infancy, 305–306
  insanity, 306–309
  intoxication, 309–310
  necessity, 311–313, 314, 315
  self-defence, 313–314
defences in tort, 61–63
  acts of God, 61
  consent, 62–63, 70–71
  inevitable accident, 61
  lawful authority, 71
  necessity, 61–62, 71, 95, 131
  self-defence, 71
  statutory authority, 62
  trespass to the person, 70–72
  volenti non fit injuria, 63
defendant, 57, 264
definition of nurse, 12, 29
delegation of responsibilities, 31
Department of Health, 254
die, right to, 96
direct discrimination, 385–386
directives of the EU, 15
Director of Equality Investigations, 395
Director of Public Prosecutions (DPP), 263
disability, person under, 87
  legal incapacity, 87

disciplinary measures, 44–52
  advice, admonishment or censure, 49–50
  conditions to retention on register, 47–49
  erasure/suspension from Register, 44–47
  hearing. see Fitness to Practise inquiry
  injunction applications, 50–52
  sanctions other than erasure/suspension, 47–49
disclosure of information
  anonymous data, 206–208
  confidentiality, and. see also confidentiality, duty of
  exceptions to duty, 221–235, 236
  consent, 213–219, 225
    express and implied, 214–215, 218
    informed, 215, 218
  court, in, 221–225
  criminal detection and investigation, 250
  data protection legislation, 248–258
  emergency situations, 234
  family or relatives, to, 215–216, 217
  health professionals, to, 209–210, 212, 225–226
  insurance industry, to, 215
  judicial proceedings, 221–225
  law enforcement officials, to, 235
  non–medical health professionals, to, 225–226
  patient's interests, in, 225–226
  permitted disclosure, 209–212, 213–219. see also consent (above)
  exceptions to duty of confidentiality, 221–236
  personal health information, 204–208, 213–219
  professional guidelines, 234
  public domain, information in, 209
  public interest, in, 226–234
  refusal to permit, 215, 253, 255, 256
  serious harm, risk of, 226–234
  sharing of identifiable information, 209–210
  statutory tribunal, requirement of, 221
  telephone/inquiries protocol, 216, 217
  third parties, to, 218, 219, 253, 255, 256
  unauthorised, 209, 211, 212
disclosure of risks, 73, 77, 108–124
  American approach, 110–111, 113, 118, 119
  benefits of disclosure, 120–121
  best interests test, 122
  Bolam test, 112
  burden of proof, 122
  causation test, 118, 124
  doctor–oriented approach, 112, 113, 123
  elective and non–elective procedures, 113–119
  empowerment, 121
  English approach, 111–112, 113, 119
  inquisitive patient, 110
  Irish law, 113–119, 124
    practical implications, 119–120
  law of disclosure, 110, 119
  material risk, 111–112, 118–119
  materiality, test of, 113, 117
  nurse, role of, 120, 121, 123
  patient–oriented approach, 111, 113, 123
  prudent patient test, 112–113
  reasonable doctor test, 78, 127
  reasonable patient test, 111, 113, 117–118, 124, 127
  record of consultations, 120
  relatives of patient, to, 122
  therapeutic privilege, 122–123
  'understanding', meaning of, 110
discovery, 264
discrimination, 383–396
  complaint process, 395
  concept of, 384–385
  direct, 385–386
  equal pay, 391–392
  fair, 394–395
  gender, 387–390
  indirect, 386–387
  occupational requirement defence, 392–394
  positive, 394–395
  retirement age, 395
  sexual harassment, 390–391
dismissal, 322–323, 350–363
  constructive, 352–353, 355
  fair, 357–361
  health board officers, 363–366
  lawful, 352

private sector nurses, 367
procedures, 338
public sector nurses, 363–366
summary, 352
types of, 350
unfair, 352, 354–363
wrongful, 350–352, 370
District Court, 261
    preliminary examination, 265
DNR (Do Not Resuscitate) orders, 84–86
    advance directive, 84
    American approach, 85–86
    immunity, 86
    implementation by doctor, 85
    nurses and, 85
    review, 85–86
    UK guidelines, 84–85
    witnesses, 85
doctor-patient relationship
    nature of, 240, 241–242
doli incapax, 305, 306
dominus litis, 263
drugs, 286–303
    abuse of, 31
    administration, 289
    clinical trials, 291
    community nurses, transport by, 300
    complementary therapies, 301
    criminal law implications, 300
    dispensing and supply, 289, 292–293
    guidelines (Nursing Board), 289, 298–302
    imported or exported, 291
    intention to supply, 288–289
    intravenous administration, 289
    lawful use, 292–293
    medical preparations, 289, 291, 292
    medication errors, 301
    medication management, 298–302
    medicinal purposes, used for, 291
    midwives, administration by, 293
    offences, 286–289
    over the counter drugs, 291
    possession, 286–287, 288–289
    prescriptions, 291, 295–297
    private institutions, in, 300
    protocols and practices, 301–302, 303
    raw form, 291
    recording of, 297–298
    register, 298
    schedule 2 drugs, 291, 300
    schedules of controlled drugs, 290, 291
    storage, 301
    supply of, 287–288, 289, 294
    use, 287, 292–293
    written requisition, 294
duress, 65, 126, 130
    defence in criminal law, 310–311, 314
    threats, by, 310
duty of care, 57, 135, 140–151. *see also* standard of care
    alternative practitioners, 148–150
    confidentiality, 193
    criteria, 143
    employer, 321, 397–398
    establishing, 143–144
    existence of duty, 140–141, 143, 144
    extent of, 144–145
    foreseeability, 142, 144, 150–151
    Good Samaritan cases, 143, 422
    joint duty, breach of, 182, 183
    knowledge available, 145–148
    neighbour principle, 140–142, 143
    policy considerations, 144–145
    pre-existing relationship, 140, 143, 144
    precedent, 143
    reasonable updating, 146–150
    reasonableness, determination of, 144–145
    strangers, to, 143
duty of confidentiality. *see* confidentiality, duty of

economic loss, 60
education, 9–10, 33–36, 125
    degree programmes, 34–35
    essay writing, 427, 439–444
    EU requirements, 35
    evolution, 34–35
    examinations, 33, 428–438
    Galway Model, 34
    general nursing, 35
    role of Nursing Board, 33–34
    training hospitals, 33, 34
    voluntary consent, and, 129, 130
eggshell skull rule, 189–190
electronically stored personal data. *see* data protection
emergency evacuation, 411, 412

emergency treatment, 62, 131–139
   consent, and, 72, 78, 95
   disclosure of information, 234
   DNR orders, 84–86
   implied consent, 131
   necessity, defence of, 72, 95, 131–133, 315
   negligence action, and, 144
employee
   common law duties, 334
   definition, 410
   dismissal. *see* constructive dismissal; dismissal; unfair dismissal
   emergency evacuation, 411, 412
   employer's vicarious liability, 416–424
   express and implied authority, 415–416
   fixed–term employees, protection of, 379–381
   health and safety duties, 401–402
   hours of work, 373–376
   legislative protection. *see* employment law
   part–time employees, protection of, 378–379
   resignation, 352–353
   self–employed, distinguished from, 320–333
employer
   common law duties, 334–335
   control test, 322
   definition, 411
   duty of care, 321, 397–398
   health and safety duties, 399–401, 403–406
   vicarious liability, 321, 416–424
Employment Appeals Tribunal, 322, 323
employment contract, 319–339
   common law duties, 333–335
   contract of services/for services, 320, 321–322, 339
   control test, 322–325
   enterprise test, 326–327
   integration test, 325–326
   mixed test, 327–328
   reality test, 328–333
   tools of the trade, 330–331
   dismissal. *see* dismissal
   express or implied, 335
   fixed term/specified purpose contract, 340–341
   nature of, 320–333
   office holder, 320
   self–employed, 320
   specific performance, 350–351
   staff nurse, 342–348
   termination, 349–370. *see also* dismissal
   terms of employment, written statement of, 336–338
   verbal or written, 335
   wages, written statement of, 338
   written records, 335, 336–338
employment equality, 383, 384. *see also* discrimination
employment law, 372–382. *see also* discrimination; dismissal; health and safety; unfair dismissal
   fixed–term employees, 379–381
   minimum notice, 372–382
   national minimum wage, 376–377
   part–time employees, 378–379
   payment of wages, 372–373
   redundancy payments, 377–378
   rest periods, 374–375
   working time, 373–376
English law. *see* UK law
enterprise liability, 421
enterprise test, 326–327
equal pay, 391–392
equality. *see* discrimination
Equality Officer, 395
equity, 192
erasure from Register, 44–47
   appeals, 45, 46–47
   criminal conviction, 49–50
   High Court, role of, 45–46, 47
   subsequent restoration, 46
essay writing, 427, 439–444
ethics. *see also* Code of Professional Conduct
   confidentiality, 194–195, 196, 221
   exceptions to duty, 221–234
Ethylmorphine, 291
European Convention on Human Rights
   confidentiality, 195–196
European Court of Justice (ECJ), 27
European Union (EU), 14–15
   directives, 15
   education and training of nurses, 35

harmonisation directive, 25–28
legislation, 14–15
mutual recognition of qualifications, 25–28
evidence, 267. *see also* burden of proof; privilege
  subpoena, under, 220, 221–225
ex parte applications, 50
examinations, 33
  questions, 428–438
excusable homicide, 284
executive, 4
express authority, 415–416
express terms, 99, 319–320

factual causation (actual cause), 179–187, 191
fair discrimination, 394–395
fair dismissal, 357–361
false imprisonment, 70
family/relatives
  consent to treatment, whether right to, 94–95
  constitutional rights of family, 102, 103, 217
  disclosure of information to, 122, 215–216, 217
  gifts or favours from, 31
FAS levy, 321
fees
  non-payment of, 44, 52
  Nursing Board, charged by, 23
felonious homicide, 284
fiduciary relationships, 240
Fitness to Practise Committee, 11, 22, 38, 39
  bias, 39
  evidence, 40
  independence and impartiality, 39
  powers, 41
  procedure, 40–44
  report, 40
Fitness to Practise inquiry, 10–11, 37–53, 367
  applications, 40
  contempt of court, 41–42
  findings, 41, 44
  grounds for, 40
  immediate suspension, 50–52
  natural justice, principles of, 38–39
  notification requirements, 41, 43–44,

45, 46–47
  powers and privileges of Committee, 41
  procedure, 40–44
  ultra vires actions, 38–39
  witnesses, 41–42
fixed-term contracts, 340–341
  employees, protection of, 379–381
force, use of. *see* self-defence; trespass to the person
forced treatment, 126
foreign qualifications
  recognition of, 25–28
Forensic Science Laboratory, 292
foreseeability, 232, 233
  causation, and, 189, 190, 191
fraud, 65
freedom of choice. *see also* voluntary consent
  education and, 129
Freedom of Information Act 1997, 254–257
  CEO, powers of, 255
  prohibition of access, 255
full and proper disclosure. *see* disclosure

Galway Model, 34
Garda Síochána, 263
  disclsoure of information to, 235
gender discrimination, 387–390
general damages, 175–177, 178
general defences. *see* defences in criminal law; defences in tort
general election, 3
General Nursing Council for Ireland
  dissolution, 8
  establishment, 5–6
  extension of term of office, 8
General Register of Medical Practitioners, 12
gifts or favours, 31
Good Samaritan acts, 143, 422
gross negligence, 285
gross salary, 371
guardian *ad litem*, 99, 105
guilty but insane, 308
guilty mind. *see mens rea*

harm, assault causing, 278–279
Harvard System, 443
health and safety, 397–414

health and safety, *continued*
  competent fellow staff, 398
  consultation with employees, 409
  control devices, 413
  danger zones, 413
  definitions, 410–411
  design of workplace, 402
  display screen equipment, 413
  employee's duties, 401–402, 410
  employer's duty of care, 397–398
  employer's general duties, 399–401, 403–406, 410–414
  equipment, 397, 412–413
  judicial formulation of principles, 398–399
  manual handling of loads, 413
  manufacture of equipment, 402
  origins of law, 397–398
  personal protective equipment, 413
  reasonably practicable, meaning of, 403–406
  regulations, 410–414
  safe place of work, 398
  safe system of work, 398
  Safety, Health and Welfare at Work Act 1989, 399–410
  safety statements, 406–409
Health and Safety Authority, 409–410
health board contracts
  fixed term/specified purpose contracts, 340–341
  officers, removal of, 357, 363–366, 370
  staff nurse, 342–348
  unfitness/unfitness to practise, 367–369
health data. *see* data protection; medical records; personal health information
health professionals
  sharing of information, 209–210, 252
health promotion, 31
High Court
  appeals to
    conditional retention on Register, 48
    erasures/suspensions from Register, 45–46
  civil proceedings, 261
  injunction applications, 50–51
  wardship procedure, 95–96

Hippocratic Oath
  duty of confidence, 194–195
HIV
  intentional infection, 281–282
holidays, 375–376
homicide, 284
hospitals
  emergency evacuation, 411, 412
  safety. *see* health and safety
  training hospitals, 33, 34
hours of work, 373–376

illegality, 65
immunity, 58
  statutory authority, 62
  witnesses, 42
implied authority, 415–416
implied terms, 99, 319–320
  confidentiality, 193–194, 211, 212
  reasonable care, 211
incapacity, 38. *see also* Fitness to Practise inquiry;
  mentally incapacitated adults
  finding of, 44–47
incapax, 87
in camera proceedings, 50
incontrovertible presumption, 305
indemnity insurance, 416
  Clinical Indemnity Scheme (CIS), 421–423
independent contractor. *see* self–employed
indictable offence, 266
  conviction for, 49–50
indictment, 262, 265
indirect discrimination, 386–387
inevitable accident, 61
infancy, defence of, 305–306
infant mortality, 5
infanticide, 284
infectious diseases, 5
information. *see* confidentiality; data protection; disclosure of information; medical records; personal health information
informed consent, 73–79, 120
  American approach, 74, 75
  battery, and, 75–76, 78
  'best interests' test, 93–94, 96, 122
  children, in respect of, 102, 104–105
  capacity, 77–78, 80–86

child, 82, 100–102, 104–105. see also parental consent
consultations, record of, 120
disclosure of information, 215, 218
disclosure of risks, 77
DNR orders, 84–86
doctrine of, 67, 74, 78
duty to explain, 74–75
full and proper disclosure. see disclosure
law of, 74
mental disability, and, 82, 88–97. see further mentally incapacitated adults
nurse, role of, 76–77, 78, 91, 120
child patients, 106–107
refusal of treatment, 83–86
relative capacity, 82–83, 88
relatives, role of
mentally incapacitated patients, 94–95
requirements, 77
tests
mentally incapacitated adults, 90–91, 93–94
voluntariness. see voluntary consent
welfare principle, 94
informed judgment, 30, 31
injunction, 50–51, 87
inquisitive patient, 110
inquisitorial system, 172
insanity, defence of, 306–309
guilty but insane, 308
McNaghten Rules, 307–308
Institutes of Technology, 34
insurance companies
disclosure of information to, 218, 219
medical reports prepared for, 253
insurance indemnity
Clinical Indemnity Scheme (CIS), 421–423
integration test, 325–326
intellectual disability. see mentally incapacitated adults
intent
criminal law, 309
intention, 270–271
assault, 278
civil and criminal law, 267
meaning, 270

mens rea, 272
murder, 284
intention in tort, 60, 68
interim injunction, 51
intervening act, 58–59
intoxication, defence of, 309–310
intravenous medical preparations
administration of, 289
involuntary manslaughter, 284, 285
involuntary treatment, 126
Irish Medicines Board, 254

judicial precedent, 108–109
judicial proceedings. see legal proceedings
judicial review, 45, 46
judiciary, 4
junior colleagues
responsibilities to, 31
juries, 262, 266
juristic persons, 14, 16–18
justifiable homicide, 284

Labour Court, 395
Law Reform Commission of Ireland (LRC), 310
lawful authority
defence of, 62, 71
legal capacity, 16, 87
legal causation (proximate cause), 179–180, 187–190, 191
legal issue, determination of, 430
legal personality, 16
legal proceedings. see also civil proceedings; criminal proceedings
civil and criminal law, distinction between, 262–269
disclosure of information, 221–225
documents, 264–266
in camera hearings, 50
initiation, 261–262, 264–265
intention, 267
juries, 266
public and private law, 262–263
legal professional privilege, 221
legal subjects, 16, 17
legal system, 172, 174, 237–238
legislation
employment. see employment law
nursing, 4–13
safety. see health and safety

legislature, 3–4
liability, 57. *see also* civil liability
   criminal and civil liability, 59–60
   immunity from, 58
liquidation, 319, 321
litigation, 172, 173
loads, manual handling of, 413
local election, 3

McNaghten Rules, 307–308
male nurses, 5, 6, 12
malicious motive, 60
mandate, 213
mandatory injunction, 87
manipulation, 125
manslaughter, 272–273, 284–285
   actus reus, 284
   mens rea, 284–285, 313
   voluntary and involuntary, 284, 285
manual data, access to, 247, 250, 251.
   see also data protection
manual handling of loads, 413
marriage law
   consent and, 126–127, 128–129
material risk
   disclosure. *see* disclosure
materiality, test of, 113, 117
maternal deaths, 5
matron/acting matron
   dispensing and supply of medicines, 292, 293, 294
Medical Council
   Guide to Ethical Conduct and Behaviour and to Fitness to Practice (6th edition, 2004), 221, 234, 368
medical details. *see* personal health information
medical expenses, 175, 178
medical negligence. *see* negligence
medical opinion, access to, 252
medical preparations. *see also* drugs
   administration of, 289
medical records, 238–24
   access to, 225, 238–246
      Canadian approach, 241–243, 244, 245, 246
      child's records, 257, 258
      common law, 238–246
      English approach, 243–244, 245, 246
      exemption, 253
      freedom of information provisions, 254–257
      prohibition of, 255
      refusal of, 253, 255–256, 257
      restriction on, 254
      statutory right, 254–257
      third parties, by, 218, 253, 255, 256
   confidentiality, 29–30, 31
   court order, production under, 235
   data protection, 239–240, 248–254, 257–258
   ownership of, 238–242, 243, 245
   private patients, 239
   public patients, 239–240
   proprietary interest, 238, 241–242, 243
Medical Registration Council, 7
medical treatment
   consent to. *see* consent
medication errors, 301
medication management
   Nursing Board guidelines, 298–301
   principles, 299
mens rea, 60, 271, 272–273, 274, 285
   aggravated assault, 279
   assault, 278
   basic and specific intent, 309–310
   intentional conduct, 272
   manslaughter, 284–285, 313
   murder, 284
   negligence, 273
   recklessness, 272–273
   syringe offences, 281–282, 283
mental handicap nursing
   training, 35
mental illness
   insanity, defence of, 306–309
mental incapacity, 82, 87, 88. *see also* mentally incapacitated adults
mentally incapacitated adults
   informed consent, 87–97
      best interests test, 93–94, 96
      carer's rights, 93–94
      family and relatives, role of, 94–95
      legal and medical approaches, 88–91
      necessity, defence of, 95
      nurse, role of, 91, 96–97

partial incapacity, 92
phobias, 92
relative capacity, 88
schizophrenics, 88–90
specific incapacity, 92–94
status approach, 88
sterilisation, 94
tests for, 90–91, 93–94, 96
ultimate decision, 94–97
wardship procedure, 95–96
welfare principle, 94
withdrawal of treatment, 95–96
lucid intervals, 88–89
midwifery, 4–5, 6–8
emergency procedure, 8
misconduct, 7
nursing profession, part of, 8, 12
Roll of Midwives, 4, 5, 7
rules, 7
midwives
drugs, dispensing of, 293
midwives badges, 6, 7, 9
Midwives Committee, 9
Mill, John Stuart, 204
minimum notice, 372
minimum wage, 376–377
minor
consent to medical treatment, 99
minors
contracts by, 98–99, 99–100
definition, 99
misconduct, 352, 358, 365, 366, 367, 368–369. see Freedom to Practise inquiry; professional misconduct
Misuse of Drugs Act, 286–303, 303. see also drugs
contravention of, 302
lawful possession or supply, 292–294
offences, 286–289
prescriptions, 295–297
recording of drugs, 297–298
regulations, 290–298
schedules of controlled drugs, 290, 291
mixed test, 327–328
Morphine, 291
motive, 273–274
murder, 284
mens rea, 284
mutual recognition of qualifications, 25–28

National Authority for Occupational Safety and Health, 409–410
National Drugs Advisory Board, 292
national minimum wage, 376–377
National University of Ireland, 34
natural justice, principles of, 38–39
necessaries
contracts in respect of, 98, 99–100
necessity, defence of
availability of defence, 133
Canadian approach, 132–133
criminal law, 311–313
emergency treatment, 131–133
mentally incapacitated adults, treatment of, 95
statutory defence, 312–313
tort, in, 61–62, 71–72, 72
negligence, 58, 59, 135–139
balance of probabilities, 136–137, 139
burden of proof, 136–137
burden of taking precautions, 145
Clinical Indemnity Scheme (CIS), 421–423
consent, and, 91
duty of care, 57, 135, 140–151. *see also* duty of care
elements of, 135–136
emergency situations, 144
foreseeability, 142, 144, 150–151
gross negligence, 285
magnitude of risk, 144–145
mens rea, 273
neighbour principle, 140–142, 143, 150
reasonableness, determination of, 144–145
res ipsa loquitur, 137–138, 139
standard of care, 152–171. *see also* standard of care
utility of defendant's conduct, 145
neighbour principle, 140–142, 143, 150
nemo iudex in sua causa, 37, 39
net salary, 371
New Zealand
no–fault compensation, 173
NHS (England)
ownership of medical records, 239
Nicocodine, 291
Nicodicodine, 291
night workers, 375
no–fault compensation, 173–175

Non–Fatal Offences Against the Person
    Act 1997, 276–284, 285
  assault, 276–278
  assault causing harm, 278, 279
  assault causing serious harm, 278, 279
  necessity, statutory defence of, 312–313
  self–defence, statutory, 313–314
  syringe offences, 279–284
non–medical health professionals
  disclosure of information to, 225–226
notification
  complaints and inquiries, 41, 43–44
  conditions to retention, attachment of, 47–48, 48–49
  erasure/suspension from Register, 45, 46–47
novus actus interveniens, 58–59
Nurses Act 1985
  definitions, 11–12
Nurses' Rules 2000, 24, 29–31
Nursing Board (An Bord Altranais), 14–32
  Chief Executive Officer, 22
  code of conduct. *see* Code of Professional Conduct for each Nurse and Midwife
  committees, 21–22
  disciplinary powers, 37–38, 47–52. *see also* Fitness to Practise inquiry
  advice, admonishment or censure, 49–50
  conditions, attachment of, 47–49
  erasure/suspension, 44–47
  education and training, 33–34
  erasure or suspension of nurse, 44–47
  establishment, 8–9, 10, 15–18
  failure or refusal to perform a function, 22
  fees, 23
  functions, 15–16
  Guidance to Nurses and Midwives on Medication Management, 298–301
  Guidance to Nurses and Midwives on the Administration of Medical Preparations, 289, 298–302
  income, 23
  juristic person, 14, 16–18
  legal personality, 16–17
  membership, 8, 18–21
  Midwives Committee, 9
  Ministerial appointments, 19, 20, 21
  Minister's powers, 20–21
  new Board (1985), 10
  nursing representatives, 18–19, 20
  officers and servants, 22
  perpetual succession, 17
  practices and procedures, 18
  Register of Nurses, 10
  registration, 24–25
  reporting and advisory functions, 11
  rules made by, 23–24
  seal, 18
  voting procedures, 9
nursing degrees, 34–35
nursing legislation
  evolution, 4–13
nursing register. *see* Register of Nurses
nursing registers, 5
  Roll of Midwives, 4, 5

obiter dictum, 108
objectivity, 64–65
occupational health and safety. *see* health and safety
occupational requirement defence, 392–394
officers of health boards
  removal from office, 357, 363–366, 370
Oireachtas, 3, 4
omission
  criminal act, as, 271
omissions, 140, 142
onus of proof. *see* burden of proof
opium, 291
Organisation of Working Time Act, 373–376
  annual leave, 375–376
  exclusions, 374
  night workers, 375
  on call workers, 376
  rest periods, 374–375
  Sunday workers, 376

pain and suffering, damages for, 175, 178
Paracetamol, 291
parental access
  child's medical records, to, 257, 258

parental consent, 98–107
   child, rights of, 104–105
   Constitution of Ireland and, 102–103, 104–105
   contraceptive advice to minors, 100–102
   refusal to permit treatment, 103–104
   substitute parent, court as, 103
   wardship procedure, 103
   welfare principle, 104–105
parental leave, 361
parliamentary elections, 3
parole, 220
part–time employees, 378–379
parties to proceedings, 264
paternalism, 64, 66
patient
   definition, 29
patient autonomy, 64, 65–70
   access to medical records, 238–246
   child patient, 100, 101–102
   consent to treatment, 66, 67, 73–86. see also informed consent
   constitutional right, 66
   disclosure of information. see also confidentiality; disclosure of information; medical records; personal health information
patient confidentiality, 29–30, 31. see confidentiality
patient information. see personal health information
patients
   death with dignity, 31
   definition, 29
   gifts or favours from, 31
   informed judgment, 30, 31
Pentazocine, 293
permanent injunction, 51
perpetual succession, 17
personal data, 248. see also data protection; medical records
personal health information, 204–208
   confidentiality, 205–208
   consent to disclosure of, 213–219
   disclosure to other health professionals, 209–210
   family or relatives, disclosure to, 215–216, 217
   permitted disclosure, 209–212
   sharing patient information, 209–210

telephone/inquiries protocol, 216, 217
third parties, disclosure to, 218, 219
unauthorised disclosure, 209
Personal Injuries Assessment Board (PIAB), 174
personal injury cases, 266
personal protective equipment, 413
persuasion, 125
persuasive presumption, 288
Pethidine, 291, 293
Pharmaceutical Society of Ireland, 292
pharmacists
   prescriptions, dispensing of, 295–297
phobias, 92
plaintiff, 57
pleadings, 261, 264
plenary summons, 261, 264
positive discrimination, 394–395
possession of drugs, 286–287, 288–289
Power of Attorney, 213
pregnancy, dismissal on grounds of, 361
prescriptions, 291, 295–297
   fax prescriptions, 299
   forgeries, 297
   instalments, 296
   offences, 297
   repeat, 296–297
   requirements, 295–297
   writing, must be in, 297
preservation of life, 31
presumption, 80, 304, 305
privacy, right of, 195
   not absolute, 200–201
private institutions
   drugs, possession or administration, 300
private law
   public law, and, 262–263
private patients
   medical records, ownership of, 239
private prosecutions, 263
private sector nurses
   legislative protection, 367
   status, 367
privilege, 41, 42, 109–110, 123, 199
   absolute, 221, 223
   legal professional privilege, 221
   relative, 221–222
   therapeutic, 122–123
Privy Council, 5

problem questions, 429–438
problem solving, 428
professional misconduct, 368–369. see also Fitness to Practise inquiry
   finding of, 44–47
prohibitory injunction, 87
proof. see burden of proof
proprietary interest
   medical records, in, 238, 241–242, 243
prosecution of offences, 263
protocols
   drugs, in relation to, 301–302, 303
provocation, 275
proximate cause. see legal causation
proximity, 233
psychiatric nursing
   training, 35
public domain, information in, 209
public holidays, 376
public interest, disclosure in, 226–234, 236
   serious harm, risk of, 226–229
public law
   private law and, 262–263
public patients
   medical records, rights of access to, 239–240, 254, 256
public sector nurses
   removal from office, 357, 363–366
public statements, 31
publicly held records, access to
   freedom of information provisions, 254–257
punishment of criminals
   aims of, 263

qualifications
   recognition of foreign qualifications, 25–28

ratio decidendi, 108, 109
re–engagement, 362
re–instatement, 362
reality test, 328–333
reasonable doctor/nurse
   standard of care, 153–166
reasonable doctor test, 78, 127
reasonable doubt, 267–268
reasonable patient test, 111, 113, 117–118, 124, 127

disclosure, and, 111, 113, 117–118
reasonable person
   standard of care, 152–166
rebuttable presumption, 288, 304
recklessness, 270, 272–273
   assault, 278
   manslaughter, 284–285
   negligence, and, 273
recognition of foreign qualifications, 25–28
redress, 349
redundancy, 359
redundancy payments, 377–378
referencing, 444
refusal of consent
   capacity, 83–86
   child patient, 101–102
   DNR orders, 84–86
   mentally incapacitated adults, 88–91
   parents, by, 103–104
   right of, 129, 130
   rights of patient, 66, 73–86, 96
Register of Nurses, 6, 9
   conditions, attachment of, 47–49
   erasure from, 38, 44–47, 367
   EU harmonisation directive, 25–28
   maintenance of, 10
   registration, 24–25
   reinstatement, 52
   suspension from, 44–47, 50–52
registration, 24–25
reinstatement to Register, 52
relative capacity
   mentally incapacitated adults, 88
relative privilege, 221–222
relatives. see family/relatives
religious or political opinion, 361
removal from Register, 38, 44–47, 367
Report of the Commission on Nursing: A Blueprint for the Future (1998), 34
res ipsa loquitur, 137–138, 139
responsibility of care, 30–31
rest periods, 374–375
retirement age, 395
Rights Commissioner, 381
Roll of Midwives, 4, 5, 7
   removal from, 7
Royal College of Nursing, 83
rules
   Nursing Board, made by, 23–24

safety. *see* health and safety
safety statements, 406–409
salary, 371. *see also* wages
Saorstat Eireann (Irish Free State), 4
schizophrenics
　informed consent, 88–90
scientific research, 292
Seanad Eireann, 3
self–defence, 71, 275, 284
　criminal law, 313–314
　force, use of, 314
　statutory, 313–314
self–determination, right to, 66, 84. *see also* patient autonomy
self–employed, 320, 321, 322
　employee, distinguished from, 320–333. *see also* employment contract
sensitive personal data, 248. *see also* data protection
serious harm, assault causing, 278–279
serious harm, risk of
　disclosure of information on grounds of, 226–229
sex discrimination, 387–390
sexual advances, 30
sexual harassment, 390–391
sister/acting sister
　dispensing and supply of medicines, 292, 293
Special Criminal Court, 266
special damages, 175–177, 178
special summons, 261
specified purpose contracts, 340–341
staff nurse
　health board contract, 342–348
standard of care, 31, 135, 152–171
　Bolam test, 155–157, 160, 161
　Codes of Practice, 166
　English approach, 155–157, 160–163
　established practice, 156–163, 166, 171
　　defects in, 163–166, 171
　foreseeability, 152–153, 154, 166
　health professionals, 153–171
　　differing standards of care, 166–171
　　nurses as 'professionals', 166–171
　Irish approach, 153–155, 157–160, 163–166
　principles, 166

reasonable person test, 152–153, 171
　doctors/nurses, 153–171
State Chemist, 292
Statement of Claim, 264
Statement of Defence, 264
statutory assault, 276–278
statutory authority, defence of, 62, 71
statutory instruments, 4
statutory offences, 275–284
sterilisation, 94
subjectivity, 64
subordinate legislation, 4
subpoena, 220, 221–225
subpoena ad testificandum, 220
subpoena duces tecum, 220
summary dismissal, 352
summary offence, 266
summary proceedings, 264–265
summary summons, 261
summons, 261
　plenary, 261, 264
Sunday workers, 376
supply of drugs, 287–289
suspension from Register, 44–47
　appeals, 45, 46–47
　High Court, role of, 45–46, 47
　immediate, 50–52
　injunctions, 50–52
　notification requirements, 45, 46–47
　termination, 46
Sweden
　Patient Insurance Scheme, 174
syringe offences, 279–284, 285
　attacks, 279–282
　contaminated syringes, 280, 281
　HIV, intentional infecting a person with, 281–282
　mens rea, 281–282, 283
　placing or abandoning syringe, 282–283
　possession, 282, 283
　threats, 280, 281
　transferred intent, 280, 281

tax deductions, 371–372
telephone/inquiries protocol, 216, 217
termination of employment, 322–324, 338, 349–370
　dismissal, 350–363. *see also* dismissal; unfair dismissal
　expiration, by, 349–350

termination of employment, *continued*
   private sector nurses, 367
   public sector nurses, 363–366
   unilateral, 369
terms of employment, written statement of, 336–338
testamentary capacity, 81
therapeutic alliance, 66
therapeutic privilege, 122–123
   nurses and, 123
thesis, 439–444
thin skull rule, 189–190
third parties
   disclosure of information to, 218, 219
   medical records, access to, 218, 253, 255, 256
tort law, 57–63
   actionable *per se*, concept of, 68
   assault, 68–69
   autonomy of patient. *see* patient autonomy
   battery, 69–70
   categories of torts, 60
   defences, 61–63
   false imprisonment, 70
   immunity from liability, 58, 62
   intention, 59, 60, 68
   legal concepts, 57–59
   liability, 57, 60
   remedies, 60
   trespass, 67–68
tortfeasor, 60, 173, 178
trade union membership, 361
training hospitals, 33, 34
training of nurses. *see* education
travelling community, membership of, 361
trespass, tort of, 67–68. *see also* trespass to the person
trespass to the person, 67, 68–70, 73–74
   actionable per se, 68, 73–74
   assault, 68–69, 73
   battery, 69–70, 73–74
   defences, 70–72

UK law, 4, 237, 238
   child, consent of, 101–102
   disclosure of risks, 111–112, 113, 119
   DNR guidelines, 84–85

   medical records, access to, 243–244, 245, 246
   medical records, ownership of, 239
   standard of care, 155–157, 160–163
ultra vires, 37, 38
undue influence, 126, 130
unfair discrimination. *see* discrimination
unfair dismissal, 352, 354–363, 369
   capability, competence or qualifications, 358
   conduct, 358–359
   deemed unfair dismissals, 361–362
   definition of dismissal, 354–355
   excluded categories of employees, 356–357
   fairness, proving, 357–361
   redundancy, 359
   remedies, 362–363
   substantial grounds justifying dismissal, 357–361
unfair dismissals, 322
unfitness to practise, 367–369. *see also* Fitness to Practise inquiry
   finding of, 44–47
University College Hospital, Galway, 34
unlawful act. *see actus reus*
unlawful detention, 70
unliquidated damages, 175
use of drugs, 287
utilitarianism, 204

Valium, 291
vicarious liability, 152, 174, 182, 183, 185, 416–424
   Clinical Indemnity Scheme, 421–423
   employer, 321
   'frolic of his own', 419–421
   indemnity insurance, 421–423
   requirements, 417
   tests, 417–419, 420
   wrongful action by employee, 417
vitiation, 125
void and voidable contracts, 98–99
volenti non fit injuria, 63
voluntary assumption of risk, 63
voluntary consent, 73, 77, 125–130
   duress, 126
   education, 129
   freedom of choice, 129, 130
   institutionalised settings, 129, 130
   marriage law, 126–127, 128–129

notion of voluntariness, 126–129
nurse, role of, 128, 129
refusal, right of, 129, 130
subjective test, 128–129, 130
undue influence, 126
voluntary manslaughter, 284, 285

wages
equal pay, 391–392
loss of, 175, 178
minimum wage, 376–377
payment of, 372–373
wardship procedure, 95–96
children, 103
welfare principle, 94
winding up, 319, 321
withdrawal of treatment
best interests test, 96
mentally incapacitated adults, 95–96
witnesses
Fitness to Practise inquiry, 41–42
immunities and privileges, 42
Working Party on General Nursing, 10
working time, 373–376. *see also*
Organisation of Working Time Act
workplace confidentiality, 211
workplace health and safety. *see* health and safety
wrongful dismissal, 350–352, 370